Modern Methods and Ancient Cultures

Here is a remarkable volume which takes the reader on a full and exciting tour of the ancient cultures of Greece, Burma, the Tiv of Nigeria, the Palau Islands, and the Spanish Americans of New Mexico—as they are today.

Brilliantly describing their time-honored ways in matters of marriage and religion, the position of women, the roles of money and goods, the manners of work and play, *Cultural Patterns and Technical Change* also shows how modern technological advances and scientific methods, if carefully related to the group's cultural values, can advance the well-being of the people in these old societies. The impressive work of the United Nations in abolishing hunger, want, and fear among millions of people is also discussed by the authors.

Important for understanding how under-developed countries are brought into the modern community of nations, this book also demonstrates the importance of the human element in determining the rate at which scientific improvements can be applied in communities which have lived for centuries according to ancient hallowed patterns.

Cultural Patterns and Technical Change was prepared by the United Nations Educational, Scientific and Cultural Organization, and edited by Dr. Margaret Mead, Associate Curator of Ethnology at the American Museum of Natural History, and author of such famous works as *Coming of Age in Samoa*, *Growing Up in New Guinea*, and *Sex and Temperament in Three Primitive Societies*, among other editions. A special introduction was prepared by Dr. Mead.

THIS IS A REPRINT OF THE ORIGINAL EDITION PUBLISHED
BY UNESCO

Other UNESCO Publications
of Special Interest

The Community Factor in Modern Technology
by Jerome F. Scott and R. P. Lynton

A report on methods successfully used to encourage a 'sense of belonging' in modern industrial plants. As a basis for this report, twelve case studies were made in six European countries of industrial undertakings which in practice have achieved a community feeling among their workers. $1.00.

Education in a Technological Society

The question raised here is whether and how education is preparing children now in school for the technological society in which they will have to live. Recommendations are given as to how defects in the present training can best be corrected. $0.75.

Social Aspects of Technical Assistance in Operation by M. E. Opler

The story of conference of technical assistance experts and social scientists called to examine the problems encountered in the transfer of "know how" to economically less developed countries. $0.75.

Democracy in a World of Tensions

An expression of opinion throughout the world on the meaning and application of "democracy." Contains thirty-three essays written by authors from fourteen different nations, each representing a thoughtful and stimulating dissertation on all or part of the many aspects of this subject. $2.50.

To Our Readers

The first three books listed above may be ordered from International Documents Service, Columbia University Press, 2960 Broadway, New York 27, N. Y. The fourth is published in the United States by the University of Chicago Press, 5750 Ellis Avenue, Chicago 37, Illinois. All four may be obtained through your local bookseller.

CULTURAL PATTERNS
AND TECHNICAL CHANGE

{From the Tensions and Technology Series}

A Manual prepared by
The World Federation for Mental Health
and edited by MARGARET MEAD

Reprinted as a MENTOR BOOK
By Arrangement with
The United Nations Educational, Scientific
and Cultural Organization

A MENTOR BOOK
Published by THE NEW AMERICAN LIBRARY

FIRST PRINTING, JUNE, 1955
SECOND PRINTING, AUGUST, 1957
THIRD PRINTING, APRIL, 1958
FOURTH PRINTING, SEPTEMBER, 1959

Reproduction of the UNESCO colophon has been authorized by the United Nations Educational, Scientific and Cultural Organization.

Library of Congress Catalog Card No. 55-8727

MENTOR BOOKS are published by
The New American Library of World Literature, **Inc.**
501 Madison Avenue, New York 22, New York

PRINTED IN THE UNITED STATES OF AMERICA

PREFACE

The words *technical change* have come to symbolize for people all over the world a hope that is new to mankind. Through the centuries most of the peoples of the world have lived close to fear—fear of hunger, of cold, of chronic illness, of ignorance. In those societies or at those periods which later have been called *great,* a small proportion of the population have been elevated above some of these fears; their food and drink, the care and protection of their children, their control over the knowledge that mankind had accumulated so far was assured. The others, ninety-nine per cent, remained relatively wretched; the most that the beneficent leader or monarch, priest or prophet, sage or artist could do was to alleviate their misery, giving them law or splendour, sacrament or messianic vision, wisdom or beautiful intricate form, within which life remained worth living in spite of hunger and thirst, cold and want. It is only very recently, actually only since World War II, that we have been able to share the hope that the peoples of the world need be hungry no longer.

But with the hope that misery can be prevented has come a new fear, a fear which is strongest perhaps in the small proportion of the human race who, exempted from the common misery, have been the custodians of the fine flower of human civilization, acutely aware of the patterns of culture—so fragile, so all of a piece—which they have guarded. If the abolition of hunger and want were to be bought only by industrialization, by urbanization, by mechanization, by westernization, by secularization, by mass production, would not the cost be too great? Of what use to introduce a tractor which made the yield of the grain fields greater, if in so doing the whole distinguishing fabric of life which had characterized a society would be ripped into shreds?

These questions have been asked by the literate and privileged in old societies where the majority of the population is illiterate and unprivileged; by the members of Western societies who, valuing the graciousness of their own past, recoiled before the crudeness of an as yet unrealized technical culture, by the specialist—the historian, the anthropologist—who warns how destructive contact has been in the past between technologically developed and technologically less developed cultures, how often the price of progress has been to turn proud, aristocratic nomads into pitifully limited factory workers, shorn of their own tradition and provided with no new values.

The conflict of these two points of view—between those whose imagination is caught by the possibility of releasing mankind from the spectre of famine and those who insist that man does not live by bread alone—finds its echo in the questions that are asked whenever technical assistance is mentioned. Eyes light up with the vision that is offered. For the first time in history there is a possibility that no man need go well-fed to his rest, knowing that his neighbour is hungry, that indeed so many of his neighbours are hungry that though he broke the bread from his own table into a million pieces it would bring no real relief for a day, for an hour. But then faces fall, as people ask the second question: *How is it to be done*—in human terms? Granted that we know the technical answers: how to redistribute land in units which can support the use of modern argicultural machinery; how to locate industrial plants in relation to population and resources; how to utilize the local food supplies to provide a nutritional diet; how to reorganize town planning and water use so as to avoid the principal epidemic and endemic diseases in the world. Granted that we know all this, what will be the cost in terms of the human spirit? How much destruction of old values, disintegration of personality, alienation of parents from children, of husbands from wives, of students from teachers, of neighbour from neighbour, of the spirit of man from the faith and style of his traditional culture must there be? How slow must we go? How fast can we go?

This is the question which is repeated in the smallest village forum where people who were yesterday illiterate, today argue about how rapidly they dare change their age-old customs, and in the universities, in the halls of government, in the corridors of the United Nations, and in the specialized United Nations agencies. All over the world, this question has become a primary one as political leaders plan in terms of change or of resistance to change, as young technicians choose between a secure but uninteresting post at home and an adventure in tropics or desert, as families or communities skimp and save to send their young people away to learn—and bring back—the new skills.

It is for this reason that a manual on how to introduce a new food crop, a new system of public health, a new system of wage labour into some remote part of Africa or Asia, is of significance to the man in the street in New York or London, Topeka or Coventry, Vancouver or Wellington or Brisbane. He himself will not, in ninety-nine cases out of a hundred, come close to the problem of the people of a faraway village who prefer to sleep on the ground and so are afraid of hospital beds, or who fear to sleep with others over their heads and so are afraid of two-story hospital buildings. Yet this book is about problems just like these: How does the expert member of an international technical assistance team bring to a people the help they have asked for? How can the new changes be introduced with the least hazard to the mental health of those who make them? These are minutiae of expert skills which the average reader will not have to exercise—in Southeast Asia. They are nevertheless relevant to him—in two ways.

As a member of a modern nation, he faces every day changes of the same kind as those with which the expert is dealing in Burma or Iraq—the same in kind, although different in pace. We all live in a world which is being transformed before our eyes by new inventions, new forms of communication. Attention to the more dramatic instances in which the culture of a people is transformed sharpens our realization of what is happening to us.

But more urgently, we live in a world which is so haunted by the destructive powers which have been released in the twentieth century that it is of vital importance that we have reason for faith in our world, a reasoned belief in the future of human living. The speed and constructiveness with which the peoples of the world can learn to share in the skills which will free them from their age-long fears is the measure of our right to hope. Upon our ability to hope will depend our willingness to act in the living present. Such reasoned belief must be based on knowledge. To think about the question, *How can technical change be introduced with such regard for the culture pattern that human values are preserved?* it is necessary to think about these patterns, these changes, and these considered attempts to protect the mental health of a world population in transition.

MARGARET MEAD

New York
October 31, 1954

INTRODUCTORY NOTE

In view of the considerable activity at the present time in the field of technical assistance, by the more privileged to some of the less privileged countries of the world, it is indeed satisfactory that Unesco has inspired the production of this manual.

Rapid changes in the industrial or social structure in any country are apt to lead to unforeseen disturbances even when such changes are initiated or supervised by nationals of that country, When men and women with technical skills set out to help in shaping new developments in a country or a culture other than their own, there are clearly many more possibilities of producing unfortunate consequences. Sometimes great harm can be done to the people of that country, especially through the creation of social psychological stresses and the disorganization of family and community life.

The World Federation for Mental Health has always stressed the problems of prophylaxis as being in the long view even more significant than those of treatment, important though the latter are. In the understanding and solution of such problems, inter-professional teams of anthropologists, sociologists, economists, educators and others, along with psychologists and psychiatrists, are essential if mental health and good human relations are to be established and maintained.

The Federation was therefore happy at being asked to sponsor such an effort, and in the hands of a skilled team in the United States of America under Dr. Margaret Mead's able leadership a good first contribution in this field has been prepared.

Dr. Mead herself sets out the plan and arrangement of the survey, and suggests the type of reader which she and her collaborators have in mind. The World Federation for Mental Health certainly hopes that this work will be of real service to workers in technical assistance projects and in many allied fields. The book is no encyclopedia which provides answers to all questions. It does, however, suggest lines of approach to many of the cultural and social situations which will inevitably be encountered.

J. R. REES, Director,
World Federation for
Mental Health

1952

CONTENTS

CONTENTS

I. INTRODUCTION

This survey is directed toward the implications for the mental health of the peoples of the world who are involved in purposive introduction of technical change. It is therefore concerned with two new developments, the purposive attempt to cultivate mental health, and the purposive attempt to introduce technical change. All peoples have been concerned, inexplicitly, inarticulately, with the problem of the mental health of the members of their group. In every society we find practices and rituals designed to rear children so their original biological impulses will be channelled and patterned so that they can function within the particular culture, and we find devices for dealing with cases where this educational process has failed, with the individuals who are unable to function, who are variously prayed over, subjected to magical curing ceremonials, tolerated, or exiled, as the case may be.

What is new in the twentieth-century world is the conscious application of our new knowledge of human behaviour, derived from the findings of psychiatry, clinical psychology, child development, cultural anthropology and sociology, to the problems of child-rearing and adult functioning in such a way as to preserve and increase the mental health of whole populations. This new approach, which had been gaining ground in different countries as the findings of the clinician and the research team were translated into recommendations for infant care, education, personnel relationships in industry, governmental administrative practices, community organizations, and the content of mass media, was given its first explicit international expression in the International Congress for Mental Health, convened in London in 1948. The International Preparatory Commission stated:[1] and affirmed, "this, then, as we see it, is

Here it is possible only to indicate the promise which the social sciences and psychiatry hold out of reducing the toll of human waste and suffering and promoting social well being. Fulfilment of this promise rests largely on the hope of full co-operation between the social scientist and the administrator, who should be fully aware of the new vistas of human achievement opened up by the social sciences. While far more has to be learnt than is now known it is evident that we stand on the threshold of a new epoch of the science of man. . . .

[1] "World Federation for Mental Health," 1948, p. 11.

11

the ultimate goal of mental health, to help men to live with their fellows in one world."[1]

Technical change is also as old as civilization and since time immemorial the ways of life of whole peoples have been transformed by the introduction of new tools and new technical procedures, as inventions like the plough, the domestication of animals, writing, the use of steam, the factory assembly line, and the internal-combustion engine, have been diffused from one country to another. Relationships of relative dominance between two peoples, population balances, dynasties, and whole religious systems have been upset by some change in technology, just as the inventions which underlie technological change have themselves arisen from changing conceptions of nature and of man.

Nor is the attempt to control technological change new; monarchs have tried to introduce new practices among their peoples; merchants have attempted to keep within national borders some valuable technical process like the weaving of cloth; conquerors have educated the conquered so that they would fit in better with the scheme of conquest.

What is new is the assumption, on an international scale, of responsibility for introducing changes which are needed among peoples in areas of the world which can visibly benefit from the knowledge which the peoples of other areas have—of techniques which will increase production and conserve natural resources; of nutritional practices which will improve the well-being of a people; of public-health practices which will lower the death-rate, the incidence of epidemic and endemic disease, and rescue individuals now doomed to physical and mental illness. New also is the recognition and willingness to deal scientifically with the concomitant effects of such change.

Within this emerging world-climate of opinion, in which international governmental and international voluntary, and national governmental and national voluntary agencies are all playing a role, this survey is designed to provide materials which will sensitize all those concerned with this world-wide task to the mental-health implications of such introduced change in the living-habits of whole populations.[2]

The approach of this survey is based on the recognition that a culture is a systematic and integrated whole. "Culture" as used in this survey is an abstraction from the body of learned behaviour which a group of people who share the same tradition transmit entire to their children, and, in part, to adult immigrants who become members of the society. It covers not only the arts and sciences, religions and philosophies, to which the word "culture" has historically applied, but also the system

[1] Ibid., p. 30.
[2] See Appendix B for copy of original plan as drawn up on behalf of the World Federation for Mental Health.

of technology, the political practices, the small intimate habits of daily life, such as the way of preparing or eating food, or of hushing a child to sleep, as well as the method of electing a prime minister or changing the constitution. This survey is based on the assumption, itself drawn from field-work among many kinds of societies, that a change in any one part of the culture will be accompanied by changes in other parts, and that only by relating any planned detail of change to the central values of the culture is it possible to provide for the repercussions which will occur in other aspects of life. This is what we mean by "cultural relativity": that practices and beliefs can and must be evaluated in context, in relation to the cultural whole. The wholeness of a culture is not a statement that all cultures are integrated in the same way, or that all are equally integrated. Some cultures, like that of the Tiv (Section II), are so tightly integrated that any change threatens the whole; others, like that of the Palauans (Section II), are characterized by a traditional pattern of manipulating events which makes it much easier to introduce particular changes without disturbing the whole way of life. Other types of integration have been developed by peoples who have lived adaptively within the political boundaries of alien societies, sometimes for centuries, as illustrated by the Spanish Americans in the Southwest of the United States (Section II). Some societies have undergone profound recorded changes in their position in relation to surrounding peoples, and these changes in orientation, initiative, and response have themselves become part of the way in which the contemporary generation meets change. Greece is discussed (Section II) as an example of a culture in which a vivid recognition of the past is institutionalized. Other societies are in process of developing a newly won national identity after a past history of European contact, and have made the introduction of technological change an important part of their emerging modern culture. But whether a culture be tightly integrated or flexibly and loosely integrated, whether its ethics are internally consistent or profoundly contradictory, whether practices in one area of life are replicas or reversals or, when superficially inspected, apparently unrelated to other areas of life, they will be found, upon close anthropological inspection, to be interrelated in systematic ways. The systematization is provided by the nature of the human beings who must act as parents, as citizens, taxpayers, consumers, members of audiences, as pedestrians and users of transport, and who follow diversified occupations—farming, herding, teaching, administrating, etc. Because the various facets of a culture are responded to differentially by every full member of a culture, each human being becomes involved in making the culture systematic, in relating the role of action to that of spectatorship. Sometimes roles are contrasted, sometimes paralleled, sometimes other types of relationship develop. Habits of preparing food and habits of eating, habits of buying and habits of selling, each bear the imprint of having been practised over and over again by individuals who were also engaged in other related and complementary habits. This is true even where the individual is debarred from a practice, so that the position of a man who is not required to pay taxes is systematically related to the taxpaying practices in his society and differs from the position of a member of a society where no one pays taxes. The taboo on the eating of pork plays a different role in the lives of religious groups who live side by side with pork-eaters than it does in a culture of people who do not raise pigs. The position of someone who cannot read in a society where some people can read is very different from being a member of a society in which no one can read. A change from a monarchical to a republican form of government affects not only those who were heir to the monarchy, but also the status of all those who were defined as commoners, and monarchical attitudes may, of course, be preserved in another form.

Careful analysis of the habits and practices of a people shows that the traditional behaviour practised between parents and children, for example, is systematically related to practices which obtain between employer and employee, audience and speaker or actor, teacher and pupil, etc.; and that the way in which a dwelling-house is perceived is related to the way in which one's own body is perceived, with varying degrees of specificity, elaboration, and intensity. This systematic or patterned quality of culture is a function of the integrated character of human beings, who, as they incorporate cultural traits, sometimes very diverse in origin, organize them into viable ways of life.

The approach of this survey is also based on a conception of mental health and mental illness which stresses the importance of the life-experience of the individual, his relations to his own body, his parents, his siblings, peers, etc. Whatever the role of constitutional predisposition and constitutional defect or specific disease, the *way* in which an individual, as he grows, experiences his society is of great significance, especially in determining the extent to which the individual's responses will be maladaptive and self-defeating or adaptive, constructive and creative. The kinds of experiences which individuals will have and the ways of responding to those experiences which are available to them depend in large part upon the culture within which they live—so that pain may appear as an injury, or an insult, or a challenge; one may learn to respond to rewards or punishments, or merely react with terror to unusual situations; to prefer death to dishonour, or dishonour to inconvenience. Where loss of a biological parent may be a very severe trauma in a society organized on the basis of the small two-generation family, it may be much less severe in societies based on large extended families, like the Zadruga of the Balkans, or as in China. While it is still not possible to say that a given culture is less conducive to mental health than another, because of our lack of cross-culture criteria for mental disorders, it is possible to say that under situations of stress and strain, of rapid change and consequent disorientation, there is likely to be an increase in manifest mental ill health. As all social change must take place through individuals, the task of devising ways of reducing the ill effects of such change by strengthening the individuals who must function within a changing situation, and of developing ways of rearing children to whom social change is not disorienting, is a mental-health problem. So also the analysis of cultural practices, as they promote or jeopardize the mental health of individuals, the identification of practices which may once have been functional but which have become obsolete and harmful, the development of practices to replace those which, although functional, were also harmful, are mental-health tasks.

Within the confines of the cultural pattern each individual responds in terms of his own constitution and life-experiences. So, while care in changing the overt cultural pattern is a vital safeguard of the mental health of the culture, such care cannot ensure the mental health of each individual member. Cultural forms, as human beings have so far developed them, while inclusive enough so that most of the human beings who survive within them can live in terms of their institutions and values, are not sufficiently varied and flexible to protect and express all of the individual personalities—each an organized whole—in the society. It is to bridge this gap, between culturally provided solutions of the problems of each individual life and the difficulties which many individuals find in using those solutions, that individual psychotherapy has been developed and is now a recognized part of modern culture.

This survey is devoted to the implications of technological change for mental *health*, and will explore those types of planned change in which the emphasis is on educational and preventive measures rather than upon clinical and corrective ones. As the Expert Committee on Mental Health of the World Health Organization recommends:

The Committee therefore holds the view that it is only by the preventive application of psychiatric knowledge that mental health problems can ultimately be solved.[1]

This survey, therefore, will deal with the ways in which changed agricultural or industrial practices, new public-health procedures, new methods of child and maternal health care, and fundamental education, can be introduced so that the cul-

[1] United Nations, WHO, *Technical Report Series*, No. 9, p. 6.

ture will be disrupted as little as possible, and so that whatever disruption does occur can either be compensated for, or channelled into constructive developments for the future. New industrial practices, for example, may make it necessary for peasant populations to move to the city; such a removal will contain many elements of possible disruption and disorientation which must be guarded against, possibly by such measures as have been suggested for the Greeks of leaving the wives, at least for an initial period, in the villages, as Greeks are already well accustomed to situations in which the husbands must go away to earn a living. Appropriate housing and schooling arrangements which permit the unity of such a group of rural migrants to survive during a period of adjustment afford another possible way of meeting such a situation. But it must be recognized, in addition, that such a change of habitat also involves a loosening of habit which can be favourably utilized. Thus, Puerto Ricans, who clung to their traditional food habits with great conservatism in Puerto Rico, became one of the groups most amenable to change in New York City, where every condition of food purchase and food preparation differed from that to which they had been accustomed. On the other hand, members of some cultures will become more conservative in certain ways when faced with strange living-conditions, and in such cases it may be more important to provide against pressure being brought in those areas of life where the conservatism is reactive and protective than to attempt to use new conditions as leverage for change.

The emphasis, then, will be on facilitating harmonious change which will produce not too great strain in the individuals involved, and not upon technical problems of the psychiatric care of individuals, either in psychiatric institutions or in child-guidance clinics. This survey will stress a broad epidemiological approach in which the individual is seen within the society, embodying a culture through which and by which he lives.

FOR WHOM THIS SURVEY IS INTENDED

This survey is intended for the use of individuals—experts, policy-makers, specialists, technicians of all sorts, chiefs of missions and teams, members of ministries of health, education, agricultural and industrial development in countries actively seeking to guide technological change—all those who are immediately concerned, at any level, with purposive technological change. It is a guide only in that it indicates the kind of thinking and the kind of activity which may be of value in facilitating the technological change itself and in preserving the cultural integrity of those among whom the changes are introduced. It is definitely not a blue print, not a handbook to be consulted for the right answer to such questions as: When do you call in a religious leader? When do you form a new council? What is better as a substitute for a magical practice, a modern medical practice disguised as magic or one openly recognized as medicine? Such questions must always be worked out on the spot, in co-operation with members of the culture in which the change is to be introduced, in specific co-operation with members of the particular community in which a demonstration is to be made or a new practice tried out. This survey is designed as a guide to ways of going at such problems, as a guide to the *kind* of question which needs to be asked, in each culture, in each instance.

The descriptive sections of whole cultures have been prepared to give a sense of what is meant by looking at a culture as a whole, and not at isolated successful and unsuccessful practices; they are designed to sensitize those concerned with the introduction of change to the problems, to increase their awareness of the importance of taking the whole culture into account.

The survey is not directed toward policy-making, but might be helpful to policy-makers, not in determining objectives but in giving them a picture of what can happen to policy when it is translated into programmes and projects. It makes no attempt to set up time-tables for interdependent changes in different fields—as between health and agriculture, for instance —nor to deal with the very complex problems which are involved in reducing the death-rate while the birth-rate remains high. But it does provide materials showing how interdependent all changes are, occurring as they must within a culture, each aspect of which is inextricably related to every other, because they are embodied in the organized sets of habits of the living human beings who constitute that society. It is not directed to the problems of local governmental structure, but it does offer material on the way in which different types of social organization provide different types of avenues for purposive technological change.

The mental-health approach emphasizes that all changes take place in individuals, and that this is true not only of the members of communities into which some piece of modern technology is being introduced, but also of all those highly trained people being drawn together from their many specialties and formed into teams to go to far parts of the world, among people whose ways and language are strange to them. To the extent that the problems discussed in this survey become real to them, they themselves will become a part of a change which is constructive and preservative of the values and the mental health of those among whom they work. Not only is respect for the culture of the changing society necessary, but also understanding of how those habits and practices which must be changed *can* be changed; this is an important skill for the foreign members of teams which come into a country. Those within the country who have received a modern technical education will often be so imbued with the technical superiority of the measures to be introduced that they will need reinforcement from the outside team if they are to be patient with their countrymen, whose resistance to change may well seem reprehensible to them. The objectivity which combines respect for the values of another culture, a determination to bring about change in ways which promote the mental health of the population, and a certain amount of detachment from the clash of old and new values going on within the culture— these are invaluable assets which come from long experience in working with members of other cultures. Many of the members of technical-assistance teams will not, however, have had that experience, that sum total of memories of felicitous suggestions and disastrous missteps, of plans that misfired and plans that succeeded inexplicably, which make up the delicate certainty of the experienced expert. This survey is designed to provide the new-comer to the field with a part of what such long experience affords—to help the newly appointed minister, the newly appointed administrator, the soil specialist, the public-health physician, the nutritionist, or the specialist in transportation. The descriptions of various experts requested in the technical-assistance contracts demonstrate vividly from what diverse technical backgrounds the experts come who are now faced with a problem so complicated and delicate as the introduction of technical change into age-old cultures, rooted not only in the habits of the people, but also in the fit of the house to the land, in the shapes of the fields, in the relationship between temple or church or mosque and the village street, in the calendar and the vocabulary.

So, there is the possibility that the International Labour Office[1] may appoint for Indonesia "a general expert on social and labour questions"; for Pakistan "two experts on employment services and two experts on vocational training"; for Ecuador, three experts "in the fields of technical training in general, craft training and training in machine-shop work"; and for Thailand, a four-man team, one of whom will be "an expert on vocational guidance and training." On another programme, there is being sent to Pakistan[2] an "expert on geodesy: to organize geodetical work with precision gravimetric equipment"; and to Thailand,[3] a "specialist in the teaching of science: to advise on science teaching and on the best methods for the popularization of science in Thailand." And in the techni-

[1] United Nations, ILO, G.B.113/T.A.C./D.1.
[2] United Nations, Unesco, 25 EX/19, Annex XIV.
[3] Ibid., Annex XV.

cal-assistance agreements made with the Food and Agriculture Organization, such diverse skills are called for as (in an agreement with the Government of Saudi Arabia)[1] "one irrigation engineer qualified to advise and instruct on the design of wells and pumping equipment"; or (in an agreement with the Government of Syria)[2] an expert in "rural home-economics" to "evaluate existing school syllabuses and courses bearing on family life in rural areas both in government schools and in private schools and institutions, with a view to their ultimate revision"; or (in an agreement with the Government of Ecuador)[3] "an expert in all phases of sheep husbandry, including feeding, breeding and management with reference to both wool and meat production under range conditions at high altitudes."

This brief selection could be amplified in many directions, but even the smallest sample makes clear what a diversity of skilled personnel, some of whom may be inexperienced in working in other cultures, is to be drawn into this world-wide enterprise.

As experts from each of these diverse professional groups, administrators from many countries with widely different cultural traditions, and policy-makers and planners, become aware of and sensitive to the implications of change, their awareness may be expected to become incorporated in institutional practices. It is in this way that the types of recognition have developed which are now almost taken for granted in the official statements of international agencies which stress the importance of taking social change into account, of meeting the felt needs of the peoples involved in the programme, of obtaining a wide local understanding of the changes to be introduced. Procedurally, this recognition has found expression in the provision that governments must *initiate* requests for technical assistance through the United Nations Specialized Agencies, and that such assistance must be channelled through the government of each Member State. Each time such a request is put into effect and the contract is made public, the horizon of all the Member States is broadened, as one more possibility

[1] United Nations, Technical Assistance Board, Agreement of technical assistance between the Food and Agriculture Organization of the United Nations and the Government of Saudi Arabia, TA/90/Rev.1, 28 September 1950.

[2] United Nations, Technical Assistance Board, Agreement between the Food and Agriculture Organization of the United Nations and the Government of Syria for the Provision of Technical Assistance to that Government, TA 230.

[3] United Nations, Technical Assistance Board, Supplemental Agreement No. 1 between the Food and Agriculture Organization of the United Nations and the Government of the Republic of Ecuador for the Provision of Technical Assistance to that country, TA/259/S/1.

of technical assistance is presented to them, initiated on a world-scale by the far-sightedness and awareness often of a single administrative official.

THE FORM OF THE MANUAL

The survey has been organized so that any section can be read independently of the others, but these sections have been placed in the order which seemed to the editorial staff most useful if the survey were to be read throughout. The members of the editorial staff have worked as a team, bringing to the task a wide diversity of experience, a speaking knowledge of 16 languages (nine of them non-Indo-European); two members were born and educated in Europe, and three have spent years in field-work among non-Western peoples. In the preparation of the survey there has been a conscious attempt to approximate the type of team-work, cross-cultural experience, contrasts in administrative background and diverse professional interests, which are being found essential to the effectiveness of a technical-assistance team in the field. This has been done following the principle that each step in any operation must have a form congruent with each later step if disturbance in functioning, due to contrasts between hierarchical and team types of organization, is to be avoided.

Section II consists of five long studies of particular cultures, selected to present as much diversity as possible within the limits of space and available material. "Greece" has been written by an anthropologist who is Greek by birth and education, and so presents an example of what an anthropologist, after cross-cultural training, does in discussing the anthropologist's own culture. It is expected that in the world of the future anthropologists will come from many countries, contributing new insights to the whole conceptual framework and to their own particular cultures. "The Tiv of Nigeria" is based on a published study of a formal ethnographic type. "Palau" is the work of an American anthropologist, based on his own recent field-work in Micronesia, done with the conceptual tools of the mid-forties. "The Spanish Americans of New Mexico, U.S.A." and "Burma" draw on composite materials—the published work of several field-workers, interviews with members of the culture, and with field-workers on unpublished materials.

These five studies have been organized around different themes. "The Tiv of Nigeria" is a study in tight integration of a homogeneous culture before it lost its essential primitive quality. "Greece" is a study of an ancient European Christian culture with a long historical tradition, oriented towards attitudes towards the individual and the self. "Burma" is a study of a South-east Asian Buddhist culture with a newly acquired natural unity. The Palauans, although a small, recently primitive, island people, are presented in "Palau" as an example of a culture which equips its members to manipulate social change. "The Spanish Americans" is a study in the conservatism of a Catholic Spanish-speaking people in the midst of an English-speaking industrially oriented society. Together, they should provide the reader or student with some conception of the diverse value systems to which specific changes must be related, and which themselves change in pattern as new technologies are introduced.

Section III is a series of cross-cultural studies dealing with agriculture, industry, public health, maternal and child health, nutrition, and fundamental education, arranged so that specialists may have illustrative materials on the introduction of changes in particular areas of life. Here again, these discussions are intended to increase awareness and lay the groundwork for the study of new situations. No models of how a particular change should be introduced are presented, since each different culture and each different local group calls for an approach which is specifically developed to fit that situation. While the new team member without previous experience should profit from knowing the kind of thing which has worked and the kind of mistakes which have proved expensive and destructive, any attempt to follow concretely the illustrations provided here, or to avoid concretely the errors cited would be fatal. The statement that a mothers' club was a success in one society as a means of spreading an acceptance of vaccination should be taken only as a counsel suggesting that sometimes organizations of men, or women, or children, or all three, based on kinship or other associational membership (neighbourhood, common religious affiliation, etc.) may serve as a good medium of getting acceptance of a new programme which involves every individual in the community. These cross-cultural treatments are also designed to suggest that specialized experts may approach an understanding of the way in which their specialty can be integrated with a whole culture by first getting a bird's-eye view of the great varieties of cultural problems which surround land-tenure, or food preparation, etc. Once an agricultural specialist has included in his expectations the possibility that in his attempt to get land organized in fields sufficiently large for the use of agricultural machinery, he may have to take account of graves and ghosts, sacred trees, oracles, shrines, dowries, sex-habits, and unborn children, as well as inheritance, property laws, rights of way, and "ancient lights," he will then be more ready to follow out the implications of any particular resistance which he meets in the foreign country where he goes as a specialist.

In this third section the emphasis has been placed on long-term types of change—on immunization rather than on clinical medicine, etc. The discussion on "Fundamental Education" in a sense cross-cuts the others, as programmes combining literacy with learning new ways of living have been found to be increasingly rewarding

Section IV is based upon material provided by psychiatrists who have worked in situations which combined clinical psychiatric procedure with inter-disciplinary research; here the materials from the other sections are discussed from a more specifically mental-health point of view. This chapter has a dual purpose: to accent the technical mental-health aspects of the entire question of social change, and to acquaint those unfamiliar with the mental-health approach with a psychiatrically oriented phrasing of the issues.

The concluding section deals with some of the long-term problems involved in purposive social change. Mental health and cultural integrity are high-level abstractions which must be translated into conceptions of different kinds of healthy personalities who live within and embody cultural patterns which express different aspirations, different designs for living.

There is one important aspect of this problem which has been purposely omitted from this survey: the question of the extent to which the special preoccupations and value systems of the members of international teams, drawn from Western cultures or educated in Western values, affect the work which such teams are able to do. It has been felt that such discussions, which must deal explicitly and self-searchingly with the defects as well as the strengths of the value systems of professional groups in British or American, Netherlands or French culture, as the case may be, should come from inside these societies. Two volumes, directed to the problems of American technicians administering programmes of change, are in preparation.[1] These will contain a careful consideration of the special set of values which American experts carry with them into other societies, whether these are enclaves within the United States or peoples in other parts of the world.

This survey, on the other hand, has been prepared for use at the international level,[2] the point of view has been a world

[1] 1954. The first study (Edward H. Spicer, 1952) consists of case studies within the United States, together with comparative materials. The second study, as yet unpublished (Conrad Arensberg, n. d.) will deal with problems related to Point Four allowing for American cultural bias.

[2] Appendix A places the problem in its formal international context, and provides selections from significant United Nations documents, and from documents of the Specialized Agencies of the United Nations which illustrate the international climate of opinion in which purposive technological change is being undertaken. These have been presented at some length in order that the reader may have before him the relationship between these high-level statements of overall purpose and procedures and the concrete illustrative materials with which later sections of the survey deal. A chart of the way in which the technical assistance activities of the United Nations are co-ordinated has been provided as a formal backdrop to the consideration of the diverse forms

point of view, and the emphasis has been upon the problems to which the professional skills and insights of the mental-health approach could contribute. It leaves to each national group the task of making a conscious evaluation of how well its own nationals are now equipped to carry out a programme involving a disciplined respect for the values of all the diverse co-operating peoples of the world.

II. STUDIES OF WHOLE CULTURES

BURMA

The culture of the Burmese is presented here as it was represented *in the villages* in the early part of this century. Contact with the Western world began with the Burmese wars against Arakan, Manipur, and Assam, which brought the Burmese into contact with the British in India. The description, with a few exceptions, is based on the work of British observers, who commented in many different ways on the traditional Burmese culture and on the changes that resulted from contact between East and West. With the establishment of the Republic of the Union of Burma, this first period of contact came to an end, but very few descriptions of conditions since Burma became an independent state on 4 January 1948 were available at the time this chapter was written. When the past tense is used, traditional Burmese culture as it was believed to be by scholars and administrators who experienced it at the turn of the century is referred to. However, in a few instances contemporary records have been introduced.[3]

of social organization within which the peoples of the world have been accustomed to operate. The reader may keep in mind the way in which this diagram would appear to a Burmese, a Tiv, a Greek, a Spanish American, a Palauan.

[3] There are two main kinds of sources for the sketch of Burmese culture. The main body of material comes from the writings of British officers of administration covering the time, approximately, from the beginning of this century until the end of British administration. These accounts are based on intimate knowledge of the people as well as of British policy and its application and results; and they are very sympathetic. Two studies of Burmese personality, made within the last eight years, were also used. These depend largely on the interviewing of Burmese in Burma or in the United States. The material on maternal care comes from the personal observation of Charles Brant, who spent several months in a Burmese village a year ago. British Government records have also been used.

The emphasis in this chapter will be upon the impact of the West—Western law and Western economic practices—on an ancient Asiatic civilization sophisticated in religious and social practices, but technologically simple. Under contact with the West, profound changes, such as immigration and commercial cultivation of land, were initiated, and the pressure of population upon land in certain areas became a background condition for a kind of poverty and unrest hitherto unknown. Since, in the past, government had been a matter of guidance and arbitration, the introduction of government by legal precedent and direct executive decision was difficult for Burmese and Western administrators alike. The presence of the "circle of villages" under the administration of one headman looked like, and was converted into, a district form of administration, whereas the Burmese had only a personal affiliation to this headman, their leader by heredity, not delegated right.

Burmese culture was a culture of contrasts perplexing to administrators used to the patterns of European or other Asiatic cultures. Although the everyday life of the people was simple, a large proportion of the men in the villages learned to read. The official religion was Buddhism, and the literacy was associated with religion and the reading of sacred texts; a knowledge of the contemporary world outside Burma was not involved. The literacy and sophistication of the Burmese belied the simplicity of their economy, not a money economy even though there was money. Their personal autonomy belied the pattern of interdependence of young children on parents and old parents on children.

Until 1824, the Burmese were voluntarily cut off from the world, interested in trading neither goods nor ideas with the outside world.[1] They were a people without either great poverty or great accumulated wealth. Predominantly rural, they lived in villages that were practically autonomous, without policemen, without enforcement of law or external authority, and with very little crime or litigation. Their lives, like their villages, were centred about a monastery, which gave their private lives and the life of the village focus and rhythm. Most of the men were literate; the women had a great degree of responsibility in agriculture and in domestic and monetary matters. The land was rich, and wants were simple; there was much time for festivity, dancing, races, and dramatic performances. Work was performed without compulsion, and there seems little evidence of anxiety. Building a fortune was not a pattern offered to the individual. The guiding principle was to increase in merit so as to be reincarnated at a higher stage of development, and merit resulted not from accumulating but from giving, not through inheritance but through one's own achievement, not from anxiety but from doing good deeds,

[1] J. S. Furnivall, 1948, p. 15.

and not from charting new paths into the future but from going along a known route.

The first effective contacts with Western civilization were commercial. Teak was exported, cotton goods imported. Entry into the nineteenth-century money economy meant a change in the level of aspiration of the Burmese, who had to learn to want and value material things instead of concentrating on immediate states of being, to spend their money for foreign goods and their labour in making money to buy these goods rather than devoting their small traditional surpluses to religious gifts that would increase their personal merit.

THE PEOPLE

We are here concerned with the Burmese specifically. Burma, however, contains several distinct racial and cultural groups, including the Buddhist Shans and Mons, as well as hill tribes such as the Katchins and Chins who were made subject to the Burmese king after periods of war. With the expansion of commerce, there was a need for more labour and, as so frequently happens when the speed of economic development outruns any change in the traditional needs and incentives of a non-industrialized population, the Burmese were unwilling to provide all of this labour. In response to the need for labour, large numbers of Indian and Chinese immigrants entered the country. Such immigration was not only welcomed by the administration but was even subsidized upon occasion. This influx of population can also be seen as related to the relatively low population density of Burma in comparison with other Asiatic countries.[1] By the beginning of the twentieth century, about two-thirds of the population of the six large industrial towns consisted of immigrant foreigners.[2] In 1942, Christian stated that there were 2,000,000 first-generation immigrants in Burma.[3]

The Burmese were absolute believers in personal worth and

[1] According to the United Nations *Demographic Yearbook* of 1948 there were 16,823,798 people in Burma as of 1941. Today there are an estimated 18,000,000. Census figures from 1901 to 1941 show a very slow upward trend in Burma's population. The 1.06 per cent rate of increase per annum for the decade 1921-31 is fairly typical. Burma has the lowest population density in South East Asia, estimated at about 65 per square mile; census figures are not accurate because of inadequate recording and due to the loss of records during the Japanese invasion. (*Demographic Yearbook, 1948*, 1949, p. 77. *See* United Nations, Statistical Office.)

To give overall figures, however, is misleading. Actually, there is a population problem arising out of maldistribution. As a result of the change in land tenure and the emphasis on cash crops, the richest districts of the Delta are the most thinly populated, supporting about 450 people per 1,000 cultivated acres, while the far less productive regions of the Dry Zone support 50 to 60 per cent more. (Furnivall, op. cit. p. 80.)

[2] Ibid, p. 117.

[3] John Leroy Christian, 1942, p. 158.

inviolability; they did not try to impose their religion, their ways, or their knowledge on other populations. If such groups were "segregated," it was because they also preferred their own customs. If they had their own chieftains, it was because there were such autonomous units throughout Burma; all rule was by such personal allegiance, from the unit of the village circle to the association of palm-sugar manufacturers.[1] All status, except that of the king, was achieved, and achievement was open to anyone through accumulation of merits, strengthening what they called the *kan*, a term by which we might understand personality or personal potency or luck; and with a strong *kan*, education could lead to status through attainment of office, or by way of the monastery.[2]

Distinctions of rank were very important and were constantly made, but did not depend on birth. Potentially, all men were born equal, whatever their race, allegiance, or religion.

The climate of Burma is tropical, characterized by heat, humidity, and much rainfall. The rainy season is from mid-May to mid-October, and from November to February there is the relatively cool, dry season. Rainfall varies from region to region, from 200 inches in the Arakan and Tenasserim coastal regions, to the dry zone of central Burma, where only about 25 to 45 inches of rain fall in a year. According to the amount of rainfall, the cash crop is rice or oil-seeds, and agricultural improvements are welcomed or rejected as unnecessary.[3]

RELIGION

It is impossible to speak of the life of the Burmese without speaking of their religion. Traditionally, the monastery has been the focus of village life. The duty-day services at the pagoda, which the villagers with their families attended every eight days in festive array and with festive foods, punctuated the Burmese month, providing highly social occasions.[4]

The great festivals were religious. The Buddhist "Lent," a period when all festivities including wedding celebrations were interdicted and meals of the devout were limited to one a day, coloured a fourth of the year's life. The great festival marking the end of "Lent" was the occasion of brilliant celebrations.[5]

Religion affected the standard of living. The best way of spending money, the expression of a "high" standard of living, was to give, as an act of merit; not for the sake of others, but for one's own enhancement, for the strengthening of the *kan*.

---

[1] Furnivall, op. cit. p. 17.
[2] Ibid. p. 15.
[3] *Burma Handbook*, 1943, pp. 1-3.
[4] Sir George Scott (Schway Yoe), 1910, pp. 217, 218, 220.
[5] H. Fielding Hall, 1906, pp. 152-154, Scott, op. cit. p. 221.

If there was enough money, one built a pagoda; for less, one could establish a shelter near a pagoda for the devout, or a rest-house on the mountain-side, or merely a small roofed structure where jars of water could be kept for the thirsty travellers who passed. Gifts were constantly given to the monasteries by simple villagers, and food was given daily to the mendicant monks, who usually gave most of it to pariah dogs and other animals. Excess money could be spent on other deeds of merit, such as buying and liberating fowl that some Indian servant, after much searching, had bought for his master; and since this was directed first of all at the preservation of life, it was not "interference," but a deed of great religious merit for the Buddhist. The hoarding of money was regarded as evil; spiritual merit was accumulated, rather than material wealth.

Health and well-being, which were aspects of personal potency, were also bound up with religion. There were two religious systems: besides the official Buddhism, there was the relation with the *nats,* beings who were easily offended and had to be propitiated to prevent hostile acts. Within Buddhism, the individual was kept well and strong by maintaining and enhancing the potency of his *kan,* his personality; if he had had a strong *kan,* he could withstand evil. One's *kan* had been created by the accumulation of merits from a past existence. In order to maintain it, it was necessary to have an even balance of merits and demerits in the present life. But everyone wanted to increase his *kan* by having a preponderance of merits to his credit, because in this way he could reduce the number of lives he had to live before he could be delivered from incarnation.[1]

On the other hand, one had to forestall evil pending from the *nats,* and their evil intentions constantly had to be turned away through some preventive act, some small sacrifice. Buddhism punctuated life with positive deeds—acts of merit—strengthening the individual and moving him forward. But these acts were separate, not a part of every undertaking, and Buddhist ritual itself, except for the special festivals, came every eighth day only; the *nats,* on the other hand, were lurking all the time, ready to take offence, and preventive measures formed an accompanying part of daily life. These might consist merely of a yellow string tied around the left wrist to avoid cholera, or the sprinkling of the house with hallowed water, or the leaving of a morsel at a *nat* shrine; or they might be expressed in a complicated rite.[2] Some of the *nats* were household and village *nats,* and these were known and predictable. But there were many unknown *nats* whom a traveller could easily offend unwittingly. The fishermen and hunters left of-

[1] Scott, op. cit. p. 186.
[2] Ibid. p. 399.

ferings all along their way, and boat-races had a preliminary run during which offerings could be left at all the appropriate spots so that all the *nats* could be propitiated.[1] During illness, together with the medicines and the massage, rites of propitiation and expulsion were often performed. When the yearly epidemic of cholera struck, the people, at some given time during the night, beat their roofs and their drums, blew trumpets, yelled, and danced about, to drive away the *nat* who was taking revenge for some insult.[2]

These two religious systems, the official Buddhism and the unformalized religion of the *nats*, are the basis of concepts about health and illness, misfortune, well-being, potency, and achievement. The *kan*, the sum of personal merits and demerits, has sometimes been translated into English as *luck*. But there was no such thing as luck among the Burmese; there was only the deserved state.[3] An individual was born a king or a commoner or a dog because of the balance of merits and demerits in his previous existence; he was himself responsible for his own state. If he had health it was because his *kan* had been strengthened to withstand illness; if his enterprises yielded fruit, it was because they were sustained by his merits. If, in spite of strong *kan*, he suffered misfortune, it was because he had failed in his preventive measures against the *nats*, or because he had unwittingly offended them.

British observers and, more recently, American observers found behaviour which seemed to them strikingly free from anxiety. Hall noticed it even at a time of dire famine,[4] and Scott reports that when the inhabitants of an entire quarter in Mandalay were burned out of their homes, managing to save only their clothes, a minister, coming to their assistance at night, found they had set up a rude stage among the ruins and were enjoying a dramatic performance.[5] Hanks relates this lack of anxiety to an absence of historicity. Only the experienced present may be said to be significant, not its antecedents and future effects. They did not investigate causes, neither were they guided by the thought of future consequences. What life brought was deserved and inevitable, but this meant also that nothing was irreparable, for no conflagration or famine could harm one's *kan*. And deeds of some degree of merit were within everyone's power; therefore, achievement and rise in status were open to everyone: "as you desire, so you get."[6] People were born in favourable or unfavourable circumstances, but this was no cause for resentment or envy. It was the inevitable outcome of the previous existence, and the in-

[1] Ibid. pp. 233-39.
[2] Ibid. pp. 396-98.
[3] H. Fielding Hall, 1908, pp. 134-37.
[4] Ibid. pp. 123-32; L. M. Hanks, 1949, p. 298.
[5] Scott, op. cit. pp. 66-67.
[6] Hall, 1908, op. cit. pp. 135-36.

dividual could change it. A really great act of merit like building a pagoda could help a man to skip several existences in his progress toward delivery from incarnation.

The monastery and the monks were the centre around which village life was lived. The mendicant monks walked daily about the village, receiving their gifts of food. And in every household, the day's supply of food included a portion for the monks. There was no compulsion or persuasion in this; like all giving, it was done voluntarily and with enjoyment. To give was a merit, and it was the recipient who conferred a benefit on the giver.[1] At a time of famine in Upper Burma, when the villagers were given subsistence rations at government work-camps, they persuaded the many monks not to leave the villages as they had intended, and out of their meagre rations, they brought back food every night for the monks.[2] In Upper Burma every village has its monastery; but at present in Lower Burma, where many of the new villages have a shifting population of tenants and labourers, only about a fourth of the villages have monasteries.[3]

Traditionally, every Burmese boy had to join the society of the monks and assume the yellow robe, if only for a few days. Without this initiation a man's *kan* would always be one-sided, that is, his ill deeds would swell the sum of his demerits but his good deeds would not be counted as merits.[4] Some stayed on after initiation, taking permanent vows, or vows for a period of years; others returned later in life.[5] The monks formed a powerful group in Burma.[6] Traditionally, the education of all males was in their hands, education covering literacy as well as principles of conduct and inter-personal relations, and of living in general. The teaching of much theory and religion was included and some knowledge of days and months and numbers, but the material aspects of education were not covered, since monks were removed from the secular aspects of life.[7]

The monks lived mainly a life of meditation; the "work" they did was that of teaching or of copying manuscripts. The little manual work, such as sweeping and bringing water, was performed by the young scholars. The monastic life was one of abstinence. Clothing was only a necessary covering, not an adornment; food was not for pleasure but only for health and strength so as to allow more diligent attention to prayer and meditation.[8] No food was taken after the shadows began to slope eastward at noon. No one wearing the yellow robe could

[1] Scott, op. cit. p. 31; Hall, 1908, op. cit. p. 167.
[2] Hall, 1908, op. cit. pp. 124-32.
[3] Furnivall, op. cit. p. 103.
[4] Scott, op. cit. pp. 18-19.
[5] Hall, 1906, op. cit. p. 134.
[6] Christian, op. cit. pp. 196-203.
[7] Hall, 1906, op. cit. pp. 141-42.
[8] Scott, op. cit. pp. 31, 37.

be out after sundown. All sexual relations were abjured. The village respected the sanctity of the monks, who had the highest status possible to mortals; but it watched their conduct. If they did not behave as monks should, they lost all their holiness and were driven out of the village.[1]

THE INDIVIDUAL

The Burmese have been called "a community of equals."[2] Traditionally there was no one between the king and the villager, except by achieved status.[3] Within structured units, however, there is now, as in earlier years, a relative ranking which is not based on individual achievement. The degree of kinship to the host determines rank at a gathering. Within the family a child is addressed by name by the parents and responds with their kinship titles, and he addresses his younger siblings and cousins by name, while they address him by title. "Etiquette governing the relations of superior to inferior is omnipresent in daily life."[4] Traditionally, it was reflected in the language of daily intercourse itself. The ranking person must be given the high seat, must be served first, and must precede in walking.

Status is achieved through learning. Traditionally, this was monastic learning and was related to the fact that Buddhist monks outrank all other people. Even kings had to prostrate themselves before monks and to address them in a special language.[5] Office has led to status traditionally and still does. Learning, to be truly respected, must be pure learning, and the school of agriculture introduced by the Administration proved a failure because it required application.

Observers in the past as well as the present have been struck by the "autonomy," the "fierce independence," of the Burmese. This freedom of the individual is part of the pattern of responsibility for one's own state or "fate," of personal progress through individual acts of merit, and a counterpart of a certain lack of true interest in the welfare of others. No one can or does help another to strengthen his *kan*. There was profound conviction of personal inviolability carried, in Western eyes, to extremes. Hall says if a villager saw a man about to cross a bridge he knew to be broken, he would give no warning, assuming the other knew what he was about. If a man was seen attempting suicide, no one would try to stop him. If a man was in obvious desperate straits, no one would offer help; but they would be ready to help if requested. To volunteer help was discourteous; it signified an attempt to interfere with personal autonomy. The Burmese valued and sought personal strength,

---

[1] Hall, 1906, op. cit. p. 134.
[2] Ibid. p. 54.
[3] Ibid. p. 79.
[4] Hanks, op. cit. pp. 287, 291.
[5] Ibid., pp. 287, 288; Hall, 1906, op. cit. p. 131.

but not as power over others, and to offer help would be a bid for power on one hand, and on the other, a reflection on another's strength.[1]

A less sympathetic observer may see this attitude as callousness; and Hanks speaks of an absence of empathy among the Burmese. The net result is irresponsibility for the effect of one's acts upon others. When this is added to the tenet that all demerit can be wiped out through expiation, this lack of responsibility for the effect of one's acts on others meant that a man could indulge in a momentary whim to harm or kill another.[2] In March 1951, as reported in a radio news broadcast, a policeman in Mandalay found a hand-grenade in the street and threw it playfully at a crowd, where it exploded and killed several people.

In the framework of personal inviolability, cases brought for litigation concerned perhaps a word of abuse, a threat, a slap; and the Burmese would consider a fine of six months' earnings or a month's imprisonment not too great for expiation. On the other hand, a man who lost property often did not bring a complaint to court; there was no personal violation involved. On this basis, even the questions of the assessor of non-agricultural income were insufferable, as they were prying and inquisitive and, in fact, interfering. The legal systems of the West, with their emphasis upon externality, rationality, and efficiency, clashed with the Burmese way of looking at human worth and integrity.

Authority within this framework was looked to only for guidance. The Burmese were ready to be reminded to do what was appropriate, but not to be ordered to do anything. They went to the headman for arbitration, not dictatorial pronouncement. They did not judge others. They gossiped all day, but without criticism, saying, "It is his way.[3]

GOVERNMENT, LAW, AUTHORITY

Against this background, we can understand the attitude of the Burmese toward the authority of the government and the law.

When the British administrators came to Burma, they found a dual system of government: there was a king who ruled the people at a distance through an official administration which emanated from his court out to the local districts, and there were hereditary headmen who ruled by personal authority. The king had certain customary powers which were respected; beyond these he had no means of enforcing orders. There was no army, no regular police, and there were almost no prisons. His officials exercised judicial powers, but as arbitrators, not judges, referring to the law-books for guidance, not for rules.

[1] Hall, 1906, op. cit. pp. 225-26.
[2] Geoffrey Gorer, 1943, p. 34.
[3] Hall, 1906, op. cit. p. 225.

The traditional administration had not been seen—as was the new—as an external authority enforced from above, nor had the traditional system been regarded as interfering with the daily life of the people.[1]

The headmen were hereditary chieftains of a group of people who happened to live in adjoining villages, the so-called "circle." They governed people, not a locality, so that sometimes people in the villages who had come from elsewhere owed allegiance to another, and were not under their authority. Again, the groups of villages were thought of as having always belonged together and their chief as having been born to them. Their laws also belonged to them and were part of village life and structure; they were followed as inherent to a way of life, not through imposed obedience to authority. The headman guided and arbitrated, he did not coerce. He had no policemen because they were not needed here, any more than they were by the king and his officials.

To Western eyes the Burmese system appeared confused, areas of authority seemed undefined, the law seemed neither organized nor binding. The Western administrators proceeded to make changes which they thought were in accord with patterns already present, with a view to creating uniform, rational arrangements. They found it confusing that some headmen were in charge of only one village, while others were responsible for a varying number of villages. They graded the headmen into three grades according to the number of villages under their jurisdiction; and they did away with the "irrational" hereditary element and appointed the headmen as salaried government officials. They thus changed personal authority to territorial authority, placing the people as local residents under the headman. The circle, based on organic relationships between people, was replaced by the district, a local administrative unit based on space.

This system encroached upon "the autonomy of the circle by interfering with its internal administration"; however, the headmen unofficially retained much of their original authority, since it was theirs by right and tradition. By the end of the nineteenth century, these discrepancies between assumed form and actual practice had been administratively corrected. For the sake of efficiency, the district—the old circle—was cut up into villages, and the village became the largest self-governing unit. New duties were imposed upon villagers and headmen, heavy penalties for non-compliance were introduced, but no new rights were conferred. The village itself was now converted from "a social and residential unit into an administrative unit." The new system "cut at the roots of organic social life within the village."[2]

[1] Furnivall, op. cit. p. 14.
[2] Ibid. pp. 14-15, 37-38, 74-75.

Law and orderly social behaviour had been based on an accepted pattern of living which only incidentally, not directly, was seen as related to village welfare. A man acted with what amounted to honesty and uprightness because that was the way to act rather than out of social responsibility, or out of concern for others. When the organic unity of the village was shattered, when external authority with penal sanctions was substituted for the authority inherent in a traditional way of life, the traditional guiding principle of social conduct was destroyed and there was nothing to take its place. With the increase in population, and the break-down of traditional patterns of behaviour, new lands which had been set aside for communal grazing or fuel or sanitary arrangements were appropriated by individual villagers, and individual villagers interfered, for instance, with the irrigation system with a view to their own profit only, even when this caused damage to the whole village. Soon after the headmen had been transformed into salaried officials, it was found necessary to form a village police-force, and shortly after, the courts, established along Western lines, were filled with cases.[1] The Western administrators attempted to base legislation on traditional Burmese principles, but study of these principles revealed them as seemingly irrational and disorganized. The Burmese had depended upon the arbitration and guidance of the headman; if they went to court they went in search of a man who, with wisdom and authority, could help them arrive at some amicable arrangement. They did not go to find fixed legal principles and logical decisions.[2] Punishment, formerly, had been atonement, and a stay in jail was not a disgrace. Mercy and forgiveness were inadequate, since they meant that the demerit remained. Hall, who had himself been a magistrate, tells of a case of a man who upon hearing that he was wanted for robbery, came to the court to give himself up. But also the practice of magistrates of meting out particularly severe punishment by way of making an "example" of the culprit was completely incomprehensible to people who saw punishment in a personal, religious context, not a secular community one, to whom this was like washing one dirty garment twice to clean another that was missing.[3]

For Burmese custom, the rule of law was substituted, which included the British form of trial by jury. But the Burmese interpreted the jury system in their own way—instead of adhering to strict legal precedents, they applied an intimate knowledge of the individuals involved, according to their own conceptions of humaneness. At one time, when husband and wife came to court, the jury punished both as perpetual trouble-makers; when a woman brought a charge of rape, they con-

[1] Ibid. pp. 37, 105-6, 115.
[2] Ibid. pp. 14, 31.
[3] Hall, 1906, op. cit. pp. 98-99.

victed her of having seduced her attacker into committing adultery.[1]

Early in the new century, the village system had become a mechanical contrivance only, in many of the areas. The popular self-government based on organic unity had been replaced by what has been described by a British critic as "a foreign legal system unable to control the anti-social forces it liberated.[2] The early writers on Burma had been impressed by the "orderly habits of the people," the relative absence of crime and rarity of litigation.[3] The tremendous growth of crime in Burma since then is said by Furnivall to be related to several factors, all eventually connected with the loss or lack of the organic foundation of inter-personal relations, as in the case of the establishment of new villages in the Delta, composed mainly of immigrants. But the spectacular rise of crime and litigation began before the colonization of the Delta—with the accompanying displacement of population—had assumed large proportions.[4] The need for functioning within the new legal framework soon encouraged the form of higher education which the Burmese would undertake most readily without outside persuasion: the study of law—that is of Western law, including how to obstruct and circumvent it.[5] But there was no fundamental ethical commitment to this new type of law. British commentators in the past were struck by the easy acceptance of bribery and what the Western world calls corruption, among officials. Outside the village structure and the personal authority of the headman, venality in the Western sense was rampant, as sanctions against it had no cultural roots. This is reported to be true at present also.

These tendencies were of course enhanced during the Japanese occupation, as in any occupied country.[6]

VILLAGE LIFE

Burmese life was predominantly village life, and even now there are relatively few Burmese in cities. The traditional picture of this life is that it was a very happy life; with no indigents and no hard work, with gaiety and very frequent festivity. There was much sociability and few quarrels. Rich and poor had enough to eat, and ate approximately the same food. All had the same amusements: perhaps the rich paid the minstrels and other entertainers, but the poor were there to enjoy them. The villagers lived in small houses and spent as much time as possible out of doors. Any money not needed to

[1] Furnivall, op. cit. pp. 31-32.
[2] Ibid. p. 76.
[3] Ibid, p. 137.
[4] Ibid. pp. 137, 141.
[5] Ibid. pp. 127-28.
[6] Hanks, op. cit. p. 294.

cover these expenses went to pay for entertainment for the village, for silks and bangles, and above all, for charity. Burmans detest hoarding, and a miser was threatened with a fate as vile as that awaiting the parricide. Hall speaks of a man who lived with his family in a three-room house, sparsely furnished, on about 1,000 rupees a year; the rest of his income of about 11,000 rupees went for gifts.[1] At one time there was an interdiction against building grand houses, but long after it disappeared, people continued to live by choice in small, lightly built, sparsely furnished houses.[2]

Work was not a virtue, except in so far as it was a deed of merit. A deed of merit was something positive and chosen; it was done without compulsion. Girls could be heard, after dark, pounding rice to remove the pellicle, sometimes working until the rising of "the red star," and chanting happily; this was the preparation of the offering for a feast-day, a deed of great merit.[3] On the other hand, work usually ceased long before sundown. Where the cultivated land was level, rice-growing was easy and not time-consuming; the monsoon rains were retained in the soil so that no irrigation was necessary. The land was incredibly fertile. Women and children and bullocks did much of the work; the men spent much time smoking, gossiping, sauntering about, and dozing.[4] Some regularity of work was introduced at sowing- and harvest-time; otherwise, work depended on personal disposition. In the early 1900s, if the farmer thought he had enough rice for home consumption, and had sold enough for money, he left what remained in the fields to rot. Similarly, he did not give particular care to his draught-animals.[5]

At this period, there was no need to work more in the fields. At home, some crafts were practised; women cooked and wove cloth. Men also wove, and were said to produce embroideries superior to those of women. Women were the petty traders of the villages, and almost every house had a little shop. But this was not "work," and the shop was mainly an excuse to bring more people in for visits. If work as such was not valued, neither was living off the labour of others.[6] Services were not requested of others. This was probably related to the feeling of the personal inviolability of others, so that when monks had to ask that some service be performed for them, they did not say "Do this for me," but "Do what is lawful";[7] that is, work meant living according to established principles, and when it resulted in a service to others, this was only incidental.

[1] Hall, 1906, op. cit. pp. 107-8; Scott, op. cit. pp. 75-76, 558.
[2] Scott, op. cit. pp. 75, 79.
[3] Ibid. p. 81.
[4] Ibid. pp. 244-47.
[5] Ibid. pp. 80, 247.
[6] Hall, 1906, op. cit. p. 115.
[7] Scott, op. cit. p. 35.

There was much festivity in the village during the nine months when it was allowed. After an evening meal, the young people bathed and dressed in festive clothes; and almost every evening, except during the rainy season, there was some amusement, sometimes lasting through the night. There were dances and dramatic performances. Minstrels were engaged to come to a man's house or recount their tales in the streets for all.[1] The great festivals were brilliant with lights, the shrines with burning tapers, the pagodas lit by tiers of lamps, the monasteries, houses and rafts were full of lights; tiny rafts with lamps were set afloat on the river. The great festival at the end of the three-month "Lent" lasted for seven days.[2] There were, besides, boat-races, Burmese football, cock-fights, and other amusements. During the months when there was no work in the fields, the men loitered at home to receive visits or went visiting, or they gambled. Good conversation was prized.

There was much noise in the village. In the monastery, there was the loud sound of the wooden bell. And, during the teaching, there was the deafening sound of learning; the boys shouted their lessons while trying to learn them, and a really noisy schoolroom meant that everyone was working in top form.[3] In the village, a knot of men might be talking together at the top of their voices.[4] Added to this din was the strident sound of the wagon wheels. A creak of a particular whine and penetration was prized by the wagoners, and people identified the approaching wagon by the key at which the creak was pitched.[5] When a family went to the duty-day services, planning to spend the night on the pagoda grounds, they often beat a gong along the way to announce loudly this deed of merit. Noise was associated with the valued things—with religion and learning, with sociability and meritorious acts, and with bustling festivity. Noise was positive and good; and noise was used against the forces of evil, to drive out the *nats*.

Parents took care of their children and children supported parents in old age as a matter of course, though emotionally, the individual appears to have been self-centred. This accepted interdependency between parents and children contrasted with the British pattern in which parents owed support to children, and self-esteem was tied up with independence in old age.

The land belonged to the family and could not be alienated by any one of its members, and the members found it difficult to alienate themselves from the land. If they went from the poorer districts of Upper Burma to earn money in Lower

[1] Ibid. pp. 72-74.
[2] Hall, 1906, op. cit. pp. 152-68.
[3] Scott, op. cit. p. 16.
[4] Ibid. pp. 357, 361.
[5] Ibid. p. 82.

Burma at harvest-time, they were not happy until they returned.[1] They would not sell their land, however useless it might be, and under Burmese law, if they did "sell" it, it was understood that they always had the right to redeem it. They could not lose it to a money-lender. A man had security through his family and his village; he did not have to save against illness or old age, he was not afraid of plunging hopelessly into debt, or of losing the means of making a living. And although the villagers sold some of their rice, they had no cash-crop economy. Money-making and the possession of property were not an essential part of their lives.

Civilized, literate, artistic, well-to-do, the Burmese were nevertheless without many of the attitudes and motivations and pressures which are associated with Western civilization. They presented a picture full of contradictions. Money was in use, yet there was not a Western-type money economy. There was literacy, yet there was little knowledge of the world, since literacy was only for the reading of sacred texts and was associated with contemplation and the renunciation of worldly or concrete matters. There was interest in the past and the future, in advancement, but only of the individual on his way to liberation from the flesh, from the necessity to be born again. There was little interest in history or in progress in the Western sense.

Their lives were full of discontinuities also. There was suavity and graciousness suddenly turning to violent vituperation. Disciplined behaviour could yield to the whim to assault or kill. Their days were full of gay life and festivity for most of the year, but absolutely without amusement for the three months of the Buddhist "Lent." The villagers indulged with great pleasure in food and gay apparel; but there was also the village monastery, where monks had to live ascetically, dressing only to cover their bodies, and eating only to retain life and strength.

MATERNAL AND CHILD CARE

The Burmese do not have many children. A family of five or six live births is unusual. There is usually an interval of three to six years between children.[2] In the cities, Western contraceptive practices are known, but we do not know about birth-control practices in the villages, nor whether the number of children is limited deliberately and if so, why.[3] When children do come they are welcomed into the family circle with warmth and full acceptance. A baby is usually in someone's hands, fondled, enjoyed, passed from adult to adult. People play with children, give them sweets and money and coddle them.

[1] Ibid. p. 106.
[2] Hanks, op. cit. p. 290; Christian, op. cit. p. 147.
[3] Charles Brant, n.d.

Women will bathe and anoint them. Men will take them to cock-fights,[1] provided that they are their own offspring, or in lieu of offspring. Children in general are not loved, apparently; they do not evoke spontaneous affection and concern, and may even be treated with cruelty.[2] It seems that kindnesses to strange children do not fall into the pattern validating the deed of merit.

As a rule children do not come early in marriage. But everyone does want to have children. This does not arise from a desire to continue the family name, since, with the Burmese tenets of reincarnation, continuity is only personal continuity. There are no family names, traditionally, among the Burmese; neither is status derived from the family; it was the personal name, based on the individual's day of birth, that was important. For the same reason, there is no desire for an heir. Traditionally, there was no accumulated property; all wealth was the wealth of personal merits which a man took with him at death to bring into a higher incarnation. But family life was enjoyed and children were wanted. The Burmese are pictured by all writers as highly sociable, valuing companionship, conversation, and sheer human noise. Childless couples are considered unfortunate, and often informally adopt the children of relatives or friends.[3]

There is marked preference for male children; to fail to have at least one son is very disappointing. For a woman to bear a son is equivalent to her achievement of full existence as a human being. Only a male can be initiated in youth into the Buddhist priesthood and the sponsorship of this ceremony is an important deed of merit on the parents' part. Parents who have no sons of their own may sponsor the initiation ceremony for a boy whose family is poor and unable to afford the expense of a proper rite.[4]

Pregnancy is not regarded as a normal state; it appears to be equated with illness. In any case, it is a time when the woman's *kan,* in this case the balance of health, is at a low point, and the woman is therefore vulnerable.[5] A pregnant woman must be careful to have only pleasant thoughts, and not to listen to or take part in unpleasant gossip. Deeds of merit, such as her daily prayers, paying homage to the household altar, decorating the altar with flowers, and giving food to the priests, are all doubly important during pregnancy. What she does will affect the unborn child as well as herself. If she attends marriage ceremonies or sends wedding gifts, her child is likely to be still-born; if she attends a funeral, an evil spirit at the cemetery will find it easy to enter her at this period of low *kan,* and in-

[1] Hanks, op. cit. p. 290.
[2] Gorer, op. cit. p. 29.
[3] Brant, op. cit.
[4] Ibid.
[5] Ibid.

jure her child. If it is necessary for her to go to a funeral or visit a household during a wake, she must take specific preventive measures; and if she has to go past a cemetery, she must be careful: "a pregnant woman looks out of the corner of her eye three times at a cemetery."[1] After delivery, she must be purged of the "noxious humours" of child-birth.[2]

When her pregnancy is visible, she must cover herself with a blanket when priests or male strangers go by.[3] Buddhist priests must be protected from this evidence of reproductive activity; it is not clear whether there is also a question of embarrassment or modesty involved.

There are specific treatments for ills at this time. If the pregnant woman has a headache, she inhales the fumes of turmeric, sprinkled over live coals; if her neck and the muscles of her legs and feet are stiff, she is massaged. To avoid vaginal discharge, she takes her bath before sundown; and if she must bathe after sunset, she puts a live coal into the jar of bath-water.[4]

In the villages of Lower Burma visited by Brant, pregnancy is calculated from the month menstruation ceases, and it is believed that a female child will be born exactly at the completion of the ninth month. A male child is supposed to be born a few days sooner. During her pregnancy, a woman abstains from hot foods, such as chillies and pepper; meat and fowl should be eaten sparingly, and only small amounts of coconut liquid and drinking-water are resorted to, to prevent nausea.[5]

A woman in labour goes to bed. The midwife is not called until labour sets in. When she comes, she massages the abdomen and sees that the head of the forthcoming child is in the proper position. The midwife receives the baby as soon as it is expelled, and cuts and ties the umbilical cord. She bathes the infant at once with warm water and soap. The mother is fed a mixture of turmeric and water, and turmeric powder is made into a paste and rubbed all over her body. A broad piece of cloth is tied around her waist. To facilitate the discharge of blood from the womb, the abdomen is rubbed daily during the period of convalescence.[6]

Heat is extremely important during this period of child-birth and the lochial period. When a woman is in labour, a fire is made beside her bed, and heated bricks are applied to her legs and feet. Traditionally, after delivery, whatever the time of year, she had to stay in bed for a lochial period of from five to seven days, covered with blankets and heated with applications of hot bricks; and she was finally steamed with medicinal

[1] Ibid.
[2] Scott, op. cit. p. 2.
[3] Brant, op. cit.
[4] Ibid.
[5] Ibid.
[6] Ibid.

herbs. She is, at any rate, encouraged to eat "heat-producing foods" such as *ngapi* (dried fish) and fried salt fish.[1]

Traditionally, if a pregnant woman died after the foetus was fully formed, her abdomen was opened and the foetus was buried separately in a secret place to avoid disinterment by sorcerers. If a baby was still-born, its body was wrapped with a piece of iron and was buried thus, with the injunction never to return to its mother's womb.[2]

When the lochial period is over, the mother is steamed and the baby has its head shaved.[3] The naming ceremony takes place after a few days, when an auspicious day is determined. Traditionally, the name has been limited by the specific day of birth; each day of the eight-day week has a group of sounds allotted to it for the initials of names of people born on those days. On this day, the child's head is washed for the first time, by the midwife, with specially prepared water, and the guests wash their hands with the same water. The midwife receives a present and the assembled company is feasted.[4]

According to traditional practice, an exact note is made of the hour of birth and a certificate of birth is drawn for everyone, so that a horoscope may be cast and the auspicious periods of life may be known. The certificate is kept by the parents until the child is old enough to take care of it, and then it is guarded by each individual as a most valuable possession, and is consulted with the aid of an astrologer. There is a belief, also, that the particular day of birth determines the personality of the child. Just as the future is already established, so personal attractiveness is established by the day of birth. A child does not have to win approval to become a favourite; his day of birth has already determined that.[5]

In the early months, babies are almost inseparable from the mother and are fed before they have a chance to cry. The mother goes about her marketing and her household work with the baby straddled on her hip.[6] At first the babies sleep mostly in their mother's arms. Gradually, they are taught to like being held by others in the group, who are always ready to fondle and play with them, and the mother is ready to accept without comment the child who, suddenly apprehensive, is ready to come back. Bodily contact is highly valued, and is a stabilizing and reassuring factor throughout life.[7] When the baby was not sleeping in the mother's lap, he slept in a basket hung from the roof. His mother sat beside him singing and crooning lullabies which mixed dreams of glory and humble fears, in the

[1] Ibid.; Scott, op. cit. p. 2.
[2] Scott, op. cit. p. 2.
[3] Brant, op. cit.
[4] Scott, op. cit. pp. 3-5.
[5] Ibid. pp. 5-13.
[6] Gorer, op. cit. p. 26.
[7] Hanks, op. cit. p. 290.

same teasing-cherishing pattern, affectionate and rejecting by turn, which, according to recent information, characterizes her ordinary relationship with her child.[1]

Breast-feeding continues for an indefinite period, sometimes up to three or four years.[2] At six or eight months, it is supplemented by fruits, juices, and solid foods, presented lovingly. The first solid food is rice, which the mother pre-chews, forms into a ball and puts in the baby's mouth. The solid diet is increased until, at weaning, the child has the same diet as adults. But he does not eat with adults until he is about eight and has learned the etiquette of eating.[3]

Toilet-training comes early, casually, and easily. Mothers maintain that the babies train themselves "naturally." A Western observer suggests that the mother holds the baby away from her body or sets him on the ground when he gives signs of wanting to defecate or urinate. At any rate, infants learn to indicate such wishes by the time they are six months old. It is a matter of social acceptability—not soiling the adult—rather than of cleanliness. And the child is not taught to use the family privy until he discovers its purpose himself, at about the age of five. There is no pressure to grow up, neither is there discouragement. Fortitude is not stressed. A child when hurt or sick is held in the arms of those who love him.[4]

The Burmese child gets a good deal of attention, but there is neither continuity nor predictability in it. He is held and fondled much, but often by people who have no continuing responsibility or concerned affection for him. His father may be indulgent at one moment, giving him money for sweets, and brusque and indifferent at another. The same is true of the mother, who may be demonstrative or indifferent according to unpredictable whims. She may be warmly cherishing, or teasing. There is no temporal continuity or predictability, but there is the ever-present assurance of human companionship, of someone who will hold and fondle *now*. The Burmese are reported to show a complete absence of that anxiety which we associate with insecurity.[5]

PLACE OF WOMEN

For anyone who undertakes to introduce change in Burma, it is important to be aware of the position of women there. Traditionally, they have occupied a high position, and have had a very important share in the affairs of the village. Theoretically, they were lesser than men—if we are justified in arranging them in hierarchical order. For example, a good woman could

[1] Gorer, op. cit. p. 29; Scott, op. cit. pp. 85-87.
[2] Gorer, op. cit. p. 27.
[3] Ibid. pp. 26-27.
[4] Hanks, op. cit. p. 290.
[5] Hall, 1908, op. cit. pp. 123-32, 134-35; Hanks, op. cit. pp. 297-98.

hope to be reincarnated as a man.[1] The hire for women was less than that for men and, for this reason, the compensation paid for killing a woman by accident was likewise less than that paid for a man.[2] Officially, women as well as men stated that men were superior.[3]

As, according to Buddhist tenet, each man was responsible for his own acts, woman could not be considered evil for "tempting" man. If a monk met his downfall through a woman, she could not be blamed for being a woman; the monk was at fault for failing to discipline his emotions. However, when a woman brought a complaint of rape to a British court, the jury—all Burmese—punished her instead for seduction.

The fact remains that a woman had at least as important a share in village activities as did her husband. All petty trading and, in fact, practically all Burmese trading (with the exception of Indian traders) was in the hands of women. Women were responsible for most of the farming activities; men did the heavier work and the women and children did the rest.[4] Women actually were the more actively religious at the home altar, in giving to the monks, in taking flowers to the pagodas, and in religious works in general.[5] In the absence of their husbands, women acted for them, carrying out the sale of the entire rice crop to the agent of an English rice farm, or gathering the policemen in the absence of the head constable to stop a fight, arrest culprits, and send them to jail.[6]

Girls kept their own names at marriage and wore no sign of their new status. The husbands had no power over their property, whether it was brought as dowry, inherited, or earned. With regard to marriage and divorce, women were treated in the same way as men under the law.[7] Men consulted their wives and women deferred to their husbands. Marriages were good when the combination of birthdays was an auspicious one, and in general, divorce, although easy, was not common.[8] Either husband or wife could ask for a divorce. Women were easily provoked, were supposed to have less patience, and often asked for a divorce; the Burmese magistrates as a rule paid no attention to their requests, unless repeated often and with some reason. A husband might request to be divorced because he had no male issue or because his wife did not love him or defer to him; a woman might complain that her husband was poor, or ailing, or idle, or had been crippled after the marriage. The people distinguished among causes for divorce, and divorces

---

[1] Hall, 1906, p. 297.
[2] Ibid. p. 171.
[3] Ibid. p. 172.
[4] Scott, op. cit. pp. 68-69, 244-45.
[5] Hall, 1908, op. cit. pp. 102, 176-81.
[6] Scott, op. cit. p. 53.
[7] Hall, 1906, op. cit. p. 169-74, 189-90.
[8] Scott, op. cit. pp. 60-61.

based on unacceptable causes were looked upon unfavourably. It was said of a divorced woman that "She fits all men as a pot its lid" (that is, "She is easy to get"). If a man entered a monastery to get rid of his wife, he was called a "jungle runaway." [1]

The difference between men and women was given symbolic expression. Men carried loads on their shoulders, women on their heads.[2] Women did the work of the household, which was light; also they ran the store which was part of almost every village household. They husked the rice in wooden mortars, they made cheroots, they cooked. They had looms under the house where they wove fabrics, but the men produced the best fabrics, as their embroidery surpassed that of the women. The posts of the houses all had sexes; the male ones were considered easy-going and harmless, the female ones fortunate and leading to honour; the female posts were ones which were broad at the base.[3] A man's riches consisted of his learning, his family, and his good name; his pride lay in being celebrated and feared for the strength of his mind and body. A woman's riches consisted of her beauty and her pride lay in her ability to talk in a pleasant and amusing way.[4]

At the age when boys joined the monastic order, girls underwent an ear-piercing during a great three-day celebration which marked their official entrance to the status of womanhood. This was the only festival in a woman's life; there were several festivals for boys and men.[5]

In general, women were actually fully equal to men, handling their own property, acting in their own right, negotiating family matters, making decisions. They were not dependent on men, except incidentally, in so far as there was interdependence among all members of a family. During the period of Western administration, this self-dependent role of women—which differed both from European and from most Asiatic patterns—was not taken into account.

FOOD

Burmese behaviour is markedly oral. Men and women smoke a large part of the time, or chew betel. Monks are not allowed to smoke, but they chew betel all the time. Drinking does not form part of the picture. People drank water when thirsty, and some tea.[6] They did not drink anything at meal-times, and their many medications were very rarely in liquid form.[7] Pregnant women reduced their liquid consumption even further. On the

[1] Ibid.
[2] Hall, 1906, op. cit. p. 197.
[3] Scott, op. cit. p. 77.
[4] Ibid. p. 222.
[5] Hall, 1906, p. 177.
[6] Brant, op. cit.
[7] Scott, op. cit. pp. 70-72.

other hand, monks and the devout, during "Lent" had to forego all solid nourishment after the noon meal, to avoid "heating." Here there is an association of liquid with cold and the non-carnal, and of solid food with heat and the carnal. So the pregnant and lochial woman was given hot treatments and "heating" foods, while the monks consumed only "cooling" liquids most of the day.

In the villages some rice liquor was drunk, but never in the house, and since the introduction of Western civilization, some beer and other alcoholic drinks may be taken. However, a drunken Burmese is rarely seen, and drunkenness generally is disapproved of.[1] Before World War II, the upper Burman was said to be well-nourished, with good dental development and none of the signs of malnutrition. In the cities, physical conditions suffered somewhat; this has been attributed to the introduction of European foods.[2]

The Burmese staple is rice. It is eaten with a curry of vegetables, usually containing chillies, onions, garlic, and fish or meat if they are available. Traditionally, the fisher and the hunter were considered to be without scruples, since they took lives, so flesh for a curry was not easy to find. The villagers kept fowl, but apparently mainly as pets and for entertainment. There is usually, however, a preserved form of fish, a paste called *ngapi,* at every meal, and this is highly nutritious.[3] Apart from rice, this is probably the food which the Burmese identify as distinctive of their native diet.

"The family eats at a low round table, usually seated on the floor or on low stools, the father and sons eating first."[4] The food is served on individual plates and, except under Western influence, eaten without any utensils.[5] There is one meal in the morning between 8 and 10, and another in the afternoon. There are also light snacks, perhaps a fried cake or so, purchased from an itinerant seller, throughout the day. During "Lent," the devout eat only the morning meal.

The rice is still often husked by hand with a large wooden mortar and pestle. It is boiled in a large kettle of water over a wood or charcoal fire, until tender. The kitchen is usually detached from the house, and when anything is fried in oil the cooking may be done to the leeward of the house, so that the fumes will not reach other houses. There is a strong objection to cooking smells, as they are believed to bring on fever.[6]

Food is given daily to the mendicant monks, and some food is always offered to guests, however brief or casual their visit.[7]

[1] Brant, op. cit.
[2] Christian, op. cit. p. 145.
[3] Scott, op. cit. pp. 69-70.
[4] Christian, op. cit. p. 146.
[5] Brant, op. cit.; Scott, op. cit. p. 69.
[6] Brant, op. cit.; Christian, op. cit. p. 146; Scott, op. cit. p. 70.
[7] Brant, op. cit.

HEALTH

Completion of the Body

No man can assume true manhood, or even true humanity, unless he has assumed the yellow robe of the monk, if only for a few days; it usually happens when a boy is around 15. For this reason, villagers were not sure that an Englishman had achieved full humanity.[1] And no girl can become a woman unless her ears are pierced. There was a feeling a boy had to ensure his manhood by tattooing the region above and below the waist, sometimes as far down as the knees. This also enhanced his effectiveness in achievement and his endurance. Tattooing was also a charm against dangers like snake-bite.[2] This custom, however, is disappearing.[3] Soldiers and bandits would have charmed jewels and pieces of gold or silver let into the flesh under the skin; in these lay their effectiveness, and when jailers cut them out, the bandit's spirit would be broken.[4]

The Burmese were ready to add things to the body in other ways, also. Long hair was prized—that is, hair in a thick knot —and both men and women added false hair to it; it was like wearing festive clothes, and no secret was made of it. And one thing apart from deeds of merit upon which they were very ready to spend surplus money was festive apparel and personal adornment in general.

Hygiene

The Burmese bathed in the morning when they got up, and after sundown, after they had eaten the last meal of the day. The purpose was not cleanliness but to "freshen up," for enjoyment, and also as part of the preparation for the evening's amusement. Soap was not used. The hair was washed less often, as a special ceremony and with circumspection.[5] Water was used to rinse out the mouth after a meal, but it is not clear whether it was for refreshment—since no liquid is drunk with the meal—or for cleanliness.

Water was drawn from shallow wells which were not protected against pollution. Drinking-water was strained, but only to remove the visible living creatures, as a Buddhist must not destroy life. Monks carried strainers with them on their rounds. When a Western scientist showed them the teeming micro-

[1] Scott, op. cit. p. 394.
[2] Ibid. pp. 39-41, 42-47, 48.
[3] Christian, op. cit. p. 145.
[4] Scott, op. cit. pp. 43-44.
[5] Ibid. pp. 65-72.

scopic life that came through the strainer, he was told that people were responsible only for the destruction of living beings that they saw with the naked eye.[1]

There are few pit latrines in the villages, and when the villagers have been persuaded to build them, they often cannot be persuaded to use them. There have been attempts to make the people wear shoes for protection against soil-borne diseases, but these have not been successful either. Communal lands, which in the past had been set aside for hygienic purposes, have often been taken up for cultivation by the villagers since the increase of cash crops and the loss of organic unity of the village. The "privy" may be merely the ground near the house, and the pigs have the function of scavengers, disposing of human offal. In the villages, the situation is endurable; in the cities, where the sanitation problem has not yet been solved, it creates much more of a hazard to health.[2]

Medicine and Treatment

Health is one of the areas of life which are maintained through a strong *kan* and through preventive measures. By following his horoscope a man learns to be careful on his unlucky days. He takes preventive measures on many occasions as a part of the complete procedure; for example, for many people, to take a bath means to utter a charm over the first jarful of water, as a precaution against illness.[3] A pregnant woman takes more precautions, since she has to depend largely on these, as her *kan* is weak. Food is considered as affecting health, and monks, before they eat, say a grace in which they state that this is their only purpose in eating.[4]

When a man falls ill he is eager to have a physician in attendance and is ready to take medicine; in fact medication is very common in the lives of the people.[5] At their morning grace, the monks state that their medicine is necessary for their health, which is necessary for diligence.[6] So a sick man immediately demands medicine as well as other treatment.

There is a complex system or a combination of systems of treatment of illness. The two main systems revolve around the theory of the "four elements of the body" and their state of equilibrium. Treatment depends on the individual's horoscope, so that two people in the same house diagnosed as having the same kind of imbalance will be treated differently if they were born under different planets. There are, moreover, two oppos-

---

[1] Ibid. p. 343.
[2] Furnivall, op. cit. pp. 144-45.
[3] Scott, op. cit. p. 73.
[4] Ibid. p. 31.
[5] Ibid. pp. 419-20.
[6] Ibid. p. 31.

ing systems of treatment, one by medication, and one by diet.[1]
Besides, there is the treatment by massage for releasing the
"body wind" which had been trapped in one portion of the
body, causing pain and discomfort, and imbalance in the
whole body.[2] If the different systems of medicine fail, a spell
is diagnosed and a "witch-doctor" is called.[3]

Apart from massage, there is treatment by objects introduced into the body. There is a large variety of herbs, seeds,
powdered stones, etc., used as remedies. Almost all medicament consists of solids; liquids are rare, as they are in the regular diet of the Burmese. When the drug-physician fails with his
pills and other solids, the "witch-doctor" usually comes and he
also introduces things into the body of the patient; he sticks
pins into him or forces red pepper into his eyes.[4] It may be suggested that this is one reason why, although the Burmese accepted injections with ease, they resisted vaccinations.[5] Anaesthetics also would probably be quite acceptable, since they
have been given for painful tattooing.[6]

Individual practitioners are known for their special abilities
in certain kinds of disorders and for their own, often secret,
remedies. British commentators seem to feel that there is a
good deal of evidence that these remedies are efficacious; Scott
cites the case of a man in Rangoon who, after the best Western
doctors in Rangoon and Calcutta had failed to cure him of
varicose ulcers, was healed speedily by a Burmese practitioner.
It was from such practitioners that Western medicine learned
to use oil of chaulmoogra for leprosy.[7]

Death is not feared by the individual. Life and death are
one, a part of the road of existence, and to die is to take on another life. There is no religious sacrament at death. A man dies
with his family around him, and perhaps the headman comes
to say to him, "Remember your good deeds." But death is terrible for the survivors, because there is no hope of ever meeting again after death, or, at any rate, of meeting again the same
form and personality in the same relationship in which the
dead beloved was known.[8]

Attempts at the introduction of Western-type medical and
hospital care into Burma were accompanied by many difficulties. Burmese practitioners have lost the place they held
when the headman ruled the circle and gave them his support.
The land in which they searched for their ingredients is now
often under cultivation; they often have to buy these in-

[1] Ibid. pp. 417-19.
[2] Ibid. p. 421; Brant, op. cit.
[3] Scott, op. cit. p. 421.
[4] Ibid. p. 421.
[5] Furnivall, op. cit. p. 147.
[6] Scott, op. cit. p. 40.
[7] Ibid. p. 417; Brant, op. cit.; Christian, op. cit. p. 151.
[8] Hall, 1906, op. cit. pp. 281-87; Hall, 1908, op. cit. p. 139.

gredients in the market now, where they may be found to be
adulterated and ineffective. Still the villagers will not seek out
Western medicine, except as a last resort. And to go to a hospital is a terrible ordeal for them. For people to whom companionship is so important, the Western hospital rule of isolation has meant great suffering. The imposing structures alarm
people accustomed to living in houses of, at most, three rooms.
The large central hospitals mean leaving home and village behind at a time when reassurance is most needed. The physicians were usually all foreign, and so were the attendants.[1] In
addition, there are other factors. A Burmese must not have
anyone above his head, and their houses have no second floors;
further, on "duty-days" four times a month, he is forbidden to
sleep "on a high place," and so, to make sure he follows this
rule, he has no beds in his house.[2] Besides, he may be awakened
suddenly by a hospital routine which does not first allow his
wandering soul to return to his body.[3] When hospital routine
necessitates his going against his religious beliefs, this increases his already insecure position.

In recent years, health standards have been higher than
those of neighbouring countries; it has been suggested that this
is due to the generally adequate food-supply and the suitability
of housing and clothing to the conditions of the climate. In
the cities, however, health conditions are not good. Rangoon,
before World War II, was said to have the highest death-rate
from tuberculosis. In 1938, the urban death-rate was 30.18
per thousand, as compared to 19.13 per thousand in the
villages.[4]

But intensive health work shows that good results can be
obtained. When infant mortality was 225 in the cities and 176
in rural areas, Heggu township—where the Rockefeller Foundation was in operation—had an infant death-rate of 124.[5]

At the present time, the Government of the Union of Burma
is making an effort to improve and expand medical care under
a system of socialized medicine. Government hospitals, staffed
by civil-service doctors and nurses, are found in many towns
and cities, and plans call for the creation of more such facilities. The realization of these plans is very highly contingent
upon the improvement of the total economic situation of the
country and upon the ability of the government to spend increased funds for training personnel and construction of medical installations. In addition to the government facilities, there
are a number of medical establishments sponsored by missionary groups and some privately operated hospitals and clinics.
Physicians in private practice are found in the more important

[1] Furnivall, op. cit. pp. 120, 140, 148, 356.
[2] Scott, op. cit. pp. 76, 79.
[3] Ibid. pp. 394-95.
[4] Christian, op. cit. pp. 151-52.
[5] Erich H. Jacoby, 1949, p. 94.

cities and towns. The University of Rangoon operates a school of medicine in down-town Rangoon, where students, after completing a two-year pre-medical course, enrol for a five-year period that culminates in the M.B.B.S. degree (Bachelor of Medicine and Surgery). The medical school is accredited in the United Kingdom. There is a great need for expansion of its facilities and staff, and for more modern equipment of all kinds. A notable fact regarding medical education in Burma is the high proportion of women students. Medicine is a profession fully open to women. Many female physicians and surgeons specialize in gynaecology and obstetrics. Burmese women much prefer to be attended, during pregnancy and child-birth, by a woman doctor, and many at this time are extremely reluctant to be looked after by a man.[1]

EDUCATION

Before and during the early years of British occupation, the monastic schools were paramount. They were to be found in all the villages and were attended by all the boys, beginning at the age of eight. Here boys were taught "how to live," not merely "how to make a living." British observers paint a not unhappy picture of the monastic school in the past. Burmese informants nowadays emphasize the negative aspects of the submission to the authority of the monks.[2]

The British administration introduced vernacular schools, giving instruction in the villages, and Anglo-vernacular schools in the large centres, where teaching in English began after the fourth year and where all subjects were taught in English at the high-school level. Many missionary schools were also established. In some cases, these tended to alienate the pupils from their culture, as they emphasized respect for Western ways, and children attending them often found it difficult to adapt themselves to their communities after they finished school.

The lay schools provided women with some literacy. Girls were sent to learn how to keep accounts for their trading, and also to get them out of the way. Since children were sent to school as a place where they would be cared for, and since the monastic schools could be used for this purpose for boys, it was the girls who swelled the numbers of the enrolment in the secular schools.[3] However, all that the girls were felt to need was a minimum of instruction in arithmetic and the use of the alphabet, and few remained in school beyond these.

The lay schools were not adequate substitutes for the monastic schools. The latter, although they taught little that was necessary for success in the Western world, and were not pri-

[1] "Burma Facts and Figures," 1946, pp. 36-37.
[2] Hanks, op. cit. p. 293.
[3] Furnivall, op. cit. pp. 203-8.

marily set up to teach boys how to make a living, taught them "how to live." They taught discipline, morality, and inter-personal relations. They trained in equalitarian living; all within the monastery walls were equal, and performed menial duties together, played, and shared life together. The lay schools, whether governmental or missionary, stressed success in examinations above all. Morality and discipline deteriorated, and, in 1932, the Director of Education noted that districts with the best record for education had the worst record for crime.[1]

Higher education in Burma has created new problems. On one hand, it created racial consciousness, as Burmese graduates of professional schools found that they were not treated with the respect accorded their European colleagues; on the other, it resulted in a class of the educated, as opposed to the unedu-cated, and since it was mainly the urbanites who could send their children to the university, defined the splits between the village and the city, Burmese culture and foreign culture. Many educated urban Burmese know very little about rural Burma and the life of the people in the villages.[2] Furthermore, it is the well-to-do who can afford to give their children this education. In the past, there was no such distinction, since all education was free and the boys did not have to leave the vil-lage to receive it. So that now, in place of the equalitarian training of the monastic school, we see the rise of unequal classes.

Certain traditional Burmese attitudes remain, and obstruct the aims of higher education. In the traditional Buddhist schools, the purpose of learning was to show the way to an upright life; there was no dignity in applied learning. The edu-cated Burmese often carries this attitude over into an objection to the applied aspects of modern agricultural science, and even to those of medicine and education. In addition, the urbanites do not want to go to the uneducated rural areas of which they know so little. Even youngsters from the villages, brought to the city for short courses in modern farming methods, do not want to return where they can impart and apply this knowl-edge. They prefer to say in town and seek a white-collar job. This is, of course, a very common characteristic of the edu-cated groups in countries in which higher education is de-veloped before industrialization.

In the past, there was a social demand for education, and the monastic school fulfilled its function of teaching disciplines and a respect for elders and family. The lay schools substituted an economic incentive for a social incentive; but few went through enough years to be able to achieve economic advance-ment through their education. And those who did either found

[1] Ibid. p. 130.
[2] Ibid. p. 205.

opportunities for making a living through their specialized education closed to them, or found these unacceptable. So there is still little incentive for Western type of education in Burma.[1] There is now more literacy in Burma than before, but this is not the result of the lay schools, but of the prevalence of public notices, the railroad signs, and the opportunity to use one's knowledge of reading. The postal system itself fosters "a latent demand for adult literacy." For literacy to continue into adulthood, there is a need for more material to read, for a literature to be made available to the people at large, in their own language.[2]

AGRICULTURE

Cultivating the land was an enjoyable part of living. The Burmese like to be out of doors, and the cultivation itself did not take very much time, produced no pressure, and created few anxieties. In the relatively dry sections where rice was grown, there were frequently years too dry for the rice; then millet would be grown which, though less well liked, still afforded subsistence. In the sections where the flat land retained the rains of the south-western monsoons, the soil was very easy to work and exceedingly rich, fertilized by the silt. There was no need to work against time, as the weather was predictable. It was easy to prepare more land than was needed and plant more rice; then, if there was a scarcity of rice elsewhere, the surplus rice could be harvested and sold; otherwise, it would be left in the fields. To have no market for it was no calamity. The villagers usually lived well within their income, with money to spare for gaming and for deeds of merit. Pressure to save labour or to preserve every bit of the crop seems to have been lacking. The draught-animals used for threshing by treading were neither muzzled nor hurried, and not much attempt was made in either part of Burma to ensure the life of these animals when they were not at work; they were left very much to themselves and sometimes died of the heat or rain or some disease. There was a division of labour in agriculture, with the adult men clearing the land if it was necessary, and perhaps ploughing it, though quite frequently a boy would drive the plough oxen.[3] Women and children did the transplanting and weeding, and men again did the reaping.

In the dry sections, sesamum was grown as a cash crop to exchange for extra rice from the lowlands as part of the subsistence pattern.[4] There was no interest in making money, creating a fortune, or buying imported goods; in fact, there were almost none to buy. Thus, though money was in use, this

[1] Brant, op. cit.; Furnivall, op. cit. pp. 202-6.
[2] Furnivall, op. cit. p. 209.
[3] Scott, op. cit. pp. 244-46, 80.
[4] Furnivall, op. cit. pp. 15-16, 85, 87-88.

was not a Western type of money economy. Borrowing existed but only on account of poverty, not to create wealth. The individual was protected by village law against accumulating interest greater than the sum originally borrowed. He could not mortgage his farm, since, in Upper Burma at least, it belonged to the whole family, and foreclosure was a thing unknown in Burma. In spite of the cash crops, it was really a subsistence economy; in spite of money, it was a barter economy.[1]

Rice was the main crop of Lower Burma; sesamum and other oil-seeds, of Upper Burma. In Lower Burma, the region of the swampy Delta, the average farm was not larger than 10 acres, and this was all planted for rice. In Upper Burma, the average holding ranged from 5 to 15 acres, and there was variety, ensuring some crop despite the erratic rainfall.[2] Upper Burma contained a large number of established villages; Lower Burma, which could have supported a thickly concentrated population, was actually sparsely settled at the opening up of Western contact.

With the opening of the Suez Canal, Burma found a steady outside market for its rice, and the Burmese were strongly encouraged by the administration, tempted by imports, and urged by Indian money-lenders, to take up more land, and grow and reap more rice. The villagers of the Delta planted larger areas and borrowed money to buy more bullocks, and to hire reapers. There had been a tradition for Upper Burmese who were landless to go to Lower Burma for the harvest as labourers. Now more of them went down, and found that they could get wages which in about two years would enable them to own and cultivate land of their own; and there was a continuous colonization from Upper Burma. But here the villages were new, usually without a monastery, and without traditional law, and the peasants were not protected against losing their land. Unsophisticated in financial matters, unused to a money economy, the peasants soon fell into irremediable debt and lost their lands—something that had been impossible in their old villages, where, even if a man did "lose" his land, he had the right to reclaim it. The landowners now became tenants and the land was concentrated in the hands of rich men to whom it was merely another financial enterprise. For them it was more profitable to divide the land in holdings which brought a larger net produce, a surplus for export, than a larger gross produce; that is, they divided it into large holdings, cultivated by large numbers of labourers. It was also profitable to them to put the land out at auction every year, leasing it to the highest bidder. This meant that even as a tenant, a man could have no continuity with the land. And it was cheaper to hire seasonal labour, so that there was no continuity of operation either; preparing the

[1] Ibid. pp. 114, 134.
[2] Christian, op. cit. p. 110.

earth, ploughing, planting, reaping and threshing, were all done by different groups of labourers. This was just labour for money. Agriculture became an industry, and Burma became a "factory without chimneys." No longer was the cultivation of land the making of a living or way of life; it was now "earning a living." [1]

Lower Burma has actually changed more than Upper Burma. There it was estimated in 1930 that 50 per cent of the land was in the hands of absentee owners. In some sections 80 to 90 per cent of the landlords are non-agriculturists. There are large numbers of immigrants from Upper Burma as well as other countries, and a large proportion of the population is shifting. The old villages as well as the new now lack the traditional unity.[2]

Conditions in Upper Burma have changed also under the new stress on economic motivations. In accordance with Western ideas of freedom and individual initiative, individual proprietorship of land was substituted for the Burmese custom of family possession; this made it possible for the individual to borrow on his own, to leave his family, and to embark on individual enterprise. In terms of Western values, this was economic progress, which in turn meant social progress. The Burmese were encouraged to give up their traditional ways which seemed wasteful and inefficient, and to abandon their elaborate time-consuming festivals, their handicrafts, their delicately shaped and carved cargo boats—the sailing of which was an art and a joy, but which could be replaced much more inexpensively. As usually happened under conditions of East-West contact in the nineteenth century, the people came to prefer the often shoddy but inexpensive machine-made article to their own handicraft products, and learned to substitute individual economic aspirations for the traditional aspirations of their culture.[3]

Presently the organic unit was atomized. Under the stress of administrative changes, which destroyed the organic basis of the village and of orderly behaviour as the way of the village, and under the stress of economic change, which atomized the family and introduced money-making as an incentive, individuals began to take up the common land which had been protected under a subsistence economy. Now, even if there was time for the social gatherings, the bullock-races, and the dances and theatricals, there was no place to hold them.[4] The changes which resulted from Western contact did not create atomization but they did produce conditions which accentuated inter-personal patterns which were already there. Inter-personal

[1] Furnivall, op. cit. pp. 48, 89-90, 193, 293-300.
[2] Ibid. p. 298.
[3] Ibid. pp. 134-36, 298-300, 303.
[4] Ibid. pp. 137-38.

relations do not appear to be binding among the Burmese; "Brothers are often relative strangers," and "as aspirers to status, they work alone." Traditionally, as well as at present, the Burmese works for himself, does good deeds for his own enhancement. What united individuals within a family or a village was the inherited unity of a way of life; when this was gone, the individuals stood alone.[1]

Since independence, the Burmese Government has passed a Land Nationalization Act aimed at a redistribution of agricultural land to the cultivators. The act provides for nationalization and redistribution by land committees, to be "elected or appointed according to circumstances of the locality." Although because of the highly disturbed situation that obtained in Burma after the nationalization legislation was passed, less was accomplished than had been hoped for toward putting land nationalization into practice, the fact that the act was passed had important effects. The Burmese farmers are continuing to cultivate the land as usual, but are not paying rent to the landlords or their representatives. They are paying only the taxes on the land. Formerly the farmer paid the rent to the landlord, and the latter was responsible for paying the taxes to the Government. Thus the landlords are receiving no income on their lands, which are technically still their property, since nationalization has not yet been carried through and compensation has not been paid. There is, expectably enough, widespread dissatisfaction among the landlords.

The traditional implement of cultivation was the "single-barred harrow, with three long teeth of acacia wood."[2] This has been almost completely replaced by the improved metal ploughshare which was introduced.[3] The bullock and the ox are still the draught-animals, even in Lower Burma with its large holdings. An attempt to introduce tractors in that area failed. The tractors often sank into the soft earth, fuel and spare parts were too expensive, and technical skill was lacking.[4] The attempts of the administration to introduce new methods of cultivation were mainly unsuccessful; it was difficult to find technicians who were willing to live among the villagers. The agricultural shows at which the new devices were demonstrated were for the Burmese merely happy festive occasions.[5] On the whole, Upper Burma is more ready to accept change. Here the people are still close to their land and are ready to improve it; and here it is not difficult to see that there is room for improvement. In the Delta, however, with its assured rainfall and natural irrigation, and its fertile silt, it is not so easy to recognize the need for improvement; yet actually, for better util-

[1] Hanks, op. cit. pp. 296-300.
[2] Scott, op. cit. p. 244.
[3] Christian, op. cit. p. 113.
[4] Jacoby, op. cit. p. 78.
[5] O. H. Spate, 1941, p. 77.

ization of this silt, it should be spread and ditches should be dug. But the people feel no need to introduce improvements on land which they will leave in a few months, and as for the immediate crop, it is obvious that it will grow without such improvement.[1]

ORIENTATIONS

Time

The Burmese had various ways of computing time without the use of timepieces. There were the definite seasonal changes which introduced the steps of agricultural activity. Definite moons introduced and ended "Lent." The phases of the moon determined the four duty-days which punctuated the month. In the monastery, people got up at daybreak, "when there is light enough to see the veins in the hand." [2] And the day-night cycle was divided in four parts by cock-crow. The layman could tell the time by the position and length of the shadows, by the sun, or the rising of the "red star" before daybreak, or even by the activities of the monks, who always started on their mendicant walks at the same time. In all this, it was *telling* time, not *using* time, or being told to do by the time, that was involved. There is no evidence that the Burmese felt pressure of time.

Mechanization

There seems to have been no feeling against the machine as such. When a pony-express was instituted, to take people from an outlying town to the railroad station, the people refused to use it because they felt it was cruel to the ponies. They preferred to walk the long distances or to use a slow bullock-cart rather than encourage the pace of an animal. But on foot or with their own conveyances, they did go to the station and used the railroad. Buddhist monks, explaining to an Englishman their preference for monasticism, said they were like the railroad, speeding to emancipation from the fleshly existence, while the layman toiled along on foot, or like people journeying on a steamboat while the others went in simple canoes.[3] Here is shown an emotional acceptance of the machine.

Machine-made goods have won acceptance in Burma. Factory-made cotton goods were substituted for the costly silks that had been woven and embroidered by hand in the villages. Machine-made crockery replaced the beautiful lacquerware and local pottery. By 1911 the number of people employed in spinning and weaving had fallen off by one-half.[4]

[1] Jacoby, op. cit. pp. 77-78.
[2] Scott, op. cit. p. 30.
[3] Ibid. p. 107.
[4] Furnivall, op. cit. pp. 100-1.

Evidence

Traditionally, truth had been axiomatic; it required neither logic nor experimental proof. When established truths were put to the test for the sake of the English, it was to exhibit, not to prove. A Burmese would ask an Englishman to fire at a talisman wrapped in a handkerchief, only to show the potency of the talisman which he knew would protect the handkerchief from being damaged by the shot. In 1881, a young man tattooed with the anti-drowning tattoo wanted to make a public demonstration of its potency and persuaded the tattooers to throw him, bound hand and foot, into the Rangoon River. When he drowned, the court convicted the tattooers of manslaughter, but the Burmese did not blame them; they knew the validity of the tattoo—the man drowned because of some miscalculation of his horoscope, or some such unforeseen contingency.[1] The experimental practices introduced by foreign agricultural experts shook the security and faith of farmers with such a background.[2]

Responsibility

Intention—rather than an act in itself—determines responsibility. Monks, when shown by a scientist that their carefully strained water actually contains much microscopic life, countered that they were responsible only for the destruction of life which they could see. In the monastery, monks hungry in the afternoon could eat food with impunity if told by young scholars that it was still mid-morning.[3] Burmese servants felt free to kill ants when ordered to do so, since the sin was the master's.[4]

Change

Change was an inherent principle in the Burmese way of life. Nothing in the individual's position was irreparable; everyone could "do something about it." The individual constantly and deliberately effected change, but this was only in his own life, as an individual, not in terms of his relationships. The established order remained immutable. The route along which the individual could effect change in his life was prescribed. By changing himself, increasing in merits or demerits, the individual did not affect his society or standard of living; eventually, if he was reborn in a city, or as a woman, or as the son of a wealthy man, his personal experience of his society was different, but only because he himself had moved to another social unit. All the old units remained the same. What money

[1] Scott, op. cit. pp. 44, 47.
[2] Furnivall, op. cit. p. 327.
[3] Scott, op. cit. pp. 136,343.
[4] Hall, 1906, op. cit. p. 234.

he made in excess of his family's needs went toward effecting change in his own stage of life; it did not change the standard of living, or the aspect of the family house or of the village, except in so far as an act of merit, such as building a pagoda, changed the face of the village in an established and accepted way. The road was known and secure, and following it the individual could move securely.

From the outset, the changes which came through Western contact cut at the very roots of the traditional, pre-established order, by bringing change where the individual had depended upon immutability.

ADDITIONAL REFERENCES

J. R. Andrus, 1947; *Burma Handbook*, 1944; *Burma Village Manual*, n.d.; J. S. Furnivall, 1943; F. Haskings, 1944; Edward M. Law Yone and David G. Mandelbaum, 1950a; 1950b; *Memorandum on Land Nationalization Act*, 1949; Gordon S. Seagrave, 1943; H. N. C. Stevenson, 1944; *The State of World Food and Agriculture*, 1949 (*See* United Nations, FAO); Virginia Thompson, 1943; *Yearbook of Food and Agricultural Statistics*, 1949 (*See* United Nations, FAO).

GREECE[1]

The culture of the Greeks is here presented as an integrated whole. The Greeks have been selected out of the European nations now engaged in introducing technical change because they represent a unique case. They have the most ancient civilization of the European continent, yet their technical development at present is one of the lowest. The history of their industries and factories goes back more than 2,500 years, yet they now resist industrialization. They are European, yet they look toward the Middle East and share a number of attitudes with the people of this area. They are Christians but with a special kind of Christianity, highly ritualized and impersonal, and incorporating much of local origin.

Individualism is prized and rampant, yet there is no atomization. Self-esteem is paramount, and rests on freedom and self-dependence; yet Greeks do not seek freedom from the family,

[1] The study of Greek culture is based largely on interviews, correspondence, and memoranda, conducted and prepared in the autumn and winter of 1950-51. Newspapers and magazines of this time were also consulted. Two Maternal and Child Care Manuals of recent years, several collections of folk songs, and a popular humorous work were intensively analysed. Accounts by people engaged in introducing change were consulted. The writer, herself a Greek by birth and upbringing, has depended also on her own firsthand experience of the culture. The manuscript was submitted to two Greeks for comment and criticism.

and do not lose self-esteem when they are dependent on the family. They have their own unique individualism. They are highly co-operative, but the basis and formulation of their co-operative activity are different from those of the Western European nations.

The Greeks have a story that when God made the world he put the earth through a sieve and used the soil to make the different countries; but the stones that were left in the sieve he threw over his shoulder, and they became Greece.[1] The land is so mountainous, precipitous and stony that out of the 50,100 square miles that constitute the area of Greece, only 25 per cent are usable as fields, orchards and pastures.[2] Yet on this land, out of a population of 7,335,675, according to 1940 figures, 60 per cent are directly engaged in agriculture, and another 15 per cent cater to the needs of the farmers.[3] This condition, as well as a growing population, is basic to the need for technical change in Greece. Through more than 2,500 years, Greece solved the problem of increasing population on limited land by sending out her people as colonists or immigrants. In the first two decades of this century, emigration to the United States provided the main solution. Early in the 1920's two things took place which combined to make the population problem acute: the United States passed a law under which a quota was applied to immigrants, which limited drastically the number of Greeks who could thereafter enter the country; and the exchange of populations with Turkey, which increased the population of Greece suddenly by more than a fourth. Since then, the population figures from 1928 to 1940 indicate an annual increase of 1.5 per cent.[4] The traditional ways of farming and the traditional crops cannot support this growing population, even in terms of sheer subsistence. Change must be introduced at the very roots of the economy, striking at the relationship of man to the land and of man to his work, which is a close and meaningful one to the Greeks. How to do this without destroying the meaning of life is the question facing those entrusted with the introduction of change into this culture.

We give here a report of the basic structure, tenets, and attitudes of Greek culture which should be considered in applying change.

Greece has been undergoing induced change for several decades now. Before 1920, the centralization of political and civil affairs effected profound and permeating change in village communities which had been used to self-regulation, and

[1] A. W. Gomme, 1945, p. 11.
[2] *Report of the FAO Mission for Greece*, 1947, p. 85. (*See* United Nations, FAO).
[3] Ibid. p. 134.
[4] Ibid. p. 162.

where a prominent farmer spent his entire fortune to build a village school, or a school-teacher, on hearing of the appearance of the enemy in the vicinity, could, on his own initiative, pass out arms and lead his pupils to battle. After the exchange of populations with Turkey in 1922, the Near East Foundation, helping to rehabilitate the refugees, also undertook to introduce changes in sanitation, child care and the standard of living generally. Changes in the areas of agriculture and health were introduced under the direction of the Rockefeller Foundation. In the thirties, the dictator Metaxas introduced a number of changes by fiat, which ran counter to Greek values, but many of which were accepted gratefully by people wearied of political dissension and lack of leadership. World War II, with its displacements and destruction and enemy occupation, the work of UNRRA and the Greek War Relief, and more recently, of the POS agency of the ECA, have all been agents of change.

There are many kinds of Greeks. The million or so Greeks who came from Turkey and Russia in the twenties differ from the so-called "old Greeks." The city Greeks consider themselves very different from the peasants. There is a vogue for peasant handicrafts but not for peasant attitudes. Urban Greeks like to take on the ways of foreigners, to use the products of technology, even the processed foods of technology. Many French and English words are used in their speech. They take on the attitudes of the Western world, using clocked time in business and living a life relatively pressed for time, adopting to some extent the Western scientific approach and objective external limits, instead of the more animistic approach and the body-patterned limits of traditional Greek culture. There are lectures here on health and hygiene, on child care and co-operation and nutrition. In Athens, the music and the drama are excellent, and in line with Euro-American developments. There is rapid transportation. There are many associations based on foreign patterns: the YMCA and the YWCA, the Girl Guides and the Boy Scouts, football groups and hiking groups. There are foreign attitudes about travel: people go to tour the country or the world, instead of going to visit a relative or a family friend or a miraculous shrine. The difference reaches its greatest intensity as between the educated Greeks and the peasants, who, though literate, have no high education.

People of different regions have a different way of life. The mountainous terrain, the absence of easy communication except coastwise, differences in dialect and local history, and, most of all, the extreme personal independence of the people, have fostered tremendous variation from place to place. To the world at large, a man may be a Greek, but to other Greeks, he is a Macedonian, an Arcadian, or an Epirot. More than this, he comes from a particular village of which he is very proud and for whose honour he competes with other villages. In the United States, Greeks from one village, such as Mani, have organized themselves in a nation-wide organization. People from one small island speak of the people of the neighbouring island as queer or ill-mannered. This is as it should be; in Greek culture it is good for everyone to be different or, as the Greeks put it, to be individually formed.

The differences are there but the similarities are more basic. The Athenians, working by clock time, strain at their bonds, and do not allow time to dictate to them in private life; and Athenian newspapers, announcing the hour of the lecture, have to remind people that it is important to be prompt at such affairs. When they deviate from old Greek ways and values, they often do so with awareness and with regret, and the deviation is not profound.

VIEW OF THE SELF

Foremost in the Greek's view of the self is his self-esteem. It is impossible to have good relations with Greeks unless one is aware of this, the Greek *philotimo*. It is important to pay tribute to it, and to avoid offending it, or, as the Greeks say, molesting it. Everyone has his *philotimo*, as an individual, as a member of a family, and, most of all, as a Greek. On this rests Greek individualism, since it is sheer being which is respected, not position in the world or achievement. On this rests Greek democracy and equality, since everyone, both as a person and as a Greek, is equal to everyone else, neither superior nor inferior. Any Greek bootblack is equal to the king, to whom he may refer familiarly as *coumbaros,* wedding sponsor, until some political agitator points out to him that the king is not Greek by descent, and therefore does not merit loyalty or respect as an equal. This does not mean that there is lacking a balance of roles or inter-personal structuring; but these relationships of interdependence, of leader and followers, of division of areas of responsibility and work, are not cast in the mould of superiority and inferiority. Inferiority comes only with the forfeiting of the *philotimo*.

On the *philotimo* also rests Greek nationalism. A man may be ignorant and poor, but when his country is threatened, it is his right and privilege to shed his blood on the altar of Greek freedom along with every other Greek, whatever his district, however wealthy or educated. Again, he shares with every other Greek a common glorious past. A small island, speaking of its illustrious sons, lists the New York chiropractor of today next to the philosopher of 2,400 years ago. A Greek, speaking about his culture, makes statements such as: "The Greeks have been hospitable since the time of Homer." Even learned treatises, such as a paper on present-day medicine, often begin with the glorious work of the ancient Greek thinkers. This is what each Greek esteems in himself, what constitutes his *philotimo:* his personal being, his status within a family, village, district, and, second to none, his Greekness.

The Greek *philotimo* is easily bruised, or molested; and a Greek addressed in a completely objective manner, or hearing himself or his way of life described in harsh scientific terms, is greatly offended. Where an American journalist or scientist, writing about his culture, feels the need to be objective, to uncover the facts, a Greek presents each fact wrapped in some subjective, protective covering. The fact is true and dependable, but it should not be naked. A memorandum of fact by a Greek is full of such phrases as: "Then the nobleness of the Greek soul was revealed," or "The Greek peasant modestly died . . . to protect his beloved country, but his death was one of the noblest sacrifices to the idea of liberty." Or, if Greeks have to criticize, they do it with oratory also, reviling passionately, as when a mother scolds a loved one with fury but not with cold and calculating anger.

The covering of the naked fact is essential to the integrity—the absence of all molestation—of the *philotimo.* The inner core of the Greek must never be exposed; and *entrope,* the Greek word for shame, modesty, decency, propriety, self-consciousness, embarrassment, means "turning inward." This is a concept both positive and negative: you have done something shameful only because you have failed in the positive aspect, in modesty and decency. Out of *entrope,* a Greek avoids saying things and doing things which would reflect on the *philotimo* of himself, his family, his country. For example, the self-made man in Greece does not boast of his rags-to-riches progress. This would expose the poverty of his village, the inability of his family to help him, the fact that his uncle or his godfather could not or did not do his duty by him; it would expose much that should remain decently covered, and would further prove him to be lacking in *philotimo.*

The Greek *philotimo* should not be confused either with the notion of face or with that of pride. Pride for the Greeks carries with it the connotation of arrogance: "the proud bird is caught by the nose." A Greek mother is not proud of her son, she is honoured by him; the *philotimo* is enhanced through honour, not pride. There is something of the notion of face, in that it is insupportable to have one's failures and needs known. But there is more than this; what is really bad is that you yourself should expose your failure or yourself. And you have no *philotimo* if you avoid going to fight for your country, whether anyone knows this or not.

The essence of *philotimo* is inviolability and freedom. The first means that a Greek is very "touchy." In a very popular work of the thirties, which gives a humorous report of the cases in the Court of Petty Offences, a large proportion of the cases arise out of this molestation of the *philotimo*. The reaction is immediate, either in scathing invective, such as name-calling, or as physical attack. Offence against one's *philotimo* brings retaliation, not self-reproach. There are suicides in Athens for financial reasons, or for love, but none are reported as a result of molested *philotimo*.

Freedom is the positive aspect of this. Greeks say: "To be a Greek means to be free," and "Nothing is beautiful unless you are free, not even the flowers in the spring."' It gave the Greeks a great sense of freedom to defy Hitler, in the sure knowledge that their country would be overrun and occupied if they did so. During the occupation, they remained free; little children risked their lives to do absolutely unnecessary things such as defacing Nazi posters, giving expression to their essential freedom. The morale of the people was upheld by their knowledge that they had not forfeited their freedom, and that they had been defeated only technically, not man to man, but by monstrous machines. External coercion without internal submission has no bearing on the maintenance of the *philotimo*.

To suggest to a Greek that he needs aid in raising his standard of living because his ways are backward is to violate his *philotimo* as a person and as a Greek. There is need for aid now because of acts of God, not because of personal failure or Greek inadequacy. Until the government centralized aid in the Department of Welfare, and to some extent thereafter, Greek families and communities took care of their own indigents or dependents. The Greeks who emigrated to the United States before the change and formed conservative communities in their new country continued to take care of their own unemployed and orphaned; they were adapting the village pattern; besides, their *philotimo* would not allow them to expose to outsiders their failure and inadequacy. However, Greeks will accept aid when it is their right within a structured relationship; they will accept it as their share from the nation for which they have fought, or from the nation which they have helped in its war against the forces of evil; and Greeks stand firm in the knowledge that they were vital in bringing about the defeat of the Nazis by delaying Hitler's plans. They will also accept help without losing their *philotimo* when the need comes through an act of God. Their ways of making a living are adequate under normal circumstances; but now, because of destruction, occupation, soil erosion, loss of the right to emigrate, they need technical assistance to achieve a standard of living which is their right as Greeks and as persons. They can accept help also because the need is common to all the Greeks. During the war they said, not "See what I have

¹ Joanne Lee Schriver, 1947.

come to," but "See what the nation has come to!" and then their situation was bearable. The office which is in charge of the ECA activities now reminds the people of the different villages that the destruction has been nation-wide, that the need applies to all the Greeks, and so makes it bearable, and saves their *philotimo*. More than this, the government now appeals for self-participation in rebuilding the homes and the villages in the name of their *philotimo* as Greeks; to exert themselves as their sons exerted themselves in war, "to show the world what the Greeks can do in peace as well as in war."

IMAGERY OF SELF

The image of the self includes that of the body and of the personality: the person. Life is structured and experienced according to the rhythm and patternings of the body, and ethics are defined by personal relationships, loyalties and roles, just as society is structured according to the physiological relationships of the body. The imagery which a lover uses to describe the body of his beloved is that which is used to praise the personal qualities of an adored leader.

There is no reference to softness in any of the personal folk-songs of the Greeks, the dystichs directed toward a loved one, the lullabies, the dirges composed for a relative. The beloved is commonly likened to a tree, sometimes to a fruit-tree, but most commonly to a cypress—slim, straight, tall, hard, resistant—"I embrace a cypress tightly," sings a lover. The body is likened to hard, cold substances. The neck of the beloved is made of crystal, the breasts are of marble, in the rare references found in impersonal folk-songs. A lover sings: "All night I lay embracing gold."

Firmness and straightness are extremely desirable personal qualities. Babies were swaddled to keep them from going crooked and to make their backs firm. The gesture of mother-love is one of holding a firm, stiff, straight bundle against the breast, not the crooking of the arms to accommodate a cuddling body. Firm and straight also is the ideal personality. Parents are urged to be firm of will with their children from birth, and to see that the children develop steadfastness. When Eleutherios Venizelos died, the leading Athenian newspaper wrote: "The cypress is fallen."

Cold, also, is attractive as well as admirable. To call a girl "cold water" is to call her attractive and desirable. Coldness and flowers are on a par in the folk-songs, and lovers walk together among the flowers, or on snowy slopes. Hotness means a lack of control, unthinking response. Grief is hot, and tears wither the grass and trees they water. Love as suffering also burns: a lover sighs and 3,000 trees burn up. It is common for a passing youth to say to a girl, "You burn my heart."

The body image is the image of the Greek character. Fortitude and hardihood, firm will, a love of simplicity in food, entertainment, furnishings, the standard of living in general, are common traits. Greeks will smoke only a few cigarettes a day, drink within measure and eat in moderation; excess is disliked. Fortitude is an ever-present quality; the *philotimo* brooks no calculation of danger or pending pain before a step is taken. If a thing is worth doing, the price to be paid for it is irrelevant, and you are able to do it because you are strong and firm. You do not even ask yourself ahead of time whether you have the necessary fortitude; a Greek takes no inventory of himself because from the time he was a baby his parents saw to it that he grew straight and hard, and because he knows himself to be a Greek. A current book on child care warns parents not to take many toys to a sick child, not to clown for his amusement, lest this spoil him. Going to bed also is a sign of weakness except for recognized disease. A man cannot seek solace in bed for fatigue or indisposition, lest he appear to be giving in to a desire for pampering. Even to fall asleep is to give in; the term is "sleep caught me."

It is difficult to give this picture attractively, to show how there is warmth within this firmness, exuberance within the austerity, and within the discipline. Yet discipline is a positive, liberating, guiding element in the Greek personality: the simple life is a joy and is also freeing, since it creates few demands, few dependencies on the external. Self-discipline and self-control are not prohibiting; they are incentive. They are not the application of discipline to the self, but rather a way of behaving. There is nothing inconsistent with these traits when, in voting on an important issue by roll-call, a member of parliament answers, "Five thousand times, yes," or when white pigeons are released in the House by the victorious party. This is appropriate exuberance, just as the fiery reaction to a violation of the *philotimo* is appropriate and within the channel of discipline. There is joy and dignity in hard work, not compulsiveness; there is joy in walking an hour and a half to and from the field twice a day over difficult ground. American visitors are taken for a walk by a young Greek village girl or even a child, and return exhausted. There is a revelling in sheer exertion, in sheer fortitude. There is nothing grim about it, neither is there boasting. Greeks may boast about their achievements, but not of their character, which they take for granted as Greek.

The organs of highest significance are the eyes. They are the seat of the person. With them, lovers and friends communicate, and they are the pre-eminent medium of enjoyment. Love comes through the eyes, and the eyes are mentioned the most frequently in the personal poems. "We have not seen you" means "We missed you."

In the folk-songs, a beloved's eyes shoot arrows, strike with a poisoned sword, catch a man in a net, they burn the heart or break it into pieces; they lead astray, they bewitch, they destroy. Glances are rarely sweet, and never soft or gentle, in the love dystichs. Here eyes are always black, perhaps because one is apprehensive if they are blue, the colour of the evil eye. It is difficult to overestimate the joy of sheer vision. The folk-songs are full of the beauty of flowers and meadows and streams, of the sea with its fleet of sail-boats, of the blue of the sky. In villages and towns, the people go strolling after work is done, calling this not a promenade, but *syryani*, "enjoyable viewing." When a long-absent loved one is returning, people congratulate, saying: "Light for your eyes."

Next to the eyes come the lips, but, red and sweet though they be, they are primarily important because of the words which come out of them. Like the eyes, they lead astray not through making false promises, but by engendering love. Speech is of extreme importance to the Greeks, since it establishes and fosters the all-important personal relationships. Almost everyone creates songs; love-songs at the village festival, dirges, lullabies, songs of the way of life, songs of work, songs of one's village and of nature. It is important to find the graphic word in the most ordinary speech, and to turn a spicy phrase. Utterance will take the form of a small oration without creating self-consciousness; an answer is often incisive repartee. There are orations in the coffee-house, and wherever a few people gather together. Even learned papers or scientific journals, when not under foreign influence, are often couched in oratory. *Couvenda*, conversation, is a recognized form of "passing the time," of entertainment, perhaps on a par with *syryani*. *Couvenda* is rarely desultory, or the mere exchange of information. It is usually contrapuntal virtuosity, incisive, combative, loud; and loudness is such a familiar quality of conversation that radios are turned on much too loud for the ears of foreigners. A statement or a question is countered by a challenging question. Tact and gentleness have no part here, insults are hurled, attacks are made, within the appropriate limits. A discussion is a battle of personal opinion, and its end is neither to reach the truth nor to reach a conclusion; its end is sheer enjoyment of vigorous speech.

The hair is a focus of erotic attraction. In the folk-songs there is often the picture of a girl letting her hair down as a ladder hung for her lover. For the man, the moustache is a symbol of his manhood and attractiveness. The beard is not important, and in a folk-song, a priest's wife calls her husband a bearded goat. A man without face hair is called a *Spanos*, and is a figure of derision in the folk-lore, and sometimes of fear.

Beyond the features of the head, very little of the body is

mentioned in the personal folk-songs. Genital organs must never be mentioned, and many women know no names for them. Out of over 400 love couplets analyzed, only one mentions the breast, "your breast is like Paradise." Formally, as a general division of the body—the chest—the breast is named in the same way for men and women and the term can be used freely. In its form of a female breast it must not be mentioned, as none of the sexual areas are mentioned. Its functional term, however, the nursing-breast, *vyzí*, is commonly used without embarrassment and when a mother is nursing, there is no embarrassment about exposing the breast for suckling.

The sense of smell is extremely important to the Greeks. In the personal folk poems, there is much mention of sweet-smelling flowers, herbs, trees: "musk and cinnamon, a beautiful girl she is" says a rhyming game. An unexpected guest will be offered a "smell" of whatever the housewife is cooking or the family is eating. And it is smell which makes the cravings of a pregnant woman not to be denied. A neighbour automatically puts aside a bit of her cooking to send to the pregnant woman next door; and in a grocery-store, a customer often offers a "smell" of the olives she has bought to a pregnant customer.

Orderliness is a highly valued quality. Love-songs mention the orderly hair, the orderly teeth. The most recent book on child care lays great stress on avoiding the disordering of a child's teeth and facial contours, giving several sketches and photographs of wrong ways of laying the child in bed or postures in sitting at a school desk which might lead to crookedness, and detailed descriptions of specific distortions and their causes. In houses which contain only one room, areas of work and living are carefully specified and maintained through scrupulous order. The Greek equivalent of "set to rights" or "all right" or "under control" is "in order."

The covering of the *philotimo* and the covering of the naked fact find their counterpart, if not their basis, in the body. The body is never naked or, perhaps, only when absolutely necessary. Mothers often arrange to bathe and change the baby without undressing it all at once. The new pediatric practices and the new books on child care demand immersion, but it is all a matter of hygiene; no joy in the naked baby is mentioned anywhere. Conversely, dress, and particularly festive dress, "dress of splendour" and ornamentation, are of great importance, and in fact, are essential to complete the body. When beautiful girls are described, their clothing and their jewelry are given at least as much place as their bodily charms, and are not treated separately; and when a brave youth, a *pallicari*, is mentioned, his trappings are part of the picture. Jewellery and brilliant clothes, woven with gold and silver thread, figure largely in the lullabies, as well as in the love-songs and wedding-songs. And the lower world which holds no joy is a place where there are no ornamental trappings. The naked body, like the naked word, is stark and grim and incomplete.

The body and the self, the Greek person, delimit, pattern and give shape to relationships and experience. All relationships start with the body and continue along lines of physiological relatedness. They are extended along lines of concrete personal contact. Greeks travel, but mainly along a chain of personal relationships; they go to see a friend of a relative of a friend, and the end, however distant is concretely linked through persons with the original person. Progress is amelioration of the concretely experienced, or the benefit of immediate relatives or friends or linked persons. The new can be introduced, not for the benefit of mankind or even the Greeks, but for the benefit of people along related lines, and better still, it can be introduced by a known and respected intermediary.

Figures on a chart mean very little to Greeks, and when they refer to people, may even be offensive. Foundations, such as the Near East Foundation, which have recognized this, have been successful in their relations with Greeks and in the introduction of desirable changes. They realized that they had to use not impersonal scientists but people who were predominantly leaders, with scientific knowledge, people who were willing to go and live in the villages, and make the acquaintance of the peasants over coffee in coffee-houses. And the villagers fell in with the proposals for new hygienic methods and child care and artificial insemination because they had respect for and faith in the man who made the proposals. And where schemes introduced in the name of self-interest did not succeed, those introduced in the name of the respected leader did. "For your sake" is a common sanction. The continuous presence of the leader is not, however, necessary once the personal loyalty is there. In recent years, foreign experts have made the mistake of operating mainly from Athens, living in hotels catering to foreigners, of moving in foreign circles, and making no personal contact with the Greeks, thus creating difficulties for themselves and raising obstacles to the effectiveness of their missions. Greek families receiving CARE parcels impersonally make great efforts to attach a person to the name of the sender; they often write very personal letters, trying to send photographs of themselves, "so that you can see us." In Greece there are no political bosses, since a man's vote is too personal, too much bound by personal loyalty, to be swayed by self-interest. On the other hand, we do find demagogues, who by sheer oratory and force of personality can inspire loyalty to themselves, and thereby, to their ideas. If there are irregularities at the polls, they come about not through the selling of one's vote, but through an attempt to vote several times in an impassioned effort to ensure the election of the chosen candidate.

Greek ethical conduct is personal also. A plea in the name of humanity or of kindness is meaningless to most Greeks; and only recently, in Athens, which has been affected by foreign ideas, did a plea in the name of the suffering peasants find true response. An organization called Friends of the Village was formed, and the aid given is by specific persons to specific people or families, in terms of a personal relationship. A peasant woman, writing to such a "Friend" in Athens, accepts the gift with ease and gratitude saying: "You are now my sister, and your family is my family."

Americans, who excel in impersonal kindness, are always surprised to see their human, warm, generous Greek friends remain unmoved and unresponsive in the face of suffering strangers. Greeks, on the other hand, are surprised to see their kind American friends giving according to figures on a piece of paper, according to what they can afford. In giving, Greeks deprive themselves of the very necessities of life, impoverish and even bankrupt themselves; but they recognize their responsibility to give only where personal relations are involved.

This is also true where truthfulness, honesty, loyalty and obedience are concerned. Greek parents are agreed that the principal thing to teach their children is to be honest and to tell the truth; but this, of course, means to be honest in their dealings with their parents and other relatives and all the friends of these, and with people who value them and trust them as persons. Honesty in abstraction is not a virtue, and may even be branded as foolishness. Loyalty also is never to something abstract, like the government, which is equated with impersonal law. Loyalty is to the Greek nation, to Greece, the mother of the people, to personified freedom, but not to "the Greeks" who are unknown. Profiteering and dealings on the black market were not considered bad, because they circumvented only impersonal law and showed disloyalty only to the government and to the unknown Greeks; actually they were good in terms of the family, to whom an individual owes his loyalty.

Responsibility is not social responsibility but family responsibility, or it might be extended to friends and to the village. With loyalty evoked only in personal relations, it follows that Greeks cannot be impartial in awarding jobs or distributing goods. To take care of one's own first, irrespective of merit or of an order of priority, is one's duty; it means fulfilling one's role. Yet impartiality, just because it is so difficult to maintain in the face of strong forces and temptations to "bend," and devotion to an abstract ideal of honesty, just because it is saintly, are highly admired in Greece—though perhaps not by the immediate relatives of the impartial man. Such people inspire what amounts to worship.

Co-operation in this framework is actually mutual aid, one person helping the other; or it is loyalty to the leader who initiates a co-operative undertaking, with men contributing their work for his sake, and women bringing gifts to him, which can be used incidentally for the undertaking.

Obedience is very important and is taught to a child almost from birth; but again, this is obedience within a structured whole, to the parents, older siblings, and to people who stand in this relationship, that is, to friends of the parents or of older relatives, or appropriately introduced older people. Authority comes only from place in this structured whole, and obedience is only to people. Government is not personal, and the law is external to the organic, structured whole. It is not the voice of Greece. There is therefore no obligation to obey the law; the guide to conduct here is expediency, and the ability to circumvent. Before the political centralization, there was obedience and lasting loyalty to the school-teacher. Now he represents only the interfering authority of the government, and it is an accepted thing that the students should try to circumvent his authority in every way they can, playing tricks on him and otherwise treating him as an enemy, since he is outside of the web of their loyalties.

WORK

Attitudes towards work, time, planning and spending arise also from the person or body as pattern and definition.

Work is life for the Greek. It is the person in function. Things like sports, week-ends and vacations, or like "leisure" in the Western sense, are the recent introductions of foreigners. There are times when work or certain kinds of work are interdicted, but this is part of religion, not a claim to leisure time or idleness. And leisure is an attitude, a dimension of all work, and in fact, of all life; it is not confined to a time of day but is the constant expression of internal freedom while at work or at rest.

Diligence is part of the image of the self; it is a personal quality, warmly admired. To call a girl *procommene*, diligent, is to say something about her attractiveness. A poem which schoolchildren used to memorize spoke of the joyous little housewife, the little girl who got up early to set the house in order. There was nothing of the repellent goody-goody about her, and nothing strange about calling industriousness joyous. The Greek folk-songs, often sung as accompaniments to the dance, picture such work situations: a group of young girls laundering at the beach, spreading the clothes and playing in the sand; or the woman singing at her loom. Folk-tales make cruel fun of the lazy wife who comes to grief. Visitors to Greek villages bring back a picture of a busy, happy life, of the girls and women gossiping at the fountain in the village square as they wait their turn; of the mother weaving in the shade of the grape-arbor while she watches the food cooking on the outdoor brazier, of her daughters working beside her and the little children running about, playing or running errands; of husband and wife walking to the fields an hour or so away, the little children running by their side, the swaddled baby hanging stiffly at the mother's hip, swinging with every step. They show a picture of shared family work as the medium of family life, as the way in which the growing child comes to belong to and identify himself with the unit of his birth.

Diligence is an internal attitude; it rests on self-discipline and free incentive, it includes interest and enjoyment. It does not mean a valuation of work for its own sake; it is the personal quality of diligence, not work itself, which is good. To work compulsively is to be a slave to work; and what can be worse than slavery? Even to work under the compulsion of work as a virtue is to deny oneself prized freedom; all work under pressure, such as the pressure of a time limit or the dictates of an employer means loss of freedom. Industrialization and work in urban centres usually run counter to this value. Greeks who emigrated to the United States to earn money for their sisters' dowries, or for land needed by the family, worked incredibly long hours, but neither through external nor through inner compulsion. They worked at their own shoeshine booths, or their own fruit-stands or restaurants; they took on unfamiliar occupations such as cooking, rather than submit to an employer.

TIME

Greeks "pass" the time; they do not save or accumulate or use it. And they are intent on passing the time, not on budgeting it. Although city people say that this picture is changing, that they are now made aware of the need to use time, the attitude is still widely prevalent, even in the area of private life among the urban groups.

The clock is not master of the Greek: it does not tell him to get up, to go to the field. In most villages, in spite of recent changes, the peasants still get up at sunrise or dawn to go to the fields, and return at sundown. The day is made for work. At night women visit and gossip; men join them or go to the coffee-house; there is story-telling, and ardent political discussion; and as for any work done after dark, "the day takes a look at it and laughs." Wherever there is no law to the contrary, a man opens his store in due course, not by the clock; however, in the cities he now functions under clocked time because he comes under government and union regulations. Even in the United States, though conservative Greek business men have adapted their business life to the time of the clock, in their private life and at social gatherings they function irrespective of the clock.

It is distasteful to Greeks to organize their activities according to external limits; they are therefore either early or late, if a time is set at all. At church the people are not impatient while waiting for Mass to begin; and the church fills only gradually. They know when to go to church; yet when a foreign visitor inquires as to the time of a certain Mass, the subject creates a discussion; and eventually the answer will be something like: "Between 2 and 3." And when Greeks who follow their traditional ways invite, they say, not: "Come at 7 o'clock," but: "Come and see us." To arrive to dinner on time is an insult, as if you came just for the food. You come to visit, and the dinner eventually appears. Among urbanized Greeks, this custom now seems burdensome, and there are many cartoons on the subject.

The dinner is not planned to appear at a predetermined time; and the housewife does not cook by the clock. She tells by the smell or the consistency, or the colour, or the resistance against the stirring spoon; or the passing of time is gauged by the intervening activities. Conservative Greek women in the United States, even after a residence of many years, banish from the kitchen the interfering clocks which are introduced by their American grandchildren. Greek men and women work expeditiously, as a rule, but do this best at their own rhythm; any need to hurry is external and interfering; it introduces fuss and disturbance. Efficiency can usually be found when it is not a conscious end.

To introduce an awareness of time into a meal is particularly abhorrent to Greeks, though this has to be done where factories set time limits. Dinner is served when it is ready, and without regard to efficient consumption. The fish is not filleted, the nuts are not shelled, the fruit is not sliced. The eater will spend a long time removing infinitesimal bits of flesh from the head of a small fish. All this is part of the process of eating, which is more than the naked act of consumption. He will end his meal with an orange which he will peel with virtuosity, leaving the peel in one piece; to consume an orange in the form of juice is to take all the meaning out of the act.

Greeks in the city, in some circles, find the need of hurry entering their lives. They are not at home with it. For the Greek traditionally, to work against time, to hurry, is to forfeit freedom. His term for hurry means, originally, to coerce oneself; and a visitor arriving out of breath may say, "I have hurried," but the form in which the word is more often used is, "Don't hurry." One does not admonish another to coerce himself, and a mother does not constantly ask her child to hurry up, unless perhaps she is following the new books on child training which say that a baby must not be allowed to set his own pace. But a Greek has other linguistic ways of expressing expeditiousness. There is the gentle hint, "Won't you make speed?" There is the reassuring, "I have finished," meaning "I am coming to the end as fast as I can," and there is the urgent call for help: "Arrive!"

There are many clocks and watches in Greece now, both in the city and the village. Watches are an important part of a man's trappings, and of a girl's adornment. Clocks are necessary to complete the furnishing of a house. It is not essential as a rule that they keep good time, or that they run at all. If they are in good running order, and are in use, their function is one of reference; they do not shape the household life. They give information and satisfy curiosity; they do not tell the wife that it is now time to start cooking or serve the meal. However, there are exceptions to this, particularly among the few mothers who follow the child-training directions for rigidly scheduled feedings and bedtime. Villagers speak of hours and minutes, but these are merely references to the passing of time, rather than its measure. Visitors, asking how far it is to the next village, find that "five minutes" may mean half an hour or two hours, but they find that the answer "A cigarette away" does provide an accurate measure.

In spite of the prevalence of timepieces, the church bell and the school bell, and even a cannon blast continue to have active functions in calling adults or children to pre-arranged gatherings or communal village work. Even in the cities, people are called "Englishmen" when they turn up on the dot at meetings or appointments. People often arrive an hour late to an appointment to find that the other person is also just arriving, or if they find him gone, they usually accept the fact with neither apology nor frustration.

STANDARD OF LIVING

The standard of living is set not by a scheme, but by the needs of the person, shaped and channelled by family role, as well as by disdain for softness and love of simplicity. Greeks do not budget, except for a very few who like to follow American ways. They spend not according to what they have, but according to the order of what they want, and, on principle, they should want little. Simplicity and frugality are expressions of fortitude and self-discipline, and they are also really enjoyed as dimensions of living. Greeks are not motivated by the thought of great or vague or schematic future benefits; however, since the family is central to all planning, and since it extends into the future, Greeks try to see to it that there are means for the education of the son or the dowry of the daughter, or for an added field or a gold ornament for the wife. They have no faith in the future, and know that it will not take care of itself. So, as a rule, they buy only what they can pay for now and will not expand either business or standard of living on the basis of future profits.

Greeks go in debt for subsistence and what they consider necessities. They do not like to borrow for luxuries, or for the creation of wealth. If they have enough for necessities, then any rise in income is sheer surplus. It does not have to go towards relieving the strain on the budget, or to pay a dreaded instalment on a radio, and, as a rule, it does not raise the standard of living. The Greek likes his life; he does not see why he should give up his lunch of cheese and bread, or his delicious *commatiasta* (stews) just because now he can afford roast lamb every day. Such things belong to festive occasions. The surplus will be put back into the business, or saved intact for the family, or given in beneficence.

The wealthy Greek "of good family," that is, who has been properly brought up, is not distinguished by luxurious living, since luxury is soft and ostentatious. He is distinguished by his gifts to his country or village, by the battleship or stadium that bears his name, the village fountain or health centre which he established for his district. Large sums of money are sent annually to Greece by its emigrated sons for these purposes, as well as for the support or education or dowering of relatives, by people whose wives do their own housework. Greece has counted on these sums as an important source of income, and the economy of Greece now suffers from the effects of restricted emigration, since American-born Greeks lose contact with their parents' country, and fewer such sums are now being sent back.

THE FAMILY UNIT AND ITS EXTENSIONS

I do not envy others for their vineyards and their gardens,
I envy only those who can stay in one place
And most I envy those who have brothers and first cousins
To grieve with them and rejoice with them
And to help each other when anything befalls.
(Cretan folk-song)

Greek society starts with the family, and is patterned on it. It extends outward from it. A child is born into a group and remains part of the group through no effort of its own, through no attempt to please. Work and play, eating, conversation, celebration, are all in terms of this unit, and are the way in which belongingness is taken on and reaffirmed. Wider contacts come through the family and its extensions. A child's friends are the family friends and their children, and the relatives. He goes visiting and to social gatherings with the family, by day or by night, though pediatricians protest against the latter practice. He goes to church with the family, attending the regular liturgy, not a Sunday-school for children. Even when great religious ceremonial occasions come late at night, such as the Mass of the Epitaph on Good Friday night, and the Mass of the Rising of Christ at midnight, the children are present. Except where foreign customs have been taken over, a Greek child does not celebrate his birthday. What is celebrated is the day of the saint after whom the child is named, and it is his family who celebrate. Old and young come to congratulate the family, and to wish that it shall enjoy the child for many years. The family containing the child is the focus, not the child himself.

The Greek family is family-oriented. It makes room for the child, and the mother expects to spend much time nursing the child, expects her cooking to be slowed down because of the constant presence and participation of the child. On the other hand, the child is not the focus, and the rhythm of activities does not change with the coming of the child. There are no special meal-times for the child, neither are the family meal-times shifted to accommodate its needs. If the father leaves the fields or closes his store on the child's name-day, it is because the *family* is celebrating. The child in the family is neither outstanding nor disruptive; but he is important, since he is accorded a definite place within the structured family.

In a Greek family the members spend much time together. The children learn to enjoy being with the adults, and to listen to their conversation, which is not trimmed down to meet the children's interests. In the village, a house often consists of only one room, so there is no physical privacy; and even when there are more rooms for summer living, the winter room is one. And shared living is prized. There is no craving for aloneness, although aloneness is accepted without complaint when necessary, as a hardship to be borne with fortitude. Sisters like to share a room, and even a bed; mothers like to work with their daughters, whom they do not consider to be underfoot. It is not contrary to peasant ethics for children of mixed sex to share sleeping quarters. Family matters are discussed by all, and children over 10 often have a voice in important decisions such as the buying or selling of a field.

Greeks value freedom and self-dependence, but the unit of self-dependence is not the individual but the family. The family is an organic whole, a system of delicately balanced roles and interrelationships. Older siblings are responsible for younger siblings, males for females. A Greek never ceases to have a claim on his family; a married son or daughter cannot be poor, starting at the bottom of the financial scale, while the parents thrive financially. A married son asks his father for help in business without losing *philotimo* or becoming dependent in character. A daughter asks for the things she cannot afford to buy. This is not dependence, it is one's rightful place within a structured, balanced whole. There is no virtue in being self-dependent in relation to one's family. But the family must be self-dependent in relation to the world, except in so far as it has a claim on government aid.

Equality within the family is a matter of personal essence, not of fairness of apportionment. An uneducated older brother is proud without bitterness of the younger brother whom he helped make a doctor. The family may impoverish itself for the education or dowering of one of the children, and the successful life of these children brings honour to the whole family. It is not uncommon to find that a man has remained unmarried so as to support his widowed sister and her family, or in order to earn a dowry for a large number of sisters. The need for obtaining these dowries was one of the main incentives for emigration to the United States. The responsibility for younger relatives is also at the base of the apportionment of positions and appointments of people who are not fitted by training or deserving by merit. A man who has been educated by older brothers who have stayed in the village working in the fields and vineyards, and who now holds a high government position, owes it to his family and to his role within it to find positions for his nephews. If he does not, he fails his family, he does not uphold the family *philotimo*, he is not a good Greek.

On the other hand, a father does try to see to it that he gives some property to every child, to sons for farming, to daughters for a dowry. This is at the base of much of the agricultural difficulty facing Greece at present, since fields have been divided, often into strips measuring a fraction of an acre, and require consolidation before effective use of mechanized farm implements can be made, as well as for contour farming and efficient fertilization.

"We moved to Athens as a family," said an islander, "my mother, her sisters and brothers, my grandfather, all the family." The Greek family is extensive, and in each case the term must be examined to find out what it includes. Second and third cousins are often in contact, and responsibility is felt for them also. They form links in the chain of relationship, so that personal contacts can be initiated. If a boy goes to Athens to attend the university, "if he has no uncles or other relatives, he rents a room." A Greek giving news usually speaks of "we" and the stock phrase beginning a letter is addressed to the plural "you," and refers to "we."

The father is in authority and he must be obeyed by all. A mother must be obeyed by the children, except when the oldest son has assumed the headship of the family. Older brothers are to be obeyed by the younger siblings. In conservative groups a son, whatever his age, has to be circumspect in the presence of his father; he may not smoke in his presence if the father objects to smoking. A father may not revel with his grown son at the tavern, and a considerate man, finding his son there, leaves the place. A wife waits upon her husband, and does not question his acts. If he fails her, if he becomes a drunkard or gambles away the family money, her *philotimo* will not allow her to reveal this, except, perhaps, to the priest. This is a matter of role and loyalty; it is not subservience. Greek women by tradition wait upon men, expect them to drink from the fountain first and to cross the bridge ahead of them; this does not make for inferiority, just as it does not make the American man inferior to wait for his wife to enter first, or to bring her water. The mother is a powerful and dominant figure, upholding fortitude and *philotimo,* sustaining her children in moral strength. There is no chivalry toward her in the village because there is respect for her. If her husband rides the only donkey, which she brought as dowry, while she walks behind him to the fields, it is because he considers her strong and able to do so. In the folk-songs, girls are jealous of their rivals because they can wait on the man they love; this is the coveted role.

The relatives by marriage, the *sympetherica,* are also important in the Greek relationship group, and the older brother-in-law often functions as an older brother. The whole family is therefore concerned with the marital arrangements of the individual. Arranged marriages, with great stress on the dowry, were the rule until recent years, and are still common. The dowry persists, even when the marriage is individually arranged, and often interferes with higher education for the girls; money is spent for the sons' education, but must be saved for the daughters' dowry. Whether the dowry is demanded or not by the groom's family, it is to the honour of the bride's family to give it. In conservative areas and circles, girls still meet young men only in groups, still communicate with them only with their eyes or in secret correspondence and secret meetings; however, there is increasing freedom in the lives of young people, particularly in Athens. Yet here too the web of relationships and extended responsibility is so wide-spread that the family, in effect, has its eyes on the young people wherever they go.

MATERNAL AND CHILD CARE

The Greeks love children. Boys are generally preferred, traditionally, sons are a sign of family vigour. Besides, a family not only loses its daughters, it has to pay out property with them. Childlessness is a terrible calamity, and the woman is held responsible. People say "the poor man," pitying the husband for his wife's sterility. A recent magazine report on current scientific discoveries combats this belief, telling its readers that potent men have been found to be sterile and that therefore wives are not always at fault for the childlessness of the family. Women fear to have anything done to their reproductive organs and will accept "maternity difficulties" without asking for medical help, lest this might somehow harm their fertility. A book on maternal and child care, *For the Mother,* urges that before marriage, both family histories be examined for possible sterility.

For the Mother urges young people to choose mates with a view to progeny. As a sanction, it mentions that the ancient Greeks urged eugenic marriages; and that the term "eugenics" was invented by Xenophon. Young people are advised to see a doctor before making the final decision. They are further advised to choose according to firmness of flesh and orderliness of features and limbs, for seriousness tempered with cheerfulness, for optimism implemented by effective energy. Marriage with kin, and with people having family histories of tuberculosis, syphilis, alcoholism, psychasthenia, is to be avoided.

According to this manual, a young woman beginning a pregnancy is expected to notice first an indisposition, accompanied by the non-appearance of the menses: this the husband diagnoses for her with great joy. Next come the food whims and the nausea, and this is the time to go for obstetrical advice. The first two months are the critical ones for the life of the embryo; therefore, a mother is urged to take a vacation in the second month. After that she may resume her normal activities, taking care only to avoid over-exertion and jerky movements. In the last month she should not immerse herself in bathing, because of the danger of infection; for the same reason she should avoid sexual intercourse in the last three weeks. In the last two weeks she should avoid all exertion. She should sleep eight to ten hours daily during her pregnancy, never more, lest she become listless and melancholy. She should avoid large social gatherings, she should not play cards, she should drink nothing stronger than light wine, she should eat meals as balanced as is consistent with her means and her normal diet. Her relatives should see to it that her days are calm and happy, and that she is surrounded by pictures of beautiful scenery and beautiful people, so that her baby will be beautiful.

Pregnancy is pictured here as a period of joyous anticipation. In the morning, after the fourth month, the mother is awakened by her gambolling embryo, who is saying to her, "Wake up, Mama; don't be in a hurry; I am coming gradually and constantly." She takes care of her breasts, massaging them and elongating the nipples, thinking of her baby. She prepares the layette, embroidering the pieces, caressing them and showing them to her visitors, taking joy in them.

Throughout her pregnancy a woman is expected to eat everything she craves. She can knock on any door where she smells cooking food and ask for a "smell." The satirist reporting on the Court of Petty Offences describes a case where a man complains that his neighbour has been pregnant almost steadily for four years, and that her pregnancies are too great a drain on his purse; the judge advises him to move to another location. The case is unusual, but not far-fetched.

There are prenatal clinics as well as well-baby clinics, maintained by the state in the cities and provincial centres. Midwives are trained in a state institution and work in close co-operation with obstetricians. In many villages, however, there are no trained midwives available, and there is recourse to the "wise woman." The manual *For the Mother* gives a list of things to be prepared for a home birth; but many women in the cities, when they can afford it, prefer an obstetrician and a hospital delivery.

Child-birth is an occasion of great importance. The mother has something of the Madonna about her now, and is idealized by all, and particularly by her husband, who offers her a second courtship at this time, bringing her special sweets and ornaments. The word *lecho*, describing her through her lochial period, is emotionally charged. Traditionally, a *lecho* is bed-ridden for eight days, and is under special regulations for the first 40 days. She may not go out until the "40 days" are over, and then she goes first to church. In some areas, no one is allowed to enter the house after sunset, until the 40 days are over.

Greek babies are swaddled except in very rare cases where a completely foreign manner of upbringing is followed. The newest manuals suggest half-swaddling for the three months, that is, swaddling only of the trunk of the body, with legs and arms free. But this much is at any rate considered essential for a straight and firm back. In Athens there is a range of swaddling; simple people often swaddle completely for at least three months, but may leave the baby's arms and legs free by day after the fortieth day. In the village, the old swaddling is practised for the most part, along with the newer ways. Traditionally the baby is swaddled all over, until it is a stiff bundle. Each knee is straightened out; in many regions, each leg is wrapped separately, and then the two are wrapped together; the arms are pressed against the sides and then the swaddling cloth is wrapped tightly over all. Swaddling is imperative to make the baby grow straight, tall and strong; most of all to prevent it from becoming crooked.

As we have mentioned, traditional and scientific opinion

agree that the baby must never be held nestling in the crook of the arm until it can sit up by itself. The gesture of mother-love is not that of the curved arms. Even an unswaddled baby is held like a long stiff bundle against the body within an imaginary swaddling-band. In villages, babies are often carried in slings, lying stiffly against the mother's hip and swinging with her walk; or they are carried standing in the sling against her back. The Greek cradle is a swing, which can be moved near to where the mother is working, so that she can pull the rope to rock it. At night it is put beside her bed. The pediatricians inveigh strongly against its use, considering that it spoils the baby, urging the use of bassinets and cribs.

It is important that the baby be breast-fed; in fact this is taken for granted. According to the child-care manuals, it is extremely rare for a mother to have no milk, and slightly less rare that she have not enough milk. The city pediatricians find it necessary, however, to make impassioned pleas for the mother's own milk, pointing out the dangers incurred in engaging a wet-nurse, the criminality towards one's own baby, who has an inherited right to his mother's milk, and the crime against the baby of the wet-nurse, who has been left in the village without a mother. Women are reminded that the great Homeric mothers, Hecuba and Penelope, suckled their own children. Some factories have baby nurseries, mainly to enable mothers to nurse their own children. When supplementary feeding is needed, it is to be given with a spoon, lest the baby find the rubber nipple easier and refuse the breast. Asses' milk is recommended as nearest to the mother's milk; cow's and goat's milk are recommended next to this.

Traditionally, the baby is given *glykanisso,* anise water, and camomile the first day, and is allowed to suck the colostrum the second day. Pediatricians urge that all ingestion should begin with suckling and that no other food be given. Babies are to receive no solid food until the sixth or even the eighth month. Nursing is recommended until the fourteenth month, or even up to two years; and the two-year period is traditional. Weaning is gradual; pediatricians as well as tradition recommend the smearing of bitter stuff, perhaps quinine on the nipple, or the offering of sweetened milk. Nursing need not be interrupted for a pregnancy and, in fact, may be good for the growing embryo. Juices of every variety of available fruit are recommended at three or four months, as well as strained vegetable soups. Traditionally, the baby joins the family at meal-time as soon as he can sit up; he is allowed to eat of the family meal, given choice slowly and carefully. At first, hard crusts and bones only are allowed, so that fragments will not lodge in his throat. The pediatricians urge against this practice. They also urge rigid scheduling of feedings. The behaviourist principles of child-rearing fit into the value of firmness, the feeding schedule falls in with the training of fortitude, and is introduced in the name of self-discipline, as well as for giving the mother freedom, that is, leisure and freedom from encroachment. Few mothers, however, fall in with these schedules.

Toilet-training is not mentioned in the two current manuals on child care. Mothers report that they begin training for urination at five or six months. Training for the bowel movement does not come until the child can sit by himself. Help in learning how to speak is suggested and described at length, but none for walking. Greek mothers do encourage their children to walk, however, and a folk rhyme says that a baby, "lest it be shamed," takes to the wall and walks at seven months. The manuals devote much space to character-training; obedience is taught first, almost from birth; it is the parents' task to mould the character of the child, to be firm and unyielding. Mothers are urged not to be indulgent or over-protective.

The manuals devote about a third of their space to illness and home care. Under illness are listed sleeplessness, enuresis, thumb-sucking, night terror, lack of appetite. Enuresis is said to come from irritation of the urethra, thumb-sucking to begin around the fifth month from irritation of the gums.

In recent years, mothers have been urged to spend more time with their babies and to do more things for them. Among the urban well-to-do this means that mothers are urged to bathe, feed, and suckle their babies themselves. For other groups, this would mean a displacement; the children are usually with the mother, working with her and sharing experience with her; but to give them her undivided attention she would have to change basic attitudes, the accepted place of the child within the family and his assumed share in all its functions, and she must reorient the entire system of roles within the family.

The mother apparently takes no delight in the naked baby, in touching its skin or watching its movements when freed from the swaddling cloth. Traditionally the baby, like the adult, is never naked. The baby's bath is not a special occasion of delight. In her lullabies, the mother shows no delight in any part of the child. She speaks of the joys of gardens, flowers, herbs and trees, but most of all, she tells of the rich clothes and adornments she is ordering from strange lands. She dreams of her daughter's wedding and her son's education. To the visitor, the baby consists of arms and legs; she says, first making appropriate allowances for the evil eye, "How his arms and legs have grown!" The mother coos and signs to her baby and smiles a special smile; she kisses his hands, she holds him in her arms. She calls him "My little gold, my little angel, my little bird, my little love"; she uses no terms derived from the sense of taste, unless she is a refugee from the interior of Turkey. On the other hand, she will say, "That I might eat you!"

It is extremely important for a child not to shame its parents. A mother, after a visit is over, will say to her child: "Bravo, my good child, you have not shamed me!" or "Bad child, you have shamed me." A child is addressed as *"my* good one," but when naughty, merely as "bad one." In fact, children usually learn early to behave in the presence of visitors. They are used to hearing their mothers praise them in their presence, and they expect to be asked to stand up on a chair and recite a poem or sing; such performances are carefully praised, with the precaution of symbolic spitting, to circumvent the evil eye. Children are also used to hearing themselves criticized bluntly by visitors.

The Greek child is given freedom in his behaviour, with the limits supplied by personal relationships. It is not wrong to be boisterous and noisy, but it is wrong to be so when Father does not like it, or during a visit, or when it disrupts Mother's work. The child is always on the periphery, never in the centre; the wishes of the elder members come first. A good child listens to his parents, runs Mother's errands. He may be rewarded with a piece of candy, but small gifts of this sort are given so freely that the reward does not stand out. He is told folk-tales of the little goat who disobeyed his mother, or the little lamb who obeyed, or the mother may invent such moral tales for the child.

Obedience to the father, the mother, older siblings, the older relatives and friends of the family in general, is very important. The disobedient child "eats wood," but it is probably only the father who might pick up a stick with which to strike the child. A mother certainly does not give the child the equivalent of a whipping, though she may strike the child with whatever she happens to have in her hand. Usually she will merely shout at the naughty child, threatening to kill him. The child will run away, the mother will run after him, catch him by the ear and pull him back, or reach out and slap his face (*batso*, slap-on-the-cheek, is very common, as is ear-pulling). The child howls, but presently comes back to the subject of the disagreement; he is not cowed. After a series of violent threats and withering curses, the mother will hug the child. This is not seen as rejection, and any lurking hostility is given full vent.

Every baby is baptized as early as possible; until baptism the child is called a "little dragon"; it has no name. Naming comes only with baptism. The occasion is an important religious and social one. The godparent is chosen carefully, since this is a relationship which lasts for life, and broadens the all-important relationship circle for the child.

When a new baby is expected, the mother may tell the knee baby[1] that he is to have a little sibling; or she may simply wait until the birth, and explain that the midwife brought the sibling. The knee baby is openly expected to be jealous, and visitors inquire in his presence whether he is so. When he sees the mother suckling the new baby, he may cry for suck too; in this case the mother will invite him to suckle on the other side, or offer him a piece of bread; or, if she knows him to be jealous or sickly, she may invite him on her own initiative. Such jealousy apparently does not last long. The knee baby is already used to having his mother shout at him and then treat him with warmth and gentleness; he does not find this condition changed. The mother makes no effort to hide her delight in the new baby, to share herself equally, with fairness. Instead, she invites the knee baby to share in her wonder and excitement over the new baby. He has already been sharing in her everyday life and work, and he shares in this also. Gradually, he takes on her attitude, the cherishing, loving, responsible attitude which characterizes the relationship of older to younger siblings in Greece.

There is a magazine addressed to parents, now in its fourth year; but Greek newspapers carry no child-care sections, either on week-days or Sundays. Of the magazines, only those catering to non-intellectuals, such as *Romanza,* carry child and maternal care information; the articles are usually translations from foreign articles. The material is generally developed on behaviouristic principles, stressing scheduling and isolation of the baby.

EDUCATION

Education is perhaps the most prized good in Greece, and above all, professional education. The doctor, the lawyer, the engineer and the specialist have high standing and command large dowries. A university professor has high standing; a school-teacher has the respect of the people, but has lost some of the standing which he had before education became centralized. The printed word is very important, even revered. It is traditionally so; the calends of Saint Basil, sung on the night of 31 December, represent the Saint as carrying a book and paper and an ink-well. The lullabies often promise the baby boy a high education, the baby girl an educated bridegroom. In a folk-song, a girl, rejecting a suitor, says she will marry only an educated man.

There has been universal compulsory education up to the sixth grade since 1911,[2] but the peasants, particularly the women, are reported to be largely illiterate. This is due only

[1] "Knee baby" is a term used for the penultimate child, who stands at the mother's knee while the youngest child is held on her lap.
[2] John Maurogordato, 1931, p. 85.

in part to the fact that money for girls goes into dowry rather than for further schooling. Not all the older peasants attended school as children, or attended it for more than three or four years; and often what literacy they did have was lost in the course of time, because they had no opportunity to use it. There are no libraries in the villages or in most of the provincial centres. There is also no pattern of reading the Bible, which has maintained reading knowledge in other lands. In Greece the translation of the Bible into modern Greek was forbidden until recent years. The men, however, do read the newspapers with care, when they find them, and they have a detailed knowledge and a private opinion on international and national events and policies; politics, well understood, forms the basis of most discussions, in village or city. The satire on the Court of Petty Offences reports a case where two simple workers on the bus, engrossed in a discussion of the Spanish Civil War, use the perspiring back of another passenger as the map of Spain upon which to follow the manoeuvres of the two armies. The incident is amusing, but not surprising to Greek readers. A book on nutrition urges housewives to pattern their planning on the principles of the British monarchy, not those of the Italian monarchy, assuming knowledge of the principles underlying the difference.

In the cities, there is much intellectual activity on a high level. Many people write articles or poems or stories for their own satisfaction in their leisure time. Conversation presupposes wide reading. The inexpensive paper-bound volumes of Greek works, as well as of translations of foreign works, old and contemporary, make such reading possible. There are 10 daily papers in Athens, and a number of magazines catering to literary tastes, or addressed to simpler people. Magazines carry reports of new scientific developments throughout the world, and a number of educational articles. Those addressed to the *cosmakis,* the simple people, carry articles on child and maternal care, have cooking and sewing hints, as well as columns of personal advice. The newspapers maintain a high literary and scholarly standard.

RELIGION

Religion and the Church are almost synonymous for the Greeks; and the Greek Orthodox religion is entirely synonymous with Greekness. When the Greek says: "Is he a Christian?" he means "Is he a Greek?" The Greek Church is the main factor in Greek continuity among emigrants nowadays. Throughout the past centuries, the Church has maintained Greek consciousness in many communities in Asia Minor, where the people spoke Turkish as a mother tongue and followed Turkish customs. The few Protestant Greeks occupy an ambiguous position and find it difficult to explain that they are really Greek, since they do not conform to the tradition of Greekness.

Religion permeates Greek life, punctuating it with ritual. No Greek, urban or rural would think of initiating anything important without a religious inauguration. Schools open with the inaugurative *agiasmos,* "making holy"; the foundation stone of every house is laid with *agiasmos*; merchants begin new undertakings with the proper religious inauguration. On Epiphany, the sea is made holy for those who journey on it. In the country, blessed water is carried from the Epiphany Mass to sprinkle on the fields. The Virgin and the Saints are invoked, but not mainly as correctives; their main function is to endow an undertaking with good and success, it is not primarily to prevent or correct. When a loved man, husband, son, brother, father, beloved, goes away with the merchant marine, or in the sponge-fishery, a woman makes a vow to the appropriate Saint, to be fulfilled on the safe return. The islands are studded with small chapels which were promised on such occasions. However, priests are called in, and Saints and the Virgin invoked, also, when difficulties arise. Vows are made for the recovery of a loved one; the priest is called when the family has had a run of misfortune, to "make holy" and exorcize the evil. Priests conduct a rain litany to break a drought.

Traditionally, Sunday services are attended regularly by women and children, perhaps less faithfully by the men. Ceremonials, however, draw the entire family. The ritual is not bolstered by strict limits of time or rules of silence. Mass starts in due course, a little early or a little late, not on the dot of an appointed time. Children run in and out between the aisles, and mothers whisper endearments to babies. A woman will break into a dirge during the Good Friday Mass of the Epitaph, mourning the death of Christ, or addressing herself in sympathy to the bereaved Virgin. The Mass before the midnight preceding Easter is tense with expectation; there is great release and spontaneous joy when Christ is announced to be risen, and the "Christ is risen!" with which all are greeted is a true, joyous message, full of the wonder and the reassurance of the renewed miracle; the candles lighted from the sacred light at this time are carried home with true concern for saving the flame from extinction.

Religion is so firmly entrenched and unquestioned that it can be taken with casualness and a lack of self-conscious effort. It is accepted and ever-present, like the air. One talks about Masses and preparations for litanies, but not about religion. Religion is not a personal matter, nor is it a guide to conduct. People consult the priest, but in matters of human relations, or, at any rate, relations which are regarded as secular, not because they are assailed by doubts. Young men do not talk about the meaning of Christ in their lives, nor do young girls dream of entering a convent. On the other hand, the Saints and the Virgin often figure in speech: a man singing of his beloved likens her neck to an altar, her arms to church tapers, or he tells her that he worships her like the Virgin. A derisive Dodecanese anti-Mussolini song, composed during Italian occupation, makes casual reference to God and the beloved Virgin of the Island.

HEALTH

The stock phrase for beginning a Greek letter is "We have health and health we wish for you." A frequent form of greeting and good-bye is "Health to you," and this is also said to anyone who sneezes. Anyone wearing a new article of clothing is greeted with the wish that he may wear it with health. The questions "How are you? Are you well?" asked upon a meeting with someone, are real questions, requiring an answer. Health is good and important, it is desired, but it is not a preoccupation. The wish for health is not a sanction; one of the child-care manuals uses this sanction in urging mothers not to let their young children play with the neighbourhood children for fear of contracting infections, but the other urges the mothers not to worry about microbes, since association with others is of primary importance. In general, however, health is not a motivation in nutrition, recreation, or housing. And human relations are definitely more important. It is terrible to send a member of the family to the hospital unless, of course, it is necessary for an operation. Because of this attitude, tuberculosis often spreads through the family, since very often not even the barrier of self-protection will be introduced between the ailing and the well. Added to this is the fear that if tuberculosis is known to be in the family, it will be hard to get a son-in-law. However, if an operation is required, a woman will go alone from a village to a hospital in Athens. There is no rejection by her family involved here; in addition, the pattern of fortitude is evoked.

In general, people do not go to a doctor unless something is very wrong. They do not go for a general check-up, although the habit of going to maternal and well-baby clinics is gaining ground. If anyone is unwell, home remedies are first resorted to, and probably the wise woman who knows about herbs is called in. The manuals on child care have long sections, covering about a third of the book, on home care and the diagnosis of disease; and they urge the use of traditional remedies: cupping, the use of camomile and other herbs. When a serious illness is recognized, the doctor is called and vows are made to the Virgin or the appropriate Saint; a mother may vow a foot pilgrimage, or 40 daily obeisances over a period of time, or the gilding of the hands of an ikon. Much illness arises from the evil eye or magic spells, and can be counteracted by magical practices.

The tuberculosis division of the UNRRA mission to Greece reports the impression that there was only half the amount of tuberculosis in the provinces as compared to the cities, and Greeks interviewed gave as their opinion that this was true of the health picture generally.

Doctors are very highly respected. There have been women doctors in Greece, as well as women dentists, for many years; but the village image of the doctor is one of a man. However, a woman is much freer to discuss gynaecological difficulties with a woman physician. There is great reluctance to mention the genital areas, and many women do not even know the appropriate terms to use. The acceptance of the *metrica*, the maternity difficulties, may be partly due to the reluctance to have this general area exposed and examined.

The handicapped are not easily accepted in Greece. To be crippled, blind, lame, means that one is not quite a person. Children might even jeer at the handicapped without being reprimanded. Amputation is therefore a terrible calamity, because it makes a person incomplete. Such a person cannot be accorded the respect that goes with the ability to assume responsibility. Parents may discourage their daughter from marrying a one-armed man whom they otherwise like in every respect, and who is perfectly capable of making a good living. Such people are assumed to be dependent. Greeks were bewildered by an UNRRA one-armed worker. Not only was he in the wrong function, but he could not fall into any known pattern of relationship, since he insisted on being physically self-sufficient. Since he would not accept help, the Greeks were uncomfortable with him, not knowing how to treat him.

Malaria, the great scourge which increased tuberculosis through lowering resistance, and which decreased production by sapping the energy, is now almost completely defeated by the spectacular DDT campaign. In the beginning of the campaign, the specialists, unaware of the peasants' love of sleeping in their orchards on hot summer nights, sprayed only the interiors of houses; when breeding grounds were also attacked, however, the campaign was totally effective, and has been of inestimable value for the introduction of further changes, since it won the confidence of the people.

Traditionally, there is no connexion between hygienic measures and health. Cleanliness is part of being well-ordered and well-groomed, not a matter of removing germs. And cleanliness is patterned. There is a day for scrubbing the kitchen floor, for changing sheets, for changing underwear, for going to the bath; there is a time for washing the face and the hands. There were never many latrines in rural areas and the situation has been aggravated through the war; in 1948, it was reported that 98 per cent of the farmers had no latrines.

NUTRITION

The Greek meal is a family ritual. It is a social occasion, a communion of the family, which does not have to be enhanced by special titbits, additional dishes, or special table arrangements. It is an occasion not to be treated lightly. Everyone down to the smallest child is present, and sits at the table throughout the meal. Everyone crosses himself at the beginning and the end of the meal. A blessing is called upon the meal, and absent members are remembered at this time. To quarrel at the table would be like "quarrelling in Church." Food is one aspect of this total situation, but it is not the entire end of the meal; and dinner is much more than food. Breakfast is not a meal but a light snack for individuals. The true family meal comes after one's day's "work" is over. Where people work until 2 p.m. and then stop for the day, as in offices in Athens, there may be two family meals a day; but the family meal is usually the evening meal.

The meal is the supreme medium of hospitality. All hospitality involves the offer of some food—a spoonful of preserves, coffee, brandy, nuts, fresh fruit, according to locality and time of the year. The meal goes beyond this. Visitors helping to re-establish refugees in their devastated villages report that the peasants kill their only hen for them, and fill their pockets with the few nuts they have. To invite a friend to dinner and take him to a restaurant is an insult, even in Athens. Restaurants are for foreigners and those who ape their ways, and for those unfortunate travellers who have no relatives in the city. There are also eating-places known as kitchens, where men who work too far from home can get a homelike meal. A group of friends on an outing or out for a dance may also eat together, incidentally, but this is a different matter.

Traditionally, food is not nutrition. Food is good, not good for you. In the cities there are at times articles published on nutrition. The mothers read maternal and child-care manuals which mention and describe nutrition, and perhaps they read the book by Dr. Katsigra on Food and Life, which tells them that all Greek food recipes destroy food values and transform the food into poison. Very few other Greeks are aware of these writings, or mention such things in conversation, however. In the cities, where mothers have been taught to stress nutritional values, to feed their children by schedule, and to keep them from the social communion of the family meal, feeding problems are well known; in the villages such problems are not reported. Children there are not urged to eat, and are not tempted with special foods: "Why should children not want to eat? Isn't food good?" If they do not like the eggplant dish particularly, there is always bread, and no one has ever heard of a child who does not like bread.

Greek meals are traditionally simple. There is always bread, and every mouthful of food must be eaten with a bite of bread. Greeks at foreign tables find it very difficult to face food, even potatoes and spaghetti, without the traditional mouthful of bread; apart from distaste, there is a feeling of guilt at eating food without bread. In the villages the bread is brown and home-baked, and it may form the complete meal, with olive-oil for dipping. If there is any other food, there is only one dish, containing a variety of ingredients which usually make for balanced eating through the day. The hot bean dish *(fasoulada)* for example, contains olive-oil, parsley, onions, tomatoes, and other vegetables, and, eaten with brown bread and perhaps olives and cheese, provides a complete nutritive meal, except that the proteins are not animal ones; and the writer finds it fit for a king. The Greek meal is not structured climactically. It may end with fruit, or a leaf of lettuce, or cheese; this, however, is nothing to look forward to but, at most, puts a period to the meal. It is the bread, the "food," that is the point of the meal. Greeks in foreign parts, who have taken on rich foreign desserts, often top their meals with a bite of bread.

In the provinces, very little meat is eaten. Through the week it is served, if at all, as a small ingredient part of one of the special vegetable dishes—dishes which are named after the main vegetable they contain. On Sundays, or when guests arrive, or on other festive occasions, there may be roast and potatoes; these are baked together and constitute the whole meal, with the ever-present bread. Fish is eaten in the villages wherever it is available. Processed fish—salted, dried, canned —is a great favourite, and salted roe, made into a "salad," is greatly enjoyed, and forms a regular item during Lent. Milk is consumed in the form of cheese and *yaourti,* a custard-like cultured milk; little is drunk. But the milk used is that of sheep and goats, which, according to Kaloyereas, is richer in fat and protein than cow's milk. In the villages, fruit and vegetables are eaten plentifully when in season; dried fruits and nuts are eaten, olives, cheese while it lasts, and a variety of legumes. There is skill in cooking, and since variety within a meal is not valued or demanded, the simple meals are much enjoyed, and wealthy emigrants who have succumbed to the luxuries of the American meal pattern often long for their peasant meals.

In the cities, the Greeks have learned to eat meat and to drink more milk. Here cow's milk and a taste for it have been introduced, and in the country around Athens and Salonika, the peasants raise cattle. Foreign packaged goods are in vogue in the cities, and people, in their desire to take on American ways, eat foods which are contrary to all Greek principles of texture. Oatmeal is eaten by young children and invalids under one of its American trade names, Quaker Oats, pronounced unrecognizably. As *vromi*, it is food for animals, and the word is reminiscent of "stench." According to Dr. Katsigra, much foreign fruit is also imported, and this has led to a demand for perfection in the appearance of the Greek fruit eaten; this means that the Greek fruit for the city is now picked unripe. City people eat mostly white bread. In general, city food, which conforms in externals more closely to the list of the nutritionists, actually seems to be inferior to that of the provinces. And city health is reported to have been much below that of the provinces, even at a time when the villages were suffering from the deprivations of the civil war.

Lent does not affect nutrition significantly. Where olive-oil is not allowed, olives are; where fish is not allowed, fish roe is. In the provinces, not much meat is eaten, even before Lent; in the cities many of the people fast only on a few of the important days of Lent. However, now that mothers have been taught the importance of giving their children daily milk, Lent does have an effect in this area; milk is forbidden during Lent, and children have to fast at least during the latter part. Unicef has made successful efforts to persuade mothers to give their children milk during this period. It achieved this with the co-operation of bishops who drank milk during Lent to show mothers that, if the cause was good, it was not a sin to drink milk; only one archimandrite refused to do so, afraid to take on the responsibility of possibly leading the people astray.

Greek holidays each have their appropriate food. It is essential for the welfare, the religion, for the Greekness of the people, to have this food at that time. At a time when the Bureau of Welfare was set up to function only during emergency, it offered funds for the indigent at holidays for the purchase of the indispensable festive foods. If Greeks have any money to spend at such a time, these foods have a priority over everything else.

ATTITUDES UNDERLYING ACCEPTANCE OF CHANGE

Greeks do not place a value on unlimited progress; what they want is the better than the present, or than the known. Modern Greek has lost the superlative of ancient Greek. To express *the best,* one now says, *the better of all the others.* And this expresses what is actually wanted. The American says, "the sky's the limit," but the Greek wants to reach the ceiling instead, something that he can touch and know ahead of time. The rest is a dream; he speculates about it as he speculates about what he would do if he were President of the United States; and he uses the subjunctive, not the future.

In this way, the attitude toward change is related to the place of the plan in Greek life. On the one hand, that which is a plan to an American, organizing and inciting to action, is a dream to the Greek, leading to quiescence or to oratory. The Greek mother of an American adolescent is shocked to hear her daughter express as plans, in the future tense, what she herself expressed in the subjunctive of the dream. Plans introducing agricultural and other change are formulated by foreign or foreign-trained technicians who say: "When I get to be . . . I shall do . . ." for people who say: "If I were . . . I would do"; there is a chasm between these two views of life.

On the other hand, the plan based on the non-experienced, on abstract calculation, is meaningless to people for whom experience is body-patterned. More than this, such plans represent external limits and directives, and to this extent are hampering and even frightening. Charts and diagrams are now common in Greek books, but the lineal diagram as a blue print of action is not within the framework of Greek life; the nearest most Greeks come to a diagram is a map, which is diagrammatic of something concrete. Foresight is good, and is extolled in proverbs; preparation is always present. But this is following along a known trail, repeating a known pattern with all its steps. For example, when a girl is 10 or 12, she may start working on her dowry; a good mother may start weaving for her daughter soon after birth. But this is to follow the Greek pattern of life, to behave as girls and mothers are supposed to behave. In the same way, a farmer has foresight according to occasions he expects to arise within a known situation. The planning is internal, arising from the rhythm of life; it is not something external to which the rhythm must be forced to conform.

This attitude presents difficulties, such as, for example, in industrialization in the area of food-processing. Greek farmers will not deliver food for canning according to plan or schedule; they will use what they need and deliver the surplus. But factories and exporting houses cannot readily function without supported expectations.

Again, Greeks are motivated by demonstrated, concrete results, not by diagrams of future benefits, or by statistics. The great success of the DDT programme was due to its quick, clear, obvious results. Much of the success of new practices initiated under the auspices of the Near East Foundation may also be attributed to their principle of demonstration.

Another attitude concerned with the introduction of change is that of coping with what is there. Americans are ready to change anything that does not measure up to specifications, or even anything that can be exchanged for something more efficient, more convenient, newer. Greeks accustom themselves to inconveniences and cope with them; they do not do away with them. Greeks, after a visit to the United States, see their countrymen putting up with the same difficulties, the same time-wasting operations, the same discomforts, but when they ask, "Why don't you do something about it?" they are immediately branded American. Anything that still works can always be patched up and used; a chipped dish can still hold food, a suit may have a few spots and still be clean, a woman may have a number of ills and still have health, and people can still travel when the steamships are crowded three times their capacity, and cannot provide the beds for which the passengers have paid; why make a change? As there is no superlative, so there are not exclusive oppositives, and one learns to cope with the common ailments, the common inconveniences. So the man whose task it is to introduce change often has to point out the mote to which the peasant's eye has become accustomed, and even has to take in consideration the fact that the eye is actually adjusted to the mote, and that its removal would mean at least temporary disruption.

There is another side to the picture with respect to coping. Greeks are tenacious and resourceful in making the best of what they do have. A visitor reports that a gasoline tank that sprang a leak on the road was repaired with *loukoums,* the sticky Near Eastern candy; she reports having seen two men pushing freight cars along a railroad track, as the engine had been destroyed in the guerrilla warfare. This attitude can be harnessed productively, and with benefit for people who derive a sense of enjoyment and achievement from it.

The sanction of the Church in inaugurating any change is essential; and so too, is that of the past, in endorsing practice, as well as a precedent for the introduction of change. It is well to remember that Byzantium and its civilization was part of the Greek past; and to remember that Rome was not. The Romans were barbarians; the manual on child care which urges mothers to suckle their babies like Penelope and the Trojan Hecuba also urges them to give up the custom of swaddling the child's limbs, a barbarous and tyrannical custom practised by the ancient Romans. The past is mentioned in learned articles, in newspapers, in letters, in the oratorical conversation. It is part of the festive dressing of the naked statement.

The areas of vulnerability of the Greek *philotimo* must be remembered in all suggestions of change, as well as the pattern of relationships within which dependency is good and taken for granted. Greeks are ready to be treated as sons or nephews or younger brothers, within the balanced system of interdependency, and the United States Economic Cooperation Administration (ECA), which has been giving welcome aid to Greece, just now is often spoken of as Uncle Truman, after the President of the United States; but it would be an insult to treat them as poor relations who are dependent through personal failure. Again, to be treated mechanistically, impersonally, is offensive; there is resentment at the fact that some of the foreign experts stay at hotels catering to foreigners, associate only with Greeks who follow foreign ways, and treat the rest of the people like figures on a chart.

It is necessary to bear in mind that the Greeks have a deep attachment to their way of life, however much in need of change it may be in terms of more recent scientific and economic developments. There are reports that in the provinces people who can afford to pipe water to their houses will not do so because they do not want to deprive their women of the social visit at the fountain, and of the walk back and forth. There are communities that decide not to have electricity, not to build a hotel to accommodate the tourists who are attracted by the beauty of the place, so that they can retain the ways they like, time-consuming as they are.

The framework of experience and the structuring of the thinking processes must also be known before change is acceptably suggested; at any rate, it must not be taken for granted that these are the same for the Greeks as they are for foreign experts. For example, a child-care specialist in the United States is inveighing against the prevalence of bottle feeding when she urges mothers to suckle their babies, but to the Greeks, she is, naturally, inveighing against engaging a wet-nurse.

It is helpful also to know what can be discussed publicly, and printed in the newspaper, without offence. The government calls artificial insemination "artificial reproduction." An attempt by the writer to elicit information on the subject under the term "insemination" from recently and previously emigrated Greeks, met with failure, since the women (coming from sections other than Athens and Salonika) had not heard of the programme, and were hesitant to mention it to their husbands; they obviously felt that the investigator, as a woman, could not approach the men with such questions.

There is a recognized variety among Greeks; and the differences are a matter of pride to them. They do not want to be treated as if they were all the same. There is also a difference in the attitude toward change. The intellectuals, the men high in the administration, do believe that the main part of the Greek population is backward, and are often ready for drastic and iconoclastic changes. For example, late in 1950, when Attica was suffering from drought, the government considered having the clouds seeded. But the peasants have always had a solution for drought: the priest and the villagers walk in a rain litany around the place. Different regions also vary in their acceptance of the new; the Greeks who came as refugees from the coastal areas of Asia Minor are, as a whole, more ready for the new; they are more enterprising, more ready to take a chance on the future.

One of the Greek attitudes deeply imbedded in their social structure is taken up here at greater length, since it is basic to many of the proposed changes; this is the phrasing of co-operative undertakings.

The suggestions for changes in agriculture, industrial developments, for the introduction of sanitary measures, demand co-operation and participation by the people concerned in bringing about these changes. The conception of co-operation as developed in the urban, scientific cultures of Europe and North America is not usual in the rest of the world. This conception involves a collective working toward an impersonal, abstract end; the joining of a group created with a view toward a future end; and the ability to trust the other members of such a group to act according to abstract, impersonal honesty, as, for example, to act believing that the statistics others present are objectively sound, and are not coloured by personal considerations.

The traditional Greek pattern, however, is that individuals work not collectively but within an intricate web of interdependencies and mutual aid. The abstract end, unless it is part of the immediate, concrete situation, and unless it is implemented in terms of persons, is meaningless; what is meaningful, for example, is for the family group to work together toward the continued education or the dowering of one of its members; or for the village community to rebuild its destroyed coffee-house together. A leader who has won the respect of the community, consulting and guiding rather than commanding, can create a co-operative unit derivatively; he enlists the personal loyalty of the people; the people will work for his sake and, incidentally, for his idea and proposed end. This remains within the personal framework.

Again, Greeks are *born into a group,* and many Greeks, except under foreign influences in the city, never *join* a group. They are born into the family, into the circle of family friends, into the village community; they do not have to please in order to belong, or to follow regulations. If they fail in their roles within these units, they are bad sons but they do not lose their membership. Only if they forfeit their Greekness in some way, perhaps turn traitor or change their religion, do they run the risk of being disowned. These are the units of co-operation, but they are rooted in the past, not created. There is no Greek equivalent of the word "group" so common in the speech of Americans; words such as *omas* (mass) and *somateion* (body) are used technically to apply to organizations. In school, the class becomes a group only in its opposition to the enemy, the teacher, in playing cruel tricks involving co-operation; otherwise, what we find, even in this opposition, is cheating for the sake of a weaker student, or support of one student by another. There are individual friendships here, individual evocations of honesty. The American Farm School at Salonika works hard at making students realize that they actually form a community at the school, and at teaching them to co-operate within this framework; and the school reports that eventually the students do learn the new co-operative pattern.

Honesty exists, and is expected and respected, only where kinship and personal relations have been established, on a basis of trust and respect for personal worth. In American schools in the cities, American teachers have managed to convince the students that they can trust them as friends, and have thus changed the teacher-student relationship into one of co-operation and honesty. Foreign technical assistants have often lived in a world of their own, in foreign circles, and failing to establish personal relations, have evoked mistrust and dishonesty. Honesty toward fellow-members in a created group can be achieved as the result of honesty and loyalty towards the leader of the group. However, it should not be taken for granted; neither should the Greeks be charged with dishonesty. Their framework of honesty is different from that known to the industrialized society of the United States and Western Europe.

There is at present a paradoxical situation in Greece. There is pride in the many co-operatives, spread throughout the country; there is delight on the part of some of the technical assistants because the groundwork for the introduction of necessary change is there. And there is dismay on the part of others that the Greeks do not know what co-operation means, that they have to be compelled to work for the benefit of the village, to be prevented from destroying its resources, and to be coerced to co-operate even in efforts for their own welfare. There is distress over the number of pressure groups created to get whatever they can from the government. All this is true. According to their own phrasing of co-operation and within the framework of the meaningful units, the Greeks were, and to some extent are now, completely co-operative. Families and villages were responsible for their own indigent; a prominent peasant would impoverish himself to build a village school or improve the water system. They made their own decisions and carried them out; they chose their own leaders. The first co-operatives were started on local initiative in the last century. But later, the central government began to institute co-operatives on a foreign pattern, taking no account of the existing units of co-operation, or of the existing patterns of self-participation. The villages were not allowed a responsible role in creating the co-operatives—in fact, in co-operating. The state-financed Agricultural Bank has been in charge of creating local credit co-operatives but the peasants have felt that this was a government affair. Actually the rate, which was 8 per cent at the time of the establishment of the bank in 1928, and is now as high as 18 per cent, with incidental fees, which peasants get from the bank through their credit co-operatives, does not seem to have been set with the welfare of the farmers in view, or according to their decision. In 1936, more than 3,000 of the 3,761 were credit co-operatives under the central supervision of the state. The others, such as the producers' co-operatives, were mainly compulsory. Such were the citrus growers' associations in Crete, the wine growers' association in Samos, Levkas, Attica, and Chalkis. There are now marketing co-operatives and machine-owning co-operatives, as well as a growing number of processing co-operatives. In general, the co-operatives are firmly controlled by the central government and the farmers are not even allowed to co-operate to the extent of electing their own officers. As a result, the attitude toward external authority has been evoked, and, in most cases, co-operation has to be compulsory, as all government legislation has to be compulsory, and the so-called co-operative decisions are circumvented like all government decisions. Another attitude has also been evoked, particularly among those Greeks who welcomed the dictatorship; deprived of responsible decision and participation, these people fell into the pattern of accepted dependency; such people, unaware that they are "co-operating," say: "The government is taking good care of us." The government itself, aware of this shifting of responsibility and lack of participation, urges the people, in its organ, *The Battle for Survival,* to work for their own welfare and to turn to the state only for guidance, or when they can do no more for themselves. It tries to put this co-operation on a par with war, both in the title of its bi-weekly publication, and in the phrasing of its admonition. But the disrupting centralization, the hated interference, remains. "Compulsory free labour" is demanded of the farmers, and there is a whole class of compulsory co-operatives for the betterment of the villages. These are circumvented with the ingenuity born of long experience. However, we also have a recent report of a village where everyone gets up when the church bell rings at four in the morning, to work, without compulsion, on some village project with pride and enthusiasm. The work is done under the leadership of a villager respected for his ability and disinterestedness. It appears that when the co-operative pattern which is already present is utilized, the villagers will work together for the common welfare.

ADDITIONAL REFERENCES

G. F. Abbott, 1903; Harold B. Allen, 1943; Koste Charitaki, 1948; Willie Snow Ethridge, 1947; Lucy M. J. Garnett, 1896; Kathleen Gibberd, 1944; Peter Gray, 1942; Marshall Hertig, 1950; Socrates A. Kaloyereas, 1948; Georgion I. Karmoule, 1926; Anna Katsigra, n.d.; Georgion N. Kazave, 1940; N. C.

and C. N. Kokkolatos, 1947; B. J. Marketos, 1945; J. B. McDougall, 1947-48; Henry Morgenthau, 1929; N. P. Polites, 1914; D. Psatha, 1937; Malvina I. Salvanou, 1926; Frank Smothers, William Hardy McNeill and Elizabeth Derbishere McNeill, 1948; C. S. Stephanides, 1948a, 1948b, 1948c; Athena Tarsoule, 1947, 1948, 1950; Clayton E. Whipple, 1944.

THE TIV OF NIGERIA[1]

The Tiv are an African tribe in southern Nigeria, who farm the rolling savannah country to the south of the Benue River, and a strip along the northern bank.[2] They are under British administration. They offered effective resistance to British occupation over a long period, not through organized resistance, but through their very lack of central organization. The tribe has a strong sense of unity, based on the tradition of common descent from a single original male ancestor; but there is no political unity, so that, in a tribe numbering over half a million,[3] the largest unit under a single authority numbers not more than 6,000.[4] The British had difficulty in dealing with the Tiv, because they were not a centralized group. The tribe was finally brought under British rule, and, by 1923, it was possible for travellers to travel through the country without protective escort.[5] But the basis of Tiv unity was not understood; serious mistakes were made in the administrative and jurisdictional units, such as in delegating authority to a young man who had not earned the right to exercise it; and these mistakes did much harm before they were corrected.

Little technical change has been effected among the Tiv. However, a shattering social change was introduced through an edict forbidding exchange marriage. This, more than anything else, gave the younger generation the opportunity and the ability to question traditional ways, authority of the elders, the kinship interrelationships, and in general, the very foundations of the culture. So, though technical change itself was not directly introduced, the mental attitude which makes such change acceptable, which allows an individual to carve his own

[1] The sources for this study consist of a general account of British administration in Nigeria, two accounts of the Tiv by British administrators, and a "history" of Tiv society by a member of the tribe, who went about questioning the elders, and gives his own experiences when growing up in this society, before and after the coming of the British. The "history" is voluminously annotated by a British administrator. The combined accounts by insider and outsider furnish unusually rich data; sometimes the same occasion is described independently by the Tiv and the British writers.
[2] Rupert East, 1939, p. 13.
[3] Margery Perham, 1937, p. 152.
[4] Roy Clive Abraham, 1940, p. 102.
[5] Perham, op. cit. p. 123.

future with new tools instead of taking his place in the security of a pre-established pattern based on human relationships, has already been introduced.

We give below a sketch of the broad outlines of the Tiv culture as it was before the edict of 1927 [1] which interdicted exchange marriage; and as it has been to a large extent since then, in spite of conflict and disruption. We also describe the far-reaching changes effected in the culture through manipulation of one of its traits, to show the interdependence of the different aspects and attitudes among the Tiv.

RELIGION AND PERSONAL DEVELOPMENT

Basic to the very existence of the Tiv, to their personal development, their human relationships, their agriculture, was their assumption of continuity between an individual and his kinship group, and between man and nature—the land, the animals, the non-human forces. This aspect of their culture we shall call the religious dimension of their life or, more briefly, their religion. It should be understood, however, that it was an ever-present aspect of their everyday activities, of the interpretation of all experience and behaviour.

There were two systems of religious rites, basically different and complementary. One had the function of tapping and internalizing the potency existing outside the individual, in society and nature. This personal potency was known as *tsav*, and people engaged in activities which enhanced their personal potency were known as *mbatsav*. Such people with strong *tsav* were able to wield influence over those with lesser *tsav*, and particularly over the empty-chested, the people with no *tsav*. *Mbatsav* could also have power over natural forces, and for example, could bring on rain. *Tsav* was positive and creative. It could enhance welfare, add to the power of natural forces. It could make yams grow bigger than normal, make women more fertile than ordinary, make a craftsman outdo himself in skill. Possessing *tsav*, a headman or chief could "make right the land" under his leadership.

All men contained the rudiments of *tsav*, but not all went through the arduous and dangerous process of developing it. To develop one's *tsav*, it was imperative that one eat human flesh. This immediately involved a man in the flesh-debt, the obligation to supply a human victim for ceremonial cannibalism, and to offer the head to his creditor, that is, the man who had killed the victim of whose flesh he had eaten. To clear a flesh-debt, a man had to kill a close younger relative, perhaps his son or younger sibling. As soon as he was known to have incurred a flesh-debt, he was feared and suspected by his near kin; and when one of these died, he was liable to be

[1] Abraham, op. cit. pp. 146-47.

accused of inflicting the death. Clearing oneself of a flesh-debt meant plunging others into a flesh-debt; and increasing one's *tsav* meant further sharing of human flesh, and the incurring of further flesh-debts. So an elder in a family group was held in high esteem and feared, partly because his strong and mature personality engendered respect, partly because he could at any time use his *tsav* destructively to punish or avenge a wrong, and partly also because the stronger his *tsav,* the more flesh-debts he had to pay off and therefore the stronger the menace he offered to the life of his younger kinsmen.

Tsav, however, was not antisocial in itself; neither was personal potency acquired primarily for individual ends. It was the common potency of the kinship group, living and dead, concentrated and incorporated in varying degrees mainly in its male members for the benefit of the group. Antisocial *mbatsav* could and did use their potency for their own purposes and destructively; but ideally, they held their *tsav* in trust for the benefit of the group. If the land and the women were to remain vital and fertile, *tsav* was indispensable to the group, and had to be implemented through the organic medium of individual persons, as representative of the ancestors as well as of the group of the living; and the dreaded flesh-debt was actually the mechanism for increasing the usable *tsav* of the group.

The main communal function of the *mbatsav* was to perform the rites of revitalizing the land. Each patrilineal kindred and, within this, each patrilineal family owned a sacred pipe made of the bone of an ancestor, and held by the head of the unit. Only the members of that particular unit could ever look on the pipe. The pipe itself was considered to represent a link between the dead and living members, as well as with the land to which the unit belonged and which belonged to the unit; with it was bound the fertility of the land and of the women of the unit. It had to be revitalized annually, and periodically in between, with fresh human blood; in recent years, the blood of an induced abortion was used. The shedding of blood was actually a part of the other religious system, the *akombo,* but for these rites of the ancestral pipes men strong in *tsav* were needed, and they maintained their *tsav* through eating of the flesh of the victim. Apart from this main function the *mbatsav* used their power against antisocial people and forces, for divining and predicting, for bringing rain, and otherwise for increasing welfare.

One was initiated into the society of the *mbatsav* through the eating of human flesh. But *tsav* itself was a personal quality, non-transferable. (It should be added here that, despite rigorous investigation, disinterment, and laboratory analysis of the implements of ritual killing, the British officials never discovered evidence of actual, physical killings on these occasions.)

The other religious system was concerned with the *akombo,* the supernatural agencies which were liable to interfere with the natural functioning of things. "A man's normal condition is one of good health, the nature of women is to bear children and that of the soil to produce good crops."[1] Any lapse from this course, or even failure to achieve the optimum, was due to intervention by the specific *akombo* of this area of life. To protect from and prevent such intervention, or to expel the evil once it had entered, there were specific rites to be performed.

The *akombo* rites, then, were negative. They did not add to the existing welfare; but they helped ensure welfare through protection and purging. Evil and interference could come automatically through lack of protection; more commonly, however, evil could be set in motion through the conscious or unconscious breach of *akombo*-protected ancestral taboos, causing pollution. The meaning of *akombo* was not clear-cut, as the term included the pollution, the evil, as well as the rites and emblems which overcome or expel the evil; it was applied, in addition, to the agency itself.

Akombo rites were necessary for protection during periods when the individual was particularly vulnerable. They were performed at intervals during pregnancy, for example, and at child-birth; *akombo* was "washed away" [2] before a boy was circumcised, as Western medicine would apply sterilization. When a man had bad luck with hunting, or in fishing, or in finding buyers for his wares, or with accidents such as falling down, he had the appropriate *akombo* "set right." [3]

Each family group had its *akombo* emblems and its *akombo* rites. When a man became ill, or was persistently unlucky, he discovered by divination which *akombo* he had offended,[4] and paid a fee to the man who controlled that *akombo* to have the appropriate expulsive rites performed. To control an *akombo,* that is, to have the ability and the right to perform the appropriate rites, it was necessary to be initiated into the unit through payment of a fee, as well as to buy the right to perform the rituals.[5] Successive initiation into the *akombo* cults to which he was entitled by birth was the way in which a man progressed along the stages of social maturity after his marriage. Initiation into a cult gave an individual control over a particular *akombo* —not through increasing his personal effectiveness, but through giving him knowledge and a right to apply it.

[1] East, op. cit. pp. 178-79.
[2] Ibid. p. 30.
[3] Ibid. p. 180.
[4] Ibid. p. 31.
[5] Ibid. pp. 208-9.

The *akombo* and *tsav* systems met in the ritual of the ancestral pipes. These were actually *akombo* pipes, inherited within the patrilineal kinship unit; but the rights were performed by the *mbatsav*. For the performance of these and equally great *akombo*, it was necessary for a man to be very strong in *tsav;* personal potency had to be commensurable with *akombo* power. A man, therefore, however wealthy and able to pay the initiation fees, could not rise too rapidly in the *akombo* scale; he had to have enough potency within himself to support his position. If he did rise unduly fast, he incurred the disapproval of the men with stronger *tsav,* who might thereupon destroy him.

Both *tsav* and *akombo* united in working for the benefit of the community, one increasing the good, the other protecting from evil. In addition, *akombo* emblems were set up to protect from the evil use of *tsav,* that which we commonly call witchcraft. The men strongest in *tsav* and highest in the *akombo* scale were naturally the senior elders. And herein lay the sanction and the source for their authority. The leader of the kindred knew the rites of all the *akombo* of the families constituting the kindred; he also knew the secrets of all the *mbatsav* societies, and had eaten human flesh with all; he had acquired the knowledge by right of his personal development. Through this he derived his position of leadership within the council of elders. Because of this, the welfare of the land and of the group was vested in him, so that if he failed in any respect, if he did not maintain and refresh his strength, he "spoiled" the land.

A grasp of these religious systems is essential to understanding the Tiv concepts of life and death and health, of personality development, of law, of authority, as well as of political structure, since all political organization and administration rested on a socio-religious base, on kinship structure sanctioned and sustained through the religious rites.

SOCIAL ORGANIZATION

All the Tiv were one in the person of the ancestor Tiv who was felt to be embodied in his half-million descendants. The individual was continuous with his community and his community was continuous with the ancestors, who diminished in actual count until the whole society was limited to the two sons of Tiv, and finally, to Tiv himself. A Tiv spoke of the two sons of Tiv or of the two divisions of the tribe interchangeably;[1] and in the same way, he spoke of the living head of a lineage and of his lineage interchangeably. It was in this, not in political organization, that the unity of the tribe lay; it was, in a sense, an organic unity.

[1] Ibid. p. 19.

The Tiv were not organized politically; they governed themselves according to an already present kinship. The largest unit under a single authority was that which has been called a kindred. This was a group of four or five extended families tracing their descent from a common ancestor. The elders of these patrilineal families constituted the kindred council; at its head was the elected chief, whose function was to implement the will of the group. He was not an executive head. He was more like the chairman of a committee; but with this difference—that power was not delegated to him, but was incorporated in his person; it was organic.

The Tiv could not understand a political grouping which was based on geographic contiguity, even though their own unit is actually contiguous. Neither could they understand authority which was conferred by someone else, as for example, by a superior authority. Their chief had authority because of what he was; he was strong in *tsav* and high in *akombo*. It was because of this that he had been elected to chieftaincy; it was not through his chieftaincy that he had authority. This was the administrative grouping which was misunderstood by the British officials, who, seeing a localized political unit with a chief, considered that they had found a basis for creating administrative units according to district. They chose as their representatives "promising" young men, who had neither strength in *tsav*, nor adequate *akombo* control. In the eyes of the Tiv, the unit itself was not valid, and the young representative could have no authority. The results were eventually recognized as destructive and an administrative change, more in accord with native concepts, was set afoot.[1]

The elders of the related families which constituted the kindred, met in council to discuss cases of witchcraft, questions arising out of exchange marriage or out of the proposal to sell one of the members into slavery, and other such matters. In none of these meetings did the chief render his own decision; rather, he gave voice to the decision of the elders, as the spokesman of group authority. It was even possible for him to be less strong than some of the other elders of the council, as such chiefs were elected by rotation from among the heads of the lineages composing the kindred. Each patrilineal family included both living members and the dead, remembered and remote, who continued in the character they had while alive, so that they helped their descendants or interfered with them as the case might be. As each elder in the council represented the original ancestor of his group as well as all his descendants, so the chief of the council represented all the members of the kindred, and might be identified with and addressed as the common ancestor of the entire group.

The patrilineal lineages composing the kindred consisted of

[1] Ibid. pp. 405-11; Perham, op. cit. pp. 156-59.

a group of close relatives whose common ancestor was still living or well remembered if dead. They usually consisted of an old man with his wives and their immature children, his sons and their wives and children, and perhaps even his married grandsons. If the group reached an unwieldly size, or if it contained too many elders of influence, it might break into a number of smaller units which built adjacent compounds.

It was the members of this patrilineal lineage who lived in daily face-to-face contact with one another. They owned the land in common; actually, the senior elder, the head of the council, was said to own the land, the women, and the children, for whose welfare and fertility he was responsible. They lived in one large compound, or in a group of adjacent compounds. Here a man built a separate hut for each of his wives, a large meeting-hut in front of his chief wife's dwelling, and a number and variety of storehouses. His sons built huts for each of their wives as they married. The group might be numbered in the hundreds; in the larger lineages there might be as many as 2,000 members. These were the people who inherited rights to common *akombo,* and could eat of the meat of the same animal killed for the *akombo* purging. The affairs of each were the affairs of the group. They shared in the work, they ate of the special dish prepared by the wife of one, and drank of the beer brewed by the wife of another. At night, they sat around a common fire, while the women spun cotton and the children exchanged riddles, until some older man began to tell myths. The Tiv referred to this group as that which ate the same *akombo*.

Within the *akombo,* there were often a number of smaller lineages—those consisting of a man, his wives, and his married or marriageable children. This sometimes was coextensive with the *akombo* group, sometimes more limited in numbers. It was known as the group which ate the same *ingol,* that is, the group which had common rights in the women born into it—the *ingol* or wards—who could be exchanged with members of other groups to procure wives. The group was bound in a web of interdependencies and interrelationships leading to and resulting from exchange marriage, which will be described below. Within it, a man thought of himself and acted, not as an individual, but as a member of the group.[1] Everything he did, his success, his breach of taboo, his wishes, his thoughts, the intentions which he did not put into practice, affected the group, and himself only incidentally, as part of this group. The more potent the man, the more potent his effect on the land and the group.

The individual was completely dependent on the group for his development. To achieve adult status, he had to marry; and to make a valid marriage, so that his sons could inherit full

[1] Roger Meaden Downes, 1933, p. 53.

membership in the group and a right to the great *akombo,* he was dependent eventually on his father to supply him with a daughter to be given in exchange for a wife. He could achieve social stature only through initiation into the group cults; he could achieve a strong personality only through physically incorporating his near relatives. He felt secure only in his group. The Tiv can emigrate only in groups; otherwise, "any Tiv found living outside his own country is a social and spiritual outcast." [1]

However, there was also another side to this grouping; the younger members lived in constant fear and suspicion of their elders. "Age is *akombo,*" and the *tsav* of the elders evoked respect, but more than this, it was within this group that the *tsav* killings took place. A man who was not satisfied with the *ingol* he had allotted to him, or who had a grievance, who felt slighted, could use his *tsav* against the offender, or persuade an elder with strong *tsav* to act for him; and in a group so tightly interdependent, such occasions occurred frequently. Besides, everyone was aware of the elders' need to pay off flesh-debts. This fear and suspicion found expression in the great crises of life, when the individual was vulnerable. During these, a member of the mother's group was asked to officiate, preferably a man strong in *tsav,* because the father might take advantage of this opportunity to kill his own son.

The binding principle within this grouping, recognized in the naming of the group, lay in the sharing of the *ingol.* The binding principle within the larger grouping, consisting of members of *ingol* lineages, lay in the sharing of the *akombo.* For a valid claim to the *akombo* of a group, a man had to be entitled to them through both his parents. This would seem impossible in view of the fact that descent was patrilineal and marriage exogamous; but continuity within the unit on both sides was made possible through giving to incoming women, that is, the mothers of the members of the group, a valid place in the kinship structure. This was accomplished through the institution of the exchange marriage.

Exchange marriage was the only valid marriage among the Tiv; and only the wife acquired in true exchange had high status, could be a chief wife, and have the great *akombo* of fertility and protection set before her hut. Only the children of such a wife were entitled to initiation into the great *akombo* cults; that is, only they could become great within the group. Through this system a man exchanged a sister, or some other woman who was directly descended through his mother, for a wife; and the wife entered the group as the complete representative of the sister, becoming a true daughter to her parents-in-law, so that she could inherit the group's ancestral emblems through her husband's mother, as a true descendant. Only

[1] East, op. cit. p. 400.

through exchange marriage could a woman assume this position, so that on the one hand she introduced no discontinuity within the living group, and, on the other, could pass on complete and unbroken to her children the continuity with their dead and living kin.

The whole group therefore had a stake in its marriageable women, its *ingol* or wards, though specific individuals had primary rights in their disposal. So important was this community of interests in the *ingol*, that the group which the British administrators considered to be a village or an extended family was regarded by the Tiv as an *ingol* group, as the group which shared the wards and could divide them among themselves for the acquisition of wives.

A man gave his daughters as *ingol* to his sons to get them wives; however, after he had provided two sons with wives, his immediate duty to his children was usually over, and he could use the rest of his daughters to get more wives for himself. Also, there were cases where there were more sons than daughters. Under these circumstances, the younger brothers had a claim on the daughters of the older brothers. The youngest brother might have long to wait, but would probably acquire more *ingol* in the end. The younger brothers would eventually supply their older brothers, who were the source of their own wives, with daughters to be used as *ingol*. There was an intricate and strong net of interdependence here, creating, strengthening, and continuing the kinship which bound the group.

The marriage arrangements were themselves an expression of the unity of the *ingol* group. The elders of the two groups conducted the arrangements, speaking and acting as though it were they who were the bridegrooms. During the ceremonies, the two groups celebrated, feasted and danced, as if they constituted the bridegrooms, not as though they were guests at a celebration. "Staying the night" in the girls' compound, which was an integral part of the marriage ceremony, meant that the whole group stayed the night. There was no implication of sexual rights in the bride on the part of the group. It was an expression of the vital concern of the group, which was getting a substitute link in the chain of continuity, and ensuring the validity and effectiveness of the *akombo* rites.

The whole purpose of all this was to acquire children; as far as the group was concerned, it gave up a woman through whom it could not get children for a woman through whom it could get them. If, therefore, a woman had no children, the marriage was not complete and her husband could return her and demand his own *ingol* back. Again, if the number of children born to the pair exchanged was markedly unequal, the slighted husband might request one or more children from those of his *ingol.* Children were valued as *ingol,* if girls, as descendants to perform ancestral rites, if boys; and merely as offspring, they were valued in themselves.

Exchange marriage meant that the younger men had to wait long before they could marry. It also meant that they could not initiate a marriage when and as they wanted it, since they were entirely dependent on their father or brothers. This hardship was mitigated or even circumvented in a number of ways. Two clans, consisting of a group of *akombo* tracing descent to a common ancestor, but having no political unity, would make a treaty allowing their young men to seek wives in each other's area. A young man, then, with the aid of his age-mates —a grouping which cut across the structured framework of precedence according to the principle of generation and of seniority within generation—sought out, courted, and eloped, with a girl from another clan. After the first child was born, the man's group was ready to accept her as a link, and provided a suitable *ingol* to validate the marriage. This was not the preferred form, and went counter to cultural pattern in giving individual freedom of initiative and choice.

Another solution was for a young unmarried man to buy sexual rights in a woman of the same group. The girl was usually distantly related, and the relationship was known as sister marriage. Such unions were temporary, and the children belonged to the mother's group. There was a permanent form of marriage by purchase, but that occurred only when a man actually bought a woman as a slave from a distant clan, having complete power of life and death and disposal over her.

No man could reach full maturity unless he was the offspring of an exchange marriage. After marriage, a Tiv achieved wisdom and status only through progressive initiation in the *akombo* of his group, until he reached the highest of these rites. But no man could perform the great *akombo* unless he was the child of an exchange union, since his right to them, his continuity with the ancestors, would be adulterated.

There was often dissatisfaction involved in exchange marriage. If a man thought his wife was not equal to his *ingol,* he might demand some gift in addition. There was the question of the equality in the number of children, or even of their equivalence as persons. There were unmarried brothers who felt wronged by their married brothers or their fathers. There was the upheaval resulting when a wife who had no children was returned, thus breaking the marriage of her own brother or other relative. Also, the two exchanged women were rivals, and frequently bitterly jealous of each other. Such difficulties might give rise to quarrels and the attempt to kill by sorcery. When matters came to a head, however, they became the concern of the family head, who took the matter beyond the family to the kindred; it was discussed in council, the wronged individuals aired their complaints, and things were usually brought to a workable solution.

There was another grouping, cutting across organization by family affiliation, and protecting a man from the *tsav* of his elders and, in general, giving him some support for behaviour which was not structured by kinship. This was the group of age-mates, who went through the stages of boyhood development more or less contemporaneously. A boy had to have his ears pierced, his teeth filed, he had to undergo circumcision, and to have his skin scarified. As soon as one of these operations was performed, he went about taunting those of his age-mates who had not undergone it, using the prerogative of his new status to forbid them anything he chose, until they too had reached this status. Usually, age-grade status was equivalent to age status; but a man strong in *tsav* could push his son rapidly through the stages to which the young man was not organically entitled, knowing he could support him against disapproving *mbatsav*.[1] Age-mates grew together, played, hunted, worked, assumed responsibilities together and, at about the age of 15, the young men of a large kinship unit participated in a feast and formed a society, pledging mutual aid. A man could call on his age-group when he needed help on his farm or in his marriage affairs; most important of all, perhaps, was the protection this group offered against the dangers of one's own family, since it took it upon itself to avenge the *tsav* death of its members.[2]

BIRTH AND REARING OF CHILDREN

A Tiv married to get children. The production of numerous children was the main function of life.[3] A man without children was sneered at and called useless, however successful he might be in his other undertakings. A woman, however excellent otherwise, would be despised if she was childless.[4]

A pregnant woman was "a woman with closed body." She was a thing of fear, open to danger. Her husband took her to her group for *akombo* rites as soon as her pregnancy was known, and for more rites thereafter. There was a series of such rites which purged the woman of any pending evil occasioned by unwitting offence against the *akombo*. When the first rite took place, the people around washed out their mouths with water, purging themselves of any grudge or thought which, even though it might not be a deliberate curse, or wish for evil, might nevertheless interfere with a successful deliv-

[1] Ibid. p. 40.
[2] Abraham, op. cit. p. 124; Downes, op. cit. pp. 24-26; East, op. cit. p. 45.
[3] East, op. cit. p. 312; Abraham, op. cit. p. 117.
[4] Downes, op. cit. p. 31; East, op. cit. p. 315.

ery.[1] When a first mother felt quickening, she complained of
the sensations and accepted proffered cures for them.[2] A woman was expected to cry with her pain, and if a man quailed at
pain he was called a girl. When child-birth pangs set in, the
woman groaned continually.[3] According to the Tiv writer,
who is a man and may be presenting a man's limited knowledge, labour usually lasted two days; and if it continued for
more than five days, *akombo* interference was suspected and
the diviner was called.

The woman lay in bed while in labour. When the child was
about to be born, the midwife was sent for. She made the
woman sit up straight and rubbed her stomach "to cause the
child to turn around,"[4] and when the child was actually emerging, a boy was sent to get a fig leaf for the baby to fall on. If
the baby did not cry immediately, cold water was thrown over
it. The midwife cut and bound the umbilical cord, bathed the
child in hot water outside, and massaged the navel. When the
afterbirth had emerged, the mother went outside and bathed
her vaginal region with hot water. The afterbirth was buried
by a boy, at the left of the entrance. And thereafter, whenever
a mother washed her baby, she did so over the place where the
placenta had been buried. To cure the child of "dizziness" and
"fear" she threw it up two or three times after its bath and
then held it head downward by the feet. When the umbilical
cord fell off, that of a boy was buried under a red-pepper
shrub so that he should be fierce, brave and dangerous, and
that of a girl under a pawpaw or a fig, so that she should be
gentle. The child was not taken out until the navel cord had
dropped off, in about three days, and no one could come visiting during this period.[5]

The new mother bathed and massaged her breasts with hot
water, and rubbed them with camwood to bring on milk. Until
her milk came, other women fed the baby. In the beginning, a
baby received only milk and water.[6]

A suckling baby slept between his parents; later he slept
next to the wall beside his mother. A woman was not allowed
to have intercourse with her husband until the baby walked;
but if she had not begun to menstruate again, she could have
intercourse before she weaned the child. But she should not
become pregnant while the child was still nursing, lest her milk
be poor and the child be weak and bring disgrace to the
parents.[7]

Children were much enjoyed; father and mother, as well as

[1] East, op. cit. p. 298.
[2] Ibid. pp. 227-29.
[3] Ibid. p. 301.
[4] Ibid. p. 302.
[5] Abraham, op. cit. pp. 150-151; East, op. cit. p. 302.
[6] Abraham, op. cit. p. 152.
[7] Ibid, p. 152.

other nurses, took care of the very young. The baby was encouraged by all to start walking, and people remarked on his early steps. He learned very early to swear, to the pride of his mother, who showed him off to everyone's amusement. He soon started to go about with other children, and a boy soon learned to kill crickets, hitting or trapping them. At this point, he began to contribute to the family meal, as crickets were a delicacy; if there was no other meat available for dipping sauce, the elder sent a boy to get a cricket, and shared it with his guests. As he grew a little older, a boy learned to shoot lizards with a sharpened raffia midrib. When the boys were ready to start shooting birds, their fathers made them bows that were easy to string, and arrows tipped with sharpened cornstalks. Although the boys were given freedom to roam and a share in the responsibility for supplying meat, they were treated as not very capable. Their welfare and security rested on the strength of their father's *tsav;* and the fathers saw to it that the boys' weapons were safe and not demanding.

Girls spent their time with their mothers, learning their role by watching and working with them. A mother guarded their chastity strictly, and tied a protective shell around their necks at the onset of adolescence, to ward off the advances of men,[1] this shell was not removed until marriage.

Children were warned not to walk about after dark, lest they be bewitched. They were warned to be respectful to their elders, as age was *akombo*-protected. An elder admonished his children as they sat together in the evenings, and the admonition was mainly negative: don't. This word was so commonly used that it is said to have been the baby's first word. Children were also admonished not to commit adultery, and never to dip into the sauce set before their elders.[2]

Punishment was mainly in retaliation, rather than disciplinary. A woman could withhold food from her husband's son if he, afraid to go out in the dark at night, made a mess in her hut when spending the night there.[3] *Mbatsav* who were annoyed at a child's impudence might afflict him with some ill, sore eyes, or a pain.[4] A parent, when angered at his son, might curse him, taking away his luck, until the son could effectively petition for peace.

THE STATUS OF WOMEN

Women were highly prized, as they were essential for the procreation of children,[5] in the old days, the Tiv are said to have refused no woman, however ugly, as long as she was capable

[1] East, op. cit. p. 309.
[2] Ibid. p. 344.
[3] Ibid. p. 244.
[4] Ibid. p. 246.
[5] Ibid. p. 313.

of bearing children and had a good character, although now she has to be pretty and her child-bearing ability is not important.[1] Women were also prized for sexual reasons; continence is a great hardship for the Tiv. "Women and food are the two things about which a Tiv will boast." Imprisonment and death itself are hard chiefly because a man leaves his women behind.[2] Yet wives were not well cared for unless they were sister substitutes acquired through exchange marriage. Otherwise, they might be left to starve or go without clothes, and be treated without respect or consideration.[3] Such wives could be mistreated with safety since, being no blood-kin, they could not inflict *tsav* death; the exchange wife, however, having assumed the kinship rank of the sister, could do so.

According to Western standards, women were not equal to men. If a murder was compounded, instead of being avenged, two women would be accepted by the unit in the place of the dead man.[4] Women were owned by the men of their family, and even after marriage, when their "waist" belonged to their husband's group, their "head" still belonged to their "owner's" group;[5] but men were not owned. And a man who managed to seduce the chosen bride before the completion of the marriage, while he was sleeping in her hut, might refuse to marry her, whereas he himself was not blamed. Submitting to seduction meant that a woman had no strength of will.[6] If beer was sweet, it was rejected by men as the beer of women and children, as not being "good beer."[7] Women had no part in making their own marriage, though actually they were formally questioned during the marriage proceedings; and they sometimes tried to kill themselves, as the only way out of a dreaded marriage.

Yet women did have a high status. They had complete control of the food-supply of the village; their authority in domestic affairs was hardly ever questioned; they had their husband's respect and co-operation when they had been honourably married; they usually accepted their place as exchange wives, within the structural interdependence of the unit; and some were members of the *mbatsav* group.[8]

FOOD

Eating and drinking were highly social. Most of the meals were social occasions, with the family eating together along with others of the group. The early morning meal might be a

[1] Ibid. p. 112.
[2] Ibid. pp. 313-14.
[3] Ibid. p. 313.
[4] Downes, op. cit. p. 74.
[5] East, op. cit. p. 115.
[6] Ibid. pp. 112-13.
[7] Ibid. p. 74.
[8] Ibid. p. 170.

solitary affair, but even at daybreak feasts were sometimes given, when a wife prepared a special dish of *shuma* beans to which guests gathered, invited and uninvited. Eating was a part of the exchange-marriage proceedings; a gift of a chicken was taken from one group to another and it was eaten by the group. The flesh of sacrificial animals was shared by those members of the lineage who were initiated in that particular *akombo*. A guest from another clan was always offered food if he was a friend, or a friend of a friend. Drinking was also social, and a man who gave a beer feast was highly praised by his guests. Beer feasts ran late into the night and were very convivial occasions. Beer figured in patterned festivals also.

Eating was enjoyed, and there is no suggestion in the litera- ture that there were any feeding problems for children. There were general preferences. Pork was the favourite meat, but was taboo to most women. There were special recipes for the large variety of greens, seeds, tubers, and condiments which were a part of the diet.

Certain regulations accompanied eating. The guest followed a special etiquette, showing no undue eagerness for the food, and giving special portions of the chicken to the cook and the housewife. More stringent regulations applied to the dipping into gravy eaten by the elders; children were warned against doing this, and if they did so, *ruam* and pepper-sauce were flung into their faces. In this way, the danger of sharing in a dish which might contain human flesh was brought home to them.

Women were the cooks on ordinary occasions, and they were considered to be the owners of the food. On ceremonial occasions, however, as when a chicken was killed for a guest, or in the case of an animal sacrificed in an *akombo* rite, the men were the cooks.

The staple food was *ruam*, a pudding prepared of pounded yams or pounded seeds cooked in water. This was prepared at noon and in the evening; in the morning, a wife cooked and peeled a yam for her husband. With the *ruam* there was usu- ally a gravy seasoned with vegetables or condiments, and per- haps containing some kind of meat. Fish and game, including birds and crickets, were eaten when available. Domestic ani- mals were killed and eaten only incidentally; their main func- tion was socio-ceremonial. However, the flesh of foreign cattle, butchered by foreigners, was just food, and could be eaten more freely; a woman might even overlook the usual taboos on eating the head of an ox. Older men, who were initiates of a number of *akombo*, ate meat during the frequent *akombo* rites; boys foraged for themselves, killing crickets, lizards, and birds. Women had less meat and, in a number of groups, eggs and black fish were also taboo to them.

Thus the eating of flesh enhanced the continuity between the body and the rest of nature. This was the principle behind ceremonial cannibalism, where the victim's potency became part of the eater. And in pregnancy, if a woman ate the flesh of a brave animal, her child would become strong; or if the animal eaten was timid, the timidity would be imparted to the child.

WORK AND CO-OPERATIVE PATTERNS

Tiv children mixed work and play from earliest years. Little boys went about killing crickets, lizards, and birds, learning to track, observe, and hunt, foraging for themselves and also bringing home some of this small game at the request of elders, for their meal. But this was not work in the eyes of the Tiv. Children ran many errands, and had special sections of an undertaking allotted to them in house-building, agriculture, and even at child-birth. On his own initiative a boy might bring wood for his father's meeting-hut; but otherwise, the work that these children did carried no responsibility for initiating or bringing to an end. Only when a boy made his own yam heap, when he was quite grown, did he really start to work, according to Tiv concepts.

For full-grown men also, the yam heap was the test of work, and when a man went beyond this and thatched the yam heaps, then his wife knew that he loved her. The rest of the farm-work was often arduous; but the Tiv spoke of it as part of the ordinary course of living. Hard work and the ability to do it formed an aspect of the admired personality, particularly in women. When Akiga describes the woman who got up at break of dawn to bake and peel a yam for her husband, who spent the day bringing wood and water and working for the *ruam* and working in the fields, and who sat spinning at night by the firelight while her husband told tales, he paints a glowing picture of the good wife. The sound of the pounding of the *ruam* was the sound of village life, punctuating the flow of time.

The ordinary day was patterned for the woman, who spent it in dealing with her housework and the seasonal work in the fields; with variety coming from special occasions, such as arrangements for weddings, *akombo* rites, the excitement of a divination into a *tsav* death. Festive days themselves had their own pattern, since they were concerned with ritual activities. A man's day was not patterned in this way, but his particular activities were. Each crop had its own farming pattern, each type of hunting its sequence of operations. But the work which an adult was called upon to do was often that of performing *akombo* rites for unpredictable interference, so that a man's day could not be expected to follow a familiar routine.

There was division of labour in Tiv society, and there was co-operative work; in both cases, whether work was done by an isolated individual or in a group working together, work was social in nature. A woman worked to fill her husband's needs and to help him get wealthy by spinning cotton for him to weave into cloth for sale. She also took care of his children for him. A man cleared land for his wife, built her a frame for a house, and worked for her in a variety of other ways. When boys caught small game for their own eating, they were not working. On the other hand, even when a man worked at developing himself, reaching the various stages of *akombo*, or working at *tsav* activities to increase his own potency, he was actually working for the group, furthering its welfare and the effectiveness of its operations. A young man depended on his group for the acquisition of a wife, and on the group elder for carrying through the negotiations. If he got a wife through capture and later exchange, he depended on his age-mates to woo the girl for him and make the capture effective; and if he courted the girl himself, it was his father's praises that he sang when he spoke of himself. There was an interlocking system of dependency in work, so that the wife could not have a garden if the husband did not do his share; and the husband could not weave cloth if the wife did not spin for him; and here the changes of recent years wrought havoc. For example, now that cloth is to be had for money, and now that a man earns money, the wife expects him to use his money to buy cloth for her, instead of enabling him by her services to save it for her and for his own economic benefit.

Each operation had its own division of labour. In house-building, for example, the man's role was set, as well as the specific task for the lad who helped his father, and the share for the wife. The wife drew the water for the mud, a boy made the balls and handed them to the builder, a group of kinsmen put on the framework for the roof and dug the holes for the rafters, amid hubbub and excitement; the wife then finished the interior.[1] And with the work concerning each crop, the roles of the husband and the wife were clearly known. With beans, for example, the husband chose and cleared and prepared the ground for planting, but thereafter the wife alone was concerned with the work and the crop, and it was she who invited to a bean feast.[2] With other crops, the husband farmed up to the harvest, and the wife, with the help of her children, took over the reaping.[3] There was also a larger co-operative pattern, as when the entire family group cleared the land for yams and cultivated them, sometimes working together in the fields, sometimes with the wives in the village preparing food for the workers.[4] In all this, though the adults had certain known areas of work and responsibility; the children were help-

[1] Ibid, pp. 53-56.
[2] Ibid, pp. 66-68.
[3] Ibid. pp. 69-70.
[4] Ibid. pp. 83-91.

ers who were asked to perform individual tasks as they arose.

In general, children had no responsibility for initiating and carrying through an operation; women knew their area of work and were responsible for performing it, but were not responsible for its effectiveness. For the effectiveness of any operation, *akombo* knowledge and the right to use it were imperative so that the work could run its natural course to its conclusion without interference through *akombo* or evil machinations. So even in women's work, men were necessary to ensure good results. Responsibility ultimately rested with the chief of the kindred, who was identified with the welfare of "the land."

MAN AND NATURE

A Tiv was continuous with his society and with nature. He was also a unit within himself, so that mind and body were one and thoughts and overt acts were equally effective.[1] Overt acts and hostile thoughts, even when involuntary or unconscious, were equally dangerous to the community and "the land," since they were equally polluting through setting in motion forces of evil and interference; so a man accused of killing would admit having done so, since he himself could not depend on remembered intention or conscious experience to tell him whether he had done so. The total environment, human and non-human, with which the Tiv were continuous, was referred to as "the land." Every act or thought of the Tiv went beyond the material limits of his body to the community or "the land"; and what happened within this *continuum* affected him. The potency of man and of the whole social unit embodied in its *mbatsav* meant enhancement of the potency of the fields and "the land" in general; and the misdeeds of man, his breach of *akombo* taboos, set evil loose upon "the land."[2] All illness, apart from common transient ailments, came through thought or act of man. Whether it was deliberately directed evil or unconscious breach of *akombo* regulations, such illness might affect the man responsible, or someone in his community, or the fields, or domestic animals, or luck in hunting.

It was this continuity which was basic to the religious systems: the *akombo* cults, which were based on continuity between the dead and the living and were effective within a *continuum* of man and nature; and the *tsav*, which could exist and increase and become effective only through concentration in the body of one with whom the others, whose potency had been incorporated, had been continuous. It was a continuity based on the body, existing ultimately among all those who came from the body of the original ancestor, Tiv, and more intensively among the people of the family group, whose origi-

[1] Ibid. p. 235.
[2] Downes, op. cit. p. 75.

nal male progenitor was alive or, at any rate, vividly remembered. Everyone who had come from this body, whether ancestor or descendant, or collaterally related, was continuous, and *mbatsav* killing was effective only among these. There was continuity also with the food one ate and with the land on which this had been grown, except when it was the food of foreigners. What emerged from the body carried this continuity. Elders forced to travel away from "the land" carefully preserved and brought back some of their excreta, not for fear of evil witchcraft, but so that the potency inherent in the excreta should benefit their own land.[1] A baby was continuous with its placenta, and for some time after birth was bathed over the spot where the placenta was buried, and the water left in the vessel was then poured over the spot so that the body-dirt could go towards refreshing the placenta.[2] A man established his children's body continuity through procreation with an exchange wife, and once he had a child by her, all subsequent children born to her were in this line of continuity, even long after he was dead. It was this line of body continuity, basic to every aspect of Tiv living, which was maintained by exchange marriage, since only through taking the place of the sister—as continuous with the body of the parents—could a woman pass on unbroken continuity to the children of the union. It was this continuity at which the abolition of exchange marriage by the British edict struck disastrously, so that the elders could justly say that the British had "spoiled the land."

Man enhanced the well-being of the farms through his *tsav*, and ensured the natural order of things through his preventive *akombo* rites; and the earth also healed and prevented ills. Mud was smeared on a part of the body at all *akombo* rites—on the big toe, or the stomach, or the navel, or the wrist; its purpose was to give healing. The excreta from the entrails of a domestic animal killed for sacrifice were also used in this way.[3] Water was the purifying and purging agent; all *akombo* rites were performed beside running water, or beside a vessel of water, which was then poured out. Water was taken in the mouth and then spat out, by way of washing away lurking resentments of litigants, or unconscious ill thoughts and wishes, which might bring pollution during a delivery, for example. However, usually it was not necessary for the water to be in physical contact with the person to be ceremonially cleaned.[4]

HEALTH

Health is treated here under a separate heading only because, as a separate concept, it is important operationally to Western

[1] Abraham, op. cit. pp. 17-18.
[2] East, op. cit. p. 303.
[3] Downes, op. cit. pp. 12-13.
[4] Ibid. p. 63; East, op. cit. pp, 29, 30-32, 235.

workers. There was no such concept among the Tiv, apart from the natural order of things.[1] It was normal for people to have a moderate degree of fertility, for crops to be attacked by only a few pests, for people to recover soon from a small common ailment, to have some good fortune in hunting and only an occasional accident, to be good craftsmen. If they had luck above normal, if their yam yields were particularly fertile, if a child were exceptionally proficient, then everyone knew that the individual had *tsav* which enhanced nature. If a man had persistent ill luck, however, whether in health or as to the number of accidents which befell him, or in his fields, then he suspected *akombo* intervention, and found out through divination which *akombo* he had offended, paid the man who controlled that rite for a performance, and hoped to have things "repaired." If there was no improvement, then he knew that *tsav* was being used against him. This applied to any area of life, not to health alone. If nothing interfered, all was well throughout all aspects of living.

Disease, when prolonged or out of the ordinary, was interference, just as an influx of red monkeys into a field was interference. Therefore most of the medical practices were agricultural practices as well. However, there were ordinary, non-ritualistic medicines for natural illness, used internally or as ointments,[2] and these applied specifically to disease. Common to the treatment of all interference was the assumption that this was an evil which had been set in motion by some breach of *akombo* taboo, and that it could be forestalled by preventive rites—purging the individuals who were concerned with a delivery, for example, of any disruptive thoughts which might set polluting evil loose; or that it could be cleaned out through cleansing agents, i.e., *akombo* rites where beer and blood were shed and water used to carry away the pollution. Interference with ordinary well-being came also through *tsav* workings; and since the *mbatsav* were concerned mainly with getting human victims to enhance their potency, the *akombo* rites were frequently performed at a time when an individual was especially vulnerable, to make the environment magically aseptic.

Except for its religious rather than scientific interpretation, Tiv medical practice was very much like modern Western medicine in its assumptions. Its main stress was on prevention; this was effected through the great *akombo* rites, which "set right the land" and were much like a general immunization in principle. Blood was shed over the ancestral pipes to prevent "the land" from losing its potency, its fertility, and its resistance to evil. The right to perform these rites was reached only by a few senior elders, after initiation into lesser *akombo* and after

[1] Abraham, op. cit. p. 84.
[2] East, op. cit. p. 182.

increase in *tsav;* and they were performed for the whole unit and its land. A householder performed the rites which protected his own household against evil.[1] Apart from prevention, there were the sterilization rites, performed particularly when blood was to flow.[2] There were then the specific rites for a disease which had already set in; the diagnosis identified not the nature of the disease itself, but the causal factor, and the cure was directed toward removing the cause rather than merely treating the symptoms; the symptoms, however, were relieved through the application of secular medicines. These concepts were not essentially different from those of Western medicine; but there were also specific requirements for making the treatment effective which were purely Tiv. No *akombo* treatment was effective unless the patient, or his group, had paid a fee for it. It was not effective unless the practitioner had inherited the right to perform it, had reached the right degree of maturity, potency, and *akombo* grade for becoming initiated into it, and had' paid for the right to perform it and for the knowledge it involved.[3] The Tiv had their own hospitals. And here also a man had to buy the right to take patients, had to buy instruction for putting up the proper shelter, as well as to pay for all the steps involved in running the hospital; and he had to be paid for the sake of the patient, since otherwise the cure would fail.[4] For the preventive rites performed at times when the individual was particularly vulnerable, because his blood was shed, there were additional rules. An operation such as circumcision, for example, was preferably performed in the mother's village, since a man's own close kin were always on the lookout for victims to pay off their flesh-debts and were, naturally, particularly dangerous during this vulnerable state. If one stayed in one's own village, it was only because one could go for the operation into the hut of a man of particularly strong *tsav* who could be trusted to protect, not to kill, his patient.[5]

The man who performed the operation should have bought the right to do so,[6] and had to be someone with good blood, that is, a man whose wounds healed quickly; this was an inborn trait which was known to others by observation.[7] The operation had to be performed in the cool of the morning, since blood, like oil, is thick when it is cool, and does not flow easily.[8] The patient was supported by a man who sat behind him and held him in his arms;[9] but he could not cry out, since

[1] Downes, op. cit. p. 63.
[2] East, op. cit. p. 31.
[3] Ibid. pp. 19-20, 208-9.
[4] Ibid. pp. 357-61.
[5] Ibid. pp. 30, 31, 122.
[6] Ibid. pp. 208-9.
[7] Ibid. p. 27.
[8] Ibid. p. 43.
[9] Ibid. p. 33.

he was a man, and crying was only for girls.[1] If he was hesitant about having the operation performed, an age-mate who had already had it performed could taunt him into it. This taunting was recognized and sanctioned; it carried with it the right to command, and particularly to forbid, anything to the person who had not gone through the same patterned experience, and it worked as a powerful incentive to effort and fortitude.[2] None of the treatments were administered by an individual upon himself. Someone else was called in to diagnose and perform the *akombo* rites, the more potent and the further initiated to perform the rites for the lesser; and the chief of the kindred, at the peak of potency and *akombo* power, administered the treatment for "the land" which was embodied and represented in himself, so that when he treated "the land" he treated himself.

European hospitals and medical practices ran into difficulties when one or all of these rules were overlooked; and they were successful without trouble when they fitted into the Tiv pattern. This was true in the case of smallpox vaccination. The principle of inoculation was inherent in the Tiv *akombo* rites; and inoculation against smallpox, specifically, was known and practiced before the coming of the Europeans. Yet, in some regions, during an epidemic of smallpox, natives fled in terror at the approach of a vaccinator; markets broke up in panic if so much as an employee of a European appeared on the scene.[3] East's explanation of this is that the conditions under which vaccinations were performed were magically septic in every way,[4] and the people naturally dreaded exposing themselves to magical death. In one region, the people refused to be vaccinated on the ground that the head of the family group had performed the appropriate *akombo* rites. The British administrator wisely dealt with this man as well as his senior, the head of the kindred. When the family head was persuaded that European vaccination was advisable, he told his people, and they came easily of their own accord, without the need of persuasion, since prevention was in the hands of the family elder and he had decided what was necessary to achieve it.[5]

DEATH

Though some amount of illness was within the natural course of events, death was never natural except for the very old. At the death of an old man there was feasting and dancing because the old man had gone to help the ancestors in their beneficent work for "the land." At the death of anyone else

[1] Ibid. p. 34.
[2] Ibid. pp. 27-29, 37, 41.
[3] Ibid. p. 352.
[4] Ibid. p. 353.
[5] Downes, op. cit. p. 41.

there was grief.[1] All such death came through the *mbatsav,*
except for very young babies,[2] since all others had some *tsav*
which helped them to withstand *akombo* interference until
this could be recognized and expelled. And no death could
come unless the *mbatsav* so decreed. When someone became
ill and did not soon recover with ordinary medicaments, a
diviner was called to find which *akombo* was interfering with
recovery. If the appropriate *akombo* rites were carried out and
there was still no recovery, then *tsav* was known to be at
work.[3] In such a case, only *mbatsav* could effect a recovery by
deciding to withdraw their killing *tsav;* and only they were
responsible when illness eventuated in death. For this reason
European physicians were never given credit for a recovery,
and neither were they blamed for a death. They could ease
pain and give other treatment, but recovery and death were
beyond their responsibility.[4]

Individuals could bring about their own death by incurring
the vengeance of the *tsav,* or defaulting in the payment of a
tsav death. A man on his death-bed, therefore, might call his
age-mates around him and solemnly pronounce, "I have taken
no man's wife, I have bewitched no one, nor eaten human
flesh with any . . . yet death is killing me for no cause." If
he had eaten human flesh with anyone and had not paid off
his flesh-debt by killing a close relative, he had forfeited his
own life, and then admitted that he was responsible for his
own death.[5] Otherwise, if he was killed for "no cause" his age-
mates could see to it that the killer was discovered, and might
even inflict death on him.[6] A life which gave no offence to the
elders protected an individual against death; but, more than
this, his age-group—cutting across family solidarity—protected him through the threat of their brutal retaliation upon the
killer.

Men and immature girls died in their own village; a wife,
however, was sent to the village of her birth to die among her
own kin, who could then be held responsible.[7]

COMPLETION OF THE BODY

A baby could not be born successfully without *akombo* rites,
and could not be complete at birth without them. At the rite
immediately following conception, the closing of the sutures
of the skull was ensured. At birth the body was still not complete. Girls were cicatrized and had their teeth filed before

[1] Ibid. p. 20.
[2] East, op. cit. pp. 250-51.
[3] Ibid. p. 182.
[4] Ibid. pp. 182, 362.
[5] Ibid. pp. 220-21.
[6] Ibid. pp. 329-30.
[7] Ibid. p. 253.

they became complete.[1] For boys there were more operations, which were a means of creating and symbolizing the continuity of the body and the group. Boys of approximately the same age went through the successive operations at approximately the same time, following the prescribed path of maturation. There was ear-piercing for specific ear ornaments; next came teeth-cutting, circumcision, and cicatrization. The cicatrices were tribal marks, badges of Tivhood.[2] At this time, the group met together to feast and ceremonially drink beer, cementing itself into a unit pledged to mutual help and support. After this, maturation was not in terms of completion of the body, but in terms of acquiring membership through initiation into the successive *akombo* cults of the unit, and in increasing *tsav*. The abolition of exchange marriage worked havoc in this area through giving free choice to the woman. Women found the tribal markings unattractive and preferred newly introduced foreign markings; this, on the one hand, broke the bond with the unit and, on the other hand, set the younger men with their non-tribal markings in opposition to the men of the older generation.[3] Before this, though men had been grouped according to approximate age, there had been no secondary grouping of younger grades together, as against the grades of the fathers. Now, at a time when the young had the greatest reason to fear the elders of their family group, they had lost the age-grade unit based on contemporaneous completion of the body, which protected against the family *tsav*.

Blood was potent, whether that of human beings or domestic animals. The greatest proportion of meat eaten in the old days was that of sacrificial animals, whose blood, as well as beer, was shed over *akombo* objects at all *akombo* rites. Water could cleanse away the infection of evil; but only blood could repair and restore health and potency. So blood was used both in agricultural *akombo* and in those concerned with human health and fertility. For the greatest *akombo* the blood of a human victim was required, and this was sometimes the blood of an abortion induced through *tsav;* otherwise, chickens, goats, rams were killed. Sacrificial blood was also used at a marriage; it was shed on the threshold of the bridegroom's house before he entered it.[4]

Blood was used to cement a new relationship. When two clans made a pact, old men from each clan shed blood from their cut hands onto a grindstone, mixed this with other ingredients, and ate it. (Beer, which is associated with blood in the rites, was drunk ritually by a group.)

The blood of a menstruating woman was dangerous to men's hunting *akombo*. It was best for a menstruating woman

[1] Ibid. p. 42.
[2] Ibid. pp. 26-42, 49.
[3] Ibid. pp. 44-49.
[4] Ibid. p. 49.

to sleep in a special bed in a special hut at the back of the village. Such a woman could not enter the meeting-house where the hunting *akombo* were kept; and no man could eat of food cooked by her, or even touch her, for fear of losing control of his hunting *akombo*.[1]

AGRICULTURE

The Tiv have been farmers traditionally. They practised secular techniques of farming in the ordinary course of events, using boys to watch against ordinary pests; and they used *akombo* rites for extra-normal intervention. Yams were the staple, and the food most steeped in myth and ritual.[2] They were planted and cultivated communally and their care was patterned. A number of *akombo* rites were concerned with them. Yams started the rotation of crops, with fallow land cleared for their planting. In the village there was a yam storage house for each household.[3] There were probably 100 varieties of yams cultivated.[4]

Bullrush millet was planted on land from which yams had been harvested, and was followed, in the same year, by Guinea corn. Next came beniseed, then *Pennisetum spicatum,* and after that the land lay fallow for five to eight years.[5] Beans were not included in the rotation cycle; they were always planted on newly cleared ground. Though the husband chose and cleared the land for cultivation, beans were considered the woman's domain. The wife planted them, harvested them, and took them home with appropriate respect in a basket, to store in the "bean store" beside her hut.

The head of the kindred performed two great *akombo* for farming, one at seed-time and one at harvest-time. He and his elders took an oath: "If I cause the land to be harmed, let *Swam (akombo)* kill me. If amongst you any man does evil for the land, let *Swam* kill him."[6] Doing "evil for the land" meant even an unconscious breach of *akombo* regulation, so that if a man's farm became prey to destructive animals, he sinned against the head of the kindred, who was identified with and responsible for the land; and he sinned thereby against the community, because this was indicative of some disobedience on his part.[7]

The *mbatsav* were apt to do damage to a field which was greener and richer than the farmer's *tsav* entitled him to have it be;[8] to protect against *tsav*, as well as against thieving and

[1] Ibid. p. 211.
[2] Abraham, op. cit. pp. 125-26; East, op. cit. pp. 70, 79-88.
[3] Abraham, op. cit. pp. 119-20.
[4] Ibid. pp. 125-26.
[5] Ibid. pp. 125-26; East, op. cit. pp. 83-90.
[6] Downes, op. cit. p. 64.
[7] Abraham, op. cit. p. 16.
[8] East, op. cit. p. 47.

other destruction, *akombo* emblems were set to guard the property;[1] transgression against them brought specific illness, such as syphilis or dysentery. Since the thieves would be of the farmer's own group and probably have control of any *akombo* into which he had been initiated, a man from another district was often called in to place an *akombo,* and this meant that the farmer himself could not touch the crop until the owner of the *akombo* came to remove it.[2]

Before any of the new crop was eaten, some of it, such as a head of grain or a yam, had to be laid on the *akombo* emblem outside the house.[3]

The old way of cultivating the land was with a wooden hoe.[4] It is difficult to tell how the substitution of iron tools has affected agriculture. Iron was magical, a thing of awe,[5] and was highly protective, particularly against *tsav.*[6]

TRUTH AND EVIDENCE

Truth was not arrived at by observed evidence, but by divination and ordeal. A man did not depend upon the evidence of his senses and experience. Truth existed, irrespective of his memory and experience and intention.[7] Akiga tells how he attended a dance to see his brother wearing his dead sister's skin, but found him displaying only a woman's philter; everyone present at the dance, however, who had known that the brother was to wear this skin, saw him displaying the skin, and reported he had done so.[8] Men accused by British officials of *tsav* killings admitted to them; and when asked to produce evidence, they manufactured it to please the officials, and stop them from asking the unbearable questions that attempted to uncover the truth.[9] At one time, a whole group of men testified as to a mutilated corpse. Pressed with questions, men even described the specific parts of the corpse which they had eaten; yet every time the British officials opened an indicated grave, they found the body intact. The accused explained this by saying they had reconstituted the body.[10] Men dug up strange skulls by way of producing evidence against themselves;[11] they produced human slaughter slabs which they manufactured carefully for the occasion, squeezing red vegetable juice over

[1] Ibid. pp. 185-86.
[2] Ibid. pp. 83-87, 91-92.
[3] Ibid. p. 92; Downes, op. cit. pp. 61-62.
[4] East, op. cit. pp. 65-66.
[5] Downes, op. cit. p. 64.
[6] Abraham, op. cit. p. 99.
[7] Downes, op. cit. p. 75; East, op. cit. pp. 235, 298.
[8] East, op. cit. p. 272.
[9] Ibid. pp. 277-78; Downes, op. cit. p. 75.
[10] Abraham, op. cit. p. 52; East, op. cit. pp. 284-89.
[11] East, op. cit. pp. 277-78.

them by way of making them realistic.[1] These were carefully tested in laboratories for human blood.[2] The Tiv could not understand the British magistrate's passion for asking questions, and sometimes feigned sickness to avoid them, since even admission of guilt apparently did not always put a stop to them.[3] They finally adopted the policy of denying everything, and particularly of never changing their testimony, since the British magistrates seemed to mind contradictory testimony.

In the old Tiv councils, there had been no question of arriving at the truth. This was already known, either because it seemed to be the obvious deduction or, if the case were serious, through divination or the oath and ordeal. The purpose of holding the council was the shifting of responsibility from the elders, who were responsible for "the land" and therefore for all deaths, to the actual culprit.

EFFECTS OF CHANGE

The Tiv have liked change. For as long as they can remember, they have introduced new ways of government, new forms of decoration, new techniques, copied from neighbouring tribes. But their basic pattern remained the same; radical changes, usually finding no place within the pattern, were discarded; the cultural basis did not support them. It was only when the conquerors introduced change by fiat, actually striking at the very root of Tiv culture itself, that change ramified into every aspect of the culture.

The specific changes introduced by the British seemed to be small, and in line with what they believed to be already present in the culture. One of the first things that the British introduced, after establishing administrative districts, was district courts. They knew of the councils of the elders; they knew also that courts were found in many African cultures, and considered them therefore in harmony with Tiv culture. But the Tiv had never had courts. The councils of the elders had been for the purpose of discussing community affairs, rather than for the purpose of judging, or even of discovering, a culprit. Everyone had known all along who was at fault; but the responsibility for the act could not be laid at his door until the elders, who as owners of the land were generally responsible for everything, came to a decision to lay it there. Nor were the councils held over the question of meting out punishment; rather, the elders often had to decide which was the offended *akombo*, so that they should know which rites had to be performed to put the land right. Matters were

[1] Ibid. p. 282.
[2] Abraham, op. cit. pp. 50-52.
[3] East, op. cit. p. 163.

usually brought to an amicable solution after discussion in private or public.

When courts were established, the Tiv began to bring every small matter to them, glad to throw the responsibility for the solution upon an outsider. Many matters which would have been settled normally after some enjoyable discussion were now brought to the district court. The British officials were overwhelmed by the amount of litigation, and very much impressed by the fact that practically every case involved, at some point or other, an exchange marriage, or a difficulty over an *ingol*. They were shocked to discover that daughters and sisters and nieces could be handed over without choice of their own for the procurement of a wife, that they were "owned" by their male kinsmen. And it seemed a travesty of human rights that a young man should be entirely dependent on the goodwill of his brother or father for a wife, that he should sometimes have to wait until middle age to get one, while his father could enjoy 10. They worried about the young children who could be turned over to their uncle in another village if this man's wife did not bear many children to him. To British eyes this went counter to the rights of the individual, and against human good. As they saw it, all these difficulties sprang from a custom which was not essential, since it had an alternative form. They saw exchange marriage as only one of several forms of marriage. They saw that marriage by purchase was a wide-spread African custom, they saw it in existence among the Tiv, and they decided that it would be perfectly safe to declare it to be the only valid form. In the interest of human rights, they told the women that they were now free to choose whom they would marry, and free to divorce a man who was unacceptable; or so, at any rate, the Tiv women interpreted the ruling.

The new marriage edict was welcomed by the young Tiv; in fact, these had been consulted and had been enthusiastically in its favour. Since the coming of the British, with the laying of the railroad through Tiv territory and the paid employment it involved, the young men had discovered that they could get wealthy without the aid of their elders; and with their earnings they knew that they could acquire wives under the proposed law. Some of the elders, for various reasons, also supported the proposed edict; and presently, a law was passed making marriage by purchase the only legal form.

The immediate result of the new edict was that there was even more work for the courts. They were flooded by a new kind of case. A stream of accusations was brought in, charging older men with killing by witchcraft. The accused readily acknowledged the accusation, furnishing terrifying details, producing witnesses in support. They were eager to convince the young men of their superior prowess, to hold their traditional place through inspiring fear, because, through the new edict, the delicately balanced equilibrium of roles and statuses had been thoroughly upset.

The abolition of exchange marriage meant the introduction of individualism. A man could now get a wife through his own efforts, without waiting his turn, which depended upon the priority of claims within the group, and without dependence on his father. In addition, to get a wife he had to please a woman; his acts were motivated by future aims, not by the established past. It was not enough for a man to become more and more Tiv by going through the pre-established stages of social development. It was not necessary to incorporate the community any more, or to act as a member of a unit. The past, embodied in the elders, had lost its meaning. Women did not insist on ear-ornaments; so, ear-piercing, a stage of the progress towards adulthood, fell into abeyance; they did not care for circumcision, so this important rite was no longer essential for development. Identity with the group through increasing participation in it according to the traditional procedure no longer provided the motivation; the future, not the past, became motivating. Change now received a sanction from the women; they chose the men who had the newly introduced form of cicatrization, as well as those who had the new type of vaccination mark. They used these marks to distinguish the young from the old; incidentally, this provided a reason for their continuance. So now, the great avenue through which all had developed into stages where they had power of choice and of action was by-passed. The elders, who had reached the point where they were entitled to choose or to speak before others at a gathering, or to take a wife without help from others, through slow organic increase in being, through incorporating society and nature, bitterly resented the fact that men and women who had not attained this right within their persons were suddenly given it by British law. Women could now interrupt an elder in the midst of a speech, since British law had given them "claws to scratch with"; a woman could leave her old husband, since the British had said that "women could do as they wished."[1] What the British did in this case was what they had done when they chose native officials and delegated authority to them, conferring power from the outside that had not grown organically within the body of the person. And the elders retaliated as they did when a man with insufficient *tsav* acquired high *akombo* power; they turned their *tsav* against him. Their claims of inflicting *tsav* deaths were sustained by the actual state of affairs, since at this time the country was swept by a wave of epidemic deaths.

To the elders, the abolition of exchange marriage had

[1] Ibid. p. 45.

meant that the British decisions had "spoiled the land" for other reasons, also. Without exchange marriage, the family group faced discontinuity; no longer could the wife be continuous with the mother, since she did not take the sister's place as a link in the chain of continuity. This meant that a man could not set the great *akombo* before any of his huts, since no wife was entitled to them. It meant that no son was entitled to initiation in the great *akombo,* and these rites could not be performed to set the land and the group to rights. People were now exposed to the dangers of pollution, women to miscarriage, the land to pests and drought; the machinations of evil *tsav* could not be forestalled. The group had lost its ancestral right and power to protect itself from evil.

Women could now choose young husbands. But the new marriage did not give women the dignified position which the British administrators had envisaged. They did not now have the status that exchange marriage had given them, since they did not occupy the place of the sister. As the true representatives of the sisters, they had been respected and given consideration, and they had been protected by the group *akombo.* More than this, the form of marriage chosen by the British administration from the Tiv forms had been one where the pattern was either one of impermanence—as when a man purchased only temporary sexual rights in a "sister"— or one in which the woman was a purchased slave in whom her group had abjured all rights, so that her very life was owned by the group of her marriage. So women now try to achieve position through power over their men, through the threat of divorce; that is easy to conceive in a pattern whose essence was impermanence; and many, afraid of the *tsav* of the group and lacking the protection of the *akombo,* do leave. Before the new marriage laws, the women's own lineage was intensely interested in the permanence of her marriage, since if it was broken, her father or brother would have to return his wife and disruption would come to the group; now the group is not concerned in maintaining the marriage. Sometimes it actually encourages a break; if a woman has borne a child, she can leave her husband without returning the bride-price; and through a series of marriages in which she bears one child, she can enrich her patrilineal unit.

The new edict also creates a dichotomy, a "younger" generation which had not been present in the culture before. Age-mates had banded together, forming a group which could frustrate the evil *tsav* of the intensely interrelated kinship unit. But this grouping, though it had actually set itself against the elder members of the family, was not a grouping of younger versus older; not all members of one generation were united in the age-grade, and the family as a whole included people of all ages. So the age-mates of a middle-aged man might combine for retaliation against a slightly older brother. A regrouping and a redividing took place, then, which was disruptive of the structure of the unit. In the same way, the equilibrium between husband and wife was upset. Whereas before the wife had been concerned in adding to her husband's wealth, spinning cotton for him to weave into cloth which he could then sell, now the young men complain that their wives expect them to spend their earnings on them, demanding that they buy them cloth and other trade-goods, upon threat of leaving them.

PALAU[1]

INTRODUCTION: PLACE AND PEOPLE

The Palau Islands lie north of New Guinea and east of the Philippines. Babelthaup, the largest of the islands, is over 150 square miles of rolling volcanic hills whose highest elevation is under 700 feet. All of the islands are narrow, the widest one being only 18 miles across.

Palau was politically autonomous prior to the nineteenth century. No outside group had ever attempted to conquer it, and it had no aspirations to conquer any outside group. There were intermittent migrations into the islands from surrounding areas and continuous transactions with neighbouring peoples. During the past century and a half, Palau has experienced cultural contact with many peoples who were among the world-powers. Spain formally exercised control over Palau from 1885 to 1899; Germany for the next 15 years; Japan during the 30-year span from 1914 to 1944; and, since then, the United States. The relative brevity of the Spanish and German eras, in addition to the absence of Spanish officials and the small number of German ones—in contrast to the Japanese—limited the extent of the influence of these two powers on native life. With the end of World War II, the American forces assumed full administrative responsibility

[1] This study is based on field observations made in Palau during three trips to the islands. Dr. John Useem initially served as a Naval civil affairs officer during the invasion and occupation in 1944. He returned in 1946, to undertake a survey of the human and economic resources of Palau, as part of a total exploration of the former Japanese mandated islands, sponsored by the U.S. Commercial Company, Reconstruction Finance Corporation. His third trip, in 1948, constituted one project in a series known as the Co-ordinated Investigations of Micronesian Anthropology supported by the Pacific Science Board, National Research Council. The Office of Naval Research, the U.S. Navy, and the administrators of the American Trust Territory provided generous assistance and co-operation.

for all of Palau, and this group of islands was transferred formally to American trusteeship; the Trust Territory came into being legally in July 1947.

There are now a few more than 6,000 inhabitants living in Palau, including, in addition to the indigenous population, Chamorros from the Marianas, peoples from other islands of Oceania, and from Korea, China, and Japan. In Palau eyes, anyone who settles in Palau with the intention of remaining indefinitely, and who accepts the duties and way of life of the native population, is a member of the society. It is a violation of etiquette and a technique of abuse to remind individuals of their origin. The largest foreign element in Palau before World War II was the Japanese and Okinawan populations.

The population of Palau was formerly many times larger than it is at present. Numbers fell sharply during the early years of contact with the outside world, and then slowly began to recover. There is little prospect of an over-population problem in Palau as a whole in the next few generations. However, within Palau there is a wide range in density between localities which may make for population pressures in particular places: population density ranges from 24 persons per square mile on Babelthaup to 333 on Koror. The man-land ratio cannot be computed realistically without taking into account intervening social and economic factors which determine the accessibility to resources, the utilization of available land, and foreigners' decisions concerning land allocations, etc. For instance, the combination of inter-village conflicts over land use and the mining of phosphate on the island of Angaur has reduced sharply the land available for raising food there, and has made for pressure of population.

Every class and household on Babelthaup now has access to land. With the decline in population, a landless class no longer exists.

The size, composition, and distribution of the population dropped to a point where it seemed doubtful that the society would survive. More than 150 villages disappeared, for there were not enough people to perform the traditional functions and to qualify for the various specialized roles contained within the ancestral social order.

There has been comparatively little opposition to the introduction of modern medical care and sanitation. The recent trend of growth has led some clans to reactivate extinct households and districts and to make plans for the re-establishment of ancestral villages. Planning for the future was notably lacking in the society, but now people say: "It isn't our custom to worry about the future, but we know we are in a new day and must work for the future."

The crude death-rate has declined, especially among females

of child-bearing age. The mortality rate for infants and children has continued to be rather high. There are twice as many deaths among male as among female children.

Although the locations of districts, villages, and households are relatively fixed, the populations who make up the social groupings have a high degree of mobility in contemporary Palau. Everyone has a village to which he "belongs," yet it is often not the one in which he resides or works. Seldom does a person remain in a community throughout his entire lifetime. Each day, craft of all types transport several hundred people in various directions. Hospitality patterns require the host, who is usually a relative, to provide shelter and food.

These incessant movements give a special character to Palau life. To an outsider, communities seem nearly empty during the course of the average day, and vessels skirting the coasts seem to be overloaded with passengers. From infancy on, individuals learn to adjust to a semi-mobile life. Parents usually take one or all of their children with them on visits. By adolescence young people make frequent trips around Palau on their own. Even the very old spend much of their time travelling from branch to branch of their clan.

ECONOMIC TRENDS

Since the beginning of contact with the West, Palau has developed a dual yet integrated economic order; one segment consists of a subsistence economy using a tradition-oriented handicraft technology; and the other is a commercial economy with a foreign-oriented, machine-made technology. The two sets of patterns are structurally interlinked and functionally interdependent. There has always existed a degree of commercial enterprise in the traditional economy. Today the foreign economy is regarded as being as much a part of Palau's tradition as the subsistence one. The majority of adult males engage in both types of gainful work, whether concomitantly or at different stages of their life-cycle.

The daily pattern of living exhibits various combinations of the two schemes. High-speed motor launches are used to transport baskets of sweet potatoes to a neighbouring village for a traditional social festival. The aboriginal adze is used to carve out a canoe alongside the gasoline-driven sawmill turning out 100 feet of plank. An industrial plant mines phosphate close to women who plant taro fields as they have done for generations. Natives drive trucks and pound typewriters so that they can earn enough money to offer the customary gifts to their wives' clans. A sorcerer, except in matters concerning the weather, chants aloud and waves his arms to turn away a local shower at so many American dollars per day. Fishermen toss hand-grenades into the sea to catch fish, and then sort their catch according to those which are taboo, those which go as tribute to the *élite,* and those to be sold on the open market or consumed. A nativistic leader waves a red flag (an ancient symbol of power over one's fortune) to deflect the course of bombers overhead. A Japanese-trained local business man produces with chain-belt methods handicrafts of traditional style to acquire sufficient American money to purchase a piece of Palau money so as to enhance his family's prestige and bargaining power in competition for the headship of a district. Sears Roebuck catalogues are consulted for buying implements to substitute for those which they have forgotten how to, or do not wish to, make. A meal may be comprised of a mixture of American canned and South-East Asian derived foods, prepared in Spanish iron pots, placed in Japanese dishes on a table made of Philippine driftwood, eaten with German silverware in a commercial restaurant housed in an American Quonset hut which has been financed by a Japanese credit pattern and is operated by a native clan as a family enterprise, while a Japanese version of an American phonograph plays African-derived dance music. These are merely illustrations of the interconnexions between the traditional and newer forms of economic patterns in contemporary Palau.

Contact between the foreign and native economic systems began with the intermittent visits of private traders, who were eagerly welcomed by the natives; and the German and Japanese eras brought about the dual economy. Production for profit was made a central theme; the virtues of the work ethic were indoctrinated into the younger generations through schools; incentives for output were offered in foreign goods. Numerous new crops and livestock were introduced. Scientific experiments in agriculture were undertaken and the findings taught to native farmers. Implements suitable to the local industries were sold at a modest price. Sudsidies were granted to expand land under cultivation, and where these proved an insufficient incentive, persuasion and some pressure were used. Joint governmental and private capital concerns built installations, factories and transportation facilities. Joint native and foreign associations were formed to market native products, to import manufactured goods from abroad, and to foster commercial enterprise in the islands. Groups of foreign experts were sent in to explore the potentially useful resources and to work out feasible means for their development.

As Palau's output increased, exports rapidly mounted and surpassed imports, which continued their upward trend. The gains of this expanding economy were evidenced in the steadily rising level of living for the entire population. Natives built new homes, dressed in foreign clothes, bought many luxuries, and dreamed of an ever-improving level of living.

World War II temporarily, and rather sharply, disrupted the existing economy. Since the end of hostilities the subsistence economy has been restored more rapidly and more fully than the commercial one. Economic rehabilitation is, however, under way, and production for the market is steadily mounting.

The division of labour within the subsistence economy involves specialization in some production. For each family to send some one of its members out to fish, for example, would be deemed an unwarranted duplication of effort and time. The rising prices of local commodities have benefited the producers for the native market, and, as a result, villages with goods to sell have experienced a decided increase in their income. Those families which rely primarily on wage-work have felt pressed. A rise also has taken place in the price of imported commodities.

Those in a position to do so have stepped up their use of traditional Palau customs to secure additional income to ffset their deficits. For example, during one three-month-interval study, two-thirds of the families had contributed under mutual-aid patterns and but one of four families secured income by these means. Because the circulation of funds under these patterns is not an equal one, pressure had been keenly felt. This in part explains the mounting discontent among members of the younger generation, who are primarily wage-earners and who are not in a position to use the mutual-aid patterns as a source of income.

Occupational mobility is the expected pattern in the course of a man's lifetime. One reason for this is the comparative ease of migration and the availability of homes and relatives for temporary or even lengthy stays. Another is the fact that the kind of work a person does is usually less important than the amount of income derived from the employment. The prestige given to various kinds of work is in terms of the social status of the employed individuals. Foreign-learned skills are not in themselves prestige-giving. The Palau groups that want income opportunities to expand are not as concerned with a question of securing a particular type of employment as with the income that would come with it.

While the possession of wealth is a source of envy, the expenditure of wealth for the glory of the family and clan brings added honours from all quarters. A feast given for some occasion which draws a very large number of people will be widely and favourably discussed as proof that the donor is really well respected. No self-respecting village would build its own club-house and few men would consider constructing their own homes in spite of the possession of necessary skills. The community pays another village of equal social rank to perform the task, and the man who wishes a new home hires others to construct it.

SOCIAL ORIENTATIONS TO THE WORLD

The dominant foreigners have encouraged the people of Palau to participate in newly introduced programmes and to assimilate foreign ways, and the people have welcomed each incoming group as a valued addition. There has been little hostility and no conspiracy to oust the foreigners. Foreigners have made no systematic attempt to destroy or suppress the native social order; official policy has been to support Palau's basic patterns. This has made it possible for individuals to gain foreign goods and training without depriving themselves of the traditional security of the ancestral subsistence-reciprocity-mutual aid system. In the course of a life-cycle, the young have worked with foreigners and then, when older, have retired to their home village. Cleavages in interest have occurred between the foreigner's economic and social plans and native wishes, but these have been fewer than those which have occurred in other comparable areas of the world.

The natives point to the progress they have made in the change-over from Spanish to German, and from German to Japanese, rule. They know that the United States is a far wealthier country than Japan, and hence have greater hopes for the future. Gains are judged both in social life and in material goods. Foreign items have great prestige in Palau and are welcomed as valuable additions, even when less efficient than their own. The demand is for more outside exposure and more introductions. There is little nostalgia for the ancient era and an impatient eagerness to accelerate the pace of "advancement." The changes brought about by the foreigners are regarded as having modified the social architecture of Palau without having undermined its cultural foundations. For example, the outlawing of native warfare and of female guests in the men's club-houses seriously changed patterns and created problems but did not dislocate the entire social order. There is in no sense total bewilderment or cultural collapse.

The foreigner is today viewed as the source of ultimate sanctions in the political order, as superordinate in the hierarchy of power, and as the primary force for social change. In the earlier period of cultural contact the foreigners were scolded for violating the local ways and, on occasion were cut off and killed. With the attenuation of traditional religious institutions, the figure of the foreigner replaced that of the indigenous religious functionaries and their supernatural spirits. This substitution of symbols was accomplished by transfer of some of the emotional effect surrounding ultimate authority and also by the utilization of traditional techniques in the new relationship.

The imposition of foreign rule did not generate a new kind of social structure totally alien to native schemes of social organization. Hierarchy was already there, and the coming of the foreigners meant adding a new apex to the established social pyramid. They occupied the peak by virtue of the combination of superiority in power and wealth, values which allocated status positions in the traditional culture. Social change is expected to stem from the top rather than from below.

THE INNER ORIENTATION

Despite the pervasive effects of the foreign on native life, most individuals are born, reared, and spend much of their lives in villages where Palau values prevail, and the foreigner is viewed as an outsider.

There is a pattern of expectancy that Palau will continue to change and yet remain the same. This apparent paradox stems from a readiness to accept new ways, paralleled by an unshaken conviction that new ways do not mean the dissolution of Palau society. It was only during the great crisis of the recent war that many turned back to ancestral patterns, and, once the emergency was past, the present orientation reasserted itself. The Palau people display ingenuity in reworking social arrangements to incorporate the new into the old in a satisfactory and workable manner.

Life's social changes are said to be both limited and competitive; the values which are most esteemed, such as titles, power, prestige and wealth, are considered quantitatively finite. Hence the gains of one person are viewed as reducing the prospects of others. This outlook is institutionalized in the social system of rank which provides a limited number of status positions. Group rivalry has been institutionalized in some activities. At the individual level, the existence of the struggle is publicly denied and privately accepted as a fact of life. Aspirations of individuals are enshrouded in disclaimers of self-interest and couched in terms of striving merely to advance the well-being of others, e.g. family, village, Palau, etc.

Social transactions are rigidly stylized and some call for "bargaining" through intermediaries. Elaborate negotiations surround the establishment and termination of social relationships and the occurrence of major social events. Transactions usually involve the transfer of money, both the native and foreign types, as well as food, gifs, social rites, and semi-formal contractual agreements. The network of social ties requires large numbers of relatives to share in the costs. Failure to fulfil one's obligations is a source of social disgrace.

Most human affairs are subject to manipulation, and those who display virtuosity in the handling of persons and processes in social situations are greatly admired. Deceit is both legitimate and expected, and even honoured if the outcome is successful.

Foreigners sometimes confuse symbolic acts of "going native" as proof of entrance into the native world. Natives, in turn, occasionally think of themselves as moving into the foreigner's world by taking on the styles of speech, costume, and behaviour of foreigners. There are matters which are seldom revealed by natives to foreigners or by foreigners to natives.

There are foreign-facing and native-facing officials with parallel social organizations to facilitate the co-ordination of the two worlds. Those traditional structures which have been revamped by the foreigner's rules combine both the foreign and the native ones. Incorporated into the social structure are those foreign-derived institutions known as the school, the hospital, the store, the police, the mission, and congeries of governmental agencies. These have become social centres where people congregate informally, and contain within them as much that is Palauan as is foreign. The local representatives, such as school-teacher, church deacons, and constables, have distinct roles in community life.

The existence of a power structure that has effective means for legitimizing its decisions, and executing them, makes possible collective action when issues threaten to disrupt the social fabric. This power structure is manned by skilled political artisans who are adroit in devising effective means. Everyone is enmeshed in a constellation of connected groups and may be activated to respond in an expected way.

Foreigners, unaware of the complex social structure, of the subtlety of all social intercourse, of the sophisticated manipulations of affairs, have blundered upon occasion. A labour-relations expert, hired by an engineering company, violated Palau ethics in his attempts to create good relations. He vaunted authority and crudely threatened coercion to people who respected only suave, indirect methods. He joked and teased informally, he gave crude public demonstrations of affection in a society where this was tantamount to indecency. He playfully tousled the hair of ranking men, an act equivalent—in Western terms—to unbuttoning a man's fly in public. On the other hand, generous treatment evoked the traditional pattern of reciprocity and graciousness; and when the American military government, which fed, clothed, and sheltered the people, asked for volunteers in the work of reconstruction, people responded but no pay was accepted, even though there was a long experience in modern money economy.

CLASSES

The class structure of Palau is caste-like in character, but it is not completely closed. Upward and downward mobility occurs, although in principle social positions are hereditary. Each locality has its own determinants of social status; the individual's social rank is defined through membership in a village or a district. Thus a person belongs to the *élite* by virtue of a title in a particular locality, and there is no way he may hold this status apart from it. He has no legitimate authority to act in his capacity as a title-holder outside the confines of his locality. The same individual may inherit several status positions in different places, and so rank in the upper class in one village and in a lower class in another.

For every male title-holder there is a female complementary title. Children traditionally follow the class rank of their mothers. Through the progressive inheritance of higher titles, a person can advance from a lower to a higher status. The wealthy class without titles gain or lose status in accordance with the proportionate amount of property held.

Individuals inherit eligibility to a title, but they must be approved by the leading members of their household, clan, and the council, as possessing the prerequisite qualities, and may be rejected if found wanting. The title may be withdrawn for failure to perform the duties of the office properly. An additional test has been established for the senior titles by the present administration, in the form of a popular election. In one district several candidates were voted on, and one of the junior men in line of succession was elected. In most localities, however, the individual most eligible to succeed to the title has been chosen.

There are both village and district titles. The relative status of the village or district determines the rating of the title. Since the onset of acculturation and accentuation of the district unit in the administration, district titles have increased in power at the expense of village titles, but their authority has increased more than their social prestige.

The same person can have several titles concomitantly or progressively but no more than one title can be held in a single place. One cannot have two titles in the same village.

Immediately below the *élite* class is a sub-*élite* class. This and the lower sections of the social pyramid consist of those without titles. There is the group of the "true men" who possess a reasonable number of relatives and amount of property, and have the ability to discharge social obligations. Here also are the wealthy men who are more likely to use Palau money as currency in business transactions than for social obligations. The rest, an inchoate "lower class," are people who lack titles, property, money, and relatives.

Vertical mobility in the titled class is of two general types: advancement through inheritance—the "approved" form—and climbing by manipulation, which is always accompanied by what is regarded as the lowering of others. Commoners are reluctant to work for a wealthy man or one who has such aspirations of climbing, for they feel it would be benefiting the entrepreneur and thereby detracting from their own modest likelihood of advancing.

There is little envy of the *élite* by members of the lower class, for these positions are beyond the levels of aspiration of the ordinary person; but some of the wealthy do have unannounced ambitions to enter the *élite*, and have been able to gain titles. Until the Japanese era, the *élite* looked down upon the wealthy without titles, but now the wealthy are more acceptable as mates for children of the *élite*, as political advisers, and as economic associates.

A lower-class woman who marries an *élite* assumes his social standing only as long as they are married. In some clans, by mutual consent, the husband's family may adopt the children of such a marriage when there are no other heirs. Lower-class men cannot afford to marry *élite* women, and such marriages are strongly discouraged. The prospects of a lower-class person becoming wealthy is today limited.

The senior titles of the major localities are known throughout Palau, the lesser ones are not. Children are aware of the social system by the time they are 12 to 15 years old. Young people decide which kinship line to follow, if they have a choice, after ascertaining the lineage which offers them the highest future status. In games, the children of the *élite* serve as leaders, and when organized programmes take place in the schools, especially if the teachers are not present, they assume the headship. A lower-class child who has a fight with an *élite* child is scolded by his parents and warned that it may bring reprisals from *élite* parents. The lower-class parents will visit the *élite* parents to apologize and make amends. *Elite* parents urge their children to exercise the role of leadership as a means of preparing themselves for the future life-work. There is little inter-class competition within the schoolroom, for the *élite* know their station in life is assured and feel no need to excel over others in academic activities.

Class position does not determine the location of the household within the village but it does affect the quality of the home. During the early part of the Japanese era some of the wealthy class built homes like the *élite*. These were burned down and their owners fined. Today the wealthier members do not face this opposition. The American Quonset hut has tended to erase the differences between classes in housing and the limited supply of foreign luxury goods has curtailed the differentials in household possessions. One of the most conspicuous signs of social status in the pre-war period was the possession of chinaware. *Elite* homes would have as many as several hundred dishes on display whereas the ordinary household would have only those actually used in daily living.

Class standing does not wholly determine an individual's occupation. The *élite* women care for their own taro patches, and it is the aged rather than the *élite* who are the leisure class. Those with high status are expected to work harder and personally do some of the most disagreeable and dangerous jobs, for their role is that of providing models for the rest. The recent tendency of some of the *élite* to withdraw from such activities has brought forth condemnation and the accusation that they are more inclined to work with their mouths than with their hands. A lower-class person may be more skilled at an occupation but ordinarily he does not assume the managerial function. When foreigners have chosen labour bosses on the basis of technical ability, irrespective of class, the appointed lower-class head of the work detail has found his role a difficult one. A few skills were hereditary monopolies of the *élite*; working with the foreigner as civil servants is the newest type of semi-monopoly.

The governing of native affairs has, in the past, been concentrated in the *élite* class. Their right to rule was symbolized in titles of office, by five entrances to their houses, by the possession of valued pieces of native money, by a special type of hair-comb, by membership in the community council, etc. In all social relationships the *élite* expected to be treated with deference and accorded special privileges; commoners stepped off the pathway when members of the *élite* approached, half-crouched in their presence, contributed choice portions of a fish catch to them, submitted to their orders, and accepted the doctrine that only the *élite* had the authority to determine what should be done in village and district affairs. Chiefs are the senior-ranking members of the *élite* class. They are the personification of power, the formal heads of institutionalized groupings, the first leaders in social activities, the arbiters of social controversies, and the representatives of their communities in negotiations with outsiders.

While chiefs outranked other title-holders, their right to rule was circumscribed. No chief was supposed to act without the prior approval of at least the second-ranking person. In some districts the veto and the right to argue in open meetings of the council was the inalienable prerogative of the head of an even lower-ranking clan or village head.

The *élite* exerted direct control through their headship of organized groups and indirect control through the interlocking of associations.

Fines, banishment from the group, and the death-penalty could be ordered by the *élite* against those who violated their regulations. Perhaps the most effective technique of social control was, and still is, the use of open scolding which puts a person to shame. The loss in reputation reflects not only on the person involved, but also on his parents, clan, and village. Because the individual is so highly dependent on groups and can do so little as an isolated being, he is most anxious to retain his good standing. A person could not run away and start all over again among total strangers. It might be better to move to another district, but this would require the approval of the chief of the new locality.

The primary defence open to those who offended was a verbal one. Fabrication of the facts was and still is a well-developed art. A more common procedure is to acquiesce overtly to any orders given but actually to evade their execution while verbally simulating compliance. The order might even be enthusiastically applauded and then either "misunderstood" or worked at without ever being quite accomplished.

There are distinct differences between districts in the way the *élite* functioned. One prominent district was renowned for the use of violence in administration, whereas in another, equally outstanding, direct fines were more common. One chief was said to rule by resorting to coercion to secure obedience; another, by employing flattery and persuasion to activate others, skilfully working out social arrangements, even inventing new customs which met the needs of everyone.

Everyone concedes that an effective leader uses some deception and trickery. Many rulers maintain that to confide in the common people or to invite open discussion of issues brings agitation, unrest and confusion, for ordinary people know little about Palau regulations. Moreover, they point out, the Palau people are quick in enthusiasm for any new idea. It would be proof of weakness rather than strength of character for a chief to fail to issue firm orders. Ambitious rival clans are alert to any opportunity to grasp the titles of those above them, and no greater disgrace could befall a chief than to be responsible for his clan's losing out to another. No one actually advocates complete equity in the distribution of rewards, and there are no records of anyone openly urging any major reforms in the power structure—until the coming of the foreigners.

Neither the foreigners nor the natives possessed any strong motives for the abolition of the traditional schemes for political management in Palau. The foreigners were concerned primarily with questions of how to utilize and supervise native government effectively. Some form of centralization and concentration of authority appeared to be the rational solution, and as Palauans themselves were eager to take advantage of the opportunity to enhance their status they readily responded.

This development contributed substantially to the decline of the control of the *élite* class over the chiefs.

The challenge to the men in power in Palau was to invent new techniques or refashion old ones to fit the changing social scene. The foreigners recruited and trained natives to serve as administrative assistants, interpreters, clerks, constables, medical assistants, school-teachers. Because they were close to the seat of ultimate power they were in a strategic position to influence policies. Native interpreters, for example, controlled most of the channels of communication between the foreigners and the natives. They became not merely translators, but arbitrators and explainers, experts in knowing what to say. Palauans expected the interpreters not to convey precisely what was told them but to offer advice on what tactics to pursue. The leading clans of the *élite* class early perceived the advisability of placing some of their most able members in these positions. Still the *élite* were not fully protected, for some of these young men were captivated by the foreigners and began to place their allegiance to the "modernization" of Palau even above their own clan or class interests. Various corrective remedies were attempted. One individual who proved too informative to the foreigners was killed. Indirect influence was applied through negative sanctions affecting the individual's prestige. A civil servant invited in to advise a district chief is in the category of distinguished men of wisdom; nevertheless, he lacks the prescribed right to argue with chiefs and he is compromised at once, for the agreement reached in these conferences is binding. Only the most skilful politicians among such civil servants consulted by chiefs have been able to manoeuvre this situation to enhance their own interests. The civil servants are not a highly cohesive group with a single set of loyalties. This fact too has helped to limit their collective power. But perhaps most important of all, the civil servants number but few who would like to change the *élite* system; the majority lean towards the development of a foreign-educated, modern-oriented *élite*.

The diffusion of foreign goods and money threatened to disturb the customary concentration of wealth and the differential levels of living. The initial reaction of the *élite* was an attempt to forbid commoners to use foreign incomes to acquire certain prestige goods. For example, commoners caught using umbrellas or wearing selected types of foreign garments were fined. But this as well as attempts to limit currency in native social ceremonies proved unsuccessful eventually, and the *élite* shifted their efforts to extracting as much as possible of the foreign moneys from those who secured them. The traditional customs of Palau gift-exchange and related patterns were converted by a series of inventions and adaptations into taxation enterprises capable of producing sizable sums.

The introduction of foreign schools has provided an orientation for youth, which exalts foreign models of life over native ones. Spearheaded by the school-teachers, many younger people have increasingly favoured changes in Palau, many of which would undermine the ruling class. Despite their criticisms of the *status quo,* these groups of educated young men have not yet emerged as the dominant political force. They submit to the pressures of their superiors. Their right to attend or speak at high-policy meetings is not recognized.

Democratic precepts introduced by Americans have given Palau politics a new dimension. The younger generation, for example, has employed the theme of liberty to gain greater freedom from authority. The Palauan authorities have countered with the argument that the right to do as one pleased was not inherent in the concept of liberty, for surely the victorious foreigners in the recent war exercised group discipline. The inauguration of democratic procedures such as the popular election of chiefs has had few immediate consequences, but may have far-reaching effects in the future.

FAMILY AND PERSON

There are five interlocking kinship systems which combine blood and social affiliations in varying ways. The fivefold units will here be referred to as the nuclear family, the extended nuclear family, the household, the clan, and the extended clan.

The nuclear family consists, ordinarily, of a wife, her husband, their children, and her children by previous marriage. Since the German era, the tendency has been for married sons, especially the younger ones, to live separately. The younger generation prefer to stress the nuclear family whereas the older ones are more oriented toward the extended nuclear family.

Most men have but one wife at any one time. Polygamy under ancestral law was restricted to the *élite* and was permissible only in the senior-ranking districts; more recently anyone with sufficient wealth could have two wives, but today the decline of social ceremonies and clan functions has reduced the need for plural marriages and the foreigners have tried intermittently to discourage or outlaw the practice.

Marriages before the age of 40 are rather impermanent and last, on the average, between two and three years. Marriages which have lasted as long as 10 years are not lightly abandoned. Despite the high incidence of marital change, there are cases of a couple who married young and continued their marriage for a lifetime.

Marriages today may be either love-matches or arrangements between representatives of the two families; and the families of the two spouses become heavily involved in financial and social transactions.

A girl reaching the age of about 15 is advised to have a sexual liaison. To remain a virgin, she is told, may make her ill and will keep her single. A young man learns the arts of talking and gift-giving, which are helpful preludes. He is expected to have several sexual liaisons, but is admonished not to assault a female and to select girls with due regard to status, affinities, etc. Traditionally, sexual intercourse among pre-adolescents was discouraged; now many of the foreign-educated and deeply Christian parents anxiously attempt to delay their children's engaging in sexual intercourse until a later age.

While early marriages seldom last, they are entered into in the hope that they will, for one's reputation is impaired by having too many divorces. Two to four marriages is a fairly typical life-history.

No woman is forced to marry, but no known adult woman was found who had never been married. Widows who have lost several husbands are sometimes called the "lucky ones," for they have yielded several payments to their older brothers in settling for the loss of their husbands. Unmarried adult women are regarded as an economic burden on their households. Most such women live in the household of their senior brother, turn over their wealth to him, and must learn to be "blind and deaf" in order to withstand the obvious suggestions that they are not welcome for an indefinite period. In one-fourth of the current marriages of Palau, the husband is 10 or more years older than the wife. There can be no doubt at present of a sense of insecurity among women. There is a feeling that while it is easier than in the past to perform their economic functions, there is still little assurance that marital fidelity and hard work will mean any protection of their interests, and with the decline in the solidarity of the clan, women have less ultimate security than formerly.

Fathers today play a more active role in the rearing of their own children. It is less common now for an irate mother to inform her husband that he has no right to discipline the children, and to threaten to return to her family. Children, in turn, are less likely to escape to their mother's family to avoid the discipline of their father. There is also a decided growth in the father's desire to pass on his wealth to his own children rather than to his sister's offspring. Several attempts have been made to establish new native codes to settle this question, but thus far none have been universally accepted.

Many younger parents of commoner status have been eager for their male children to enter the expanding wealthy class or secure civil-service employment, or acquire the skills and some of the ways of foreigners. At the same time, the child is warned not to fail to conform to the traditional expectations of a member of Palau society, and parents endeavour to inculcate into their children knowledge and respect for Palau mores at an early age. Children subjected to unwelcome parental demands respond in several ways; the most common is unenthusiastic outward submission to orders where the values are, in conflict. This is often accompanied by evasion through a simulated acceptance of the imposed edict, and pursuit of personal plans beyond the presence of the parents. Deviations are explored to ascertain the maximum attainable without provoking discipline; direct conflict is avoided as far as possible.

The system of rewards and punishments is basically like that of the past, with some modifications. Children are cautioned "not to stand in one spot while their companions run," and the returns of having a good reputation are stressed. Little children are threatened with potential dangers of pigs, cows, goats, and cats. The *élite* remain an important threat for the children of commoners, and to this group the foreigner has been added. Fines imposed by the foreigner are interpreted as a social disgrace to the whole family and even the village. Two other types of punishment have declined; the threat to withdraw the right to inherit a title or wealth, and corporal punishment.

A major and continuing source of division between parents and children stems from the contrasting types of training a child receives at home and in school. The home education is oriented around traditional Palau customs, whereas the school's emphasis is on "modern" values. Native schoolteachers are acutely aware of this discrepancy and have sought to obtain a policy declaration from the native and foreign leadership, but have thus far been unable to do so.

Today men's work is the principal source of cash income, and the traditional opportunities of women to acquire wealth have been circumscribed or eliminated, which in turn has reduced their social power.

If a marriage is infertile, efforts are made to secure children through adoption. One out of every six children has the status of an adopted child. The traditional pattern is for a young couple to present a child to infertile relatives and friends, or elderly relatives. The newer patterns involve the foreigners. Japanese and Okinawan parents in a number of instances gave their children to Palau families prior to their evacuation, fearing that life would be too hard for children in the defeated homeland, after having been raised in Palau. War-orphaning of Oriental children, and broken mixed marriages in which the Japanese mate returned home, also led to some adoptions. Half-American children are now given, in some instances, for adoption. Two unrelated families who are linked by adoption have a special bond which in some cases has formed the basis of an affiliation between two households.

The firmest ties within the family are between the mother and her children and among the siblings. As other kinship affiliations have weakened, these have been strengthened. The loyalty between brothers is one of the strongest social attachments in Palau.

Outward expression of one's inner feelings towards a loved one in the presence of others is regarded as bad taste. (This applies in other relationships as well.) Mothers and grandmothers may be openly affectionate to children; the fondling pattern is usually stopped around the age of five. After a son reaches the age of about 15, a mother "cherishes her affection in her heart." The boy is expected to avoid lingering around the home in the day, and to sleep out of the home frequently. On Korror, Peleliu, and Angaur, the younger women are reported to have the reputation of being "wild and crazy," for some have adopted the dating patterns exhibited by the foreigners and the foreigners' movies. It may be noted that this reputation does not apply to the men in these districts.

The extended nuclear family is the second kinship grouping in Palau. The typical matrilineal extended nuclear family consists of a male head, a senior-ranking woman (usually his sister), his other sisters, the children of his sisters, and his brothers (but not their children). It is an important unit in all social and economic transactions; the inheritance of wealth, titles, and status comes through this unit. The male head is responsible for the general welfare of its members.

The Japanese attempted to re-allocate land to the nuclear family units and to encourage wage-workers for the foreigners to keep money within the nuclear family rather than turning it over to the head of the extended nuclear family. But even where weakening has occurred in the extended family, token obligations are still customary.

A household has its own name, home, land, hereditary titles, and membership. In actuality not all of these attributes occur in every household today. Persons may never live in their "household" and yet will always refer to it as their home. Since the foreigners defined the household as the conjugal family with dependent relatives occupying a particular site, and encouraged the re-assignment of conjugal families to separate dwellings, the household has shifted in many communities to a symbolic rather than a functional unit.

The clan is a combination of households related by blood and political ties within a district. Clans are ranked in two social systems, the district and the village. The same clan may have a high village rank and a low district rank or vice versa. This unit is important for the inheritance of titles, the senior-

ranking of which become village and district officers. An individual can rely on his clan to give him a place to stay when
he moves about in the district and can be called upon to give
him aid in all economic and social transactions.

The extended clan is the largest, most extensive, and all-
inclusive kinship grouping. It consists of a network of con-
federate clans from two or more districts. The extensiveness
of the extended clan is correlated with class position. The
senior-most-ranking extended clan of Palau has units in every
district. Loyalty to the group and even awareness of its position
is much less among this younger generation than among the
older ones. Despite these losses, it continues to serve as a
mutual-aid group.

There is a constellation of leading positions in all kinship
groupings. The one role which has great emotional significance
for the individual is that of the *m'as*. She is the female head of
any kinship or sub-kinship unit. The position is passed from
sister to sister, and after the sisters die, the oldest daughter of
the senior sister assumes the position. However, in those cases
where a daughter of a deceased sister is about the same age or
older than her aunt, she may be selected. The qualities stressed
for this position are: having been married (it does not matter
how often or what her current marital status is, or whether or
not she has children), her reputation in the district, her ability
to control other women, her record as a worker, her mental
capacities, her stability and her reliability. The future *m'as* of
an important clan or extended family is carefully trained from
childhood on. The newly appointed *m'as* must leave her husband's household and return to her own. She usually brings
her husband and children with her. A *m'as* cannot retire from
office nor can she be removed.

The prestige of the *m'as* is immense. She is an honoured
person in Palau folk-lore and appears more frequently in
legendary accounts than any other figure. There is an adage
that a male title-holder is respected for his power but a *m'as* is
loved because of her spirit. Her idealized qualities include the
following: (a) she makes people relatives in spirit through her
gentle talk and actions; (b) she prefers peace to conflict; (c)
she offers wise advice in all affairs, even men's business and
political activities; (d) her calculations and manipulations are
not for her self-glory, but for her family; (e) she wishes to hear
only the good news about people; (f) she grows the food on
which everyone lives; (g) she is famous for being good to all
children; (h) she is the "mother" of all social units.

The official authority of the *m'as* is less today than in the
past, but her actual influence is still great. The *m'as* of the extended clan issues orders to the *m'as* of each sub-clan, who in
turn directs the *m'as* of each extended family. Together with
the male head, she shares the responsibility for formulating

plans for the kinship group, and few males would dare make a major commitment without first consulting the *m'as*.

The *m'as* of an extended family traditionally directed the activities of the women of the various nuclear families, and of the wives of her sons, in regard to food-raising. With respect to money, the son's wife obeyed her own *m'as*.

Since the dispersal of the sub-units of the clan, the formal supervisory role of the *m'as* has decreased. Women in the fields are less responsive to her orders. Her control over young women has diminished; many of them say that the *m'as* has not caught up with the times. If she is aged, they claim that her views are the outmoded ones of ancestral Palau; and if she is middle-aged, they argue that she is too much like the Japanese. The *m'as* is held to be the custodian of knowledge which makes individuals powerful in Palau or Japanese ways, whereas only the schools offer knowledge which enables one to be powerful in American, modern ways. However, when a *m'as* joins a particular foreign church, the rest of the family will become members; she is still the trustee of important information about the kinship unit and exercises an influence over the style of living in the household.

SOCIETIES

There are approximately 50 active societies in Palau; they include a majority of the adult population. The degree of active participation required is less than in the past. Persons with private enterprises, those working for the foreigners, may be called upon to contribute funds or to assist in some emergency or special celebration, but in other respects they are free of further obligations. Individuals residing outside of their home district may be invited to join the society of the locality in which they are staying.

Men's clubs no longer serve as the organized garrison forces of villages, and the social status of villages now depends on elements other than the number of war canoes its societies can put into the sea. Women no longer serve as guests in men's club-houses, and their own societies have abandoned many of their prior functions. The schools have taken over the education of the younger generation and those charged with this responsibility within societies are mainly foreign-trained individuals who know little of the traditions. The reduction of the number of dances and other social celebrations made for a further loss in the role of the societies.

Despite these trends the social life of most individuals is intimately linked with the societies. Friendships are usually formed within the club, and the preference for group-organized activities provides the psychological foundation for the perpetuation of societies. Societies are primary instruments by which districts and villages engage in organized projects. For the men in power they constitute an effective control over the man-power of the district, since orders issued to societies ordinarily cannot be disobeyed.

Most societies are at present organized on a district-wide basis. Many communities maintain club-houses as social centres without having any going societies. Members of district societies living in the same village act together in local affairs even though they may not be formally organized within the village. Every district possesses societies and each society has its own distinct title. Societies are organized on the basis of three principles: sex, age, and status. Within these, further subdivisions occur, depending on the size of the population, the usage of traditional competing groups, and informal arrangements within the districts.

Men's societies, prior to the Japanese, were subdivided into *élite* and commoner groupings; leadership positions in both groupings were offices inherited along clan lines. They were further subdivided into a dual division, and within each half there was an additional subdivision into two units, and within each of these units there might be several clubs; from 6 to 12 commoner groupings were not uncommon at the district level.

No man could qualify for a title unless he had been reasonably effective as a head of a commoner society. The leadership of each commoner society formed a council for it and they were expected to assume responsibility for duties assigned to or appropriate to the group, such as warfare, manual labour, etc. However, the leaders were to be the first in exposing themselves to risks, were expected to be more proficient technically, and were to be models of stoicism and industry.

The leaders of the commoner associations kept records of which families might have offspring who were eligible for membership. Upon the birth of a child, the heads of competing clubs raced to the home of the new-born to ask the parents to pledge the offspring. The first to arrive won, for it was impolite to refuse. A man did not become eligible for active membership in a senior-age commoner society until reaching the age of about 30. After the age of six, boys were informally attached to their club and performed minor duties; at late puberty, they began sleeping in the club-house and assumed additional responsibilities. The leaders of the clubs were responsible for the boys' training.

Elite societies were fewer in number but had a comparable set of patterns. *Elite* societies were the "thinking" and "inventing" organizations and they had the authority to issue orders to the commoner clubs in their moiety. They had an informal division of labour within their groups.

Spirited rivalry existed between the societies and competition between them was fostered by the officials. Each of the major clubs possessed a club-house which was the centre of activities. Commoner societies had the right to discipline their members and to undertake certain actions, including military expeditions, without the consent of the *élite* clubs; but if the undertaking failed, the leaders were subject to fine. An injury to a member was deemed an attack on the entire society and compensation had to be made.

The Japanese rearranged these societies into age-grades and combined the groups; the young men's societies became widely popular, and men well beyond the prescribed age clung to their membership in these. With Japanese encouragement and in response to a declining population, consolidation took place in the number and distribution of societies, and some localities gave up the dual division and placed their formal groupings on a district-wide basis.

The general tendency since World War II has been to restore openly the *élite* societies (which had persisted underneath) on a village basis and to have a combination of commoner-youth society for the district as a whole. Within the Japanese-reorganized societies, the Palauans worked out a new pattern which incorporated the ancestral forms of men's societies. But regardless of what scheme was officially used, in nearly all cases the leaders came from the *élite* class and usually from the senior-ranking clans of the high-ranking villages. Each age-grade society had two sub-groupings based on the traditional *élite* and commoner status groupings.

Since the end of the Japanese rule, additional changes have taken place. The district has combined the youth and commoner clubs into a single district organization but retains the Japanese-introduced age distinctions. The Japanese-introduced age-grade system is no longer adhered to formally in many districts and one district has abolished the youth societies. In a few districts, men's societies have become the principal administrative organization. One district, for example, had 10 official meetings of its men's society in one year to consider copra production, the use of land, road and school repairs; to make arrangements for the transportation and marketing of produce; to discuss operations of their co-operatively run saw-mill; to settle a dispute; and to make general plans for the future.

Women's societies parallel men's organizations. They were once powerful independent units, but now most of them have become inactive and exert relatively little influence. In some districts, every girl must belong to the youth club until she is pregnant or married or leaves the district. Women's societies were never as dominant a force in the women's lives as the men's societies were in theirs.

VILLAGES

The ordinary native's world still continues to be mainly that of his village. It is the centre of most social activities and it is one of the most cohesive social units in Palau. Loyalty to the home village is second only to that of the family. Though village solidarity is less intense than before acculturation, it is more resilient than wider loyalties.

Individuals are subject to the regulations of the village in which they reside. A person whose clan is in one village, who works in a second, and lives in a third, is subject to the last. However, if he commits an offence in either of the other two villages, he may be punished by its chief, and the chief of the village in which he resides has no authority to intervene. The consent of the village chief must be obtained for permanent migration in or out of the village.

Villages are ranked in social position within each district. Persons who are contemplating a move usually prefer to settle in high-ranking villages. The Japanese officially abolished village rankings, but the major change was merely that the ranking system became unofficial. On the whole, the older generation are more village rank-conscious than the middle or younger age-grades.

There are 72 villages with inhabitants; formerly there were three times that number. Uninhabited villages still count as villages with respect to landownership, legal residence, formal political structure, and inheritance of titles. There are communities in which the population consists of several distinctly separate villages for administrative and social functions, although there are no geographical divisions between them. In some communities there are separate chiefs and separate councils for each village unit within it; other communities may have several chiefs and but one council; in still others, the chief and council of one village will act for the others within it.

The larger and more isolated villages tend to have fully developed institutions, whereas the small ones adjacent to other small or larger villages have relatively few.

Some villages are physically and socially isolated from the larger society. They have relatively few visitors and, in turn, do little visiting elsewhere. Commercial transactions with the outside world are limited to a small number of items, production for the market is incidental to subsistence enterprises. Members of such villages have no ambitions to rise to dominance and they cling tenaciously to their own self-dependence. A second group of villages are nearly the opposite in their orientation. They are often the "mother" or senior-ranking village in the district, or have aspirations of achieving ascendancy. A constant stream of visitors comes to the community. Trips to other places are common. Local resources are used exclusively to produce goods for export and the demand for foreign articles seems unlimited. Foreigners are especially wanted as residents and acculturation is manifest in most aspects of life. There is great pride exhibited in the construction of public facilities and in their decoration. Mixed scorn and pity is felt toward the conservative communities. In between the two extremes are the majority of Palau's villages.

The relationships of village to district organization are most variable. The least common, but a major recent development, is that of complete domination of the village by the district. This scheme enables the district chief to issue orders to the villages which they must accept, and permits the district officials to remove village chiefs. In such districts the village chiefs are primarily local agents of the district officials and some village chiefs are used full-time as administrative assistants for the district and perform few village duties. More common is the pattern in which district chiefs are followed when there are questions relating to the foreigner and to district-wide actions, and village chiefs are paramount in purely village affairs.

DISTRICTS

There are 14 districts with both a name and a title, at the present time. Among people of the older generation, the titles are still used, as it is more dignified to refer to a district by title and name. Following the Japanese land surveys, maps marked with names only were used in the schools, and as a result the younger generation tend to use only the district names. Districts are ranked within their confederation.

The areas which make up the districts have, according to tradition, changeless boundaries dating back to ancestral times. The actual composition of districts has, in reality, shifted in a number of instances. It was not until the middle of the Japanese period that a fixed line was drawn for the islands between Koror and Peleliu which had come under two districts.

Today the district is the primary political framework in Palau, but it is not equivalent to the Western concept of "state," as by native customary law it does not have complete sovereignty. The most common pattern is one in which the district has complete control in some specified spheres and restricted power in others. The trend has been towards the expansion of the district's political-social functions at the expense of the village.

The district at present contains an average of five villages with a range from 1 to 11 villages. The median population is about 300 persons, with one district having less than 70 and the largest being in excess of 1,000.

The districts which suffered the greatest losses in the very early period had either to devise methods for maintaining their status or to suffer a decline in position and wealth. They could not put as many war canoes into the sea and hence were more vulnerable to attack, as well as lacking in bargaining power. When the foreigners established their industries they had less man-power to contribute to the labour market, and could produce less native goods for the market, and were at a disadvantage in the rivalry for foreign money and goods. The foreigners located their schools in large population centres in the initial period, a further contribution to the decline of prestige among the smaller populations. Today, several small districts with an eye to the future are resettling their old sites and exploring ways of hastening their growth.

The traditional council and the foreign-oriented council now constitute the two principal political bodies of the district. In theory, both are legislative and administrative. The foreign-oriented council developed on a limited scale in the German era in a few localities and was "officially" established in some districts in the Japanese period. Conflict between a chief of a powerful district and the Japanese administration precipitated the decision. The Japanese removed the chief and "elected" in his place a man from the male line of the same clan who by tradition could not head the ancestral council. In order to form a group he could more easily work with in collaboration with the foreigners, he organized the foreign-oriented council made up of village chiefs. The traditional council was made up of senior-ranking titles in the district and there was little overlapping between the two. As an outcome of rivalry between the two councils, the traditional council became an organization occupied with traditional affairs while the foreign-oriented council concentrated on modern affairs. Other districts soon followed this lead. The ancestral district council has proved to be a resilient social organization, however, and there is some sentiment among the *élite* that eventually it may be restored to its former dominance or incorporate the foreign-oriented council.

The role of the district chiefs also is a study in plural systems. There are a few districts in which the district chief is merely a symbol created because of the demand of the foreigner, in a few others the chief is the dominant figure. In some districts, there are dual chiefs, one who faces the foreigners, the other the Palauans. In several districts, the chief has become involved in larger political arrangements and has turned over his district duties to his administrative chief. In many districts, there are assistant chiefs, established partially in response to demands of the foreigners which the native chiefs could not carry out.

Those who control the districts are the most important political figures in Palau. Though they are limited by village leaders and foreigners, they are the leaders of contemporary Palau.

PUBLIC OPINION

People and events are the continual subject of conversation in Palau. When individuals meet, the first question they ask is, "What is the news?" Topics are not merely social facts. They are accompanied by further comments and speculations on the actors involved. By this process, reputations are made. Important political personages are rather sensitive about invented rumours, for once they are started, the opposition may be able to use them for its own ends, and they may produce general unrest in the village or district. Although everyone is a part of the communication network, there are certain people who are known to be rumour-mongers, expert in character assassination. There is a division between men's and women's news, and distinction by age-grades and social status. Thus the older men of the *élite* class have selected subjects they are especially interested in, and which they transmit within their own circle. A young woman of commoner status would not serve as an intermediary between members of upper classes even though she knew the facts and was the first person to travel from the source of the story to a distant place where there was no prior knowledge.

People are cautious and calculating in expressing their views for fear their opinions may be used against them, or may run counter to those held by the more powerful, or may otherwise be used to their disadvantage in some future relationship. The polite way of talking in Palau is to say whatever the listener wants to hear. Only the foolish and the brave speak bluntly. In the traditional meetings of the council, views were not expressed for open discussion but were whispered to special messengers who carried the opinions to the proper recipients. The exchange of opinions is often accompanied by the agreement to keep the matter confidential. Many of the crucial conferences are held in closed groups, and sometimes secretly.

In sum, Palau exemplifies on a small scale those non-Western societies which have adapted to the modern world and offer to the individual members means for working out personal adjustments to contemporary life within a traditional framework.

ADDITIONAL REFERENCES

John Useem, 1945a; 1945b; 1945c; 1946; 1947; 1948a; 1948b; 1950.

THE SPANISH AMERICANS OF NEW MEXICO, U.S.A.[1]

Note. The culture presented in this section is the culture of an enclave. The Spanish Americans constituted the population of the State of New Mexico when this was annexed by the United States. In the face of a differing dominant culture, of rapid technological change around them, they maintained the values, the concepts, the attitudes of their fathers, not through ignorance of another way of life, but by choice. They accepted a few traits from the "Anglo" culture, plucked them out of context and gave them their own background. They took electricity for their houses, but in general they rejected running water and plumbing, because these were manipulations of nature, with which they were familiar and intimate. They play basketball, and light a candle to the saint for aid in winning. They accepted schooling, but not the "Anglo" motivations for education—the higher standard of living, the better job. When the latest technology came to them in the form of atomic explosions at the New Mexico testing-grounds, many of them had never seen a train or a steamboat. When they become urbanized, they reproduce their village community, and buy a piece of land to till. They choose and reject according to their system of values.

When the United States annexed the State of New Mexico in 1848, the non-Indian population consisted almost entirely of Spanish-speaking people. They were descendants of immigrants who had followed the Conquistadores from Mexico, and had settled in Indian territory in the borderlands along the Rio Grande. By the end of the seventeenth century, they had founded many communities such as those they had known in Mexico. They lived in villages centred around a chapel dedicated to a patron saint. Their cultural contacts were with Mexico. Many villagers tilled their own small plot of land, and also worked on the land of their *patrón,* often a wealthy relative, who had been given a large land-grant, and had assumed a position of responsibility toward the poorer villagers, the *peons.* Not until the middle of the nineteenth century, when New Mexico became part of the United States and the Santa Fe Trail was opened from Missouri, was there any shift in orientation north-eastward to the United States.[2] The original village *peon-patrón* pattern of Spanish American life was not greatly altered by the rancho-trader-army settlement patterns of the first "Anglo" migrants, the English-speaking Americans. The Anglos came into the same territory but with such selectively different goals that the two cultures continued for a period with little intimate contact and with comparatively lit-

[1] This study is based largely on unpublished notes and reports of observers who lived in Spanish American villages, sharing in the daily life of the community. The published material, much of it by members of the United States Department of Agriculture, centres generally upon community socio-economic relationships and problems.

[2] Paul, A. F. Walter, Jr., 1938.

tle friction or functional interrelation. Even in the latter part of the nineteenth century, Spanish Americans began to be drawn into the Anglo economy. In the twentieth century more and more Anglos have come into the region, until today they outnumber the Spanish Americans. Their dominance is more significant in terms of the human relations or technological matters. In place of the entrepreneurs and adventurers of early days are their settled descendants; in addition there are Anglo labourers, employees, carpenters, mechanics, government men, school-teachers, military personnel, members of all the professions. Characteristically, most of these have come with their families to make their homes, and hopefully their fortunes. The whole fabric of the American social system is represented. This has meant the growth of urban centres, of communications, of service trades, of industries, of wage-hour living, of railroads, highways and tourism, of schools, of research and scientific centres, of large military installations.

The shift of cultural emphasis in New Mexico has been rapid and recent. Potentialities for change in the lives of the Spanish Americans have suddenly been vastly increased. What then is the picture in Spanish American communities today? Are changes taking place? In what directions? To what advantage? At what cost? How is it that the Spanish American culture remains so clearly defined in spite of the impact of the Anglo-American way?

Here in New Mexico two peoples live and work side by side, yet each has a recognizable way of life of characteristic vitality. One is an enclave, the other the dominant culture group, the Anglos. The Spanish Americans are in daily contact with the dominant group, at work and at school, and in all political activity. Through sharp legalistic manipulation by members of the dominant group, the Spanish Americans have been deprived of much of their land. They are now suspicious of the dominant group; they fear its schemes for land improvement, its legal papers, the Anglos who ask questions for their records; yet they are in daily contact with this group, and are taking on many of its ways. And, historically and geographically, they form the fringe of another group, the people of Latin America, whose culture, language and religion they share.

THE STRUCTURE

A VILLAGE PEOPLE

The basic cultural fact of traditional Spanish American life is the village. To be Spanish American is to be of a village. There is no keen awareness of special national or cultural identity. Each village has its patron saint, who is a kind of companion-protector for the village as a whole and its individual members.

The average size of the villages is 200-250. Only two of the Spanish American towns studied in a Tewa Basin survey were over 600.[1] A "village" is actually a series of small settlements (*placitas*) recognizing a common centre. Houses are clustered along the river or irrigation ditches or clustered at intervals down the roads. Scattered farmsteads (*ranchitos*) and each small settlement are thought of as an integral part of a particular village.

These villages which are the old Mexico of New Mexico do not stand out from the surrounding countryside. The sandy brown of old adobe and straw, the tan plastered walls, dark poles of the corral fences, merge with the prevailing natural colours. Beyond the squares of the fields and the lines of the irrigation ditches, lies the randomness of sage-brush and tumble-weed, wild flowers and grasses. Signs and billboards are absent, since these towns and villages are not for the chance stranger. They belong to people who depend on one another for their livelihoods and their diversions. To get news of local events, one must become acquainted with the villagers. No local newspaper tells which family has a new baby or has just lost a member; these are vital events but not vital statistics.

FAMILY

To be Spanish American is to belong to a *familia*. "The central structuralizing principle is seen to be that of loyalty and responsibility for all members. And although the first loyalty and responsibility is for members of the immediate or extended family, the principle extends to all persons related by blood or marriage."[2] "Immediate families tend to set up separate households, each with its two or three room adobe home. But not far away are their neighbour-relatives. As the village is felt to be a unit though made up of several settlements, so the *familia*, made up of several households, is felt to be a unit and functions as such. Sons build their own houses when they marry, with the help of their father, brothers and other relatives. . . . But one's 'own house' is an extremely nebulous thing as far as the particular persons in it are concerned. Visiting back and forth goes on constantly. The grandchildren will stay overnight at their grandparents' house, will clean, wash and iron when they are there. It is rare that someone from another household has not dropped in even for breakfast early in the morning, and from then on the unannounced visiting continues."[3]

[1] *Tewa Basin Study*, 1935, Vol. 2. (*See* United States, Office of Indian Affairs.)

[2] Florence Kluckhohn, c. 1941, pp. 22-24.

[3] Ramah Project, n.d.

In the small household, the father is the central figure of authority and under the strongest obligations to support his wife and children. The elder brother (*hermano major*) is recognized apart from the other children and may have authority and obligations which are almost parental at times, explicitly so in the case of the death of the father.[1] The pattern of the father's life keeps him away from the house a great deal of the time, tending to the farm, helping his relatives, working for wages. His leisure time is spent with other men around the plaza or in the bars. He may have to be away two or three months at a time herding, sawmilling, or on some other job. When not too far from home, he may have a son or nephew along with him, but relationships with his young children are distant and inconsistent. The father may be indulgent but he is also domineering.

The pattern of the dominant father is carried beyond the small household to the larger *familia,* and beyond that to the village, providing the structure for the *patrón* relationship.[2] The Church structure uses the same concept of the father (*padre*) as leader, and where there is no resident priest, the *patrón* is apt to function as head of the local church.

The continuity of household life depends upon the mother, whose place is in the home as a matter of course, and whose function is to bear children and care for them. Women also care for small gardens and some domestic animals. They may go and help a neighbour or relative, but they do not work for wages outside the home.[3] In case of the mother's death, a female relative may take over, usually an aunt or a grandmother; it is important that it be an adult, who will nurture the family.[4] But an older sister may take on the care of the family, or even a brother in his teens.[5]

There is a flow of neighbourhood interaction; a woman will go to consult her mother on big and little matters.[6] She accepts her maternal role, which is patterned after a continuing close relationship with her own mother. She may go with her husband to a local dance, or to town; but even on these occasions, children are along and she is not merely a wife; the mother role is ever present.

It is not too unusual to find some children of large families adopted by relatives who have none of their own. Every adult woman is expected to be a "mother" and adoptions bring the childless woman into harmony with the general pattern.

[1] Munro Edmonson, 1950.
[2] Kluckhohn, 1941, op. cit. p. 98.
[3] Sister M. Lucia van der Eerden, 1948, pp. 5-6.
[4] Edmonson, op. cit.
[5] Alice Marriott, 1949, p. 206.
[6] Van der Eerden, op. cit. p. 18.

The specialized roles of woman are concerned with motherhood and the care of others; i.e. midwifery and curing. These specialties are in no sense "careers." Any adult woman, usually one past childbearing age, may gain the reputation of being especially successful in helping her neighbours in child-birth or illness. Gradually she is called on more and more, until she comes to be thought of as a *partera* (midwife) or *curandera* (specialist in curing disease).[1]

Spanish Americans love children and want to have many of them. Birth is a normal process, in a different category from physical pathology,[2] and the *curandera* is never called in—only the *partera*. From the beginning of a baby's life, he is brought into contact with the extended family. Another woman is called on for first nursing, as colostrum is believed not to be good for the baby. Traditionally the mother should stay in bed for 40 days.[3] Even though not strictly adhered to, this necessarily means a great deal of care of both mother and child by others. A child receives attention when it cries and is not taken away from the group for nursing. The person nearest to a baby will pick it up and comfort it if it cries.[4] When the next baby arrives, this warm prompt care is transferred to the new-comer. This does not appear to establish sibling rivalry. Kluckhohn reports that she found no cases of conflict among sisters and almost none among brothers. The sibling relation is a cherished one of affection, companionship and interdependence. Marriott describes how a group of siblings, given a ride to school, arranged themselves in the car without any of the scramble for the desirable positions which is often found among a group of Anglo siblings. There is pride and concern and spontaneous responsibility in the relationship; a 13-year-old boy, having to braid the hair of his little sisters, or to cook their meals, shows no sign of finding this a "burden" or a "duty."[5] Cousins fit into the sibling picture; and brothers, sisters and cousins learn to take care of each other when young, and continue the pattern in later life. There is an identification of interests, and a general equality; and on inheritance, property is divided in equal shares. When an older brother has to assume the father's place, however, he also acts with the father's authority, rather than with the brother's permissiveness.

Children are not separated from the adults and take part in whatever is going on as far as their development allows; only when important guests arrive do they withdraw with the women. Their activities are seldom the centre of interest, their

[1] Ibid. pp. 13-14.
[2] Ibid. p. 8.
[3] Ibid. p. 46.
[4] Ramah Project, op. cit.
[5] Marriott, op. cit. pp. 201-20.

achievements are not demonstrated before admiring relatives. Children are admonished to have *"vergüenza"* (shame, pride, modesty), not to push themselves forward. It is threatening to stand out from the group. *"No te rejis"* (Don't blow your own horn) is a constant piece of advice in Mexican songs.[1] In school they do not vie for marks, and when they are adults they do not exhibit their produce at fairs, nor do they centre their lives in individual aspiration and achievement.

The earliest care of the baby is permissive, and later relationships between parent and child seem generally "easygoing." Obedience is not enforced by parental sternness and high seriousness, the Anglo-Saxon way. School is not set apart as a special area of achievement. A child may decide not to go for a while; he does not have to be sick or make a show of illness.

Discipline of Spanish American children centres in the father. The child is not constantly told that his behaviour is either "good" or "bad"; and when he is corrected, it is because he is "bothersome"; and the mother warns the child to act in such a way that he does not annoy his father. It is better to behave than to oppose.

The mother phrases discipline so that she is on the side of the child. It is not that she is against what he is doing, but what would happen if his father should catch him? She draws on "bogey-men" and "Anglos" also as threatening figures.[2] This identification of interests of mother and child has a replica in the way Spanish Americans think and appeal to the Virgin Mary, as on their side and in a position to intercede for them.

There is no "child's world" in Spanish American life. Play is not a separate activity. Work is not something children are not permitted to do, but neither are they pushed into it. Spanish American children take part very early in the work of the home and maintenance of the family, not "allowed to help" by a rewarding mother, but making a real contribution. There is neither pushing into adulthood, nor postponement of adulthood.

Boy-girl relationships are ideally strictly controlled and highly formal. There is none of the "dating" pattern typical of America today. Adults provide no models for adolescent intersex behaviour, emphasizing as they do the *father-mother* roles rather than the *husband-wife* roles. There is no explicit "sex education." Girls and women go together to dances and sit along the sides of the hall. Men and boys stand around the door. The boy approaches the girl, stands in front of her looking away, and holds out his hand. The girl, also not looking directly at her partner, puts her hand in his. When the dance

---

[1] Edmonson, op. cit.
[2] Ramah Project, op. cit.

is finished, the couple separates. Thus boy and girl solve the problem of being together by formally ignoring one another.[1] This pattern of segregation of the sexes is characteristic of many aspects of Spanish American life. Premarital sex experience is prohibited by these patterns, but the prohibition is reinforced not by moral sanctions, but by retaliation. It is all right if one can get away with it. But don't get caught.

Courting is through go-betweens. One young man may ask another to write a letter asking a particular girl to be his girl friend. Tradition prescribes that marriage be arranged by parents and through go-betweens, and the Church rules that a person must marry outside of the second-cousin degree of relationship.[2] Divorce is prohibited by the Church, and is actually rare. Where it does occur the man is apt to leave the community permanently.[3] The marriage bond is a strong one, centring in the welfare of the family rather than in the "individual happiness" of the members, and powerfully reinforced by the sanction of the Church against breaking it.

When parents have many children they know that they will not be lonely in their old age; their children will live near them, and they will have grandchildren about them.[4] As children give respect to their parents, grandparents command the respect of their grown children and have a somewhat indulgent relationship with their grandchildren. Age in itself is valued and honoured. Children are not expected to go farther and faster than their parents, but to listen to their advice and learn from their experience, to consult the old people and heed their words. The truly aged are cared for by their children and other relatives. There is no traditional community system of welfare beyond the *familia*.

The Spanish American has two major links with the world beyond his village. Both of these are derived from the *familia* system. He is known through his relatives. The ties of brotherhood ensure his comfort and make him feel at home within the larger Spanish American society. His father, even more his *patrón*, is the link with the total community, Anglo and Spanish.

AUTHORITY

Leadership is provided through the *patrón* system, whereby the leading man in the community, whether because of his financial status, his knowledge of the outside world or his personal power, assumes a position of responsibility for the villagers. The *patrón* system reproduces the family picture for the community, and the *patrón* holds the position ascribed to the father

[1] Edmonson, op. cit.
[2] Ibid.
[3] Kluckhohn, 1941, op. cit. p. 1.
[4] Van der Eerden, op. cit. p. 5.

in Spanish American culture. To be Spanish American is to be a father or to be dependent, or both, in different contexts. For most fathers, it is to be dependent on a *patrón*. The older, in general, are in authority over the younger, men over women, and, to some extent, the rich over the poor.

In the more eastern villages, there are no glaring inequalities in wealth; the largest holdings are perhaps 12 acres, and almost all the people are landholders or small farmers.¹ In such communities, the *patrón* principle is less clear, but even here there are positions of power for the man of a dominant *familia*. A *mayordomo de la acequia* is elected annually to supervise the ditches, to see to their cleaning and direct the release of water to the various landowners. A group of commissioners is also elected annually to handle claims which arise between ditch boss and landowners. But they function only when complaints arise and do not otherwise review the work of the boss.

The *patrón*, however, is not elected. He may own the local store, and control credits. He may dominate the local church; the *padre* will stay at his home when visiting the village. He will be political boss, dispensing political jobs. The longer he maintains his status, the more his contacts extend to the larger community beyond the village, the less his activities are understood by the villagers. His position becomes the more threatening, his behaviour more unpredictable. He can say with more assurance: "But if you don't vote the straight ticket, I don't give a damn, because I got plenty more votes in my pocket."²

Throughout the structure, authority and responsibility for leadership, power and obligation for dependents, tend to focus on one person. There are no voluntary associations here, with elected leaders. Society is characterized by already present units: the paternalistic kinship group, the village with which it may prove to be coextensive. Within this, in the appropriate position, the *patrón* rises in authority.

There is no evidence of any comparable dominant role for women. Their status depends on that of their father or their husband, or both. The control exercised by the *patrón* varies as between communities. The more western villages are centred around a rank economy. Here the *patrón* principle is most highly developed; many observers call the situation "feudal." Tremendous property-holdings are concentrated in single families which occupy positions "of benevolent paternity in the minds of the population."³ Dependent households have tended to their own homes and small subsistence farms in the village while working for the *patrón*. Traditionally the

¹ *Tewa Basin Study*, 1935, Vol. 2, op. cit.
² Edmonson, op. cit.
³ *Conservation Economic Series* No. 2, p. 6. (*See* United States, Department of Agriculture.)

patrón allowed these families to graze small flocks or herds on the open ranges and to have free access to water and fuel resources. Dependence on the *patrón's* kindness has been accompanied by dependence on his power, the fear of his ruthlessness, his unpredictability. It would be dangerous to oppose him.[1]

The dominant male has something of a reputation for cruelty, but this is not regarded as the ideal pattern of dominance. It is the "good" *patrón,* the "good" husband, who is praised; and violence has not been patterned. On the part of the dependent, it is better to submit than to act in a way which will evoke anger and possibly violence.[2]

COMMUNITY

To be Spanish American is to be a brother. The basis of this system is again the *familia.* It relates to the solidarity which is set up over against the father-figure—originating in the unity of mother and children. By extension, it is "my group" against others who may dominate. But it includes the atmosphere of fraternity as much as of opposition. The way in which Spanish Americans perceive themselves as members of the same, or of different groups, defines the situations of co-operation or conflict within the system.

The primary group to which every Spanish American belongs is the family. The conflicts and hostilities which arise are inter-familial and particularly between unrelated families.[3] Families may join in opposition to others on one issue, and oppose each other on another issue. Those held together by such interests may disagree over a proposed marriage. In opposition to the family principle, the women of the community make up one social grouping, the men another.

Characteristic of the Spanish American community is the absence of other formalized interest groups. The one exception to this is the *Penitente* organization. This is a religious brotherhood, its members in general being the poorer men of the community—probably those whose interests are least well represented by the *patrón,* and whose influence is otherwise negligible.[4] The leader of this group is called *hermano mayor,* not *patrón,* emphasizing the brother relationship (the brother to whom authority is delegated, rather than the dominant father relationship). The *Penitentes* function somewhat in opposition to the established Church. They bury members free; the Church charges $10. Where the family-*patrón* system fails to provide adequately for economic security, the *Penitentes* take care of members who are hard up, making

[1] Kluckhohn, 1941, op. cit. pp. 94-96.
[2] Ibid. pp. 26-28.
[3] Michel Pijoan and Antonio Goubaud, 1942, p. 44.
[4] Edmonson, op. cit.

loans, giving relief. *Penitente* membership gives prestige where the established order fails to provide sufficient "social" security.[1]

Though there has been a pattern for young men to go out into the world in search of a job, subsequently returning to the village, Spanish Americans, in general, do not go far beyond the known social community; they do not go into a world of strangers. When they travel they seek out relatives. Even distant relatives may arrive uninvited, fully expecting to be provided with food and lodging for several days.[2] This farthest extension of the *familia* joins members in one village to those of another. It makes mobility possible.

Marked anxiety is expressed over being alone—*solo*. It takes the form of a brotherly concern for others who may be alone as much as for oneself. This is seen in the patterns of visiting and hospitality, of adoption, and pity for childless couples. One Spanish American man urged a field-worker to bring his parents over for a visit "so they will know you have some friends here . . . so they won't think you're all alone."[3] Few persons go out into the larger society to "make good" on their own. A state law in New Mexico requires that sheepherders be hired in pairs.[4] Sheepherding in itself is not very hard: *"Es solo y triste . . . muy triste."* (It is lonely and sad . . . very sad.)[5] A man who must go away to work usually goes along with friends or relatives. He goes to make a little money and come home again, not to "be a success."

The Spanish American *patrón* who gains power and political prestige achieves it through the support of his friend-neighbour-relative following. Even he is not *solo*.

There is constant intercourse within the community. Neighbours drop in to borrow, to help, to consult, to discuss news, to bring a loaf of freshly baked bread. There is an interchange of gifts and services. Even Anglos, when accepted by the community, find that their neighbours accept as graciously as they give, and that they are not satisfied until they have returned a gift. If they borrow a car, they will refuse to be paid for replastering the fire-place; if they bring fresh eggs, they will be ready to accept a gift of sugar before they leave.[6] To give a return gift is a sign that the original gift was appreciated.

There is much visiting whether people are working or not. The attitude toward work allows for personal intercourse during the work, so that men visit together either at the job or at the bars, and women visit in the home, at work or idle.

The weekly dance *(baile)* is a major institution. In the more

[1] Ibid.
[2] Pijoan and Goubaud, op. cit. p. 28.
[3] Edmonson, op. cit.
[4] Carey McWilliams, 1949, p. 148.
[5] Edmonson, op. cit.
[6] Marriott, op. cit. p. 179.

remote centres these dances begin at sundown and end by midnight. In other communities they begin somewhat later and last till early morning. At *fiesta* times, celebrations may last most of the night. The people of the village gather at a central hall and a local orchestra plays. There may be fights among the men outside, particularly with men who are from other villages. This is true so often that it seems almost an institutionalized pattern of defence of the women by the village men. One field-worker was told:

They don't like strangers around here and we figured you better get to know the boys before you go to a dance. There are always a few who get drunk and they start pushing around the first stranger they see. . . . It isn't because you would dance with the girls, but because you're a stranger. It isn't because you're an Anglo either.[1]

Church services, school meetings, political rallies and *fiestas* bring the whole village together. The church service is not, however, highly developed as a social occasion. It is an authority situation. When the service is over, the women go directly home. The men may stop to visit or to warm themselves at the fire in front of the church.[2]

School meetings, political rallies and *fiestas* are different. The Spanish American enters into such community activities without obligation, and without typical Anglo restraint and self-consciousness. At a rally, the *patrón* is seeking favour more than dispensing it. He identifies himself with local interests: "All the time we are for the People and against the Public."[3]

Fiesta is the occasion when the patron saint is honoured and celebrated; it is traditionally a time of colour and gaiety. The honour of the village is involved in honouring the patron saint is cherished, more than appealed to, less a *parent* and and the role may vary with the situation. At *fiesta* time, the saint is cherished, more than appealed to, less a *parent* and more a *brother*. Festivities are much in the spirit of baptismal or wedding celebrations when a new member is added to the family, but on a larger scale. Feasting and dancing go along with religious observation. The people are gay, and there may be some who are aggressive.

Fiesta demonstrates most clearly that the Church does not function simply as an external authority in Spanish American culture. The *Santos* are of the villages. They are both revered and beloved. Through them the sanctions of the Church as an institution are personalized and translated into the sanctions of the familiar community. And the relation to the saint is a personal one, imbuing daily life so naturally that only the

[1] Ramah Project, op. cit.
[2] Edmonson, op. cit.
[3] Ibid.

observer notices that one aspect is religious, one secular. For example, a boy describing a basket-ball game blow by blow includes casually in his description the statement that he burned a candle for his side before the game began.[1]

THE STRANGER

New priests, government officials, new landowners are accepted in the village through the sponsorship of the *patrón*; political candidates are introduced through his endorsement.

The newly arrived leader must demonstrate a tireless concern for the welfare of each member of the community, and an interest in daily personal and family problems. He cannot repudiate his leadership obligations. He must be the conservative initiator, the person who will be blamed as well as honoured. To a far greater extent than Anglos, Spanish Americans are ready to assume a dependency relationship with a person in a superordinate position.

The Anglo, assigned a superordinate role, is self-assertive and expects assertion in return. Instead he gets agreement; but this does not mean that his words are heeded when he is not around. For the Spanish American "yes" does not mean "I understand and I agree," but "You are the boss, so I agree."

To enter into a Spanish American community in the brother relationship is more difficult. Familiarity with the mutual expectations of family members is essential. In time he may build up friendship relations which may fall into the brother pattern, and this relationship may be carried to neighbouring villages. He must expect, however, to find himself placed also in the structural situations of opposition of the family of his identification. He can avoid these only through re-assertion of his stranger role.

Acceptance of the stranger can never be complete, "unless he becomes related to permanently established families through marriage. The conduct of transients is frequently criticized, and people comment: 'They have no relatives here.' When permanent members of the community do anything wrong, the tendency is to find excuses for them."[2]

ORIENTATIONS

TIME

Spanish Americans do not regulate their lives by the clock as Anglos do. Both rural and urban people, when asked when

[1] Marriott, op. cit. p. 203.
[2] Kluckhohn, 1941, op. cit. p. 107.

they plan to do something, give answers like "Right now, about two or four o'clock."[1]

Work for wages or in the fields for men, or school attendance for children, regulates the time for meals. Except in winter, breakfast is prepared by seven. In winter some households eat only breakfast about 10 and dinner about four. Children may go to school without breakfast, and sit down to their first meal at noon. In the spring the head of the family may ask to have dinner served when he comes home from work at four. The children will probably be fed when they return from school at about five.[2]

There is a round of seasonal activities, correlated with the sacred calendar, and set within this established framework.[3] But a definite future date unrelated to the patterned round of activities does not have much meaning.[4]

Spanish American culture puts its major emphasis on the established present. Things are as they are because "These are the customs." The past is not venerated, it validates the present; and the future is expected to be like the present.[5] An observer has called this the *"mañana* configuration." But to translate *mañana* as "tomorrow" leads to misunderstanding. The Spanish American does today what can be done only today; he does not put that off till tomorrow. But he frequently does put off the things which will bring him future benefits, which can be put off for *mañana,* for tomorrow, or any date in the future.[6]

There is little place for planning in this framework. Gatherings, celebrations, are usually spontaneous. Children are sent from house to house announcing the dance or the *fiesta* or the "spread," borrowing implements or crockery, asking for help. Though Anglo ways, seeping into the village through the school and through wage labour, are introducing the need for planning, private life still appears to run along the old spontaneous lines.

The orientation of the Spanish American *patrón* is not greatly different, although at first it appears to be. It is not so much that he looks toward the future, but that he takes more advantage of the present. He is an opportunist—not a planner or a visionary. For he must not only make a living, he must maintain *el honor,* the honour of his family and of his village.[7] He must therefore perform with distinction in whatever situation may arise, as it arises.

[1] Ibid. pp. 18-19.
[2] Pijoan and Goubaud, op. cit. pp. 28-29.
[3] Ibid. pp. 41-42.
[4] Kluckhohn, 1941, op. cit. p. 19.
[5] Ibid. p. 27.
[6] Kluckhohn, 1941, op. cit. pp. 17-18.
[7] Edmonson, op. cit.

WORK

Work is an accepted and inevitable part of everyday life. It is a certain amount of trouble but there it is. No need to go out after it. Then it becomes *mucho trabajo* (much work). Spanish Americans are good, persistent workers when they see a reason to work, but they do not consider work itself a virtue. It is not common sense, in their view, to work just so as to keep the hands occupied, or even to earn money when there is money for the current needs of the family because some other adult male is employed. There is no moral corruption in being idle, or in staying away from one's job. A worker may stay away from wage-work, but may spend the day repairing a neighbour's door or helping build a hen-house for nothing. This is needed work and within the framework of community co-operation.

Everyone is expected to do his part, but there is seldom any explicit mention of expectations. Duties are not discussed ahead of time and few verbal directions are given while working, even where a good number of people are working together. The sons usually find something to do or may be assigned duties, but they are not reprimanded if they are idle.[1]

Working-hours are not specifically defined. The day begins between six and seven o'clock and people begin to be busy doing something. Since most of the people do about the same things, according to age and sex, each is familiar with the work of the other. When one member of the family cannot get to work, another will go instead. With jobs much alike, "the job" has little prestige value. In the types of work Spanish Americans are equipped to do, wages will not vary significantly as between jobs.

Although there is a clear distinction between men's and women's work, women will do men's work around the place when the men are away. Men who are off herding or working in towns live together and share the tasks of cooking and minimum housekeeping, without embarrassment. Boys will watch their mother at work in the kitchen and become acquainted with her methods.[2] Fathers are ready to cook for their motherless children, if there is no one else to do this.

There is little anxiety about the future, as far as work is concerned. In this is combined the inevitability of work, the "present-time" orientation, and a dependent psychology. Relief-work in the depression was not thought of as being "different." No one was shamed. No one was "going to the dogs."

Work is shared. People do not want to be alone. It is common for a number of neighbour-relatives to gather first at one place, then at another, for butcherings or plasterings and

[1] Ramah Project, op. cit.
[2] Pijoan and Goubaud, op. cit. p. 29.

even for more everyday activities. This is much preferred to working separately at the same tasks. Tools of work are likewise shared. Co-operation on some occasions involves the whole village. "Though a man can be forgiven for a clandestine affair, he will long be condemned for refusing to lend his farming tools to a neighbour, or for failing to appear for annual clearing of the irrigation ditch."[1] Working for oneself, and not for an employer, is thought of as desirable, because then one is free to work at one's own tempo. "I like to work a little, rest a little."[2] Traditionally, work and rest were not in opposition to one another, but were often part of the same process. There was no eight-hour work-day, no special time for a siesta, no set bedtime for anyone, no time for work and time for rest. Rest and work were both in the nature of things, according to the demands of the present.

FOOD AND NUTRITION

Chillies, beans, *tortillas* and coffee with milk and sugar make up the typical Spanish American meal. The main body-builder in the diet is considered to be the cereal food, and green vegetables and meats are a relish, a luxury food, eaten for the sake of their flavour alone.[3]

The Spanish American raises his own chillies, and blue corn or wheat for *tortilla* flour. Home gardens also provide a wide variety of vegetables in season and onions, cabbages, peas, potatoes, turnips, carrots, etc., which can be stored for use through the winter. In small orchards, peaches, apples and apricots are raised. Each household keeps a few chickens. On a festive occasion an old hen may be killed and eaten. A pig may be slaughtered in the fall, so that pork and bacon are available for a time. Beef is the main kind of meat eaten, usually ground up in chilli. Milk is generally just for babies except for the little taken in coffee. Only a few households own milch cows. Cakes, cookies, candies, puddings are served on ceremonial occasions.[4]

Food in the Spanish American household is set out when people want to eat. The father may ask that a meal be served. Otherwise it just appears. Men may or may not eat first, and often not everyone present eats at the same time.[5] Neighbour-relatives may come in unannounced for any meal with the household. An important guest is apt to eat alone with the head of the house; the rest of the household and local visitors will eat later. Children can help themselves to food at odd times,

---

[1] Olen Leonard and Charles P. Loomis, 1941, p. 19.
[2] Ramah Project, op. cit.
[3] Pijoan and Goubaud, op. cit. p. 38.
[4] Ibid.
[5] Ramah Project, op. cit.

eating a piece of *tortilla,* or a slice of raw potato, or a dish of cold beans.[1]

There are frequent and casual gifts of food between relatives and friends. A visitor may arrive with some *chili con carne* she cooked, or the remains of an open can of fish which would spoil if not eaten that day. Such gifts, like all gifts, are returned, often on the same day.[2]

Nothing is wasted. Scraps go to the animals and the same food will reappear on the table until it is consumed.[3] Meals are not elaborate family gatherings in any ritual sense, except that no one gets up from the table while the meal is in progress. One of the women stands by to refill the pots.[4] Even the *banquete* of ceremonial occasions seems comparatively informal. When there is a large group, everyone does not sit down at once; lunch is made ready and passed around or people help themselves.

The typical low-income diet, patterned by cultural factors, is expressive also of the subsistence nature of the economy. A detailed dietary study of one Spanish American community has revealed pronounced deficiencies. The diet is low in animal protein, as well as in vitamins; it contains green vegetables only occasionally. The lassitude, easy fatigue and poor weight-gain common among growing children, and the irritability present among the younger infants, have been ascribed to the dietary inadequacy.[5]

HEALTH AND SICKNESS

"Better health" for the individual or the community is not a Spanish American concept. The Spanish American considers himself a whole person. He does not have to attempt to perfect himself in this aspect of life any more than any other. So long as he has relatives around him, he is all right.[6]

In Atarque, Florence Kluckhohn found that the presence of ill health was accepted as part of the picture of life. Very little attention was paid to colds, stomach disorders, and other such frequent ailments; only when people, children or adults, were too ill to move about did they go to bed. Doctors were very infrequently called, and only for very grave illnesses. At such times, there was much excitement and visiting, and the patient was given none of the quiet and isolation which is generally advised by Western medicine.

The reluctance to call in a doctor stems partly from the attitude of acceptance which is present throughout the culture.

[1] Pijoan and Goubaud, op. cit. p. 29.
[2] Ibid. p. 27.
[3] Ramah Project, op. cit.
[4] Ibid.
[5] Pijoan and Goubaud, op. cit. pp. 66, 71.
[6] Van der Eerden, op. cit. pp. 17, 35.

As one of the members of the community said: "I do not want a doctor. If the Lord intends that I die, I will die." Actually, Kluckhohn found that in Atarque most adults died of old age. In a 10-year period there were four deaths between the ages of 1 and 34, two of congenital difficulties, one through murder, and only one through the contraction of illness, and that an illness contracted away from the village. There was no typhoid fever in this period, in spite of the unsanitary water supply. In spite of the crowded living-conditions, the malnutrition, the frequency of colds, the only case of tuberculosis reported was contracted during service in World War I. An epidemic of whooping-cough in 1933, which affected almost everyone, took no lives.

The acceptance of illness apparently was supported by this picture, because when, in 1934, for the first time in memory a woman died in child-birth, it was a shock to the community, and, since then, many women call in a doctor for delivery.

The attitude toward infant mortality, however, did not change. As in rural areas of Mexico, there is acceptance of infant deaths. There is no feeling that an infant should be saved at all costs, and little is done to keep a frail infant alive. Infant mortality in Atarque was 30 per cent; and if a mother lost no children at infancy, she was pitied because now she must lose them when they grew older.

There is a sort of persistent hypochondria, not surprising when considering the general health of the population. But it is not characterized by general complaints of feeling bad "all over." It takes the form of practical discussion of localized ailments. Something is wrong with the feet, the stomach, the jaw, the back. By projecting the trouble onto a specific body-part, totality is protected. The vagueness with which the Spanish American regards the future puts the emphasis on the discomfort of the present rather than upon the possible complications which may develop later. Accidents are the source of considerable anxiety, for to be cut or broken in some way damages the whole person.

For the treatment of illness, there is a wide variety of specific herbal remedies, as well as a dependence on general cure-alls. Syrups and garlic-water are general remedies.[1] There is satisfaction in effective home treatment, but the help of a herbalist (*curandero* or *curandera*) may be sought. One practitioner may be preferred to another, but not because to use a special one brings prestige to the patient. Factors of skill and relationship are involved in the choice.[2]

A sick person does not withdraw from the group, for this would make him feel worse instead of better. Being ill has no secondary advantages of care or coddling. The danger of

[1] Ibid. p. 16.
[2] Ibid.

illness or harm is perceived as coming from outside (as, witches in other villages), from the impersonal physical world (as, the light of the moon), from the unknown (as, the evil eye). A person identified as a witch within the community is thought of as protecting the interests of the group. Contamination by members of the in-group is not feared. The group does not ostracize or avoid a sick person. Houses are kept clean and swept, and everyone washes morning and evening; but this seems to have no relation to any idea of germs—of the possibility of contamination from familiar things or activities.

Many of the remedies for illness, those of the home and those of the herbalist, consist of something to drink; a large number are cathartic in effect.

Illness or harm is prevented by wearing proper objects or performing certain rites. Special care is taken to keep children who are too good-looking from coming to harm.[1] The pregnant mother should wear keys on a string and wear a band of cloth tight around her waist.

Charms of the saints are worn around the neck or carried by both men and women, not only against illness but against the hazards of the unknown. Observing the ritual calendar, being filial, being a good Catholic and a good member of the community—all of these seem to have something to do with keeping things right, whether in health or in other aspects of life.

EFFECTS OF CONTACT

The consequences of Anglo contact have not been exactly the same in any two Spanish American communities, and individuals vary greatly in the retention of their original culture. Yet the total image of Spanish American life in the South-west today clearly reflects the importance of cultural values in defining types and directions of change. The Spanish American family that eats beans and chilli may be doing it from preference as often as from necessity. There may be the community that wants a school and "education" for its young people, but nobody gets around to see about it: it will have the school —*mañana*. The man who calls on a *curandero* as well as on a doctor is making peace with himself as well as with his relatives.

When Spanish Americans move from village to city, it is generally to a peripheral Spanish American community. But they do not move readily, and for the most part they do not want to. They often make other types of readjustment, when changes are called for by the changing times.

The first type of change evident in the gradual shift from an

[1] Ramah Project, op. cit.

agrarian economy to wage-work, which began over 75 years ago, was the development of migrant labour. The families remained in the villages; the men went off to work following a pattern already set in ranch life under Spanish *patróns*—the logical direction for adjustment in the villages more dependent on irrigation agriculture, as their lands became overcrowded. The land was already overcrowded in 1875, and the coming of the railroad offered a source of cash income which continued on an extensive scale until 1929. "It is estimated that one person from each family (i.e. household) was a (seasonal) wage-worker in the beet fields, the mining camps, the sawmills, the sheep-camps and on the railroad."[1] Until about 1900, most of this work was in the New Mexico area. After that workers began to go into Colorado, Wyoming, and Utah, where higher wages were commanded. Though the men have gone farther and farther from home, many of the villages have kept a high degree of solidarity.

A second type of adjustment has been the development of crops for market. Since chilli alone is regularly produced in surplus in the area, this has figured prominently in the change. But chilli has not become a true "cash crop." The farmer does not sell it for money and buy goods where he chooses, so much as he trades for credit at the local store, depending on the merchant as *patrón*.

In more recent years, a third trend has become increasingly evident. This is the decline of the more isolated villages and the growth of larger Spanish American towns in more centralized locations, either along main highways, peripheral to the Anglo cities, or within them ("Old Towns"). This appears to be the beginning of rural-urban mobility of small household units but closer examination suggests that it is actually a village movement. People from the same village tend to move to the same towns and seek to re-establish traditional patterns there:

"Why did you move to Grants?"
"Because I had no land to sow. Because nothing could be raised. Very dry for that."
"Do you like it in Grants?"
"Now, yes."
"Why?"
"Because I have a little land. Because I have a house. Now I am able to work a little, rest a little sometimes."[2]

Although Spanish American *patróns* have lost much of their control of commercial landholdings to Anglos, most Spanish Americans have tended to keep their small acreages for house and garden. A striking number of families that have moved

[1] *Conservation Economic Series*, No. 19, 1937, pp. 2-3. (*See* United States, Department of Agriculture.)
[2] Ramah Project, op. cit.

to towns own their own house and land. It appears that at first the men leave the village in groups to work. Later, with increased economic pressure and bad years for farming or ranching, households actually move from the village to a town, if they are able to get a little house on a piece of land in the new centre, and if it is the town to which other members of their community are moving (and where the men have worked). Many of the aspects of village society are thus retained. In addition, there is marked increase of visiting back and forth between relatives in the original village and in the towns. This gradually accelerates the movement to town.

FAMILY

The Spanish American *familia* still functions in much the same way as in the past. Where father and mother go together, the children go along; so do aunts, uncles and cousins. Child-training changes little. In spite of an expressed interest in education, the child receives little encouragement for schooling from the home situation. "All a man needs in school is arithmetic. If he can figure that is all a man needs in his work."[1]

It is mostly young people who begin moving into the larger society and who identify with groups other than family and home-town. But though sociologists speak of their striking Americanization, the young people of 10 years ago who were obviously "going Anglo" are now the Spanish American adults. It seems that it is their children who will be Anglos—*mañana*.

In the city it is as young people that Spanish Americans come into closest contact with Anglo culture. Significantly, this includes girls as well as boys. Spanish American girls take on work outside the home—not only in domestic jobs, but as waitresses, clerks, hospital attendants—which requires them to meet strangers. It is not surprising that boy-girl relationships are changing. Young people are more on their own. Chaperoning is out; "dating" is in.

Spanish American culture depends largely on *vergüenza*—shame, pride, modesty—to regulate the behaviour of its members, and hence its first dependence is on primary groups in which everyone knows what everyone else is doing, while the Anglos around them depend more on "guilt," so that the individual, even among strangers, will be constrained to live up to his code, or suffer pangs of conscience. The Spanish American young person moving into an Anglo world is beyond his own primary group. Delinquency is one of the logical outcomes. "I don't like no city. You learn to steal in the city."[2] Delinquency is not the whole story, but is certainly one of

[1] Ibid.
[2] Ibid.

the problems of cultural change among the Spanish Americans of New Mexico. Later in life, there appears to be a re-adoption of more traditional ways, or at least "disappearance into the Spanish American community." The changes in youth are relatively temporary, and the patterns of earlier training, and the patterns of later family life and kinship responsibilities, are little changed by comparison.

The young person who seeks an Anglo adjustment not only needs new skills, he must also acquire a wholly different set of attitudes of aspiration and persistence. He must become an "interest group" unto himself. He must experience *solo*. He has grown up to be a person in need of a *patrón* and may find himself without one. If he succeeds in finding a new father-figure in the new culture, then he may move further from the Spanish American way. His training has been against any self-assertion except within the balanced rivalry structure of the familiar community, and the competition in the impersonal Anglo system within a framework of unpredictability means an increase of anxiety. If he succeeds in identifying his new interests with an "interest group" in the new culture, then he may move farther from the Spanish American way. Otherwise he tends to follow the more traditional pattern.

The father's position is still one of authority, but his actual control of the situation has diminished. Some of the awe which surrounded the father's going out of the community to work and coming back with dignity was lost during the unemployment of the depression. It is the young people more than the fathers who are the contacts with the outside world. They are the strangers at home, and undermine the father's authority; they may even look down on him, if they have adopted Anglo attitudes.

The role of the mother is still one of care and nurture. Though a woman may have worked outside the home before her marriage, it is very unusual for her to be employed afterward except in domestic work. If changes have been taking place in housekeeping and child-rearing patterns, they are in no way clear. Old people do not receive the same respect as before; but the general acceptance of more traditional patterns as people reach adulthood implies that this is more in the particular relations between youth and age rather than in the total structure. Also "some (old) people think that it is the government's responsibility to take care of them in their old age as their children are not able to do so as they once were." [1]

URBAN PATTERNS OF DOMINANCE

The Spanish American *patrón*, with his opportunism, held out only for a time against the growth of American ranching

[1] Ibid.

and trading business, and then sold out. But the villages still needed a *patrón* and expected to give loyalty in return. It did not matter so much who the *patrón* was, so long as the paternalistic relationship was maintained in a personal way. Anglos have failed to live up to paternalistic expectations, with attendant confusion and hardship.

During the depression the U.S. Government fulfilled the *patrón* role more effectively than at any other time. In 1929, approximately 12,600 men from 14,000 families of the Upper Rio Grande villages went outside for work. In 1930-35, only about 2,000 could get these jobs;[1] "government relief" came into the area to supplement a deficient livelihood. In May of 1935, it was estimated that 60 per cent of the population was receiving some form of government aid.[2]

The large Spanish American towns present what one observer has called a "false front":[3] a line of stores, theatres, cafés, bars, which provide the necessary alternatives for the *patrón* group, who may control the business firms, occupy the few professional roles and keep a grip on local politics. Even when they lose out to Anglos they retain positions of influence in relation to the total Spanish American group.

Contests for local dominance take new forms. One of the growing Spanish American towns has two theatres. They started when one family enlarged its house and began showing movies and the family directly across the road did the same thing. They put up no prominent displays or lights; and inside were bare wooden chairs and benches. There was no sign of competition in terms of greater comfort or conspicuous display; and when one house announced "Dakota" the other showed "Dakota Territory." Each theatre had a loud-speaker and the whole sound-track of the films was broadcast loudly to all outdoors; and the resulting confusion made it impossible to follow either story. It was not a question of choosing the better or more interesting picture. But the Spanish Americans had no difficulty in choosing: they attended according to patterns of loyalty. It is in such new ways that the *patrón* relation works itself out.

In state politics, Spanish Americans have participated from the start and have retained great power. The tendency to dependency and acceptance which characterizes the Spanish American personality, plus patterns of withdrawal from strangers and outsiders, have made the Spanish American *patrón* essential in the hierarchical political structure. Through county jobs, relief, and employment programmes, he has kept a hand in economic matters. Up to now, Anglos have not

[1] *Conservation Economic Series*, No. 20, 1937. (*See* United States, Department of Agriculture.)

[2] *Conservation Economic Series*, No. 19, op. cit. p. 3.

[3] Walter, op. cit.

replaced the Spanish American *patrón* in this role, which requires that the leader be identified with the community as well as apart from it.

COMMUNITY

In spite of the continuing decline of the small villages and the growth of larger Spanish American towns, the Spanish Americans continue to depend upon their community relationships for their personal security. This is the setting of meaningful co-operation and competition, not the larger American society.

For the most part Spanish Americans have identified themselves only with "interest groups" which do not cut across community ties. In the economic sphere, unionism has made little progress. This is true up to now in spite of increasing specialization of labour. There is little "professionalism" in the *patrón* group. Their relation to the local population is too intimate. There are, for instance, no societies of theatre-owners with membership drawn from several centres. Connexions with other communities are still largely based on kinship. In the "social" sphere, some local clubs have become established, but there are few linked clubs. The *Penitentes,* with their religious inspiration and with chapters in many villages, might be expected to form the nucleus of a wide-spread "nativistic" movement, but there is no indication that this is happening.

People do not tend to settle far apart from their neighbour-relatives to assert their independence. The breaking-up of extended family ties which occurs constantly in Anglo society as one brother gets ahead of another is not carried very far in Spanish American society. Indeed it seems almost inevitable that if one member of the family gets ahead, the whole extended kin group is involved in the process and included in the benefit.

Community sentiment works against members of the group who strive to "get ahead" in the Anglo sense. "A *good man* is one who does not do evil—a man who lends money . . . a *bad man* is one who does not want to help the poor."[1]

The Church seems to have less community meaning, but as much or more meaning in the structure of authority. The priest in one larger Spanish American town is having trouble getting people to come to confession, to buy the church newspaper, or to come to bingo parties.[2] But a Spanish American political leader can speak with finality "speaking as a Catholic." The patron saint, identified with the home villages, seems far less prominent. Most local celebrations of the saint have lost their fervour. Secular political meetings have increasingly provided the *raison d'être* of festivities. Yet there are festivities still in

[1] Ramah Project, op. cit.
[2] Ibid.

the old manner, but with new entertainment; speeches are given in English and Spanish, the school band performs, but the scheduled time is disregarded and the occasion is a highly social and highly co-operative one.[1]

For the Spanish American it is still the present, the known and sure, which has meaning. Even nativistic movements fail, because the Spanish Americans want things as they are, not as they were or as they should be. There is no evidence that a Spanish American is interested in "saving time." He may buy a machine or a time-saving gadget, but does not become dependent on it. While it runs, good. When it breaks down, there is no rush to fix it.

The *past* still validates the present, and operates to slow the pace of culture change. When a large landowner changed the source of the main ditch within his lands, the decision at a meeting was against him, even though it was admitted that "this change would improve the flow of water in the main ditch, thereby benefiting not only the man himself but also his neighbours." The change itself was condemned because it was a change.[2]

Spanish Americans have come to put great stress on the idea of education, but it is always "for the children." It is almost never for oneself! Soon these children are old enough to go to work, then to marry and settle down. They want education—for their children. The *mañana* pattern carries along. And in school the teachers have found it very difficult to motivate these children, as they do the Anglo children, in terms of future benefits—grades or better jobs or higher standards of living.

The persistence of this orientation to present time in the face of the equally persistent future orientation of Anglos is central to the whole process of Spanish American acculturation.

WORK, REST, AND LEISURE

Spanish Americans have gone to work in the larger economy but they have not absorbed the pressure to keep busy. They do not look forward to "time off," but incorporate their leisure with their labour. They work by the clock only when they work for Anglos; and if they have "leisure," they spend it in visiting: the men on the job, in streets or at bars, the women at home. Anglos consider Spanish Americans "lazy" and hence in large part responsible for their own difficulties; Spanish Americans consider the economic pressures of Anglo society responsible for them.

Spanish Americans react unfavourably to impersonal employer-employee contacts. "In Albuquerque, the boss would

[1] Marriott, op. cit. pp. 182-84.
[2] Pijoan and Goubaud, op. cit. pp. 22-23.

come along and say 'Hey you, get to work.' "[1] They choose to work for someone they know, in preference to jobs of higher status by Anglo standards. And higher status is gained for the Spanish American by working for a locally prominent *patrón* rather than by climbing the Anglo ladder of unskilled, semi-skilled, skilled, business and professional work.

The idea of higher pay does not immediately interest the Spanish American. There has been a shift from an agricultural to a money economy as a practical adjustment to changing times, but this does not mean that monetary incentives have been accepted. "Spanish Americans seldom, if ever, express the desire to make a lot of money and become rich."[2] There is an attitude of acceptance toward the hierarchy combined with a fear of ostracism for standing out from the group that operates to keep Spanish Americans out of competitive work situations. His status in his own community may be lowered rather than raised by achievement—and he has no other community. It is much more important to be than to do; to be a good son, or a good Catholic, or a good member of the village.

Radio, with its continuous programming, is well suited to Spanish Americans, who like listening to Spanish American "folk" music and campaign speeches. In the larger communities, there are now few or no major events which bring the whole group together. This is a striking change from village life. At home, the radio is a welcome addition.

Young people have taken over Anglo recreations, but with certain differences. At dances, there is still formality in boy-girl relationships and it is not quite right to ask directly for a date. Boys and girls may go in separate groups to a "show," as before; but they will pair off in the dark—a situation defined by the culture as permissive. From here on the new pattern takes over; it is a date and couples come out together. "It almost seems that without the movies, the change could never have taken place.[3]

When the boy and the girl marry and have children, however, they are mainly father and mother, not husband and wife. The old pattern reasserts itself.

FOOD AND NUTRITION

A wide variety of new foods is available to Spanish Americans, and a number have been incorporated into the diet; the choice has been influenced by traditional attitudes toward food. It is cereal foods—the main body-builders traditionally—that have been most acceptable: macaroni, potatoes, oatmeal, bread, doughnuts, cinnamon buns. Along with the introduction of

[1] Ramah Project, op. cit.
[2] Ibid.
[3] Edmonson, op. cit.

breakfast cereals has apparently come the development of breakfast as a special meal, of a different pattern from the rest.

Anglo foods such as ice-cream and bread have prestige, and white bread is considered a food that is more "delicate" than *tortillas*.[1] Such foods are used on ceremonial occasions. Anglo luxury foods have no place at all in the Spanish American diet.

The focus of change in food-habits has been in the items of food rather than the patterns of food-preparation or dining. The items accepted have been those which fit the Spanish American definition of what is good for you, and do not follow Anglo theories of balanced meals.

HEALTH AND SICKNESS

Spanish Americans continue to resort to a doctor only when their home remedies fail, but now they have adopted patent medicines. They tend to regard treatment by a doctor as curative in and of itself: "Mrs. G. feels better now that the doctor X-rayed her."[2] They still consider that operations endanger life and harm the body irreparably. "An operation is as if you take a clay pot, drop it on the ground and crack it; you pick it up and you still have a pot but one less useful than an undamaged one; or it may even have lost a piece, and thus be less valuable depending on the size and position of the shard. . . ." Stories may be told of cases where local remedies cured when surgery failed.[3] The people are uncomfortable when treated with the professional approach of the doctor; they take this for indifference to personal needs. In addition, women feel shame and bashfulness in the presence of a man physician or medical student. In the hospital the fear of surgery, the impersonality of the nurses, the infringement of modesty, the feeling that death is the natural result of hospitalization, all have to be borne without the constant, reassuring presence of relatives and friends.[4]

Ideas of public health and community improvement have not been adopted, in spite of the co-operative aspects of the structure of many Spanish American towns which might lend themselves to the carrying out of sanitary measures. The idea of contamination from familiar people or objects or surroundings is unacceptable.

A state programme of midwife-training has added to the procedures which Spanish American *parteras* may follow, but have not replaced old ones. "Women have been found to scrub their hands before delivery and then pass them through their hair: to boil water in order to sterilize it and next dip their

[1] Pijoan and Goubaud, op. cit. p. 58.
[2] Ramah Project, op. cit.
[3] Van der Eerden, op. cit. pp. 29-30.
[4] Ibid. p. 53.

hands in it from time to time to ascertain . . . the decrease in temperature; to prepare a sterile pad before delivery by putting it in a hot oven and then spread its contents on the hot table long before there is need of their actual use." Spanish Americans regard Anglo medicine as different from their own, but not as more valid or as a substitute.[1] The midwives have added new techniques, but the principles underlying these have not ousted the belief that pollution cannot come from loved relatives or familiar objects.

ADDITIONAL REFERENCES

Conservation Economic Series No. 11, 1937 (*See* United States, Department of Agriculture); Florence Kluckhohn, 1949; *Tewa Basin Study*, 1935, Vol. 3. (*See* United States, Office of Indian Affairs.)

III. CROSS-CULTURAL STUDIES OF ASPECTS OF TECHNICAL CHANGE

AGRICULTURE

Technical change in agriculture is directed at the resources available for cultivation, at methods of production, and at the organization of production. These three factors are interrelated, and whether we deal with water-control, the improvement of land or seed or livestock, basic to all is the work of man, his division of labour, his groupings, his traditional procedures, his relationship to the land.[2] His survival, and often also the reason why he wants to survive, depend on these. He will be the instrument of change; and all change, even in techniques and tools used, will affect his way of life and his relations with others.

The immediate need for agricultural changes arises from the great increase in population in recent years. This has come about as a result of public-health measures which improved sanitation and controlled epidemic disease, through induced changes which destroyed the practices affecting the depletion of population and maintaining the balance through abortion, infanticide, and birth-control; and in individual countries, the United States and elsewhere, through the tightening of immigration laws. If the proposed further improvements in public health and nutrition are carried out, there may be a further

[1] Ibid. pp. 27-28.
[2] Margaret Read, 1938, p. 38.

increase in population. The FAO mission in Greece antici-
pates that by the time its proposals are carried out, there will
probably be some 20 per cent further increase in a population
already dangerously high in proportion to cultivable land.[1] In
addition, there is the hope that the farmers of the world will
not only be able to support life in spite of the mounting ratio
of man to land, but that they will also be able to produce cash
crops, both in order to be able to buy for themselves some of
the many products of technology, and so that they can feed the
growing body of industrial and other non-agricultural
workers.[2]

Certain general changes are proposed, with specific suggestions for particular regions. The general changes directed at
the land and its produce fall in the following areas: soil conservation, including reforestation and contour ploughing; livestock improvement; seed improvement; pest-control; land
improvement; introduction of cash crops; mechanization. Non-
human as these categories appear to be, they actually concern
the life of people at every turn. For example, prevention of
overgrazing and of the burning of brush mean that shepherds,
abandoning the ways of their fathers, have to take on a strange
occupation out of necessity, not from choice. Water-control
may mean that the course of rivers must be changed, as it does
in Greece, perhaps moving people away from the land of their
fathers. Pest-control and seed improvement involve persuading people that these measures are necessary for a better crop.
Indians in Mexico, who see agricultural mishaps as acts of
God, often see no reason why they should not sell their good
seed, since it brings more money, and plant their poorer seed.
In the mountains of Luzon, the Ifugao, believing that pests are
a form of divine blackmail, bribe the appropriate gods to remove them.[3] In the human area changes are directed at wide-
spread ownership patterns, since in many countries share-
cropping and tenancy mean a lower yield and a greater degree
of exploitation of the land, as well as a very low level of subsistence and welfare.[4]

To introduce change effectively, it is necessary to know existing conditions. Where it involves implementation by people,
it must first be accepted. Otherwise the new proposals, however
simple, will be defeated. When pest-control is imperative,
people will nevertheless release the rats from their traps.[5]
Where immunization of cattle is necessary, farmers will hide
their cattle.[6] And where land reform is introduced without ac-

[1] *Report of the FAO Mission for Greece,* 1947, p. 162. (*See* United Nations, FAO.)

[2] William Malcolm Hailey, 1938, pp. 978-79.

[3] R. F. Barton, 1922, p. 403.

[4] Ernest E. Maes, 1942, p. 235; Afif I. Tannous, 1950, p. 263.

[5] S. A. Barnett, 1948, p. 142.

[6] *Time,* Vol. 57, No. 4, 1951, p. 74.

companying measures for a reformed credit system, the land will again be concentrated in the hands of a few within a few years.[1] And since change is proposed in the interests of human welfare, it is important to see to it that it is introduced constructively or, at any rate, with a minimum of disruption and destruction of established interrelationships and values. Basic attitudes, concepts, and values are therefore here considered.

RELATIONSHIP TO THE LAND

The relationship to the land is twofold: tenure and agricultural activity. Within this relationship is often incorporated a man's religion and entire way of life. The agriculture of the Egyptian fellahin, as Shalaby says, "is a highly integrated way of life that is deeply rooted in centuries of tradition. It involves personal emotional expression, family ties, religious sentiment, social intercourse, and firmly established habits of behaviour."[2] In most parts of the world farmers have lived in villages close together, while their fields have been scattered around, sometimes far apart. In regions such as the Middle East, a village is a tightly knit community in which most of the members are related, help one another in need, and work together in communal undertakings. For such people the significance of land "goes beyond its economic value. It figures strongly in many traditions and is the object of strong emotional attachment."[3] In terms of either relationship, tenure of land or agricultural activity, man often sees the land as a kind of nourishing mother, or as something to which he belongs.[4] In Middle Eastern villages there is always some part of the land that belongs to the village forever; it cannot be alienated.[5] This is a common attitude toward land among Pacific peoples; sometimes it is presented in the reverse form, in that man cannot be alienated from the land, as among many Australian tribes and the Arapesh of New Guinea. In general the attitude of belonging to a specific piece of land is common even among peoples who leave home for long periods, as the Greeks do.

When man has ownership rights over land, they may take a variety of forms. The ownership unit may be the tribe, as in the case of the grazing-lands in Saudi Arabia, where agriculture and individual ownership are being introduced together.[6] It may be the village, apportioning land for family use; it may be the family, including a number of adult men; or it may be the individual. There may be a combination of different types

[1] Omer C. Stewart, 1950, p. 27.
[2] Mohamed M. Shalaby, 1950, p. 7.
[3] Edmund de S. Brunner and others, 1945, p. 79.
[4] Virginia Thompson, 1937, pp. 456-66.
[5] Brunner, op. cit. p. 79.
[6] Tannous, 1950, op. cit. pp. 268-69.

of ownership, such as exist in the Middle East.[1] In Greece, as in Turkey and Cyprus, arable land is mostly individually owned, and grazing-land is village-owned.

Systems of inheritance according to which every son receives a parcel of land, or every daughter receives land as dowry, make for a continual division of fields and the scattering of the arable land of a farmer over a wide area; in Greece a farmer's fields, containing a fraction of an acre each, may lie an hour's walk away from one another. Primogeniture counteracts division of land, but creates an army of landless workers.

Property rights may differ. To give an extreme example from a primitive society, among the Dobu of the New Guinea Archipelago there is no land which a man may dispose of completely, with all the rights pertaining thereto. Village land for houses and gardens automatically goes to his sister's children. Land outside the village, which he has cleared and cultivated, can be left at death to his own children; but though he can will them the land and its fruits, he cannot will them the right to eat of its fruits. His children will have to dispose of the vegetables and fruit grown here in exchange for others grown elsewhere. Superficial similarity to known patterns of ownership may be misleading to the worker who is introducing agricultural change.

In many sections of the world we find that the land is in the hands of a few owners, often absentee owners. This condition may have its roots in a feudal past. Quite often, however, it is a recent result of the introduction of change by a conquering people. The great Latin American *haciendas*, affecting the lives of millions of the conquered Indians, came into being by fiat, as state grants. In South-east Asia, the introduction and encouragement of cash crops by the conquering peoples, the disruptive change introduced into the units of administration, the destruction of the native credit system which protected the land rights of the people, and the neglect of the introduction of a reasonable system to take its place—in short, the introduction of change without reference to the existing patterns and without a programme, led to overwhelming indebtedness, a landless peasantry, and the concentration of land in the hands of a few money-lenders, or otherwise of people whose one aim was the exploitation of the land. We find comparable conditions in the Middle East. In such regions land is worked by hired labourers, tenants, and share-croppers. Under these conditions the land does not bear as richly, and it is usually depleted without mercy. The absentee landlord hiring labourers treats land and people merely as a money-making enterprise and, not having an intimate acquaintance with the land, exploits it destructively to his own financial detriment. The share-croppers, sometimes receiving as little as 20 per cent of the

[1] Brunner, op. cit. pp. 79-80.

crop, do not exert themselves to the limit of their ability.[1] In Latin America and in the Middle East, it has been found that whenever a farmer managed to acquire land of his own, his productivity increased. We also have the farmers who, though nominally owners, are so deeply in debt as to be virtually share-croppers.

Agricultural activity is often conceived of as an interrelationship with the cherishing earth. In India the Baiga refused to use an iron plough, since this would repay with harshness the generosity of the land, tearing her breasts and breaking her belly; they found the wooden hoe more gentle.[2] The Hopi Indians do not think of themselves as wresting a living from the arid land, but rather conceive of their relationship as one of aid to the land, which wants to grow the valued corn of the Hopi, but cannot do so without their help.

When we apply change in agriculture, then, we are usually dealing with people who have such deep ties with the land itself, and for whom agriculture is not a way of earning a living but a way of life. If such people are persuaded to grow more of the things they have grown, adding to their own food and getting a cash income, this change in itself is not essentially disruptive. But when the change is from subsistence agriculture to cash crops, a number of disruptive factors enter the picture. To the superficial observer there seems to be no change, since the people are still occupied with agriculture. But actually we now have a radical change, from *making* a living to *earning* a living. And in many societies the change is further, from a value crop, around which religious life centres, to a merely utilitarian crop. Redfield and Warner say of corn cultivation in south-western Yucatan: "It is not simply a way of securing food. It is also a way of worshipping the gods. Before a man plants, he builds an altar in the field and prays there. He must not speak boisterously in the cornfield; it is a sort of temple. The cornfield is planted as an incident in a perpetual sacred contract between supernatural beings and man. By this agreement, the supernatural yield part of what is theirs—the riches of the natural environment, to man. In exchange, men are pious and perform the traditional ceremonies in which offerings are made to supernaturals. These ceremonies are dramatic expressions of this understanding."[3] This can be said of a large number of the corn-growing communities of Indians in North and South America, as well as of those growing potatoes in Peru. When we teach such people to shift to a cash crop, we deprive them of a meaningful area in their lives. Even when we only introduce new techniques we make a break with the sustaining tradition which gives security. We make a break in the

[1] Tannous, 1950, op. cit. pp. 267.
[2] Verrier Elwin, 1939, pp. 106-7.
[3] Robert Redfield and W. Lloyd Warner, 1940, p. 989.

continuity with the unit of belongingness, since identification with this is implemented in terms of taking on its techniques and specific activities. A change in techniques may make shifts in the balanced division of labour, disrupting the pattern of relationship between man and wife, father and son, unless it is introduced with awareness, and unless help is given in readjusting the disturbed balance.

THE MEANING OF CO-OPERATION

Many of the proposed agricultural changes involve co-operation of individuals and of groups. This takes the form of co-operative activity and of the performance of acts for the welfare of a unit larger than the individual or the family, as, for example, in the consolidation of scattered holdings to make the saving of long walks possible for all in the village and to enable all to use more effective implements which are too heavy to carry from strip to strip. Measures such as pest-control and reforestation mean co-operative work in terms of larger units, in terms of the welfare of the villages farther afield, and ultimately, the welfare of the nation. It means working for ends which are abstract and at best envisioned, which have often neither the safety of the known nor the security of faith in a divine plan, since they are the work of man.

Western social scientists find co-operating units in many parts of the world. But the concept of co-operation in most areas is different from that known to the West. Western co-operation refers usually to a group which has been created in terms of future ends for the benefit of the individual members; it is individual collective effort converging towards a unifying end. The co-operating units we find in Africa, Latin America, the Middle East, and China, however, are units with an organic basis deriving from the past and originating in birth, repeating past patterns, not reaching toward the future. Here an individual is born into a family, a village, a church group, and when he acts for the welfare of the unit, he is often merely filling his prescribed role; the "co-operation" is incidental.[1] To the outsider, they may appear to be co-operative, but within themselves they often are not, since they are not collective. They are units, not groups; a Greek, for example, never applies the term "group" to a family or a village. Their ends are common, and not a collection of individual ends; and they are not in the future but part of the pattern of rooted activity. For example, the Middle East peasants who practised crop rotation, terracing, and other soil-conservation measures, were not co-operating toward saving the land of the state; they were

[1] Chen Han-Seng, 1947, pp. 59-60; H. D. Fong, 1937, pp. 6-7; Ofelia Hooper, 1943, pp. 251-52; Charles Issawi, 1947, p. 80; Afif I. Tannous, 1944 b, p. 134.

practising agriculture as they knew it, and they refrained from cutting many of the trees, not as a conservation measure, but because the trees were sacred. In the Trobriands, as among the Tiv, the magical activities in agriculture were performed by the head for the social unit, and by all the members of the social unit.

In order to enlist the co-operation necessary to carry out the new measures, understanding of the existing patterns, as well as careful education, is needed. In Egypt and Arab Palestine, the proposed co-operatives are presented as the continuation of the traditional village co-operation. In support the Koran is cited, and the danger of the loss of land without co-operation stressed, with references to specific cases of such loss. The religious objection that co-operative credit societies charge interest on loans, going against Koran law, is counteracted by the argument that the interest charged is for the purpose of mutual aid, which is enjoined by the Koran.[1] In some of the Middle East countries, however, as in Greece, the government overlooked the existing patterns as well as local leadership and responsibility, introducing co-operation through the central government, patterned after the foreign concept; and the results have not been good. In isolated instances, as when the Near East Foundation instituted projects in Macedonia after a programme of education, there have been outstanding cases of co-operative activity. Not one cent of the half-million dollars which the Near East Foundation spends annually in Greece goes to hire labour; it spends money on education until the villages co-operate freely in the improvement of their land, sanitation, or water-supply.[2]

One form of co-operation particularly relevant to agricultural change is based on the communal ownership and working of the land. Opinion is divided as to the value of this. On one hand, communal ownership assures the unbroken tracts of land necessary to the effective application of some of the proposed changes, particularly for the use of mechanized equipment; in general it means economy of effort. For example, the FAO mission to Greece recommends the wide use of strip farming on the hills, with alternate strips of grass land and cultivated land laid horizontally; but the hillsides are owned in narrow strips of land running vertically. The strip farming chequers a man's scattered strips into tiny pieces, the cultivation of which is uneconomical. A communal ownership of the hillside would avoid this waste. The Panamanians resist individual ownership of land, even when the government offers it to them as a free grant. They believe the land belongs to "the people" and that individuals can only have its use; if they are told that "the

[1] Tannous, 1944 b, op. cit. p. 143.
[2] Apostolos Koskinides, 1948, p. 113.

people" are now represented by the state, they reply that they would rather rent from the state. This attitude goes hand in hand with a co-operative basis for work, which is a social occasion of enjoyment, affording security. In 1940 the First International Conference on Indian Life resolved to recommend support of the continued existence of the *ayllu,* the unit which holds land in common found in several Latin American countries, both for the advantages it affords for mechanization and because of the social function it fills.[1]

The communal ownership of land and communal responsibility in agriculture offer its members security and make possible certain valued social patterns.[2] Among the Tanala of Madagascar individual ownership was introduced indirectly as a by-product of the introduction of wet-rice culture, which made the continuous farming of one tract possible and so led to individual ownership. One of the clans, which valued its joint-family ownership and co-operative labour above material wealth, outlawed the disruptive change and returned to dry-rice culture.[3] The chiefs of Basutoland, who also prize community solidarity, discourage measures essential to the preservation of land, such as tree-planting or the fencing of pasture lands, because these imply individual rights over the communal land and may lead to individual ownership.[4]

Against the advantages, moreover, may be set the paramount disadvantage of communal ownership and the co-operative work group: its resistance to change.[5] From Bechuanaland and East Africa comes the objection that improvements such as drainage, terracing, planting permanent crops, reduction of stock as an anti-erosion measure, meet with little incentive under this system because the results of the individual would be lost to him without the co-operation of his neighbours,[6] and whereas these do co-operate along traditional lines, there is no pattern for doing so in introducing the new practices. And the individual, unable to get financial support from his group for improvements, cannot even borrow for them when he cannot give land as security. The group which recommended the support of the *ayllu* also pointed out this anti-progressive effect of communal ownership. The difficulty is, of course, not insurmountable. It can probably be overcome through education and through a knowledge of the existing structure which can be used in rooting the new co-operatives. The Inter-American Conference suggests such a procedure so as to make the *ayllu* an effectively functioning part of the changing economy.[7]

[1] Hildebrando Castro Pozo, 1942, pp. 11-16.
[2] See also Carl C. Taylor and others, 1949, p. 12, on the Bolivian *ayllu.*
[3] Ralph Linton, 1936, pp. 348-55.
[4] Hailey, op. cit. p. 868.
[5] Tannous, 1950, op. cit. pp. 263-64.
[6] Hailey, op. cit. pp. 869, 971.
[7] Castro Pozo, op. cit. pp. 11-16.

ACCEPTANCE

In many parts of the world we find cultures adhering to the belief that man has no causal effect upon his own future or the future of the land; God, not man, can improve man's lot. This view is held in different forms, from the attitude of the Ifugao of Luzon who believe that man has absolutely no effectiveness of his own, so that each step of each act has to be given its effectiveness by a specific god, to the acceptance of events as God's will or the working of fate which we find in Latin America and the Middle East. It is difficult to persuade such people to use fertilizers, or to save the best seed for planting, since man is responsible only for the performance, and the divine for the success, of the act.[1]

ADAPTATION

In many groups we find the attitude of doing with what is there rather than changing it, of coping rather than fixing. Such people see no reason why "anyt..ing should be done about it." When traditional methods produce some crops, maintain a measure of health, keep some of the soil from running off, or when a cow has some vigour,[2] it is better to cope with the shortcomings, accept the inadequacies or inconveniences, than to effect a disturbing change; in fact, it is possible that adjustment is such an automatic reaction that the inadequacy is not even noticed. It is difficult to persuade people with this attitude that reforestation is necessary until it is too late to do anything about it;[3] they adjust to a poor yield, or to the diminished vigour or milk-supply of their cow until the situation may develop beyond the help of man.

LOVE OF THE WAY OF LIFE

All of these attitudes are, of course, related to the positive value which the traditional way of life holds for many of the people. Where this is paramount, change is either resisted or, if accepted, it is kept along the fringes. Changes which increase income, and are introduced in the interest of an improvement in living-standards, are rendered ineffective by this attitude.[4] Increased income, according to reports, is often squandered while the standard of living remains the same. Labour-saving devices have been known to release time for prostitution.[5] In Spanish American communities in New Mexico, extra income

[1] Nathan L. Whetten, 1948, p. 280; R. F. Barton, 1946.
[2] Near East Foundation, 1949 a, p. 7.
[3] *Report of the FAO Mission for Greece*, op. cit. p. 140.
[4] Tannous, 1944 b, op. cit. p. 143; Whetten, op. cit. p. 303.
[5] Whetten, op. cit. pp. 234, 236.

may be changed to silver dollars and buried in some forgotten place: it does not affect living.[1] In Turkey and elsewhere in the Middle East, the aim of most farmers is to produce just enough crops and livestock for family needs and perhaps only a little over for sale to buy necessities.[2] Experts show concern for women who have to carry water from the village fountain to the home, or wash clothes on the stones by the brook; but the women who are the subject of their concern find in these functions a pleasant social activity and an opportunity to be out of doors. And their men ask, "What will our women do all day long?"[3] It is not enough to introduce more effective and more productive ways of making a living; education is necessary so that the added income and the released time can have the intended effect. Sometimes the people have levels of aspiration which have not been reached. For example, literacy and understanding of policies and processes are highly valued in Greece. Released time can be used in realizing these aspirations, but only if, at the same time, more reading matter is made available, and more centres of adult education are established within reach of the peasants. Sometimes all that is needed is guidance by a leader with an intimate knowledge of the culture with which he is dealing.

NEED FOR ASSURED RESULTS

Most of the farmers of the world are not motivated by abstract ends or speculative results. Statistics that show what will happen if vetch is planted or fertilizer applied are meaningless to them. For them, "seeing is believing." This is the principle upon which the Near East Foundation has always operated, with excellent results. It is a principle that is now being applied extensively in the Middle East. The distrust of new and untried ways is an obverse of the faith in the known, that which with all its ups and downs has supported the society since time immemorial. Unfortunately, it is also rooted in the mistakes made by the agents of change who sometimes managed to persuade the peasants to use new ways which proved disastrous because of local conditions. In Burma, deep ploughing introduced by European agricultural experts broke up the hard pan that held the water in the rice-fields. The weeding of rubber plantations reduced the sap. The new tomato, which the Burmese were persuaded to grow because it was more productive, had a flavour they did not like.[4] In Turkey, experts trained abroad persuaded some of the younger peasants to remove the stones from their tilled land; when the grain sprouted, the fields of the old men had a better crop, since, in that dry climate, the stones served

[1] Florence Kluckhohn, 1941.
[2] C. S. Stephanides, 1949, p. 196.
[3] Brunner, op. cit. p. 99.
[4] J. S. Furnivall, 1948, p. 327.

the function of preserving moisture.[1] In Greece, the wheat in fertilized fields did not resist the drought as well as the wheat in other fields, and the experts realized that earlier-ripening varieties should be planted if the fields were to be fertilized. Mistakes of this sort are acceptable to people who are willing to take the risk of trying the new; but they shake the faith of those who believe in tried and proven procedure alone.

THE VALUED

Programmes for improvement are sometimes rendered ineffective because of failure to take account of what the people specifically value. Values may range in intensity from strong preferences to highly emotionally charged attitudes of a religious significance. Spanish Americans in New Mexico should be shown how to grow more productive varieties of medium-sized cabbages rather than to grow large cabbages, because they do not like very large vegetables. However, it would not very seriously disrupt their culture if they were persuaded to grow larger varieties. At the other end of the scale we have the religious status of the cow in India and Africa. Here we have to find a way of helping without taking away from the people their faith and the meaning of life. If the sacred cows are allowed to eat the crops unmolested while the people are on the brink of starvation, the agricultural expert can give aid in making the land more productive and introduce crops which cows do not like to eat, as was done recently in Mahwa of the United Provinces by Horace Holmes.[3] If the Hindu peasants will not make cheese because this requires rennet from the fourth stomach of a young ruminant,[4] we might concentrate on finding a synthetic substitute, or on finding a different way of processing milk. When Hindus in need of nutritional improvement have refused to eat eggs because it would destroy life, the experts have introduced unfertilized eggs, as "vegetarian eggs," first showing that they did not show any sign or possibility of life.[5]

In Africa, in the societies where cattle constitute wealth, and are killed only on ceremonial occasions and are given in compensation for injuries and for women taken as brides, overstocking cannot be stopped unless this central, meaningful area of the culture is changed. Among people who combine

[1] Nuri Eren, 1946, pp. 282-83.
[2] *Report of the FAO Mission for Greece*, op. cit. p. 136.
[3] *Time*, op. cit. p. 74.
[4] D. A. Soulides, 1949, p. 26.
[5] Brunner, op. cit. p. 68.

cultivation of the land with cattle-raising, there is at least a vegetable basis for subsistence. Among those who are pastoral nomads, there are conditions described as extreme poverty in the midst of plenty, since money is non-existent for food and clothing, and cattle will not be killed or sold.[1] Among such people the application of veterinary science has resulted merely in overstocking.[2] Pastoral tribes, despising any activity not directly connected with the care of their cows, cannot even be persuaded to grow food for the lean months of the dry season, since they see this only as despised horticulture.[3] Such people name themselves after their cattle, compose songs for them, spend their leisure contemplating them, form personal attachments to them.[4] To introduce an economic conception of the cattle to these people, if this were possible at all, would be to destroy value and security. In the Chinese village described by Martin Yang, cattle are classified as members of the household and have a day set aside for the celebration of their birthdays. And beef is cheap in relation to other meat because, in spite of its scarcity, few people will buy it from someone who has committed such a near-crime as killing a cow.[5]

In many primitive societies the large amount of time and human energy spent in ritual, magic, and other religious practices seems to be wasted in the eyes of the agricultural expert. But to the native, they give him faith in his work, saving him from the anxieties which so often attend the work of the cultivator; and where agriculture is a total pattern of life rather than a means of earning a living, this means only that the areas of religion and agriculture are not compartmentalized. Instead of putting all his religion into Friday, Saturday, or Sunday, he practises it as a part of his daily activities. Even from the point of view of work efficiency, these practices may not be wasteful: Malinowski has shown how they are the organizing principle of agricultural work among a people for whom organization has to be inherent in the pattern.[6]

Sacred groves and the value attached to special trees, which have helped in soil conservation, must also be given consideration. During World War II, a United States Government agent almost caused a mutiny among his workers in a Latin American country when he ordered that mangoes, held sacred by these people, be cut down to make ground available for a crop needed for the war.[7]

It is against this background that the proposed measures should be viewed.

[1] Hailey, op. cit. p. 882.
[2] Ibid. p. 886.
[3] Ibid. p. 972.
[4] E. E. Evans-Pritchard, 1940, pp. 18-19, 36-48.
[5] Martin Yang, 1945, pp. 47-48.
[6] Bronislav Malinowski, 1926, p. 81; Bronislav Malinowski, 1935.
[7] Charles P. Loomis, 1950, p. 126.

SOIL CONSERVATION

Contour Ploughing

In Africa this goes against traditional ways and makes a break in continuity with the valued ancestors, who sanction the traditional methods. However, this same sanction of social continuity was used effectively in the introduction of contour ploughing in French Africa; men were persuaded to use the new methods in order to pass the land unharmed to their descendants. In Greece, where people have "to be shown," the Near East Foundation had terraces made on a hillside which stood when the rest of the land was gullied during a torrential rain.

Measures against Overgrazing and Burning Forested Land

These run counter to the principle of livestock as value rather than a means of subsistence. In places like Greece, to limit grazing would mean to take from many shepherds their life-work and, in fact, their valued way of life, since sheepherding is a traditional occupation, tying in with the past. Such measures need also to utilize present concepts of co-operation, or to educate in new ones. A programme involving soil conservation and the improvement of sheep breeds for better nutrition and improved economic conditions, and involving severe limitation of flocks, was carried out successfully in recent years among the Navaho Indians. Demonstration, as well as real guarantees against financial loss, went far toward persuading them to accept the new practices.[1] In Africa, teaching natives to substitute money for cattle as their bride-price is no solution to the problem; if it helps to correct overgrazing, it also means that men will have to leave the village to make money, disrupting village and family units as well as harming cultivation or crops. The growth of towns in the Egyptian Sudan has resulted in excessive cutting of trees for firewood on the outskirts, as well as overgrazing.[2]

Reforestation

Persuasion by demonstration in this area is difficult, since it takes too long for the effects to be apparent. In addition, it should be remembered that there are special difficulties, as in Greece, where the water has to be carried up to the seedlings in the summer at a time when the farmers are at their busiest.

[1] Taylor and others, op. cit. p. 15.
[2] E. N. Corbyn, 1945, pp. 188-89.

IMPROVEMENT OF YIELD

Pest-Control

Here the peasant has to be persuaded that he actually can control pests. There is also a need to learn to co-operate in terms of a wide group. In Greece, farmers are required to report the presence of locusts, and then to give "compulsory free labour" in setting down poisoned bait. As this is a measure imposed by the central government, whose authority is not respected, and since the peasant does not see that it concerns his own meaningful unit, it has not met with success. Farmers either do not report locusts, or, if they are called to work, they are often so careless in their haste to lay down bait that the livestock is also poisoned.[1]

Fertilization

In some societies, a garden greener than one's neighbours' is considered to have been achieved only by robbing the neighbours' fields of their fertility, and farmers may hesitate therefore to use fertilizer. In other regions, farmers will have to be convinced that it can be effective in the improvement of their yield.

Improved Seed

Remarks under "Contour Ploughing" and "Measures against Overgrazing and Burning Forested Land" also apply here. In addition, where new varieties of seed have to be bought, low interest-rates are needed in some areas. Practices and beliefs concerned with seed will have an effect in the acceptance of new varieties. In some areas people feel themselves to be closely bound organically to the seed of their land or of their unit. In Oceania, in Dobu and among the Trobrianders, yams descend like people within a family line, and will grow only for their kin. Among the Arapesh and Kwoma, a man cannot eat of the fruit of the seed yam which he has planted.

Crop Rotation

Writers point out that the agricultural worker must take the present patterns of rotation (as in the Middle East and Africa) into account and base changes upon them.

LIVESTOCK IMPROVEMENT. INTRODUCTION OF NEW KINDS OR BREEDS, UTILIZATION

It would be utterly destructive or useless to attempt the introduction of different kinds of livestock where the present kind

[1] *Report of the FAO Mission for Greece*, op. cit. p. 145.

incorporates the values of the society. Improvement of breed has been effected successfully among the Navaho, and is in process in Greece through the programme of artificial insemination. Here difficulty is encountered because the Greek peasants hold that an ox is a more vigorous draught-animal if he has not been castrated until he was 12 or even 18 months old; so sexually mature bullocks interfere with the attempts to improve the breed through artificial insemination.[1] Before improvement is undertaken the worker must consider that often the existing breed is the only one that will thrive under existing conditions of feed and climate.

The place of livestock in the culture varies. In Greece, cattle are draught-animals. They are almost never raised for beef. Except in the villages around Athens and Salonika, where the urban groups have learned to drink cow's milk, they are not milked either. Sheep and goats are raised for their milk and for their flesh, to be eaten on festive occasions; but wool and hair are considered only as by-products.[2] The worker should base his attempt to persuade the peasants to kill hens at an earlier age on some point other than a better quality of flesh, since the coarser grain and stronger flavour of the flesh of the old fowl may be preferred.

Agriculture experts mention the need to teach the value of keeping records on milk production, fertility, etc. However, sometimes these records do exist in forms which are not recognized. An American visitor, astonished at seeing an African veterinary send back unmarked to the herd the cattle he was inoculating, discovered that all the cattle were known to him by name individually.

The expert should not assume that the combination of cultivation and livestock will necessarily mean fertilized fields. In Greece one-fifth of the animal manure is used for fuel.[3] In sections of Africa where cattle-herding is exclusively a masculine occupation, cattle are herded at great distances from the fields, which are cultivated by the women; and manure drops where it does not improve cultivation.

INTRODUCTION OF CASH CROPS

Among many groups the introduction of cash crops has resulted in lowered nutrition, since the farmers are tempted to put their best efforts into the cash crop, or to sell the best.[4] The increase of a tropical disease, found to result from predisposing malnutrition, is more prevalent in cash-crop areas.[5] In East Africa the raising of cash crops necessary to pay money taxes

[1] Near East Foundation, 1949 a, op. cit. p. 7.
[2] *Report of the FAO Mission for Greece*, op. cit. p. 107.
[3] C. S. Stephanides, 1948a.
[4] Hailey, op. cit. p. 961; John F. Melby, 1942, p. 452.
[5] H. C. Trowell, 1950.

has forced men into what used to be a woman's area traditionally; when the men resisted this, they had to work for wages away from the security of home. In Brazil the development of cotton-growing has been destructive to social welfare and has led to increased renting and share-cropping, with accompanying exploitation of the land.[1] In Malaya, where small rubber holdings form the cash crop of the farmer, they are a source of tension in the country's economy, since when supply is high and prices are low, the farmers produce even more rubber in order to make the necessary money.[2] In the areas where the subsistence crop is of high emotional value, the introduction of cash crops meets with strong resistance.

MECHANIZATION

The introduction of mechanized tools is confronted by an obstacle in the small size of many holdings. Recent programmes of land reform have been responsible for the breaking up of holdings in a number of areas. In China, where narrow scattered strips have been traditional, the National Reclamation Farms found tractors uneconomical.[3] In Egypt the many dikes and canals that chequer the fields present an additional difficulty.

In French Indo-China the introduction of machinery into agriculture has desanctified the land for the Annamite peasants to some extent; this means that it is a little easier to persuade them to leave the land, to which they are very strongly attached, to colonize or work as contract labourers.[4] Even so apparently small a change as that from a wooden to an iron plough may have wide-spread repercussions. Hadary suggests that a heavier plough is inadvisable in Iran as it would be too heavy for the draught-animals now used, and might also expose the soil to wind erosion unless the introduction is preceded by different ploughing methods.[5] The iron plough has sometimes been resisted as an assault upon the land. In villages of the United Provinces of India, it threatens established human relationships.[6] A man inherits a relationship to a carpenter family whose task it is to make and repair the plough. This family is always invited to the farmer's feasts, and the women are given *saris*. The relationship, the "pay," the gifts continue whether ploughs are made or not. It is part of a pattern of interdependencies, and of the structuring of responsibility, so that it is not direct self-responsibility, but circular. Perhaps the farmer can be taught to repair his own plough,

[1] Carlos B. Schmidt, 1943, pp. 243-46.
[2] Erich H. Jacoby, 1949, pp. 117-18.
[3] James Y. T. Yu, 1948, pp. 297-98, 300.
[4] Virginia Thompson, 1937, op. cit. pp. 456-66.
[5] Gideon Hadary, 1949, p. 211.
[6] Morris Opler, personal communication.

but it would mean personal reorientation as well as a change in the valued relationship structure. Again, because of the extremely short ploughing season, it is necessary that there be no delays; an iron plough with brittle shears needs frequent repairs and replacements by experts who can be reached only after covering a distance over bad roads. But the carpenter is in the field with the farmer, ready to repair the wooden plough. Then too, an iron plough would require heavier draught-animals, which in turn would need more fodder than is now available. The wooden plough is light and can be carried easily from strip to strip, and a farmer has probably five widely scattered strips to plough. In order to introduce a heavy plough at all it is necessary to persuade the villagers to consolidate their holdings. The government has decreed that when 75 per cent of the villagers demand consolidation, the rest will have to accede. Until a few months ago, only one village had demanded consolidation of holdings, and even then when the farmers realized that this meant each would have to give up strips treasured because of location or ancestral association, the project fell through.

In some areas it is uneconomical to introduce mechanization because human labour is cheaper, and remains cheaper because the people themselves place a low valuation upon it. In Indonesia the workers fatalistically accept the fact that the rate of pay for buffalo labour is twice that of human labour.[1] In the Philippines, where more than half the holdings are less than two hectares, farming occupies only about 75 eight-hour days of the year for the peasant, and the absence of a diversified economy means that there is no other systematic work to occupy a man.[2] Even if it were possible, through consolidation, to make the introduction of mechanization feasible, we would be leaving the farmer with even less of the creative work of which he now has too little.

In general, mechanization can have an overwhelming effect on human welfare by rupturing the nourishing continuity of man with the land, with his own body rhythms, and with his traditional past. In cultures such as those of the Middle East and Greece and of Latin America, where desires and aspirations have limits, mechanization will probably mean not that man will cultivate more land, but that he will work less, and at a less satisfying occupation at that. Where work, particularly traditional work, is life, this may be a serious matter. Jacoby further finds that mechanization, such as the use of tractors designed for soggy rice land and the self-propelled threshers in South-east Asia, has meant the shifting of tenant labour to hired labour and has led to the dislocation of the tenant group, often separating the members from the burial place of their

[1] Jacoby, op. cit. p. 152.
[2] Ibid. pp. 90, 176-89.

fathers, from land which they had previously owned and with which they and their families had been continuous.[1]

ADDITIONAL REFERENCES

Hugh Hammond Bennett, 1939; "Contrast in Method," 1950; "Co-operative Stores in Ceylon," 1943; Moses Das, 1947; Selma Ekrem, 1947; Charles R. Enlow, 1948; "European Programs for Expanding Farm Production—Turkey," 1949; *Farmers in a Changing World*, 1940. (*See* United States, Department of Agriculture); A. Irving Hallowell, 1937; J. C. Kumarappa, 1949; Bruno Lasker, 1950; Roseric Matthews and Matta Akrawi, 1949; K. G. Menon, 1949; Near East Foundation, 1949 b; 1950 a; 1950 b; F. S. C. Northrop, 1949; Morris Opler and Rudra Datt Singh, 1948; Graham S. Quate, 1950; E. R. Raymond, 1949; "Report of a Trip to Langada, Sohos, Sckepasto, Mavrouda and Pente-Vrysses," 1950; Peter K. Roest, 1942; P. N. Sampath, 1939; Omer Celâl Sâre, 1948; "Self-Government in Turkey," n.d.; Lauriston Sharp, 1950; Afif I. Tannous, 1947, 1948, 1949 a, 1949 b; Laura Thompson, 1949, 1950; Laura Thompson and Alice Joseph, 1945; E. W. F. Tomlin, 1940; Moises Poblete Troncoso, 1940; "Turkey's Agricultural Land," 1945; John W. M. Whiting, 1938; Charles Wisdom, 1940.

NUTRITION

The low level of nutrition in most areas of the world is one of the main concerns of the present-day world. Sheer hunger is prevalent, and there is the hidden hunger of people who live on inadequate food. We do not know whether the food-supply of the world was ever adequate everywhere. Certainly with the increase in population which accompanied contact with Western civilization, with industrialization and its by-products, the supply has become inadequate. Increase of crops has not kept up with the population growth, even though since the war plans for increasing agricultural yield have been put into operation. And industrialization itself has had a great effect on nutrition. Where the concentration of population has encouraged the growth of a cash-crop economy, this has meant impoverishment of the soil, because old conservation measures were abandoned in favour of immediate cash benefits, as well as because many people entered the area of agriculture who thought of land only as something to exploit commercially.[2] In addition, it has meant that fewer food crops were planted for the farmer's own use. The wide-spread syndrome *kwashiorkor*, which causes many deaths in the tropics, is found to be correlated with a cash-crop economy in Africa.

[1] Ibid. pp. 19-20.
[2] John F. Melby, 1942, pp. 455-65.

It is uncommon in the less sophisticated areas where mixed farming is still practised.[1] In Africa, industrialization has often meant the disruption of the agricultural cycle, since the men, who traditionally helped at certain key points, were now away earning wages, and in many sections this has meant that the village has had to import four-fifths of its food. The building of railroads, on the one hand, has meant that a greater variety of foods can now come to the city, and from greater distances; on the other, it has encouraged sending fruits and vegetables from great distances, and so they now have to be picked unripe, without their full complement of nutrients, to reach the city in good condition, and they must be sold at too high a price to form a bulk item in the diet of the ordinary city worker. Katsigra,[2] writing on food in Athens, describes exactly such a condition among people who, when in their native village, had eaten mainly fruit and vegetables.

Again, the increase and concentration of population has sometimes destroyed the very sources of the food. In Greece, after deforestation came the use of manure for fuel, which resulted in less fertilizer and poorer crops.[3] In Liberia, the bush in the *hinterland* has been progressively cut down, and this means that the game, which furnished most of the meat, has disappeared accordingly.[4]

In many areas, overpopulation has meant overcultivation, and the poverty of the soil has been reflected not only in diminished returns but also in crops deficient in essential minerals. It has meant soil erosion and the carrying away of the top soil as silt, so that farmers, as in Korea, have to go now to the mouths of streams to scoop up the land by the handful and carry it back to grow their food.

Not all difficulties in the realm of nutrition are due to contact with Western civilization, however. In the Middle East and the Far East, for example, nutrition is affected by the lack of methods for preservation. Any animal slaughtered must be consumed immediately, since there is no refrigeration, and methods of storing are almost completely lacking.[5] There is some spread of meat through the year, however, since anyone who slaughters must invite guests to a feast to help him finish the meat; and this means that he in turn will be invited to eat when his guests kill their own animals. In Rumania, when cattle had to be killed because of a three-month drought, the meat had to be consumed immediately or rot.[6] We also find here and elsewhere, that fruits and vegetables are not pre-

[1] H. C. Trowell, 1950, pp. 161-63.
[2] Anna Katsigra, n.d.
[3] C. S. Stephanides, 1948 a.
[4] Don Looper, 1950, p. 113.
[5] E. J. Bell, 1950, p. 162; Afif I. Tannous, 1943, p. 252; Afif I. Tannous, 1944 a, p. 40.
[6] Nathan Koenig, 1949, p. 176.

served, so that they can be eaten only seasonally. In the Middle East, for example, figs and grapes can be eaten only two months a year. Sometimes traditional methods of preservation have been lost as a result of outside contact; more often, ways of storing new products are not known. In Africa, poor storage methods have resulted in the development of toxic elements in rice.[1]

Lack of adequate transportation has also meant poor nutrition. Egyptian fellahin need citrus products, but cannot get them even though they grow not far away. In China, a surplus of food in one area cannot alleviate famine in another, since the food cannot be brought to the hungry population.[2]

Poor nutrition cannot, then, be attacked by the dietician alone. Agricultural specialists in Greece are working for nutrition when they institute reforestation. Programmes centering around the health of the *carabao* in the Far East are aimed at nutrition through the improvement of cultivation, since these are the essential draught-animals in agriculture.[3] Or programmes attacking rinderpest and hoof-and-mouth disease may be aimed directly at the source of food-supply. In Greece, the DDT campaign was instituted partly as a measure to increase food production through decreasing the depletion of man-power in the farms, due to malaria. Workers starting a health programme in Matandan, India, found that it was useless to give medicine to hungry people, and instituted a nutrition programme.[4] And public-health workers, becoming aware of the pressing need for better nutrition, find themselves in the field of agriculture, advocating better seed and more efficient methods of preservation.

It is not enough, however, to increase the available food-supply. What has been supplied must be considered food, and acceptable food, by the people. In Africa, the British Government supplied veterinary service to cattle-raising tribes, but this did not increase their food supply at all, and actually contributed to soil erosion and depletion. These people love their cattle as they love members of their family, and kill them only on ceremonial occasions; since the ceremonial occasions did not increase in number, the saving of cattle through veterinary aid merely resulted in too many cattle on the land. Again, it is a commonplace that to increase the number of pigs in a Moslem country does not mean to increase the available food-supply at all; so ingrained is the religious prohibition against the eating of pork that there is disgust at the mere thought of eating pigs as food, and a Moslem will not do so, however hungry he may be.[5]

[1] William Malcolm Hailey, 1938, p. 123.
[2] Koenig, op. cit. p. 173.
[3] Ibid. p. 173.
[4] Edmund de S. Brunner and others, 1945, p. 69.
[5] Tannous, 1943, op. cit. pp. 254-55.

To introduce adequate nutrition, it is important to bring about changes that are in keeping with the established food-habits of the people, and are acceptable within the framework of their value system. In most societies, food is the focus of emotional associations, a channel for inter-personal relations, for the communication of love or discrimination or disapproval; it usually has a symbolic reference. Therefore, unless the place and the function of food, its preparation and consumption within the total culture, are taken into account, the introduction of change, however apparently limited and harmless, can be very disruptive. For example, in the United States in the South, mothers cook food the way each child likes it, compensating for the poorness and monotony of the ingredients; and any change in the preparation of food would introduce change in personal relationships. In some societies, the breast or other food is offered to the child after punishment; if we persuade these people to offer the breast only at scheduled feedings, or teach them that it is harmful to eat between meals, we have made ourselves responsible for finding some way in which the mother can give reassurance and acceptance to the punished child. Again, if we teach mothers to nurse their babies according to schedule, we run the risk of having the baby sleep at a distance from the mother, who cannot then exercise her customary watchfulness against smothering, getting cold, falling into the fire or out of bed.

In some societies, where meals end with a sweet dessert, mothers withhold dessert as a way of punishing the child; this results in a devaluation of that part of the meal which contains the main elements necessary for nutritional balance, and the child has to be urged to eat them because "they are good for" him. Yet mothers depend on this form of punishment, and will resist attempts to change this stress on the dessert. Again, where milk and pulped food are associated with infancy, men will resist the drinking of milk or eating of pulped foods in special diets which call for them. Where home and food are strongly identified, children reject the school meal, and men the meal at the plant; and business concerns in such countries often give their employees a longer lunch-hour, or arrange the work day in such a way that men can eat their meals at home.

Nutritional precepts have interfered with patterns of caring for children or of personal relations with the husband. Housewives may be urged by the nutritionist to cook vegetables just before serving, so as to preserve their vitamins; and by the child-care specialist to bathe their children at this time, or read to them. This is also the time when the husband, away at his work all day, comes back eager for his wife's exclusive companionship.

A study made by the Committee on Food Habits of the National Research Council in the United States during World

War II has made workers aware of the importance of the "role which learning plays in the maintenance of a viable dietary pattern. We now ask, not how we change a people's bad habits into good habits, but what are their habits, how are they learned, by what mechanisms are the self-preservative choices of some foods and rejections of others, perpetuated."[1] We have to know the pattern of the meal and the meaning of the meal in the life of the people; we have to know whether a mother is expressing her impulse to create when she produces a meal, or whether she is showing her love to her family or her husband or a particular child through the preparation of a special dish; or whether she is merely following a meaningful pattern, preparing the food appropriate to the occasion. Knowing this, we are aware that if we must make a substitution, this should also substitute adequately for the lost symbol. A dietary survey is not enough: it does not tell us who gets the lion's share, who gets the titbit, who has to settle for the least desirable— but sometimes the most nutritious—share of food. It sometimes intimidates or antagonizes people who have learned to suspect questioning as a means of setting a base for taxation, or it introduces prying in an area which is felt to be private.[2]

FOOD PATTERNING

In many areas of the world, people whose nutritional pattern appears, according to Western standards, to be inadequate, actually present a picture of health. In sections of Africa where mixed cultivation is still practised and cash crops have not been taken up, the nutritionists have been surprised to find such health and growth as presupposes adequacy of diet. In Siam, where meat proteins are not sufficient and minerals and vitamins are lacking in what are considered adequate amounts, malnutrition is, nevertheless, absent. Authorities on the Far East point out that in many areas the people actually have an adequate diet, either because they eat nutritious parts of the plant or animal which elsewhere are often thrown away as waste, or because they have achieved an adaptation to economical use of the food eaten.[3] It appears that cultures like these found a dietary balance which gave them nutritional adequacy and a basis for health. Even the polished-rice diet, which in this century was found to be basic to beriberi, was noticed only after contact with industrialization, direct or indirect. In countries like Burma and Siam, where more than one pound of polished rice *per capita* is consumed daily, the vegetables, herbs, and fish products which accompany the rice in

[1] Margaret Mead, 1950 a.

[2] Michel Pijoan and Antonio Goubaud, 1942, p. 8; Tannous, 1943, op. cit. p. 247.

[3] Bell, op. cit. p. 163; G. H. Gunn, 1947, p. 514; Hailey, op. cit. p. 1122; W. I. Ladejinsky, 1942, p. 169.

the rural areas apparently make up for its nutritional deficiencies. In Lower Burma, however, where a cash-crop economy flourishes, malnutrition is reported. In general, the introduction of a money economy has been a serious factor in nutritional imbalance. In Africa, for example, a good balance had been achieved through some process unknown to us; it depended on the agricultural cycle, the crop rotation, the ceremonial cycle, the division of labour between men and women, and between age-groups. When these cycles and the divisions of labour were disturbed or destroyed, the dietary balance was also gone. Given money as the base for creating a meal, the people have no traditional pattern on which to fall back, and, in fact, they usually have to make their choice entirely on the basis of expense and availability. In Greece also, the rural areas show unexpectedly sturdy health and longevity among those who have survived the hazards of war; but the urban areas, for all their methods of preservation and their transportation facilities, have shown nutritional deficiency in recent years. A pediatrician, writing for women who are at least moderately well-to-do, suggests that city babies be given supplementary food earlier than village babies, since the village mother's milk is richer in vitamins.

Where food patterns reflect cultural structuring and values, any change introduced into the society may produce imbalance. With many peoples, as among the Ifugao of Luzon for example, meat was a by-product of religious sacrifice, or validation. There was no difference in the meat consumption of poor and rich; however, it was always the rich who killed and distributed the meat. Where this continuity between rich and poor has disappeared in the society, the diet of the poor is thrown out of balance. And contact often makes such occasions disappear also. The Ifugao killed fowl or *carabao* only as sacrifices to buy the goodwill of the deities, and particularly to bribe them to give health. If we introduce Western concepts of disease and health and of causation, we should do so in a programme which takes account of the effect of these changes on the nutritional pattern.

It is necessary to know also the pattern of meals during the day; which eating, for instance, is unimportant, except as a response to hunger? In Greece, breakfast is not considered a focus of value as a family ritual; and change here would not introduce disruption. The patterning of each meal itself must also be known. The Committee on Food Habits found that where one item in the meal formed the emotionally charged focus, nutritional change could be introduced much more easily through the subsidiary items. In the United States, for example, where meat on a platter or in a casserole is the central item at dinner, the substitute for this during periods of shortage is not determined by nutritional interchangeability, but rather by ability to substitute in an aesthetic whole. Where large groups of women were fed in one educational institution, the substitute was often fried eggplant, detested by most of the students, but acceptable because the fried slices could be arranged on a platter in imitation of chops or slices of meat.

To know what is being eaten, as well as the meaning of the food, it is necessary to know that pattern of food throughout the year. In regions where there are many ceremonials, we often have special foods which can be eaten on special occasions. In Greece, for example, there is a special, extremely nutritious dish cooked once a year after the midnight service on Easter Eve, when Christ is declared to be risen. There is a special preparation of wheat for funerals and for frequent memorial services thereafter. There are special foods for Lent, to take the place of those which are forbidden. Meat itself, as a main item instead of a flavouring, is traditionally a festive food or food for hospitality. These foods have appropriateness, and often a strong emotional association with specific occasions. To displace them, to make them ordinary, may rob life of a meaningful part. This is what has actually happened in the cities, where the wonderful Lenten dishes are served as accompaniments to cocktails the year round. But it is part of the change which has also meant worse nutrition and worse health in the cities.

In many societies we find that one item is the staple, the basic food, without which man feels he cannot live. Throughout India, for example, the basis of the diet is a cereal of some kind, according to the area; in some sections cereal represents up to 90 per cent of the total consumption. And when rationing was strict, the black market in cereals flourished, each man selling his ration of wheat or rice for the kind of cereal he considered essential to his meal.[1] In the Middle East, where bread is a staple, everything else is merely an accompaniment, a relish. No food is eaten, or can be eaten, without bread by the fellahin, since bread is the "plate" as well as the "fork" with which to eat; anything else has to be put on the bread, which is then folded around it and carried to the mouth. In the Far East, where wheat-bread has been introduced, it has not displaced rice; it is eaten, like everything else, as a relish with the rice or, at times, in-between meals as a snack. There is usually an identification with the staple, the traditional food which is essential to life; it is a symbol of the life of the group or the individual, it is used in religious rites and in social rites, or as a mark of well-being, as when loaves of bread are placed around on exhibit at a banquet in the Middle East.[2]

People usually like special aspects of the food they eat. It

[1] Henry W. Spielman, 1950, p. 97.
[2] H. A. Baehr, 1950, pp. 206-7; Bell, op. cit.; Tannous, 1943, op. cit. pp. 252, 253.

has been useless to try to introduce unpolished rice, for example, because what people value is the whiteness of the rice. When an attempt was made to introduce enriched polished rice into Puerto Rico, this too was resisted, because it was not pure white; the processing had given it a creamy colour, and only very recently, when a reconstituted pure white rice has been achieved, has there been acceptance. In the Far East it has been found that wheat will be accepted only if it is white like rice; whole wheat is resisted as being like brown rice.[1] The special quality may be texture or taste. In New Mexico a government worker introduced a hybrid corn to Spanish American farmers, and it produced three times the yield of their own corn; since corn was here the staple diet, the worker was sure that the innovation would be welcomed. Within four years, however, the farmers had ceased to grow it, as their wives did not like the texture and no one liked the flavour.[2]

FOOD AND VALUE

The feeling which people have toward their staple often verges on, or actually is, religious. The factors of value and religion must be taken into consideration when availability of food is investigated and when any change is contemplated. Among the Hopi Indians, for example, as among most farmers in Mexico, corn is identified with living and with the good, and the attitude toward it is religious. Mexican Indians often cannot be persuaded to grow other crops on land where these would do better than corn, because they would rather have a poor crop of corn than a good crop of something that is not corn. Writers complain that needed food, although available, is not eaten by peasants in Latin America. In Mitla, a father, advised to give his sick child milk, insisted on giving corn instead, as milk would be too "strong."[3] Hopi mothers in the United States resist child-care advice because this does not allow them to give their babies corn-meal.

One-third of the total cattle population of the world is found in India, yet this does not mean that beef is really available there. Only 25 per cent of the people eat meat at all, and that mainly in the form of mutton, fowl and fish. Because of the strong religious feeling against killing and, in many sections, against eating cattle, the presence of cattle actually means less food for the people, since cows compete for the available agricultural products.[4] Even the introduction here of a cheese industry, by way of counteracting the lack of refrig-

---

[1] Bell, op. cit. p. 163.

[2] John Adair and Edward H. Spicer, n.d.

[3] Juan Comas, 1942; Epaminondas Quintana, 1942, p. 28; Nathan L. Whetten, 1948, pp. 306, 308.

[4] Spielman, op. cit. p. 97.

eration, encounters a religious objection; processed cheese needs rennet from the fourth stomach of a young ruminant.[1]

Among the cattle-owning tribes of Africa also, cattle become available as food only when a ceremonial occasion calls for slaughter. Meat is liked, but the cattle are considered friends, known by personality traits and name, loved like relatives or sweethearts; they are not meat, except when they have become so incidentally. In Assam, pork is liked and pigs are killed; yet an Englishman trying to improve the pork supply by the introduction of black-and-white Berkshire pigs failed because the Chin spirits do not like pigs with black-and-white markings. Moslems and Jews are ready to eat meat other than pork, but only if it has been killed according to certain religious regulations.[2]

FOOD PREFERENCES

There are also specific preferences and objections which affect nutrition and health as well as the introduction of any new food or way of preparation. West Africans, for example, have an aversion to food in its raw state, as fit only for cattle. The older people think it undignified to eat oranges and discourage children from eating them, as oranges will make them soft.[3] Greeks like raw vegetables and fruits, but not all vegetables are considered edible when raw. Cucumbers can be eaten only raw, but zucchini squash must be cooked; green beans and peas can never be eaten raw; cabbage is good when raw, but cauliflower is inedible. The fact that many leafy vegetables go into the salad does not mean that such vegetables belong there. In sections of Africa, meat is eaten raw, and food is seasoned with mineral salts; and both these practices lead to the spread of intestinal diseases.[4] Puerto Ricans, living precariously on too little food, often will not eat even fruit which grows wild, as they consider fruit to be poisonous, or dangerous, or a cause of indigestion. Among many, there is the feeling that fruit is "cold," a term used of something objectionable. Many feel, too, that pineapple is harmful when eaten in combination with any other food.[5]

INTRODUCTION OF CHANGE

Mistakes have been made in the past, before we knew the importance of food-habits and the cultural and social context of the food. We tried to introduce supplementary nutrients through the medium of cream soups to people who, though

[1] D. A. Soulides, 1949, p. 26.
[2] E. S. Phipson, 1939, p. 39; Tannous, 1943, op. cit. pp. 254-55.
[3] S. D. Onabanirio, 1949, pp. 122, 133.
[4] Hailey, op. cit. pp. 1146-47.
[5] Lydia J. Roberts and Rosa Luisa Stefani, 1949, p. 176.

they liked soups, would eat nothing bland and nothing creamy unless it also contained pieces offering resistance in chewing. We upset dietary balance by persuading Spanish American schoolchildren in New Mexico to eat white bread instead of cold corn *tortillas,* when their main source of calcium came from the lime-water in which the corn of the *tortillas* had been soaked. We persuaded their mothers to substitute canned spinach for wild greens, and when there was no money to buy spinach, the children went without greens. Hopi mothers were forced to wean their children if these had to be hospitalized after they were a year old; and when the children came back, the expense of giving them canned milk out of individual small cans—since no refrigeration was available—was some-times too great for the family to maintain.[1]

Agricultural experts warn of possible disruption of dietary balance with the increase of commercialization. For example, in many parts of rural India where large amounts of *ghee* butter are consumed, the farmer's family depends heavily on the accompanying buttermilk; if butter-making is to become industrialized, nutritional planning should take into account the gap this will leave in the family diet.

Child-care services have often urged new foods for children which have perhaps been good for nutritional adequacy but have made for strain in family relations. In Greece, where one nutritionist persuaded mothers to introduce raisin-bread and other unacceptable items into the family meal, this often created a split between the father's and the children's food, or brought derision from the father, or otherwise produced dis-continuity in an occasion which is essentially a family com-munion. It would probably be equally effective, and less destructive, to introduce change through less emotionally im-portant eating situations. For example, if a Greek child must eat raisins, these can be introduced into the frequent snacks, "the passing of the time" in which all Greeks indulge, as dry chewy raisins, fitting into an already present food pattern. Certainly very valuable nutrients can be added by persuading Greeks to eat more of the roasted chick-peas they like so well, and which are so easily and cheaply available. In Puerto Rico, fruit, if eaten at all, is eaten between meals, and there would be less resistance if consumption of more fruit was introduced at such times.

One commonly practised method of improving nutrition is through supplementary feeding of children and of expectant and lactating mothers. This does not attempt to change or stop existing practices. Such attempts have met with resistance in the past, as in an instance when a public-health nurse in a Chi-nese district was rejected because she tried to persuade parturi-ent mothers to eat vegetables instead of a diet of fried chicken;

[1] Laura Thompson, 1950, p. 55.

these women had been eating mainly vegetables all their lives, and had looked to this period when their special status would be acknowledged by this special diet. However, in giving supplementary feedings it is well to remember, in addition, that food is sometimes the coin of society, of social ritual, and that much of its emotional sustenance is lost when it is not part of the family meal. During World War II, the Greeks in Athens voiced a preference for eating cold food in their unheated houses rather than hot food in warm soup-kitchens. UNRRA workers found a similar preference in Germany, also.

Food preferences and aversions have successfully been taken into consideration in introducing change. In Thailand, where there is an aversion to cow's milk, canned milk did not evoke the image of the cow, and was introduced acceptably. Wheat products are increasingly being introduced in the Far East, either in terms of existing foods such as noodles and *chapattis*, or as rolls for snacks, or bread for an accompaniment to the rice.

ADDITIONAL REFERENCES

Alfredo Ramos Espinosa, 1942; Manuel Gamio, 1942; Gabriel Giraldo Jaramillo, 1942; Margaret Mead, 1950b; C. M. Purves and John C. Hobbes, 1951; Report of the Committee on Food Habits, 1943, 1945; Afif I. Tannous, 1945, 1949a.

MATERNAL AND CHILD CARE

Figures on maternal and infant mortality in many sections of the world are shocking, and reveal how great is the need for technical assistance in this area. It is necessary not only to establish systematic prenatal care, but to convince people of the need for it, and also to offer it in a way which is acceptable, and which does not destroy the frequently precarious security of this period. Well-baby clinics are also needed, and mothers must be educated in their use, in taking preventive measures, in recognizing the need for expert advice for illness before it is too late. In some regions, mothers have to learn further, in order to save the lives of infants, that it is not natural and necessary for babies to die. It may be possible to do all this, to change practice this far, without upsetting the basic meaning of life. However, reducing infant mortality meets an additional and significant obstacle; it comes directly up against the belief that personal value is enhanced and increased by living; that a child's and particularly an infant's life, therefore, is relatively without value. People who love children freely, who welcome them eagerly, may at the same time show this casual attitude toward safeguarding their lives. In the United States, prenatal as well as child care is strongly supported by the great value placed upon the future, and the equation of children with the future; but a large number of cultures value the past.

The changes proposed in the area of maternal and child care also encounter firmly established patterns of behaviour, which most often are an expression of the basic patterning of the universe, and of personal relations. However, many of the established patterns are merely different and, from the viewpoint of Western medicine, at any rate harmless. For example, there is the custom in regions of Africa, such as that reported of the Pondo of South Africa, of drinking during pregnancy an infusion of the plant with which the husband's unit is identified. Unless the plant itself is harmful, this cannot bring harm. However, under outside contact, some women have learned to substitute laxatives for this infusion, and if the meaning had traditionally represented the continuity between the father and the growing child, the laxative cannot be an adequate substitute.[1]

HOSPITALIZATION

Where houses are crowded and ill-ventilated, and where sanitary measures are inadequate, it has often seemed desirable to persuade women to go to a hospital for delivery. Maternity hospitals in under-developed areas are few in relation to population, but it is often difficult to fill even these few. Hospitals are usually strange, imposing edifices, staffed by impersonal strangers, and require all one's moral strength to enter; but during illness, or at child-birth, the individual is weak and vulnerable. A critical time in one's life is not one at which to court the hazards of unknown surroundings. For maternity cases there are further, specific objections.

A hospital is a place where death often occurs, and, unless the maternity hospital is in a special building, this holds great danger for those pregnant women who must never see a corpse or be in the vicinity of one. This is true of women in Burma and in regions of Africa.[2] In many regions, if a pregnant woman dies, it is necessary to remove the foetus and bury it separately.[3] And a pregnant woman in difficulty might hesitate to go to a hospital where the relatives might have no right to insist on this.

Each culture has its own prescribed behaviour for the mother after child-birth, and this is important for the health and survival of mother and child, or the husband, or the total unit. A Pondo woman has to lie on a bed of special grass, traditional within her clan; and for the welfare of the child

[1] Monica Hunter, 1936, pp. 147-48.
[2] Richard C. Thurnwald, 1935, pp. 119-20.
[3] Anathanath Chatterjee and Tarakchandra Das, 1927, p. 31; Hunter, op. cit. p. 151; Thurnwald, op. cit. p. 198.

she must have a fire burning near her until the umbilical cord drops off. The disposal of the lochial blood, of the placenta and navel cord, all depend on the society's conception of the body and of the continuity within the unit. Among the Tiv, for example, the placenta must be buried where it can be refreshed daily with water from the baby's bath, and where it can add to his inadequate strength. Among the Kgatla, lochial blood and placenta must be buried where they can be prevented from scorching the earth and bringing disease on the people, and where no sorcerer can work charms over them to put an end to the mother's fertility.[1] On the specific disposal of the navel cord often depends the future life of the new individual. How can one be assured that all these practices will be rightly observed in the hospital?

Among the Hopi Indians, many women are disinclined to be confined in the hospitals and will go only if they have been in labour for several days and are near death, because there they are not allowed to observe certain all-important lochial rules: to abstain from eating salt and meat, fresh fruit and vegetables, and to be protected from the sun. The hospital believes that these food items are a necessary part of the diet; and its rules forbid shading of the windows where the parturient mother lies with her infant.[2] In West Africa women find it insupportable that they should be parted from their babies, who are made to lie on separate cots; and except when they secretly take their babies in beside them, this hospital regulation is a great hardship.[3]

A missionary doctor in Africa, Dr. Maynard, overcame the fear of hospitalization. Some 30 years ago she established a maternity home which found acceptance, by first carefully winning the confidence of the women in the community. She first visited the women in their homes and helped them there; only after her work was accepted did she build her maternity home. She invited expectant mothers to come several weeks before delivery, without pay, so that the babies were born in familiar surroundings. She did not confuse hygiene with Western ideas of cleanliness; the women were allowed to continue their habit of spitting tobacco juice on the walls.[4]

Hospitalization for delivery also presents a number of drawbacks in common with hospitalization for other reasons. Under British administration in Africa and Burma, an individual usually had to go far for hospital care; the hospitals there were usually conceived of as centres to come to for treatment. There was a policy of complete isolation from friends and relatives, and hospital discipline made no concessions to

[1] Isaac Schapera, 1941, p. 233.
[2] Wayne Dennis, 1940 a, pp. 2, 29; Laura Thompson, 1950, p. 55.
[3] S. D. Onabanirio, 1949, p. 89.
[4] Thurnwald, op. cit. pp. 199-200.

strange customs.[1] The French Colonial administration in Africa initiated a system which seems to be more reassuring to the patient. Under their administration hospitals were centres to make available preventive and curative medicine to rural areas; the hospitals were small and the patients were encouraged to live with their families while undergoing treatment and even if they did stay at the hospital, their relatives brought them food.[2] Particularly where a patient is isolated, he suffers from the impersonal treatment which he receives at this time, from the fact that he is visited or treated only once a day, and from the general absence of reassuring concern.[3]

At times there are specific, positive factors making for insecurity. It is reported that in previous times in West Africa, the charms and talismans which gave a man the power to withstand evil forces were forcibly taken away from those hospitalized.[4] In Burma, where villagers built one-storey houses to avoid having anyone over their heads, and where they slept on the floor to be certain that they would not break the rule against sleeping on a high place during the duty-days, the Western types of hospitals with their elevated beds could not have been reassuring to the ill. Where modesty or secretiveness attends evacuation, people find it harassing to use a bedpan before other people, particularly if this act has always been attended by feelings of uneasiness and fear lest someone watch. In societies where all bodily effluvia are continuous with the body, to abandon phlegm, blood, or excreta to strangers may well be a source of unease. The records which have to be kept in a hospital, with the large number of questions they involve, are reported as producing distress; the inquisitiveness is a source of worry, and even the capturing of the personal name in symbols on paper has produced fear in people who have to protect themselves against magic. Where part of the definition of a good doctor or diagnostician is that he should know everything, the questions make the incoming patients distrust the doctor who has to ask before he knows. In a number of cultures, the individual never undresses completely. Even a baby in a hot climate may be bathed piecemeal, so that a part of the body is always covered. Change of clothing is effected piece by piece, and if night wear is used, the individual undresses under the tent of the night-gown.

Dr. Schweitzer, in the description of his hospital in the French Congo, brings out further points in this connexion. For example, the fact that people entered the hospital alive in the evening and were taken out dead in the morning gave

[1] William Malcolm Hailey, 1938, pp. 1173-74, 1195.
[2] Ibid.
[3] Alexander H. Leighton and Dorothea C. Leighton, 1944, pp. 56-57, 60; Albert Schweitzer, 1931, p. 35.
[4] Charles Morrow Wilson, 1949, p. 17.

rise to the suspicion that the doctor was a human leopard.[1]
He found that, on the one hand, people were mortally afraid
of anaesthetics, which they considered as death-dealing, while
on the other hand, they despised the surgeon who administered
them, since they thought that he had failed in his attempt
to inflict lasting death.[2] In this hospital discipline was slight.
"Order" consisted in having people appear every morning
for injections, or change of bandage, or other treatment. Yet
even this was considered oppressive; and patients would do
everything they could to avoid staying at the hospital. The
leprosy treatment with its long series of injections was very
unpopular, and lepers came only if they thought they would
be given chaulmoogra oil prepared for use at home. Since
dysentery meant that the patient's freedom was curtailed and
he was put under supervision, this disease was usually con-
cealed by the victim, as well as by other patients. Non-dysen-
tery patients further disobeyed the rule against sharing the
cooking with dysentery patients, and would even eat out of the
same pot with them. One such patient told the doctor: "Better
be with my brother and die, than not see him." [3] The fact that
Dr. Schweitzer was ready to help a man, however near to
death he might be, led the people to distrust him; their native
medicine men knew enough to recognize approaching death,
and refused to waste their skill on the dying, thus bolstering
faith in their infallibility; and, in addition, Dr. Schweitzer's
humaneness meant that people were confirmed in their belief
that one went to the hospital not to get well but to die.[4] These
difficulties were not insurmountable, and when the doctor returned after some years of absence, his hospital was besieged
by the sick, who came from hundreds of miles away, even before he had time to unpack his instruments and medicines.[5]

The doctors who worked with the Navaho Indians found
resistance to hospitalization among these people who, according to Dr. Leighton, are "unaccustomed to a bed, to living
by the clock, to staying in one place continuously instead of
wandering around . . . and to efficient, impersonal attention." The Navaho cannot see why "he must be fed with gruel
and milk when, if he were home, he would be fed as much
as he could eat of the best food the family could get for him."
He misses the undivided, continuous attention he has had
from the medicine man when he has been ill at home.[6] In
addition, his relatives often travel many miles to see him,
only to be told that it is the wrong time of day for visiting.[7]

[1] Schweitzer, 1931, op. cit. p. 28.
[2] Ibid. p. 160.
[3] Ibid. pp. 91, 110, 117.
[4] Ibid. pp. 28, 38, 39.
[5] Albert Schweitzer, 1933, pp. 163-64, 252.
[6] Leighton and Leighton, op. cit. pp. 56-57.
[7] Alice Joseph, 1942, p. 4.

PRENATAL CARE

In most societies, pregnancy is regarded as a normal state, and women go about their ordinary occupations until the end. However, it is often a period of vulnerability for the woman, and there are rites acting as preventive and strengthening measures. These are actually health measures, since tney enhance security and well-being. The Tiv woman has a number of *akombo* rites worked over her, and everyone around her is cleansed even of unsuspected evil intentions against her. In many societies, the social unit itself, and even the land, have to be protected from the pregnant woman, who is now so profane that she may destroy sanctity, potency, power; or whose blood is so hot that it may wither others. So a pregnant woman has to follow regulations which are essentially based on the concept of continuity found in the particular culture.

In most cultures children are wanted and pregnancy is a desired state. Where a union is not fruitful, a woman often seeks magical or medical aid, or she may be put away as useless, or another wife or concubine may be taken, according to the custom of the society. Among the Kgatla, there is a belief that there is no conception when the wife's blood disagrees with the husband's semen; so a liquid concoction is given to the woman to change her blood. But here it is not only the woman who is to blame; sterility in men is recognized, and such men are given medicine made from the roots of plants which have a red juice.

Many cultures also have practices resulting in birth-control; and changes in other areas of life have often resulted in the disruption of these practices. For example, where women must not conceive during lactation and must therefore avoid sexual intercourse, when lactation went on for two or three years, children were widely spaced; however, when such women have been persuaded not to nurse their infants for this length of time or where nurseries have been established to care for babies while the mother is in the fields, accustoming the infants to non-human milk, this works against the regulation of conception. Again, this custom was easier to maintain where polygamy was part of the picture. But where polygamy has disappeared, either by governmental interdiction or through activities of Christian missions, or through other induced change, wives prefer to go against traditional practice rather than have their husbands visit prostitutes. Contraceptive practices and special medicaments are known in a number of areas; however, where birth-control has depended upon sexual abstinence during prolonged lactation, as among the Pondo, we find no traditional knowledge of contraceptives, and women are said to be going to the trading stores asking for the contraceptives of Western civilization. Industrialization has had an indirect effect on the size of families in South Africa, through separating couples for long periods of time, through introducing the desire to spend money on trade-goods, through increasing atomization of the social group and by giving the woman a different picture of herself. Christianity, in destroying the ancestor cults, has rendered it unnecessary for people to have numerous progeny, or any progeny through whom to continue the social unit after death. Education has introduced budgeting and the need to educate one's children, and has brought attempts to limit families.[1]

Many groups in Africa "circumcise" their girls at puberty. Missionary attempts to put a stop to this practice have led, as among the Kikuyu, to a strengthening of it, as the people apparently feel that with it is involved the very continuance of their identity. The initiation rites at this time are basic to womanhood, to wifehood, and motherhood; circumcision is the physical preparation for motherhood, and is believed to improve the process of birth. Western physicians, however, believe that it complicates the process of birth and gives rise to difficulties with which native midwives are not able to cope; yet to teach growing girls to lose their faith in this rite might mean to destroy their image of their own womanhood and the security they need during pregnancy.

There are often changes in diet throughout pregnancy. Foods which according to Western ideas are essential to maternal health and the growth of the foetus are sometimes forbidden; and those which are prescribed as strengthening, while they probably improve well-being through reassuring the pregnant woman, are often not nutritive from the Western point of view. Changes in this area will have to be made with care. On the one hand, the nutritive values of many native foods are not adequately known; on the other hand, where traditional procedure is important, any change may destroy well-being. However, where cash crops have been substituted for subsistence farming, the maternal diet is reported to be dangerously inadequate, due to factors which are not rooted in the value system.

Any changes proposed in the pattern of sexual intercourse during pregnancy would run up against the society's conception of the formation of the body. Daily intercourse for a number of weeks or months may be enjoined for the complete formation of the embryo; or it may be completely forbidden, for the protection of the husband's social unit. Greek manuals on prenatal care allow intercourse through part of the ninth month, and forbid it only because of the danger of infection, along with immersion baths.

Where pregnancy is regarded as a natural state, the woman

[1] Hunter, op. cit. p. 146; Thurnwald, op. cit. p. 164.

performs her duties until delivery. We have reports, from Oceania and Africa, of women walking many miles carrying heavy loads, just before delivery. In South Africa, however, Monica Hunter found that all the women she spoke to complained that lifting heavy weights to the head during pregnancy caused them pain, and that the strenuous grinding of corn flung the child about in the womb; apparently they connect with this the frequency with which the child is born with the umbilical cord twisted about the neck.[1] In West Africa, women are absolved from carrying heavy loads, but are otherwise very active during pregnancy; one of them, evaluating maternal care, says that educated women in this group, who have accepted the European pattern of having others do their work but not the habits of sports and exercise which European women have, present a higher maternal mortality-rate.[2]

This author gives the favourable and unfavourable aspects of maternal care here as follows: the woman feels secure through the authority of the family medicine man who is a personal friend and who supervises the pregnancy. Her muscles are active, she eats little. Her genital tract has not been handled during pregnancy, so the danger of infection is reduced. She is used to pain. Her friends are with her during delivery. Against this, the author sets the fact that no one present knows how to deal with complications and unusual presentations, that there is no fresh air in the delivery-room and that hygienic measures are lacking, thus exposing the infant to infection.[3]

There have been reports in the past that among so-called under-developed peoples delivery is easy and painless. These have been discredited. If babies are born in a field two miles away from home it is only because the mother has been following her practice of doing her ordinary work; and some deliveries are unusually easy everywhere. The fact that in the United States many babies are born in a taxi on the way to the hospital, or under the supervision of a hastily summoned policeman, does not mean that deliveries are generally short and painless. Pondo midwives report that a first labour usually lasts two days.[4]

Similar reports come from all parts of the world. There is a report from Alaska that Western diet has made for a narrower pelvis among native women, and for greater difficulty during child-birth. Though labour may be long and difficult, however, we usually find that in societies where a mother participates actively in the birth process, where she takes no anaesthetic, and where she assumes a natural position during

[1] Hunter, op. cit. pp. 146-47.
[2] Onabanirio, op. cit. pp. 24-25.
[3] Ibid. pp. 32 ff.
[4] Hunter, op. cit. p. 147.

parturition, recovery from labour is quicker and the mother is able to go about her ordinary occupations much sooner than is generally the case in centres of Western civilization. The whole picture should therefore be considered before a decision is made to alter the mother's position during labour, or to administer anaesthetics. In addition, the impression—which is frequently expressed—that women in under-developed areas do not fear child-birth is also often erroneous. In many parts of the world, women fear the approach of parturition and dread the pain of labour. A difficult labour may be a result of unfaithfulness, and a sign to all observers. Sometimes all that young girls know of birth is the fearful anticipation of the pregnant women around them. In Bali, girls see birth only on the stage, with the feared witches all about.

The number of days that a woman is considered to be in childbed varies greatly, but is usually established by the culture. A woman may be delivered in her mother's or brother's home, and may be cared for by the women there; or relatives or even neighbours may come in to help while she stays in bed, or at any rate remains inactive for the prescribed number of days. In Greece the lochial period is traditionally 40 days, and it is a time when the woman can be cherished and pampered without her feeling inadequate or shamed. It is important to refrain from introducing change in such patterns unless we are entirely sure of our ground. In the United States, 12 years ago women having children followed approximately the Greek lochial pattern (a six-weeks lochial period); now they follow a pattern nearer to the Burmese four-day period. But these women belong to a society where physician and patient are accustomed to trying out new things, new fads, new gadgets, enjoying experimentation. Most societies, however, find experimentation disrupting and want the security of the proven and demonstrated if they are to include any change in their lives.

In some societies, the prenatal and lochial regulations apply to the father also. To rationally minded people these may appear wasteful and unnecessary. However, in cultures where continuity with the family unit is paramount, this is an important aspect of the father's share in the creation of the infant, and its loss may be a factor of family disintegration.

In this area, as in the areas of agriculture and industry, it is important to introduce planning. In many cultures, such as that of the Spanish Americans, the Pondo, the Palestinian Arabs, nothing is done towards the actual birth of the child until labour sets in, or even until labour is advanced. Yet hygienic measures require that clean rags shall be available, that fuel and water should be available for boiling and sterilizing; in short, that there should be preparation ahead of time. Some people feel that it would be presumptuous to plan, since

God has his own plan; some feel it would be courting disaster to act in such an assured way about a situation that holds so many uncertainties and hazards. It is not merely a question of teaching new measures, then, but one of educating the people to find a place for these changes in their systems of values and beliefs.[1]

CHILD-BIRTH

Birth itself is strongly patterned everywhere. It may be necessary for the baby to be born in a structure other than a dwelling-hut. The mother's position during child-birth is determined by the culture. She may squat or kneel or bear down on a rope suspended from the roof, or she may be supported by her husband or female relatives or friends. There may be a pit filled with ashes, or a pile of cow-dung or of rags, to receive not only the infant but the highly charged lochial blood. The baby may be slapped to provoke crying, as in the United States, or it may be gently massaged, or have cold water thrown on it, or, as an extreme measure, a wise woman may blow up its anus, as in sections of Greece.[2] It may be possible to keep some of these practices without harm, or to fit changes into the existing pattern. The slap, as in the United States, may be an act of friendly aggression, just as the baby's movements in the womb have been interpreted aggressively as "kicking." But in Greece a slap is an intrusion, a molestation; there is nothing friendly about it, or about aggressiveness. In the womb, the embryo has not been kicking the mother: it has been "gambolling," and to slap a new-born infant may be unacceptable.

CHILD CARE

In many regions infants are swaddled, or kept on a stiff cradle-board where movement is made impossible. The reasons given for this practice vary from society to society, and in each case what is communicated to the child through the practice varies with the values of the culture.[3] Studies of American Indian children who were reared on a cradle-board, in comparison with children who were not, show that such devices do not delay co-ordination and locomotion, and that they seem to give the growing infant a feeling of security. In Greece, where pediatricians inveigh against swaddling, the principle underlying the practice, the position of the unswaddled child in the mother's arms, and even the rudiments of swaddling itself, have been retained; and the change seems to be accepted

[1] Hilma Granquist, 1947, p. 72; Hunter, op. cit. p. 150.
[2] Clyde Kluckhohn, 1947, p. 42.
[3] Ruth Benedict, 1949.

without strain or distress by those mothers who are in contact with the advice and writings of pediatricians.

The feeding of infants is also deeply rooted in the cultural structuring of relationships. Suckling is not merely an ingestation of food; in many cultures it is an aspect of the continuity between mother and child, so that a bottle is no substitute. The child may seek the breast whenever he wants to participate in this continuity, and must be free to do so. Or he may be given reassurance when frightened or in pain, by being brought into the continuity through the offer of the breast. In such cultures, the baby is never denied the breast when he asks for it, and scheduled feeding would interfere with this continuity. Seen against this background, the reasons for urging scheduled feeding appear irrelevant, and the introduction of such feeding would necessitate as well the teaching of the mother to equate breast-feeding with nutrition alone. A society which phrases suckling as continuity, and yet makes it necessary that the mother be away for long periods of time, may even prefer to leave the infant hungry all day rather than allow it to suckle the breast of another woman.

Substitute milk is rarely necessary in many cultures where there is a conviction that a mother is bound to have milk, and where a mother prepares her nipples, believes she will have milk, and patiently awaits the certain filling of her breasts. A Greek manual, passionately inveighing against the foreign-introduced practice of hiring wet-nurses, tells mothers that a parturient woman always has some milk and urges that, on the very rare occasions when the milk is insufficient, the supplementary milk should be given with a spoon, not through an artificial nipple. Mothers are told that the child inherits an inalienable right to their milk. Some factories in Greece make it possible for mothers to bring their unweaned infants with them, so that this continuity with the mother's breast need not be broken. Even the breast-pump in Greece takes account of this continuity; it is designed in such a way that the mother pumps at one end with her mouth while the infant suckles at the other end.

Scheduled feeding, in addition, introduces a foreign element, an element of separation, into the rhythm of family life. Often, even in industrialized groups, we find that the family does not function according to the clock. In the United States, families of foreign extraction living in cities, where the men of the family go out into the business world, which is run according to the clock, and where the children attend school by the clock, nevertheless run the affairs of the household, serve meals, and even go to church according to a different temporal rhythm. They are people to whom time limits are intrinsic to the situation, and are not externally set beforehand. To put the baby of the family on an intrusive schedule is to introduce a barrier in a pattern where security lies in the very continuity of the individual with the social unit.

We tread on the same delicate ground when we try to introduce a special diet for the child. In some societies, it is true, the infant's diet is grossly inadequate; yet in attempting to change it, it is well to be aware of the areas that are to be influenced by such change. If to be Greek means to eat wheat-bread, or to be Hopi means to eat corn-meal, then the infant who is making his identification with his unit should not be deprived of these items of food unless this is absolutely necessary. If to be a member of the family means to share food in a family ritual, in a sort of daily communion, then the harm done by the introduction of a special child diet may outweigh the good. Reports from Greece suggest that the new diets introduced for children bring dissension to the family table, where to quarrel is "like quarreling in church."

In several countries, as in the United States and Australia, child-care manuals also give advice on toilet-training. In some cultures this training is taken casually and the mothers are not particularly aware of training their children. In others, it is strongly stressed and is considered a problem situation. In the United States there has been a change in recent years, so that infants do not have to begin training for defecation at the age of 10 weeks or two months; however, in most groups in this country the attitude of disgust at the child's excreta, the feeling that the child has done something dirty, remains, and it is considered by many to help in forming a basis for the pattern of success, of achievement as a means for winning approval. In China and Burma, toilet-training is part of the process of becoming socially acceptable. Mothers report that they do not train their children, but they watch their children closely and "catch them" in time, and—perhaps through being immediately held away from the nurse's body when they begin to defecate—they are apparently trained by the time they reach the age of six months. Greek mothers train for micturition first, and for defecation only when the baby can imitate the mother. And in other cultures learning to defecate is often a part of the process of identification with the mother: the child, when able to walk, goes with the mother when she goes to defecate, and acts as she acts.

Maternal care and child care are receiving attention from the governments of many countries. In Afghanistan, mobile clinics have been established, also a maternity ward which is increasingly used. Countries in Latin America, the Middle East, and the Far East report that they train midwives and are establishing baby clinics; many also report increasing numbers of prenatal clinics. In many areas, midwives are in close touch with obstetricians and report cases where delivery is expected to present complications, so that these women, at least, can be hospitalized. Many of these projects are government-supported. In Moslem countries, however, there are the vast private charitable organizations which have been responsible for care at this time.[1] In many countries, such as, for example, Indonesia, India, and among Spanish Americans in New Mexico, the midwives already operating have been trained in Western practices. This has not always been a completely successful programme; where hygienic principles are not understood, a midwife may learn to scrub her hands and then may run them through her hair. In rural India, midwives were reluctant to work with male physicians, preferring to work with women.[2]

Again, in many regions the place of the midwife, as someone known and trusted who treats the patients with personal attention, has been recognized, and midwives have been sent to rural areas to visit women in their homes and become acquaintances and even friends before child-birth takes place.

Hospitalization is making headway. Perhaps one of the main obstacles is overcome when special maternity homes are established, rather than maternity wards in large hospitals. Where child-bearing is in no way equated with disease or a non-normal state, it is more acceptable to go to a maternity home; this also eliminates the fear of being in the vicinity of dead or dying people at this critical time. Such a procedure is also in accord with patterns where child-birth must occur not in the family home, but in a special building, a pattern found in many regions. In the United States, the Fox Indians welcomed the opportunity to have child-birth take place away from home, since in this way they could avoid the responsibility for the ceremonies of purification after this defiling event.

Well-baby clinics, child-welfare stations, and day-nurseries are also being established. Some countries, however, find that the child is better off in the care of the home. The Government of Saudi Arabia explains that, since the family is still the cornerstone of the society and brings up the children in strict accordance with the teachings of the Koran, it is completely adequate, and is not in need of further advice on child-rearing.[3] In countries where mothers have been persuaded to leave their young children behind in nurseries when they go to work in the fields, it is probably not always to the benefit of the child. Where work is life, and working with the mother is sharing her life, and increasing one's sense of belonging with the social unit, it is probably harmful to the child to be given instead "play activity" and contrived projects, which are discontinuous with the life and work of his group. Furthermore,

[1] United Nations Secretariat, Department of Social Affairs. *Child and Youth Welfare, Annual Report,* 1948 and 1949.
[2] A. I. Pillay, 1931, pp. 23-24.
[3] United Nations Secretariat, 1949, op. cit. p. 129.

the assumption that this separation is a boon to the mother, because it frees her from the interference of the child, is open to question, since in such societies the family expands to accept the child, so that the child is not a disturbing or interfering factor; and without the child, the mother's life itself may be impoverished.

ADDITIONAL REFERENCES

Wayne Dennis, 1940b; Sister M. Lucia van der Eerden, 1948; Yang Hsin-Pao, 1949.

PUBLIC HEALTH

THE BODY

Unity of Function

"Public health . . . is an integral part of the social process," says Dr. Raymond Fosdick, speaking from the wide experience of the international work of the Rockefeller Foundation.[1] For this reason it is difficult to isolate the subject of this section, for here we are dealing with people to whom the issues of public health are all of that and more: they cover man's conception of good and evil, of the relationship of the individual to his social unit, and to the universe. Among many people, such as the Hopi, Navaho, and Papago of the south-western United States, health is the expression of harmony with the universe. And health is only one such expression; it is merely an aspect of his well-being, his effectiveness, his luck, or his potency. That which causes disease might also cause failure of the crops, ill luck in hunting, or incompetence in the building of a house, as it does to the Tiv. A Burmese villager can easily succumb to illness, or also to any other misfortune, if his *kan* (accumulated virtue and strength) is low; and an Ifugao will meet with misfortune if he has not bribed the appropriate gods with the necessary sacrifices, as will a Tiv if he has not performed the preventive *akombo* rites; illness is only one of such misfortunes. Man's being and function, his body, mind, activity, emotions, and social relations, are all one, and weakness of the person, the failure to take preventive measures or to strengthen one's person, may result in "illness" in any of these areas.

Continuity

In many cultures throughout the world man is continuous with his environment. Therefore, he is not healthy unless his environment is "healthy," or, conversely, the well-being of his

[1] Raymond B. Fosdick, 1947, p. 29.

environment depends upon his acts. For example, a Kgatla woman can scorch the earth if she lets her lochial blood drip on it; a bereaved spouse of a fruitful union needs purification before he can step on the earth because his tread scorches the ground—he injures the people, the cattle, the crops, and prevents rain from coming.[1] Or the effluvia of the body may add to the well-being of the earth, as when the feces of potent Tiv men are needed to pass on to the earth the potency of the body. To break connexion between the body and the land that is continuous with it may be hazardous or disastrous, irrespective of whether the people are sedentary or not, whether they depend on "the fruits of the earth" through agriculture. This continuity is expressed in a wide range of ways, from the Eskimo desire to die where he was born to the belief of the cattle-raising Nuer that if a man permanently settles away from tribal land he will get sick unless he takes some earth with him to drink in water mixed with gradually increasing amounts of new land.[2] The distance a man will travel for treatment may depend on which is more hazardous, lack of treatment or continuity with his land.

Again, the body is continuous with the other bodies of the social unit, and in this lies the strength and the weakness of the unit, inasmuch as when one body suffers, it exposes the whole unit to danger. Western medicine has a name for this: it calls it contagion and explains it scientifically. The medicine of other groups recognizes a different order of contagion or pollution, and acts according to a different conception. So a Tiv, unwittingly exposing himself to *akombo* danger, exposes the whole unit, as well as all its land, polluting the whole. So also the Australian Murngin will psychologically cut off any one of their members who is known to have been magically attacked; they stop treating him in terms of his place in the balanced system of structured roles; the mother does not act as his mother, the brother does not relate himself to the man who is magically stricken as his brother. The stricken one is "isolated," and the social unit thus protects itself against his contagion. Among the Kgatla we find the concept of "hot blood" which is very dangerous to land and to other human beings. People's blood is hot immediately after intercourse, a woman's blood is hot in later pregnancy and in the lochial period; bereaved spouses who are parents have hot blood. Hot blood makes the new-born "dirty" until the purification ceremony. It gives paralysis, or sterility, or even death to a sexual partner.[3] It is this continuity which is basic to the belief found in many cultures that the acts of parents, or their diet, will react upon their children, born or unborn, or that what a wife does while

[1] Isaac Schapera, 1941, pp. 224-25, 308-11.
[2] E. E. Evans-Pritchard, 1940, p. 120.
[3] Schapera, op. cit. pp. 195-98, 201-2.

her husband is engaged upon an important undertaking will help or hinder or harm him. Such a conception of continuity of body with land and society underlies the way in which medical treatment and hygienic measures are accepted and worked out.

Image

The image of the body depends to some extent on these concepts of continuity. In many societies it has no sharp boundaries. Different parts of the body may be stressed in forming the link of continuity. In Greek culture, for example, lineal continuity with the descendant is envisioned as a continuity of the internal organs, the *splanchna*, and "compassion" in Greek is derived from this word. A mother, ready to do anything for her child, will say: "He is my *splanchna*." The lateral relationship, however, is one of blood: my sister is "my blood," and blood-brotherhood is reported to have been created between friends, at least until recently, in remote sections. The organs of communication, the windows of the soul, are the eyes among the Greeks, and also among the Russians, as well as in Latin America. In Mediterranean countries and the Middle East evil flows through the eyes when an individual admires and covets.

Different areas of the body, or different sides, are associated with different activities. In certain cultures there are very strict distinctions between the things that can be done with the left hand and those to be done with the right, largely because there is a rigid separation between the areas of sexual activity and those pertaining to food. It is usual to find the left hand associated with sex, the right with cooking and eating. A Kgatla bereaved spouse has to eat with his left hand until his contamination is removed. Western medicine believes that to rehabilitate someone who has undergone amputation is largely a matter of training. But in other cultures it may be a matter of highly skilful education involving a reorientation of values.

Certain parts of the body are often more highly charged with emotion than others. We find many regions in the Middle East, the Far East, and the Pacific Islands where the head is extremely important, often sacred. It may have to be covered, or there may be regulations against allowing anyone to step over it, or even over the shadow of another's head. In Bellona two chiefs learned in their dreams that Dr. Lambert slept on the beach above them, and woke him up, since this was harmful to them.[1] The Burmese villager refrained from building two-storey houses, so as to avoid the danger of having anyone over his head. In some areas the hair is extremely important.[2] The Burmese villagers washed their hair ceremonially, treating

[1] S. M. Lambert, 1941, p. 351.
[2] Richard C. Thurnwald, 1935, p. 296.

it differently from other parts of the body, and spent much care on it. Cutting off the hair has been a symbolic act of mourning in many cultures. In Greece long hair is a symbol of womanhood, and when urbanized daughters cut their hair, the parents often react as though a sin had been committed.

The female breasts may be taken for granted as necessary for infants, or they may be sexual symbols; or, in their role of sustaining and giving solace, they may be the symbol, or source, of "the milk of human kindness," as they are among the Arabs of Palestine, where the breast is a symbol of compassion,[1] and where a woman will bare her breast to express a blessing.

It is not here our intention to list all the differences in the emotional weighting of parts of the body, but to point out that these exist and should be taken into consideration in the application of health measures. For example, if a treatment is to be applied to feet and the head, it might be expedient to introduce it through tampering with the less valued area first. If skin is to be grafted and it is unavoidable that it be applied from the lesser to the higher area, this differential in value should at least be known to the worker. The advantages of cutting off the hair should probably be weighed against the disadvantages resulting from such a procedure. In the hospital the nurse may unwittingly offend when she uses the same towel for face and pubes; fastidious Poles, in fact, use three towels to wipe themselves, one for the face, one for the genitals, legs and feet, and one for the rest of the body. It is important to know that to many people all blood is not the same: blood from the veins may be healing, health-giving, the source of life and continuity of human and natural environment, whereas menstrual and lochial blood may be dangerous and destructive, particularly to men. A patient may be greatly concerned over the disposal of such blood, or a man in a hospital, given food by a menstruating nurse, may suspect her of wishing to bring him impotence or death. Where continuity comes through blood, a patient might well be concerned over the source of blood in a transfusion.

Where continuity between man and land is strong, this should be given consideration in the disposal of body-parts. Placenta and the navel cord, for instance, may be continuous with the infant and with the land in which they are buried, and should therefore be buried under the appropriate tree or rock. Or, as among the Kgatla, they may blight the productivity of the land, or can be used by a sorcerer to render the mother infertile, and so should be buried under the house-floor.[2] It may be necessary to keep the placenta "fresh" by way of strengthening the infant until he acquires potency; in that case, as

[1] Hilma Granquist, 1947, pp. 107-8.
[2] Schapera, op. cit. pp. 224-25, 233.

among the Tiv, it should be buried where the water carrying off the body-dirt of the bathing infant can nourish it. Again, continuity between man and land is basic to the kind of substitutions which are acceptable. The Tiv, for example, may substitute mud for blood in a health rite; the Kgatla wife whose husband is absent substitutes mud for semen in the rite of strengthening the infant.

Composition

In many societies the body is believed to be created through the mixture of menstrual blood with semen. This is a common theory in Africa; for example, among the Azande, Chagga, Kgatla. To create the new body repeated intercourse is necessary. On this belief rest accusations of adultery by visiting husbands who have had intercourse only once or twice with their wives, and on it also rest the failures of attempts at birth-control.[1] The theory is also reported from Oceania. The blood and the semen are responsible for specific parts of the forming body; among the Bavenda, the blood and muscles are believed to come from the mother, the rest from the secretion of semen.

In Western thought the body is often equated to a machine. Americans speak of "fuelling" the body or "lubricating" it; of putting it in perfect "working order," of "gearing" it to a specific situation. The Burmese used mechanical analogy, but only for the course of life, the *bios*, not for the body. In Greek folk-lore, metaphors for the body derive from trees and flowers, or from hard, cold minerals, often the precious metals. The analogy to a reproductive earth is common in many areas of the world. To people for whom the body is an organic unit, continuous with nature, to speak of any exclusively local treatment is bewildering.

Completion

In many societies the body is not considered to be complete at birth. Man has to add to it, to increase it in maleness or femaleness or potency or effectiveness, or sheer adequacy. In Burma a girl traditionally could reach womanhood only when her ears were pierced. To be truly male, a boy was tattooed between knees and navel. The body of its own accord was not completely potent; many Burmese and people from the hill tribes inserted coins and other charms under the skin to enhance the person. In Africa and Oceania the teeth had to be filed or knocked out or broken or blackened, before the body was complete. In many parts of the world, the body had to be scarified and some foreign substance rubbed in. This comple-

[1] Ibid. p. 218; Thurnwald, op. cit. p. 198.

tion was not, however, for the body itself alone, but also symbolized the continuity with the social unit. It was not enough to be scarified; it was necessary to have the special design of the tribe or clan, done in the traditional way, often with the traditional tools. In Tiv society the introduction of a new way of scarification, when this became merely body completion, symbolized and intensified the schism between the younger and older generations and the break from the body of ancestors.

A very wide-spread form of completing the body is that of circumcision, and this also is often considered as uniting the individual with the society, so that a group will call itself "the circumcised," setting itself in distinction against all the uncircumcised. Where this is the case, circumcision as a health measure will need to be preceded by education; for example, Greeks usually feel that circumcision will identify them with non-Christian groups, such as Turks or Jews, and resist it strongly when doctors order it for children. Circumcision in certain areas, as in Australia, has taken a form so intensive as to have given rise, reportedly, to wide-spread sterility. Where it is applied to girls, as in certain sections of Africa, it is said to be often responsible for difficulties of delivery. To stop or change such practices, however, may mean to give the individual a sense of inadequacy or incompleteness, or to make him feel that his identity with the unit, his continuity with the ancestors, is broken.

In certain cultures clothing seems necessary to the completion of the body. A Greek village girl may never see her naked body, and may never try to see her naked baby. She delights in the clothed baby, and particularly in festive array with embroideries and jewels. Petal skin or rosy cheeks have no part in her lullabies or dirges; she sings of costly silks and jewels, and of the festive trappings of the young brave. In many parts of the world, clothing is not "shelter," as it is classified by Western society, but personal enhancement, even completion. For 30 years missionaries among the Chagga tried to introduce change in their clothing habits, so as to combat the scourge of respiratory diseases, without any success. The Chagga said that these diseases came from evil spirits, and that clothing had nothing to do with them, since its function was that of adornment.[1]

Secretions

The attitudes and concepts relating to the secretions and effluvia of the body are relevant to the introduction of hygienic measures. Saliva may be considered potent against witchcraft, as in Greece, where anyone who gives praise also at least goes

[1] Thurnwald, op. cit. p. 198.

through the motion of spitting to ward off the effect of his own possibly evil eye. The continuity of the person may be basic to the custom of conferring the leavings of food on younger, or lesser, members of the group, or to the offer of half-chewed betel nut from brother to sister, as among the Tikopia. It may also mean that one's spittle must be guarded against evilly disposed people. Among the Arapesh, food leavings are part of the body-dirt and are carefully guarded lest they fall into the hands of the sorcerer.

Feces and urine are often treated completely casually, and the introduction of latrines in such cases involves only the necessity of convincing the people of the need to guard themselves from pollution. There is often no disgust felt about handling a baby's bowel movement; for example, a Navaho girl will scrape out her young brother's diaper and then wear it on her head if she needs a head covering; and if there is a defecation on the floor, it may merely be covered with sand.[1] We find the same casualness in the Burmese village and the rural areas of China and India. The revulsion felt toward bodily effluvia in the United States has gone under the name of hygiene, but is actually deeper than preoccupation with germs. Washing in urine is reported from several areas of the world. In many societies urine, and particularly feces, must be guarded against witchcraft, and the Navaho woman, casual about the feces on her floor, is very careful to cover and hide the spot when she and her children have gone to defecate out of doors.[2] Furthermore, since feces are a part of the person, an individual can be contaminated through them. In certain regions in Uganda, people refuse to share latrines with other individuals, because it would expose them to infection from the feces of others.[3] Among labourers in India it was found that there was a deep objection to defecating in a place where a man of lower caste had defecated.[4] Here also, the people of high caste will have nothing to do with excreta, so that hospitals as well as private households have to hire lower-caste people to dispose of excreta. In India as well as Burma, nurses usually will not clean patients or provide bed-pans, necessitating the employment of a duplicate, unwieldy staff.[5]

A mother's milk, the symbol of purity, of innocence and of kindness among some groups, is in the category of excreta among the Chinese. For the Greeks, the mother's milk is a thing apart, and the term for the "suckling" of the breast is a word that cannot be applied to anything else, so that thumb-sucking and pacifiers are in a completely different category,

[1] Clyde Kluckhohn, 1947, p. 82.
[2] Dorothea C. Leighton and Clyde Kluckhohn, 1947, p. 40.
[3] George Gillanders, 1940, p. 231.
[4] B. A. Lamprell and G. C. Ramsay, 1939, p. 4.
[5] Gordon S. Seagrave, 1943, p. 45.

and are considered to have only the function of relieving irritation of the gums.

These are some of the concepts relating to the body which are relevant to the introduction of health measures, either in the field of medicine or in that of hygiene.

HYGIENE

Hygiene and medicine are here treated separately. Hygiene, in Dr. Hydrick's definition, tells people what they *should* do and tries to prevent the spread of disease.[1] Medical care has as its purpose the relief of suffering and tells people what they *should not* do.

The two fields, however, often overlap. It is difficult, for example, to place the DDT campaign in either category exclusively. Undertaken under medical auspices, it has also destroyed pests and vermin in the area of hygiene. In Iran, a farmer was heard to complain that it had an adverse effect upon farming; the flies, mosquitoes and bedbugs which had been counted upon to wake the farmers from their afternoon siesta are now gone, and the farmers do not wake up in time to put in sufficient work before sunset.[2]

Conceptions of what constitutes cleanliness, uncleanliness, and dirt vary throughout the world. In many societies death and graves are contaminating, making relatives or people who handled the dead unclean until they can be purified or until a certain period of time has elapsed.[3] Among the Kgatla, a baby is regarded as unclean for a month or more, and must undergo a cleansing rite before it can be brought among people.[4] In pidgin English, in New Guinea, exuviae, which can be used for sorcery, are spoken of as "dirt."

Habits which may seem to us expressive of hygienic motivation may be based on other factors. It is not safe to assume that because a people are given to washing often, they can be trusted to wash their hands before embarking on an undertaking which may be highly vulnerable to infection. People in Indian villages may bathe before every meal, before anything considered "clean" activity; but child-bearing is unclean, and the woman assisting does not have to wash her hands for this.[5] When villagers in an Iranian village complained that their water tasted and smelled foul, a filter was built for it under the auspices of the Near East Foundation. The farmers were told all about the dangerous micro-organisms and urged to avoid them by drinking only the filtered water. But they

[1] John Lee Hydrick, 1937, p. 11.
[2] Lyle J. Hayden, 1949, p. 148.
[3] Anathanath Chatterjee and Tarakchandra Das, 1927, p. 31; Schapera, op. cit. p. 311.
[4] Schapera, op. cit. p. 237.
[5] John S. Carmen, 1936, p. 181; Chatterjee, op. cit. p. 11.

needed no urging; they drank of the pure water because it was cool and clear and tasted good, though not because of the absence of micro-organisms.[1] A variation of this attitude, as Margaret Mead has pointed out, is prevalent in the United States, where people avoid that which looks or smells or tastes dirty as unhygienic, whereas actually the dangerous germs have neither taste nor smell and are not visible to the naked eye.

Patterned cleanliness, not because cleanliness as such is important, but as part of a way of life, is common in many cultures. A good housewife, as among the Spanish Americans of New Mexico, may be one who always keeps her house clean; the people may always wash themselves, morning and evening. But among these people, this is the way to act, part of the aesthetic picture; it has nothing to do with hygienic ends. The idea that a person they love, or familiar objects and surroundings, can contaminate them, is rejected by this group. In Colombia cleanliness was introduced in the schools as an aesthetic measure.[2] In Indonesia and the Pacific Islands there is frequent bathing by immersion throughout the day, apparently for refreshment. In Indian villages there are often tanks where the villagers can immerse themselves before a meal.[3] The Burmese villager bathes after the last meal for refreshment and as part of the ritual of making himself festive for the amusement of the evening. Burmese wash their mouths after every meal; the Hos clean their teeth with a twig every day after their first meal.[4] Cleanliness, again, may be a ritual, as with Mohammedans and Jews. Orthodox Jews must wash out mouth and hands upon arising and before eating and after elimination; the hands must be clean before they help to wash the mouth. The water must be flowing or must be poured.

From the viewpoint of other peoples, many Western habits are dirty. The British, who regarded the hill tribes of Burma as filthy for taking almost no baths, were in turn considered dirty by the Indonesians for bathing only once a day. Our Western handkerchief, used for pocketing mucus, is found revolting by a number of other societies.

There has been confusion among people of Western culture as to the meaning of dirt and cleanliness, and the extent to which they are related to hygiene. And where new habits have been pressed upon other cultures without plan, they have often reflected this confusion. Cow-dung, for example, is important in medication in some groups, such as the Kgatla, and in some Indian villages, where it is used in poulticing and for

[1] Hayden, op. cit. p. 147.
[2] *Fundamental Education*, 1947, p. 23.
[3] Chatterjee, op. cit. p. 11; Marion W. Smith, 1946, p. 588.
[4] Chatterjee, op. cit. p. 11.

the treatment of burns.[1] There is no disgust connected with it, and disgust expressed by a foreigner may meet strong opposition. Cleanliness in Western culture is often merely an aesthetic quality, or is associated with virtue, despite the use of hygiene as a sanction.

Teaching hygienic habits has been difficult where the background of science on which they rest is lacking or even rejected. A state programme of midwife-training for Spanish Americans in New Mexico found that the purpose of training could be defeated by women to whom contamination was not a reality. "These women could be taught to scrub their hands before attending a delivery, but could not be made to understand that they should not run their fingers through their hair afterward; they learned to sterilize water by boiling it, but saw no reason why they should not then test its temperature by dipping their hands in it."[2]

Hygienic measures have been directed toward teaching people cleanly habits, better housing, better ventilation, and the destruction of vermin: but the most concentrated attack since the beginning of this century has been against soil pollution and water pollution. Where people eliminated on the surface of the ground, in no specific area, and went about barefooted, they exposed themselves daily to hookworm in many areas where this is present. Rains washed parasites from the excreta into streams and exposed people to dysentery and other intestinal disorders. Flies settling on exposed excreta carried disease from person to person. The paramount need then was for the building of deep pit latrines. The attempt to educate people to the need for latrines and to persuade them to build and use them was undertaken by the Rockefeller Foundation for the Oceanic areas,[3] by the Near East Foundation for areas in Greece and the Middle East,[4] and by various governments and colonial administrations.[5] The need was wide-spread and still is. In 1948, after 15 years of an intermittent campaign for the introduction of latrines, 98 per cent of the Greek farmers were reported to be without latrines.[6] And this was in a country where the only resistance came from the people's contentment with the habitual and from seeing no need for change.

It is no easy matter to introduce latrines in the different regions of the world. Sometimes, as in the Netherlands Indies, the very idea was so curious that people could not believe that they had understood correctly.[7] Sometimes, as in India, it was

[1] Carmen, op. cit. p. 71.
[2] Sister M. Lucia van der Eerden, 1948, pp. 27-28.
[3] See Victor George Heiser, 1936; Hydrick, op. cit.; Lambert, op. cit.
[4] Apostolos Koskinides, 1948; Near East Foundation, 1949 b; Marie Puhr, 1950.
[5] Gillanders, op. cit.; Nathan L. Whetten, 1948.
[6] Koskinides, op. cit. p. 113.
[7] Hydrick, op. cit. p. 52.

ridiculous. With all the space around the village, why should the people trouble themselves to bore holes for latrines.[1] Where continuity between excreta and the individual was strongly felt in a region where sorcery was rampant, resistance was more strong. In the mountains of New Guinea, Dr. Lambert of the Rockefeller Foundation found that the people felt safe only when they defecated in the midst of a mountain stream whose water then infected the users. In Malekula he found that the fear was so strong that he had great difficulty in securing the few specimens he did, so as to find out whether hookworm was present. In Rennell, when his assistant first got a specimen in the presence of a number of people and was seen to enclose it in a covered box, he precipitated a panic; later, after careful persuasion, each man who brought in the can of specimen also waited and watched the doctor until he finally buried the material in the sand.[2] Another belief, that all illness comes as a penalty from God, carried as its corollary that it was wasteful to try to prevent disease by building holes for excreta.[3]

When the patterns of resistance and their bases are known, it may be possible to utilize them for the introduction of the latrines. For example, in Uganda many groups were found to be afraid of using the latrines because these were fixed and known, so that sorcerers could come and get the excreta for their hostile purposes. People felt safer when they could defecate at random in the bush. To use latrines indiscriminately by way of confounding the sorcerer would not work either, since the individual is continuous with his excreta, so that the feces of another in contact with his own can bring about contamination. The British medical services persuaded people to bore latrines of such a depth that the excreta would be out of the sorcerer's reach, and to cover the fecal matter after each defecation, so as to prevent contamination.[4] In one Indian village two latrines were eventually introduced for each household, and were fitted into the pattern of village industry, since in this way the latrines could be used alternately over a period of time, allowing the contents of one latrine to become composted for sale as fertilizer.[5]

Dr. Lambert in Papua, and Dr. Hydrick in the Netherlands Indies, found that wherever there was no strong resistance to the latrines, they were actually easier to introduce than other hygienic measures, since hookworm was a chronic disease which could hold their attention over a long period, and hookworm could, besides, be seen and demonstrated; its reproduction, its eggs and larvae, could be presented graphically and dramatically.[6]

[1] Edmund de S. Brunner and others, 1945, p. 72.
[2] Lambert, op. cit. pp. 52, 226, 295-96, 304.
[3] Ibid. p. 293.
[4] Gillanders, op. cit. p. 231.
[5] Brunner, op. cit. p. 72.
[6] Hydrick, op. cit. p. 4; Lambert, op. cit. pp. 32-34.

In some areas latrines appear to be unnecessary. Dr. Lambert found that where the inhabitants took care to defecate over tide-water, hookworm was absent. However, even among such people the foreign government has been pressing for the construction of latrines above the water.[1]

The campaign for a pure water-supply met a number of resistances also. In Egypt it encountered the belief that an illness is God-sent and therefore the water-supply can have nothing to do with it, and the water is God's water, and therefore is as God wants it to be. Among some tribes in the Philippines, Dr. Heiser, campaigning for the boring of wells, met with the objection that God wanted water to run on the surface and placed it there; if he had wanted it in holes he would have provided it for them in holes. The Spanish-speaking people of New Mexico, resisting all idea of the possibility of contamination from familiar people or objects, quickly contaminated the wells which they had been made to dig at great labour through 15 feet of solid rock.[2]

In Macedonia the campaign for a pure water-supply often had as its by-product the elimination of mosquito-breeding swamps.[3]

The attempt to introduce more hygienic housing has also met with various resistances. Often people lived in crowded quarters because they liked to live that way; the hope that a better income would mean better housing for the Mexican villager, for example, or for the Spanish Americans of New Mexico, was ill-founded. In Uganda the resistance was based on the religion of the people and was found to be almost insurmountable. Here in many areas the houses have no windows and very low doorways, admitting minimal quantities of light and fresh air, and thus also allowing no opportunity for the working of the evil eye, which is responsible for all illness, poverty, and death. In other districts, a husband must not sleep in the same room as his wife, so a small hut will be subdivided into a number of tiny, dark rooms.[4] Where people are taxed according to the number of huts they own, moreover, it was found that the tax results in over-crowding.

MEDICINE: DISEASE TREATMENT AND PREVENTION

Causation

The concepts of health and disease are part of man's view of the universe and his place within it. There are people who believe that the good is normal and inherent, and only man's mis-

[1] *Handbook on the Trust Territory of the Pacific Islands*, 1948, p. 33 (*See* United States, Navy). Lambert, op. cit. p. 322.
[2] Charles P. Loomis, 1950, pp. 126-27.
[3] Harold B. Allen, 1943, pp. 179, 183-96.
[4] Gillanders, op. cit. p. 231.

deed, carelessness, or sin allows evil to intrude. Among some Indian tribes of the south-western United States evil, and specifically disease, can enter when man has allowed his relations with the universe to become disharmonious, or the loss of harmony itself is a disease. So, among the Hopi and the Papago, it is imperative to have good thoughts, to avoid quarrelling and aggressive acts, for the maintenance of good relations with the universe—that is, for psychosomatic health. The neighbouring Navaho follow a large number of specific regulations for maintaining harmony and have long curing ceremonies for re-establishing lost harmony.

Among some groups disease is a punishment for sin, mainly against society; it was therefore an important factor in the maintenance of social order. Among the Saulteaux Indians, and the Manus of the Admiralties, where confession was necessary before cure could be effected, disease actually brought to light and clarified a number of hidden matters. The whole process of getting ill and being cured was a mainstay of society. To introduce a new concept of disease, and prescribe penicillin instead of confession, to people for whom illness has a significant place in the universal order is often impossible, or dangerous to psychosomatic health.

It is common to attribute disease to the machinations of witchcraft, evilly disposed people or spirits, the evil eye, or blackmailing deities desiring to be bribed. Weak *tsav* potency among the Tiv, a low *kan* among the Burmese, makes the individual vulnerable to such attack. Fright is a major cause of disease in Mitla, and its effects may be manifested years later.[1] Against a background of such beliefs, workers found it hard to introduce hygienic measures. Wide-spread also is the belief that disease can come through the misdeed of others. Among the Navaho, parents who are careless of a regulation can cause their child to become ill many years afterwards. Among the Tiv, misdeed releases evil, introduces pollution and contaminates, and any member of the unit may suffer. In several regions of Africa the birth of twins is a cause of deadly disease, and the new parents have to be isolated for several weeks and purged until their contagiousness is gone.[2]

Attitudes toward treatment rest on the conception of health and disease. The Navaho may take treatment to relieve his symptoms, but he knows he will never be truly well until he recovers his harmony with the universe. Where health is defined as an existing average, not an ideal to be achieved, much ill health will be accepted before treatment is sought. Workers among fellahin in the Middle East found that trachoma, and even partial blindness, were part of the picture of health, since these things had always been present, and anyway they

[1] Elsie Clews Parsons, 1936, pp. 120-22.
[2] Thurnwald, op. cit. pp. 295, 328.

were from God. Reports from Latin Americans and from the Spanish Americans in the United States indicate that there, too, the picture of health contains a "normal" amount of disease. This is the conception among the Tiv, where *tsav* was needed for super-normal health. It is the attitude of rural Greeks, who learn to put up with a certain amount of ill health as a matter of course. It is one which has made the teaching of new health measures very difficult, since the people have first to be taught to recognize ill health as abnormal and unnecessary.

Infection

The idea of infection itself frequently does not have to be taught, since it is present in many cultures, but the agents of infection, the routes, the kinds of things which are communicable, are usually completely different from those which Western medicine accepts. As we have noted, the parents of new twins may be considered as carrying a deadly infection; intercourse with a man who has "hot blood" among the Kgatla engenders a contagious disease known as "bad hips" in a girl, and other girls are warned not to borrow her clothing lest they become infected.[1] What is often considered to be contagious is death in itself rather than the disease which brought it on. Excreta of two people in contact may communicate disease. All this is no more difficult for Western medicine to accept than it is for other peoples to accept the idea that walking through their village without shoes will make worms grow in their bodies. There are many kinds of measures taken for the prevention of the spread of an infection. To prevent the spread of death, the home of the dead is often burned or deserted, and his belongings buried or destroyed. In many parts of the world the near relatives of the dead are isolated, and are not allowed to mix with others until they have undergone purification. From the viewpoint of Western medical practice, these measures often are actually good precautions when the death was from an infectious disease. Dr. Lambert did find isolation of people suffering from yaws,[2] but only on one of the many islands he visited in Oceania.

In many cultures where the individual is continuous with his unit, the isolation of the ill is completely unacceptable. Dr. Carl Binger reports that when he was dealing with a typhus epidemic among the Greeks of Macedonia at the end of World War I, the family would hide its sick under piles of clothing or in the cellar rather than show them to a physician who might take them to a hospital, though they knew that to keep the sick with them might mean death for the family. This attitude is reported to be present today also, obstructing the

[1] Schapera, op. cit. p. 196.
[2] Lambert, op. cit. p. 350.

campaign against tuberculosis. People do know the danger to which they are exposed, but they feel that to isolate the sick individual, or to take precautions protecting the rest of the family, would be to reject a member of the family. In West Africa "the whole family would rather contract disease and die from it than part with the infected member." [1] Spanish-speaking people of New Mexico protest that no harm can come to them from their loved ones. The Navaho feel that this is a time when a man needs his relatives around him; they do have concepts of contamination, but they also have measures for purging so that it is possible for the infectious person to join his people again soon.

Responsibility for Care of the Sick

When a Burmese villager is ill, it is he who immediately sends for a physician, for drugs, for treatment. When a Greek is ill, he does not exhibit any need for care, does not go to bed unless he is incapable of standing up, thus exercising fortitude. When a Navaho is ill, it is his relatives who decide what is to be done and make the necessary arrangements. When a Jew from Eastern Europe is ill, he must be helpless, go to bed immediately, and give his relatives the opportunity to fulfil their role in the pattern of beneficence. The worker who knows this picture addresses his recommendations to the appropriate person. It is not much use to try to persuade a sick Navaho to go to the hospital, since it is his family who will actually make the decision for him. It is cruel to tell a Greek that he must stay in bed and do nothing for himself; it is much kinder to say this to his wife or other relatives, so that the sick one should not have to be put in the position of asking for this pampering.

Treatment

There are definite patterns of treatment in the various cultures. Where disease is inflicted by the intrusion of foreign matter, of spirit arrows or snakes or fish, sucking is a common form of treatment. In Papua, Dr. Lambert found the native doctors sucking out the spirit of the hookworm and spitting it out in the form of a miniature snake. On the first contact with Western medicine, it is usual for the native medicine man to be called first and for the Western practitioner to be called only when all else fails.

Burmese take mainly solids as medicament, and have solids introduced into the body. The Navaho depend largely upon anointing, and use a variety of greases. They use pitch as a sort of poultice, and when a herbal concoction is used, it is first rubbed ritually over the body and then the remains are

[1] S. D. Onabanirio, 1949, p. 100.

drunk. Emetics and cathartics are common, as well as astringents and inhalants. The sweat-bath and the yucca-root-and-water bath are much in use.[1] Pills and powders, unless given a meaningful place in this picture, would not have much validity here. The Spanish-speaking people of New Mexico, as well as groups in Latin America, have sometimes added patent-medicine pills to their medicines, but they depend primarily on liquids such as infusions, decoctions to be bathed in, to rub on, to drink. Such liquids are used for every kind of disease, local pain, and general indisposition.[2] In various parts of Africa we find the practice of cutting slits and rubbing in medicine as curative or for increased personal effectiveness.[3]

The Western practice of going to bed when ill is not present everywhere. In some societies, such as the Zuni, one goes to bed when one is ready to die; Dr. Bunzel reports that she was thought to be announcing her approaching death when she went to bed with an indisposition while visiting a Zuni household. Sending such people to bed may be very disturbing. The Navaho, used to moving about freely, find it terribly confining to stay in bed in the hospital. Where beds consist of mats on a draughty floor, moreover, they may not be an ideal place for the ill.

A difficulty encountered in treatment is that diagnostic measures are often taken as the cure. In Sikian, in Malaita, and the Cook Islands, Dr. Lambert found that the use of the stethoscope and tuberculin injections were considered corrective measures; the people could not understand why they should submit to further treatment. And in general, one application, whether diagnostic or curative, was considered a cure, so that in the tuberculin test, people could not be persuaded to return for further injections or for inspection.[4] The Spanish Americans of New Mexico felt that an X-ray examination was a cure in itself, and that there was no need to return to the physician.

Control and Prevention

Where illness and health are determined by ancestors or deities, prevention often takes the form of periodic rites. When Western practices are introduced, it is found to be necessary to educate people first in Western concepts of the agency of disease. It is very difficult to explain what we mean by germs and microbes. Dr. Heiser found that people in the Philippines were ready to attack germs with a bolo, since a germ represented the enemy. Workers in India found it effective to present germs

[1] Alexander H. Leighton and Dorothea C. Leighton, 1944, p. 62.
[2] Parsons, op. cit. pp. 123-28; Lydia J. Roberts and Rosa Luisa Stephani, 1949, p. 131.
[3] Schapera, op. cit. pp. 211-12, 312; Thurnwald, op. cit. p. 207.
[4] Lambert, op. cit. pp. 322, 328-29.

as poison; this made sense and circumvented the necessity of determining whether the germs had true life or not.[1] Control through elimination of insect carriers met with resistance in Buddhist societies; some groups, however, may agree to destroy life if they are made to do so by someone who will assume the responsibility. In the destruction of plague-infested rats we find that, though such people will be unwilling to take life, they are ready to abandon a village until all the rats have been forced to leave, or they will lift the roofs off their houses so that the light forces the rats to leave.[2] Africans and Greeks were delighted with the dramatic elimination of mosquitoes and vermin which accompanied the DDT campaign.[3] Iranian farmers worried because pests were God-sent, and God might now send worse ones.[4]

Immunization and vaccination are sometimes entirely acceptable. Some societies have the pattern of introducing potency and resistance to evil by the introduction of substances under the skin. The practice of pricking the skin with a needle is also often present. The Burmese did not resist injections when these were first introduced, for tattooing was prevalent here, as well as the practice of introducing charms and medicines under the skin. In Oceanic regions where tattooing is prevalent, Dr. Lambert found that people came to him demanding the "needle." Among the Tiv vaccination is acceptable when the headman endorses it, and this is a region where the practice of slitting the skin and rubbing something into it prevails.

On the other hand, Seagrave encountered great resistance to inoculation among tribes in northern Burma. People deserted their villages in panic when they heard that he was coming to inoculate against a raging epidemic of the plague.

Physician

There are certain requisites for the acceptable physician. Moslem women—except where change has been carefully induced—will not allow themselves to be examined by a male physician. In Afghanistan where, out of an estimated 18 to 20 pregnancies, there are often only one or two live births, and where sterility and repeated abortions are prevalent, physicians cannot determine the cause; although venereal disease is suspected, its presence cannot be determined because the women will not allow a male physician to look upon their faces or skin, and certainly not to conduct an internal examination.[5] Before the changes introduced by Kemal Ataturk, Moslem

[1] Carmen, op. cit. p. 103.
[2] Heiser, op. cit. p. 91.
[3] P. C. C. Garnham, 1949, p. 619.
[4] Hayden, op. cit. p. 148.
[5] J. C. Cutler, 1950, pp. 700-1.

women in an Asia Minor town flocked to a Christian minister who had some knowledge of medicine, believing that, since he was a man of God and unworldly, this was no sin; but they could not go to a regular male physician. In West Africa, physicians younger than the husband cannot look at or treat a wife, but those older can do so without bringing harm.

In many cultures the physician's right to treat must be validated, perhaps by supernatural sanction, perhaps by payment. Among the Tiv, a "physician" could not treat a patient effectively unless he had paid for the knowledge and also for the right to give that particular treatment. Often the treatment itself is ineffective unless the patient makes some payment. This conception is quite prevalent, and may be important in ensuring the patient's faith in the treatment given by a Western physician. But Dr. Lambert reports that in New Guinea a patient insisted on being paid for having his broken hand treated.[1] In Africa the British administration, attempting to persuade the people to seek treatment by making it both valid and free, announced that the people had already made payment through their taxes.

Surgery

People to whom it is important that the body should be complete, perfect, find surgery insupportable. The Spanish Americans of New Mexico resist having any cut made into the body, and prefer to deal themselves with such ills as appendicitis. An operation means that the body is damaged forever; they compare it to a pottery vessel which, however carefully mended after breaking, will always present a damaged appearance. Greeks also bewail the need for an operation, for being "cut," but they are ready to undergo it when necessary, and much readier to go to the hospital for an operation than for illness, since the former is obviously indispensable, whereas the latter might indicate rejection by the family.

Amputation presents a somewhat different picture. It is not merely surgery; it changes the individual into a kind of cripple, and in many societies the crippled are despised, or at any rate, are a source of uneasiness. The Navaho feel that the cripple is out of harmony with the universe, and close contact with him might bring disharmony into one's own life. And infants who are born deformed, among these people who have a great love for children, are sometimes abandoned to die, or taken to a hospital and left there.[2] The Greeks feel that the cripple is incomplete, and allow their children to make fun of him. This is a serious problem there at present, as the number of people crippled through the war is increased daily by the

[1] Lambert, op. cit. p. 35.
[2] Leighton and Leighton, op. cit. p. 61.

farmers who are victims of exploding land-mines left behind by the departing German army.[1]

In Melanesia, Dr. Lambert found that people preferred to die of gangrene rather than have a limb amputated, because they wanted to go complete to the after-life, lest the gods and the dead deride them for being incomplete.[2]

In Burma Dr. Seagrave found that the Katchin were ready and even eager for operation when they were sure that this was desirable. At one time a man offered a great sword for the incision by way of persuading Dr. Seagrave, who was hesitating over the advisability of operating on the abdomen, saying that he would not hold the surgeon responsible if the operation failed. The need for surgery, however, was not usually recognized by these people until it was too late. For a year, everyone undergoing appendectomy died, since the patients came only after rupture; yet they did not hesitate to come, even though they knew that no one had survived this operation.[3] In Africa also, Dr. Schweitzer found that the people were ready to accept surgery, even that involving amputation, and were impressed with the dramatic cure effected. At one time a man walked 300 miles to be operated on.

EFFECTS OF CHANGE

The effects of change, and of regulations intended to bring about change, have sometimes been unforeseen. Pure-water campaigns, directed at the elimination of enteric disorders, have actually reduced malaria through removing the source of the swamp, and have resulted in better roads, as in a village in Egypt, or a village park, as in a Macedonian village. A hut-tax in Africa, and the scarcity in timber resulting from industrialization, have brought about overcrowding and possibly an increase in ill health.[4] The introduction of medicine has meant a loss of faith in the known, and when the new medicines proved too expensive, people found themselves without any medicine.[5]

Industrialization and the migration of labour, as well as the opening of roads and the establishment of improved transportation, have meant that local diseases have been spread to areas where there was no immunity. From tropical areas in Africa, tsetse infection is brought to temperate regions, and here the new-comers are exposed to cerebro-spinal meningitis and tuberculosis, and take the latter home with them. Tuberculosis in Africa has been aggravated by industrialization and

[1] Near East Foundation, 1949 b, op. cit. p. 32.
[2] Lambert, op. cit. p. 97.
[3] Seagrave, op. cit. pp. 28-29, 49, 51.
[4] William Malcolm Hailey, 1938, p. 1139.
[5] *World Health Organization Newsletter*, No. 10, October 1950, p. 4. (*See* United Nations, WHO.)

urbanization. In the home village, where work was not compulsive, where one could sit or work in the sun, where the hut of the dead was burned, conditions worked against the spread of the disease.[1]

The attempt to control or eradicate a disease has affected the lives of many tribes. In Uganda and on the Gold Coast, entire populations were moved and then repatriated as a measure for controlling the tsetse-fly infection.[2] In the Congo the movement of infected people, as well as of people to and from the infected areas, was restricted.[3] Often tsetse-fly control has resulted in the planting of eucalyptus trees near the village, so as to save people the necessity of going to and from the bush for firewood; it has sometimes also meant the introduction of brick for building.[4]

Industry, which has been responsible for much ill health and disruption, has also been responsible for many of the health programmes in colonial areas, since people in ill health or low health make wasteful workers. And the economic motivation for the introduction of health measures has been reported from rural areas also, where people have been persuaded to control flood-waters which formed breeding-places for malarial mosquitoes, only when they discovered that these also damaged the crops.

ADDITIONAL REFERENCES

M. Aziz, 1947; Wilbert Beale, 1935; P. A. Buxton, 1949; "Egypt Menaced from Within," 1948; James H. S. Gear, 1949; G. H. Gunn, 1947; A. Irving Hallowell, 1948; Douglas G. Haring, 1948; Erdman Harris, 1932; Alice Joseph, 1942; H. Nelson, 1949; Elsie Clews Parsons, 1945; *Report of the First National Sanitation Clinic*, 1948; Mohamed M. Shalaby, 1950; Willard L. Thorp, 1950; G. Tooth, 1950.

INDUSTRIALIZATION

GENERAL CONSIDERATIONS

Civilization in the last century has meant increasing industrialization in Europe as well as in the United States, and in the countries with which they came in contact, and which, courted or coerced into commerce with them, also became progressively industrialized. In both West and East the process was, for long, unplanned. The people in responsible positions had, as a rule, no view of the total picture, and no suspicion of the

[1] Hailey, op. cit. pp. 1138-39; 1199-1200.
[2] Ibid. p. 1131; K. R. S. Morris, 1950.
[3] Hailey, op. cit. p. 1133.
[4] Ibid. p. 1131

eventual results and their ramifications. Those who did either hailed the increase in material goods as an increase in human welfare, or offered romantic escapism. Even now, after long experience, and with all our awareness and intensive investigation of the concomitants of industrialization, we are astounded when we see the far-reaching results of the introduction of money into a barter economy, or of a new tool as simple as the kerosene lamp or a wooden-wheeled wagon.

Industrialization is with us to stay. We may decry its effects, as did a Venezuelan editor recently, appalled at the hidden poverty of rich, industrialized Caracas.[1] Yet, "The demographic consequences of industrialization constitute a powerful propulsive toward further industrialization. . . . It is not a reversible process."[2] And other countries, still primarily agrarian, are now drawn into the process of industrialization as a result of contact with Western civilization. Sometimes, in introducing a programme of industrialization or the building of great public works and large factories, such countries have introduced radical change in the standard of living, drastically curtailing consumers' goods.[3] Usually the effects have been much more far-reaching and costly in human welfare than this statement implies.

The areas of agricultural change and industrialization overlap in certain respects. Large plantations, usually owned and operated by people of Western origin, use large numbers of labourers, as does industry, and seeing the process merely as one of money-making, often exploit land and people.[4] In Africa, plantations are often near the labourers' native villages, so that there is no accompanying disruption of the family and village life, as there is in connexion with industry; but in New Guinea, where labourers were brought from great distances, there was such disruption, as well as demoralization, among the large groups of men living without women and without families or villages.[5] In addition, mechanization itself, whether in agriculture or in industry, separates man from the traditional processes and techniques of his social unit, from the skills which he learned as an aspect of his belongingness with his family, or of his identification with his father and his line of ancestors. Finally, even on small farms, where cash crops have been introduced, the effects of the new money economy have often been of the same kind as with the introduction of industrial wages.

Governments throughout the world have done away with the more obvious ills of industrial labour. Women may no longer

[1] *Time*, Vol. 57, No. 8, 1951, p. 39.
[2] Irene B. Taeuber, 1950, p. 292.
[3] Horace Belshaw, 1950, p. 50.
[4] Candido M. de Silva Rondon, 1943, p. 23.
[5] William Malcolm Hai'ey, 1938, p. 699; S. M. Lambert, 1941, p. 21; Richard C. Thurnwald, 1935, p. 118.

be allowed to work 14 hours a day, as they did in Turkey in 1914, or in rooms where no fresh air is allowed to enter lest the humidity shrink the cotton, as they did in Bombay at that time. But neither are they any longer allowed to bring their children to sleep or play at their feet.[1] The new laws have given workers protection, but the efficiency measures, and measures undertaken honestly for the protection of children, have worked toward breaking up the family unit during the day.[2]

The implications of industrialization for mental health are not covered by the new laws. For example, when it was proposed to a group of fellahin that a village pump be installed as a labour-saving device for the women, they said, "You say that the pump will save our women effort and time. If that happens, what are they going to do with themselves all day long?"[3] And it is not merely a question of occupying time. This is one of the components of womanhood; a woman carries water from the fountain. When Arab pictures are made for the tourist trade, they often portray a woman with a water pitcher. So also, among the Tiv, as well as the Burmese, women were identified with the pounding mortar; and the wife whom the Tiv, Akiga, pictures, was one who spun and wove for her husband. What happens to the woman, and to the man's relation with her, when she ceases to fulfil her role, to fit the picture of womanhood and wifehood? When work is neither virtue nor necessity, but merely a way of life, what happens when "labour" is saved? what happens when industriousness is one of the highest virtues, as it is with some American Indians?

Such factors must be taken into account when and if industrialization is to be introduced without undue destruction. For example, the FAO mission fund found that Greece must be industrialized and must change to a predominantly cash-crop economy if it is to be able to support its growing population and to raise its standard of living. There is a practical problem here of how best to reconcile cultural patterns with technical change. It is suggested that women in the villages be persuaded to buy factory-woven cloth, and to send their clothes to the laundry, and to support processing industries in general. Yet the laundering on the slab by the village fountain, or on the rocks by the stream, is a time of enjoyable social intercourse; one of the beloved songs of the round dance tells of such a laundering group. Again, visitors bring away a happy picture of the mother weaving under the grape-arbor in the spring, now and then stirring the cooking-pot, while her children play about. Good mothers start weaving for their daughters almost from birth. Factory-woven cloth is in use to some extent, but can all home weaving disappear without

---

[1] Janet Harvey Kelman, 1923, p. 83.
[2] Lo-Chun, 1938, pp. 241-42.
[3] Edmund de S. Brunner and others, 1945, p. 99.

impoverishing the life of the individual and of the family? And if it does, can industry provide an equally meaningful occupation to take up the released time? Again, the FAO report suggests that Greeks be persuaded to invest their money in industry, so as to make industrialization possible; but this runs counter to the Greek attitude of trusting only a sure thing, the known present. One speculates *about* the future, not *in* the future. A Greek traditionally likes his money in the form of a lump under the mattress, not as so many figures on a chart, or a number of shares of stock. And when people love their life on the land so much that the greatest gift of gratitude they can send to the United Nations is a jar of Peloponnesian earth, the displacement of the individual or the family from the village to the industrial centre could bring much distress. All these difficulties are not insurmountable, but to effect technological change with the least human destruction, these problems and others of their kind must be taken into account.

Actually, there are patterns in Greek life that allow for continuity in spite of radical change of occupation. When Greek men first emigrated to the United States, they brought with them the construct of the family and the village; in one sense they never left home. They did not become part of the community around them and barely recognized its existence. They were working for the family they had left behind, spending on themselves only what was absolutely necessary, since they were earning family money, money for a sister's dowry or a brother's education, or an additional family field. With this background to give them stability, and with the strong feeling for personal freedom, they could take up a completely non-traditional occupation, that of restaurateurs, without disruption, an occupation that did not demand obedience to the external authority of an employer, and in which the structured relationships of the family could be reproduced. This was also true of Chinese emigrants who, sustained by family continuity, could safely be away from home for many years and take on the non-traditional occupation of laundry-men.

MONEY ECONOMY

Here we must distinguish between the presence of money in a community and a money economy. For example, Burma traditionally had essentially a subsistence and barter economy, although money was in use. Money was not used to create more money, or to found a fortune, or to make the individual independent of the family; and the earning of money was incidental to living, it was not an end. Linton reports trying to buy the entire stock of pieces of raffia cloth from a trader in a Madagascar market-town, and of being refused on the ground that the trader would be bored through the rest of the day if he had nothing to sell. In addition, the buyer being a poor bargainer, was actually paying too high a price; yet bargaining is often considered the spice of social intercourse, and this too many have caused the trader to refuse to give up a day's bargaining for the sake of extra profit.[1] This is not what the Western world means by a money economy.

Technological change in agriculture, as well as in industrialization, has introduced a money economy in many regions. For example, the Navaho, who were established by the United States Government on farms in an unusually fertile strip, learned to neglect their farms so as to work for cash wages. Mothers left their children untended, gave up time-consuming preparation of their traditional foods for makeshift, processed store foods. The health of the Navaho children, it was found, had been maintained at a higher level under the conditions of a subsistence economy. In Africa, the introduction of a money economy has usually meant atomization of the individuals within the family, complete destruction of the structuring of family relationships, and of the social and economic system of the group. Where wealth lay in herds of cattle under the head of the family or the extended family, who had "earned" the right to this position organically, the growing boy had an established place within the scheme, and was dependent upon the head until he himself reached the position of headship organically. Now a boy can go and earn money to buy a cow. The money economy has meant secession and revolt, the undermining of parental authority and the authority of tradition, and this has resulted in the rise of the "younger generation" as a class apart. Marriage is often no longer a contract between two families but, particularly in the cities, one between a man and a woman. The traditional *lobola*, the bride-price, which cemented two families in interdependence and maintained strongly structured continuities within the family, is now frequently handed by the boy to the girl, closely imitating the pattern of prostitution which is prevalent in the cities.[2] Where a traveller always knew he could find ready hospitality, he now often has to pay for food and shelter, even to his relatives; or he may find that his friend, seeing a traveller arriving, has conveniently disappeared, to spare himself the expense of entertaining with bought food, or food he could sell for cash.[3] In China also, industrialization has meant that "family relations are more and more disregarded in property ownership."[4] Where a money economy has not been accepted or understood by people living in the midst of this industrial society, there is frequently a tendency toward exploitation.[5]

[1] Ralph Linton, 1936, p. 144.
[2] Hailey, op. cit. p. 605; Thurnwald, op. cit. p. 111.
[3] Thurnwald, op. cit. p. 133.
[4] Wong Yin-seng, Chang Hsi-chang, and others, 1938, pp. 21-25.
[5] Charles Wagley and Eduardo Galvão, 1949, p. 169.

INTRODUCTION OF NEW TOOLS

New tools are being introduced, whether in agriculture or industry, to save labour or to increase production, or to improve a product, but the change they effect often involves much more than this. Where technology is simple, the tool is an extension of the body; the shuttle elongates and refines the finger, the mallet is a harder and more powerful fist. The tool follows the rhythm of the body; it enhances and intensifies; but it does not replace and does not introduce anything basically different. But the machine is not body-patterned. It has its own existence, its own rhythm, to which man must submit. The woman at her hand-loom controls the tension of the weft by the feeling in her muscles and the rhythm of her body motion; in the factory she watches the loom, and acts at externally stated intervals, as the operations of the machine dictate them. When she worked at home, she followed her own rhythm, and ended an operation when she felt—by the resistance against the pounding mallet or the feel between her fingers—that the process was complete. In the factory she is asked to adjust her rhythm to that of the rhythm prescribed by the factory; to do things according to externally set time limits. The changes of processes and tools involved in industrialization have often brought a shattering break between the living and the all-important, sustaining dead members of the family unit. "To the Chinese the introduction of power machinery meant (that) he had to throw over not only habits of work but a whole ideology; for, dissatisfaction with the ways of his fathers in one particular meant doubt of the father's way of life in all its aspects. If the old loom must be discarded, then 100 other things must be discarded with it, for there are somehow no adequate substitutes." [1]

The suggested technological changes are sometimes uneconomical, as the labour they save is cheaper than the purchase and upkeep of the new tool. Sometimes they are resisted precisely because they do save labour, threatening to deprive workers of their maintenance. A Puerto Rican company which delayed importation and use of mechanical and chemical means of lowering production costs is much admired by the workers, partly because it does not displace them, partly on the ground that "the cane needs the human touch to grow well," and because of a feeling that herbicide is evil.[2] Sometimes machines are introduced without plan and fail because no provision is made for upkeep or replacement of parts, as when outboard motors were introduced in Brazil without parts for repair, and without, or with exorbitantly expensive, oil for

[1] H. D. Fong, 1937, pp. 3-4.
[2] Sidney W. Mintz, 1951.

fuelling. Agricultural machinery is demonstrated to farmers far too poor to afford its purchase and upkeep and with farms too small for its effective use, when what they need is an improved hoe or plough.[1] In sections of Africa, the sewing-machine and manufactured cloth have been introduced without the use of the needle. Africans buy clothing made on sewing-machines by Indians, but they have no way of mending them, or having them mended, since machine mending has not been introduced.

The introduction of a new tool which is completely accepted may have unimagined results. In certain sections of Uganda, the introduction of lamps meant an added fire hazard to thatched roofs and provided, in turn, fire-proof roofing: kerosene tins, which, flattened, took the place of the thatching materials which were rapidly decreasing because of the increasing use of land for cash crops. This affected the health picture, since the old roofing had harboured rats which were a plague hazard. However, the next step in efficiency has resulted in the sale of kerosene in the bulk, and people now carry it home in Coca Cola or beer bottles; the new roofing material has disappeared, and the administration of Uganda now has to experiment with suitable roofing materials.[2]

In Africa railroads were built as a measure in the campaign against slavery, particularly the slavery encouraged by the need for porters. But until contact with the West, the need for porterage had been non-existent. Slavery had been merely a form of agricultural or domestic service. The West, in an attempt to eradicate an evil of its own making, built a railroad by compulsory labour at the expense of a very high toll of life, supporting the introduction of cash crops and a money economy for its own uses, destroying traditional patterns of family living, marriage, and parental authority. Ultimately the public works were perhaps "instruments of world welfare" at best. They have yet, however, to be made instruments of African welfare.[3]

An interesting example comes from the Papago Indians, among whom a wooden wagon was introduced by the United States Government around 1900. The men quickly taught their horses to pull the wagon, and one man learned to work iron, so that they could shoe the horses and repair the metal parts of the wagon. The women had been carrying water for household needs in earthen *ollas,* from a distance. Now the wagon could be used for this, and the water used in the household increased. The *ollas* were found to break easily in the wagon, so they were replaced by wooden, and later by metal, barrels; only a few *ollas* were kept for holding the drinking-water, since their porous walls kept the water cool. The wagon was then used

[1] Brunner, op. cit. p. 129; Charles P. Loomis, 1950, pp. 117, 124.
[2] George Gillanders, 1940, pp. 233-37.
[3] J. S. Furnivall, 1948, pp. 320-22.

to transport the family to its summer camp; and in order to do this, a road had to be built. Soon the traditional practice of having the women gather small pieces of fuel (a wide-spread Indian custom, defining the role of the woman) was changed by the presence of the wagon. Now men undertook the bringing of wood, cutting instead of merely gathering, and presently they hauled wood to the nearest towns for sale, introducing a money economy, which eventually meant that the villagers began to grow cash crops to add to the loads of wood going into town.[1] What we do not know, of course, was what had been present in the culture to guide the change in this particular direction, and what hidden benefit or harm came with it.

EFFECTS ON HEALTH AND NUTRITION

The attention paid to the health of workers limits itself, as a rule, to what is considered physical health, and varies in different countries. Where the conquered peoples under Western jurisdiction have been considered an inferior species of humanity, legislation protecting the welfare of workers has often been weak. In Kenya, for example, there has been the practice of "payment by pigment"; and the wages of the Africans are permitted to be so low that they do not assure an adequate subsistence for one, discouraging the workers from bringing their families or from getting married, and encouraging prostitution. There is malnutrition, and a lowering of efficiency, which need not worry the employer when labour can be had at such low recompense. Where wages are to be paid partly in food, often only poor food is given; and during World War II employers cheated freely, since rations were fixed, thus making extra money for themselves. And when employers break the law not deliberately, but in ignorance, the effect is the same.[2] Basic to this condition is not merely industrialization but an expression of disrespect for, and exploitation of, one section of humanity by another, and it is encouraging to know that now the government shows concern over the condition of its wards. Here and in other parts of Africa, there are sometimes industrial centres surrounded by tribes where wage employment is not countenanced. To reach these centres, people from distant reserves may walk as much as 700 miles.[3] They arrive worn-out from their exertion as well as from poor nutrition along the way. Companies often bring such people up to par with rest and good food before putting them to work.[4] This is good practice from the financial standpoint. However, these same companies are ready to release

[1] John Adair and Edward H. Spicer, n.d.

[2] S. and K. Aaronovitch, 1947, pp. 106-12; Kenya Colony and Protectorate, 1939.

[3] *The Industrialization of the African*, 1937, p. 4 f.

[4] Hailey, op. cit. pp. 1120-21.

these people during a period of seasonal slackness, jobless and penniless, hundreds of miles away from home.

Where workers are considered full citizens or full members of the society, conditions are usually better. A government such as that of Egypt, for example, sees the welfare of the country as a totality, recognizes that the solution of the continuing increase in population lies in industrialization, and prepares for this by planning adequate housing for workers near urban centres.[1]

In general, the effect of a cash-crop or wage economy on nutrition has been one of lowering the level by disturbing the balance achieved under subsistence economy, introducing processed foods as prestige foods, limiting the amount and quality of subsistence crops in favour of cash crops, or the amount of time spent in preparation and preservation of food for home consumption.

ATTITUDES AFFECTING INDUSTRIALIZATION

Obstacles to the establishment of an industry are often encountered, arising from the values of the culture involved. The Masai, for example, will not work for wages, since tending cattle is the only valued occupation,[2] and cattle themselves are the highest good. In many parts of Africa the relationship of obedience to someone without traditional authority is lacking. The Zulus, considering themselves a dominant warrior race, think it degrading to accept the discipline of industrial labour; they are ready, however, to accept domestic service, since this falls within a differently structured relationship.[3] The Tiv say that only boys who are asocial and who do not fit into the group are ready to live away from home earning wages; that is, boys who are essentially maladjusted. On the other hand, when the railroad went through Tiv country, groups of people from the district concerned worked happily for wages, and revealed qualities much liked by their employers.

The assumption that all peoples have an incentive to improve the standard of living, and therefore of taking on employment, is not justified. Puerto Rican workers may express a desire to earn enough money to pay the first instalment on the installation of electric light or the purchase of a radio; yet this desire often does not counterbalance the distaste for working for wages, so that payments may not be completed, or an individual may leave his employment if he has some money accumulated.[4] This is essentially true also of the Spanish Americans of New Mexico, as well as of many

[1] René Francis, 1948, p. 24.
[2] Hailey, op. cit. pp. 604-5.
[3] Ibid. p. 694.
[4] Mintz, op. cit.

Mexican wage-earners. The incentive to improve subsistence by wage-earning is reported lacking in many parts of Africa.[1] In the Anglo-Egyptian Sudan, when peasant proprietors found their incomes increased to unaccustomed amounts, they did not know what to do with the surplus, and spent it hiring others to do their work. Their incomes had been increased through external aid, not through internal motivation such as desire for new goods and services. Or the incentive may be present, but not as an incentive to improve subsistence. For example, in China: "One large employer of a highly skilled class of labour, not long ago, was moved by the obvious physical inefficiency of many of his employees and the large incidence of sickness among them to raise wages of his own accord. The only result, as he was able to discern not long afterwards, was that each of these men was now supporting an even larger number of relatives than a person in his position was expected to look after."[2] In Puerto Rico, where the pattern of supporting a large number of dependent relatives is present along with changing values making for individualism, men prefer to emigrate alone to the United States for wage-work, so that, if they are single, they can save or spend their money as they please with no relatives to claim a share, and if they are married, they can send money home to their wives knowing that it will be used for the immediate family, since women living without men are not supposed to support dependents.[3]

In Annam it is difficult to get the original inhabitants to work in the mines, as they fear to disturb the mountain spirits; and their fears are supported by the high mortality in the mining occupation.[4]

In many parts of the world we find that one works as necessity calls; this may be the need for the day's food, or for preparation for a ceremonial, or it may be the need of the land or the growing plant which must be attended to on that particular day. But the machine has no such insistent need; so if the worker has enough food or money for his needs, he does not see why he has to go to his job. In fact, if he also has a garden, or if the fish are running in the stream, he has a valid reason for not going. This is part of a general attitude which we find also in connexion with school attendance. And it is an aspect of the different conception of time as a process rather than as programmatic. People may operate in terms of mechanical "time-saving" tools—automobiles, radios, telegraph—but this does not mean that they accept the need for speed which these implements represent; they may be only modern conveniences to these people. The exact

[1] Hailey, op. cit. pp. 604-5.
[2] Fong, op. cit. pp. 6-7, 38.
[3] Mintz, op. cit.
[4] Virginia Thompson, 1937, pp. 456-66.

minute may be unimportant, and the time "saved" using such devices may nevertheless be spent in inactivity; people "stand or sit doing very little for hours at a time." Industrialization, in the interest of good results and human welfare, must take account of such basic patterns, either working within them, or else educating people in an understanding of the Western framework of industrial work.[1]

Cultural attitudes often determine the composition and quality of the personnel in an industrial establishment. Where familial values are of paramount importance, as in Greece, China, and Japan, a man has to give jobs to relatives, choosing them neither according to ability nor according to merit. And even when the employees are not all relatives, the structure of the organization may follow the lines of the kinship unit. In China, for example, there was reluctance to discharge a delinquent employee (as one punished one's own son for wrongdoing, but did not expel him from the family)[2] there was a decided preference for punishment, and therefore businesses in China and Japan were found to be losing money. In Japan, when a business was losing money and there was not enough work for all the employees, the employer did not therefore dismiss them; he was responsible for them. (This was termed "feather-bedding" by the *New York Times*, when a financial adviser from the United States discovered that it was the pattern in government offices.) The practice was accorded unqualified condemnation; Western methods were then applied by employers in private firms, and caused upheaval and indignation on all sides.[3] In addition, when authority was part of the structure of the family or extended family, the employee did not know how to obey a foreman, and the employer did not know how to treat the employee. And people to whom honesty was a matter of personal family relations acted with dishonesty in terms of the industrial organization the validity of which as a unit they did not recognize.[4]

In Burma, the attitude against the accumulation of capital, the tendency to spend much money for religious purposes, the tenet that a Buddhist cannot make a valid will, all militate against the creation of capital needed for industrial enterprise of any major scope. However, small mills and small plants in rural areas have been increasing and fit into the Burmese pattern. Under British administration, machinery for agriculture was regarded with suspicion as another device to raise taxable capacity, but agricultural shows, where they were exhibited, were attended, since they fit into the pattern of "convivial celebration, with a few side-shows such as ex-

[1] John F. Embree, 1950.
[2] Fong, op. cit. p. 7; C. L. Nieh, 1933, p. 7.
[3] O. M. Green, 1950, pp. 76-77.
[4] Fong, op. cit. pp. 2, 3, 56.

hibitions of fertilizers and insect pests, matters to which the government attaches superstitious importance."[1] In Turkey, there was a shortage in qualified labour, and low efficiency of unskilled labour, because the worker simply did not like industry, and did not remain long enough to be trained, preferring to go back to his agriculture.

INDUSTRY AND THE SOCIAL UNIT

Industrialization affects the social unit in a variety of ways. Even in changing its tools, it makes a change within the structure, re-aligning roles in the division of labour and the interrelationships involved in the earlier processes. In Burma, the British administration pointed with approval to the "rise" in the standard of living indicated by the rising imports of cotton goods and crockery; but actually this was also an index of changes in family life, of the idleness of the loom underneath the house where wives and daughters had traditionally woven rich silks for the family, and where husbands also sometimes did so, producing more beautifully patterned stuffs. The Tiv men felt that the marital relationship had been disrupted with the coming of manufactured cloth. The traditional picture of the wife was one in which she spun by the village fire at night, listening to the children's riddles, and to the myth-telling of the men, eventually making cloth which her husband could sell to make wealth for the family; cloth-making was a service from a wife to her husband. When manufactured cloth was introduced, the women demanded it of the men; the man had to leave home to make money to buy cloth for his wife, who had ceased to fit the traditional picture of a wife. In many parts of Africa the introduction of factory goods meant the rapid disappearance of local industries, with all that these involved in the way of family relationships and village life. In Northern Rhodesia, the smelting of iron declined, and pottery disappeared, with the introduction of the petrol tin. In the Union of South Africa, the products of local industries were sold to procure money for factory goods, which became increasingly important, and after the local industries themselves disappeared, there were no goods to sell to procure money, since cattle had a value beyond money, so that cash crops and wage-labour were the only answer, with an accompanying disruption in living-patterns.[2]

When men are forced to leave the village to earn wages, the economic interrelationship is again affected. In Africa, in areas where men used to lop off the branches of large trees to burn as fertilizer for the garden, the young men are now absent and older men must take on this work, with the

[1] O. H. Spate, 1941, pp. 75-90.
[2] Hailey, op. cit. pp. 1408, 1420.

eventual result of deforestation and soil erosion, because the older men cannot climb the trees to cut off the branches, and so they cut down the trees at the root. Again, in many parts of Africa agriculture was an area of activity where there was division of labour between men and women, with the men clearing and preparing the land; women cannot make good gardens without the periodic assistance of their men, who are now absent for long periods working for wages at the industrial centre.[1]

The effect of the migration of the men on family and village life depends on whether there was a pattern for living without the men before the coming of industrialization. In Northern Burma, for example, there had apparently been a pattern for temporary migration to South Burma, among those in need of money; and it was this pattern that was followed when wage-earning became more important. Few Burmese went to the cities to work in factories or other urban wage occupations. In Greece, there was a centuries-old pattern, either of emigration of the man until he could take a wife or his family to the new country or until he could come back with the needed money; or of the man's going "on the sea." Many islands were accustomed to sending their men on the sea, as sponge-fishermen, or to man vessels. "My father used to come back every year to propagate another child," said the son of such a man. Where family ties are strongly structured, the family can build life which will take such absences without disruption, where the wife can turn to a brother or an uncle or her father, some man who has not left the community. And a Greek wife will do the work of a man when fortitude demands it. Sharing of work, rather than division of labour, is important in the Greek peasant family. In China, also, the family learned to follow its course in the absence of the male head. For the young Chinese man it has been traditional to enlist in the army or to enter a government office; the village was used to being without him.[2]

In India, too, the pattern in many sections has been for the man to go to the industrial centre without the family. Usually he did not go far, so that he could return after a few months to do the man's share in the cultivation of the ancestral lands. The men's lives were centred in the village, even though they did work temporarily in the cities—in the same way that in the traditional pattern of living, a man might have a store in the market centre and still have his life centred in the village where he had his home, his cows, and his fields.[3]

In Africa, on the other hand, there had been no precedent

[1] Ibid. p. 885.
[2] Shih Kuo-Heng, 1944, p. 43.
[3] Kelman, op. cit. pp. 91-94; Marian W. Smith, 1946, p. 577.

for the long absences of the men when industrialization came, with its demand and lure for men. Division of labour had been basic to family life and agricultural work, so that these were disturbed. The loss of production was not balanced by the wages the men earned, since these usually were spent to support the man while away, or to buy a few gifts to bring back, so the standard of living deteriorated.[1] Without the men, the home lost its place as an educational unit, and there was no way of passing on the values of the society to the growing boy.[2] With the dislocation in family life, the displacement of authority, came demoralization. Young girls, unwilling to stay in villages without men, followed the men to the cities, where they often became prostitutes.

Some idea of the sheer depletion of the villages can be gained from the figures on migration. "In 1933, it was estimated that 62 per cent of the able-bodied male population of the Mikuyu and Kiambu, 74 per cent of the Nandi, 43 per cent of the Lumbwa . . . left the reserves as labourers."[3] In China, in the mid-thirties, 50 per cent of the families in southern Shantung, western Hupeh, and northern Anhwei had been affected by internal migration, usually by having some member leave.[4]

The effect of the migration, as we have seen, differs according to whether or not the centre is at a great distance. If it is distant, the men may stay away several years at a time. In China, in the twenties, it was found that the largest percentage of the men migrants stayed away three years. In Africa, the men who work as labourers on plantations may go only for the day, or at any rate, are usually able to return after brief absences.

In some cases the whole family migrated. "Ordinarily, the migrating family, that is, the migrating immediate family, makes the most successful adjustment, but this is only true where, because of the system of relations previously in operation or the progressive changes which have taken place which have led to such a system, the immediate family is not too integrally knit to a larger structure which provided for its members a major proportion of its emotional satisfaction."[5] The Greek migrating family manages to keep its emotional balance through keeping in close touch with the rest of the relationship unit, or, as in the United States, through reproducing the village relationships in the Greek community of a large city. In Brazil, where migration of rural families was common, migration itself was not a disturbing factor.

[1] Hailey, op. cit. pp. 704-5.
[2] Edwin H. Smith, 1934, pp. 333-34.
[3] Aaronovitch, op. cit. p. 203.
[4] Hu Nai-tsiu, 1938, p. 256.
[5] Eliot D. Chapple, personal communication.

Where the tie with a social unit larger than the immediate family has been strong, however, and when the people had a strong bond with the land, the migration of the family makes for disruption. This is particularly true of Africa, where moral law often loses its validity when the tie with the land is broken.[1] It is true of the Tiv, where even elders strong in magical potency were uneasy when travelling away from the land of their unit; and among the Nuer, who feel that leaving their own soil will bring them illness unless they drink a dilution of their soil in water, mixed with increasing amounts of soil from the land of their new habitat.

What will happen upon migration depends on cultural structuring and values. In the United States, different groups of immigrants present a differing picture of strength and health; some groups, coming in families, quickly present a picture of disorientation, while others—whether in families or individually—present a picture of inner stability and orientation. It appears, for example, that some groups have the ability to maintain a construct of the unit they have left behind, and to recreate it. According to Laura Thompson, when workers from the Philippines, mainly Catholics, first went to Hawaii, they were mostly men who went alone; but when one of them got married, a large number of men stood as godfathers to the first baby, and a kinship unit was thus immediately created out of a large number of unrelated men.

The extent to which urbanization of the family affects family relationships again depends on what has been there to begin with. In Greece, the pattern of interdependence often remains the same. Whereas formerly all the sons worked in the common fields and added to the family income, now all the sons work for wages which they bring to the family, keeping only a very small sum for cigarette money. However, this pattern is reported to be undergoing change, and, in many other cultures, wages for the sons have been a wedge, introducing increasing atomization. Sons stop working for the economic welfare of the family unit, and in turn cease being dependent on the father. Eventually, grown children cease to be an insurance against old age, so old age brings indigence; or else the parents must save toward it, or the state must take care of it. This change of events, encouraged by changes in legislation and in land-tenure introduced by British administrators, took place in Burma in recent years. In the United States, internal migration has increasingly meant loneliness for the old people or unbearable displacement in their old age. An indirect effect of wages and migration has been the rise of a younger generation in opposition to an older generation. This is reported of the Tiv, of Spanish Americans in New Mexico and in Peru, and from other areas.

[1] *The Industrialization of the African,* op. cit. pp. 3-4.

SOLUTIONS IN PROCESS

The waste in human welfare which came into being as a by-product of industrialization has caused much concern among governments, social scientists, and foundations. There appears to be general agreement that decentralization of industry, bringing work to the village or to its vicinity within the framework of known associations and associational ties, will make for less disruption and, at the same time, will bring the increase in income needed for raising the standard of living.

Village industries can provide the funds for raising the standard of living, and can fill the gap created when handicrafts give way to manufactured goods. They can also, in part, be the answer to the mechanization of agriculture, which often releases time for which there is no provision. As it is, in many villages in India, China, and the Philippines, the farmers are actually partly unemployed. In the Chinese villages it is estimated that the farmers and farm labourers are unemployed for periods of six to eight months a year.[1]

The introduction of village industries is not, however, without difficulties. In India it is found that the villagers often do not want to be organized into new co-operative units, or any created units. Demonstration of the advantages of the new products is often not effective, since the demonstration party does not stay long enough in the village to make a lasting impression on people who need a long time to assimilate new ideas.[2] In China, in 1935, village industry in the district of Kiangying was working havoc in family life. Before it was introduced, the women had spent much of their time helping the men in the fields and had raised silkworms; they had done their spinning and weaving only during their free time. When home knitting with a hand-machine was introduced, women knitted late into the night by kerosene lamps, and, since they had to spend so much of their time caring for old people and young children, they had no time even to eat their meals with the family, but ate at their work. In times of crop failure, when the home industry was the only means of subsistence, the loom had to be busy all the time if there was only one loom in the house. This meant that members of the family had to work at it in shifts 24 hours a day. This was an economic solution, but one that failed on the social level.[3] In southern Hopei, also in the 1930's, it was found that commercialization had brought a shift in power and authority in the village; not the farmers and producers, but the owners and administrators, were the ruling groups. "The centre of political power of the village has been definitely shifted from

[1] Shriman Narayan Agarwal, 1949, p. 184; Chen Han-seng, 1947, p. 62; Erich H. Jacoby, 1949, p. 189.
[2] T. Bheemacharya, 1949, pp. 12-13.
[3] Lo-Chun, op. cit. pp. 239-40.

the elders and old gentry to the business firms wherein reside the trinity of usurers, landlords, merchants. Commercialization, unaccompanied by a healthy system of production, is thus shown to be a deteriorating factor in Chinese rural economy, although it at first brings a transitory period of prosperity."[1]

There have been difficulties and destruction; but through a study of the local situation, through an understanding of and respect for the existing framework, such difficulties are being solved. China's co-operatives have become increasingly successful in their social effects. The recently formulated programme proposes to carry over into industrialization the traditional co-operative relationships of guild and family; it aims at industrializing the already present village units.[2] In India, careful teaching by people who have an understanding of the need for a long period of instruction achieved the introduction of the idea of village industry. In one village, even the latrine was incorporated into the home-industry scheme, so that many homes now have two latrines, one in use while the contents of the other are being composted for sale as fertilizer. In Mexico and Ecuador, some home industries have fitted into existing, valued, and enjoyed patterns, with happy results.[3]

ADDITIONAL REFERENCES

Agrarian China, 1938. (*See* Institute of Pacific Relations); Margaret E. Burton, 1918; Chang Yu-sui, 1938; F. L. Ho, 1931; Kenya Colony and Protectorate, 1932; "Labour Conditions in Indo-China," 1938. (*See* United Nations, ILO); W. I. Ladejinsky, 1950; Bruno Lasker, 1950; L. S. B. Leakey, 1936; Lee Tse-tsian, 1938; Jose Silva, 1943; Thomas Lynn Smith, 1946; Carl C. Taylor and others, 1949.

FUNDAMENTAL EDUCATION

Until recently, the need for literacy was considered one of the most pressing in under-developed countries. But the concept has now been broadened, and literacy is regarded as the tool of education in all areas of life. As long as the function of education was to maintain and pass on to the new generation the traditions of a culture, its skills, knowledge, and principles of inter-personal conduct, its religious tenets and values, there was no need for literacy, nor for education provided and stimulated by outsiders. Parents and other relatives educated the child in his cultural heritage by giving him increasing

[1] Chi Ping, 1938, pp. 166-167.
[2] *Training Rural Leaders*, 1949, pp. 19-27. (*See* United Nations, FAO.)
[3] John Collier, Jr. and Anibal Buitron, 1949, p. 196; Nathan L. Whetten, 1948, pp. 445-47.

participation in the work involved in making a living, in community work and ceremonials,[1] as well as by giving him specific instruction. In some societies this training was supplemented by attendance at community schools for boys or for girls at special periods of their lives, often at adolescence, for the teaching of the special knowledge needed to enter adult status. In either case, the function of education was the inculcation of the established tradition.

With the impact of civilization, and particularly because of contact with Western culture, the function of education has necessarily changed. The need now is to move away to new knowledge and skills, to a new place in a new social order; education is now not for the maintenance of the old, but for change. Whether these cultures have sought Western contact or not, whether they want to change or not, the fact is that they have felt the effects of Western contact, and must now be taught how to cope with these effects. The roads built to outlying villages have brought money wages to the people for building them, trade goods on which to spend them, and often the destruction of native industries with which these goods competed, thus taking away the livelihood of the craftsmen. A desire for trade has become an incentive for cash crops, introducing an imbalance in the agricultural process which has often robbed the land of its fertility and even of its soil, and in the diet, bringing malnutrition. A lack of understanding of the principles of money and credit has led to indebtedness and loss of lands. Along the new roads new diseases travelled, while the medical aid to combat and prevent them lagged far behind. Sometimes, as in Indonesia and the Philippines, when civilization brought its sanitation, its laws, and at times its religion, this has meant a large increase in the population, on land inadequate to support it by using traditional agricultural methods.

Education is needed in all these areas to cope with and repair the destruction already introduced; and beyond this, to make it possible for the peoples, if they choose, to take their place in the community of nations, and to take advantage of the progress of science and technology in improving their standard of living.

If the new education is to fill the place of the old, it has to cover all areas of living. Native education included all growing-up: it gave instruction in inter-personal relationships, soil conservation, and ways of making a living.[2] The task of fundamental education is to cover the whole of living. In addition, it is to teach not only new ways, but the need and the incentive for new ways. For the control of water-borne disease, for example, we must teach villagers not only how to boil

[1] Richard C. Thurnwald, 1935, pp. 236-38.
[2] Robert Redfield, 1943, pp. 642-45.

their water or dig wells and install pumps; we also have to teach them how to recognize the need for this, to stop accepting all water as "water-and-therefore-good"; to recognize that *some* impurity in the water makes it bad and dangerous to health.[1] It is not enough to offer a change or an improvement; it is necessary to teach a dissatisfaction with the picture of health which includes some trachoma,[2] some infant diarrhoea, some infant death, as a matter of course.[3] It is not enough to introduce co-operatives or techniques involving co-operation; it is necessary also to teach the people to recognize as valid the created group, and to organize in terms of future benefits rather than according to established community patterns.

For many years schooling was not only ineffective, but also disruptive, because it was applied only to the young. Roles were reversed in the home, so that the children became the teachers of the parents, creating confusion in relationships, and resentment on the part of the displaced leaders. A "younger" generation in conflict with an "older" generation was created where there had been no such categories. In some societies, where the structuring of authority was felt strongly, the responsibility placed on the young to teach the old created insupportable conflict for them. Children, taught in school not to spit on the floor, to take baths regularly, to be inoculated against epidemics, lived in homes which taught the opposite.[4] With the new conception of education as covering all areas of living came the recognition of society as the unit to be educated. In China, the mass-education programme initiated by James Yen was directed at adult groups as well as children, and covered simplified reading and writing as well as public health, agriculture, and similar areas.[5]

In the United States, and increasingly in other countries, it has been the function of the Extension Service of the Department of Agriculture to educate in areas of life other than literacy. In many countries now fundamental education is carried on by teams including social workers, graduate nurses, agricultural assistants, home-economists, hygienic experts.[6]

In past years, as Margaret Mead says, education of dependent peoples was for the purpose of their successful exploitation by more advanced economies.[7] It is now recognized

[1] Edmund de S. Brunner and others, 1945, pp. 98-99.
[2] Ibid. pp. 94-95.
[3] Florence Kluckhohn, 1941.
[4] *Fundamental Education*, 1947, pp. 84-85.
[5] Ibid. p. 82; Pearl S. Buck, 1945.
[6] Elisabeth S. Enochs, 1943, pp. 20-24; *Fundamental Education*, op. cit. pp. 40-43; D. Spencer Hatch, 1944, p. 57; Ofelia Hooper, 1943, p. 252; Helen A. Kitchen, 1950, p. 5.
[7] Margaret Mead, 1946, p. 346.

that the dependent and under-developed peoples will have to be given education in literacy so that they can participate in the larger world-community. They have to be given the grasp of the framework of the economy of the civilized countries, an understanding of money and credit and the ideas of pure number involved therein, and some grasp of the implications of living by contract rather than according to established relationships.[1]

A number of factors must be taken into account in introducing literacy. The main one is the conceptual framework and the structuring of knowledge and relationships within the society. For example, when American teachers had their Samoan pupils skip a grade at school, parents were ashamed, since precocity is decried in Samoa.[2] When American teachers tried to spur Hopi and Navaho children through introducing competition, or to encourage by singling out for praise, they failed in the first case and caused intense misery in the second, since to stand out is painful and brings insecurity. The dichotomies and dualisms employed by some cultures are meaningless in others, and to present dualism as oppositive is confusing in many Pacific cultures where dualism is complementary, enclosing a whole. Concepts of success and failure are in the pattern of Western education; but in certain parts of the Orient, a "failed" A.B. is a classificatory statement of achievement.[3]

In addition, there are many questions of procedure. Should we teach literacy in the vernacular or in some world-language? To what extent should we develop principles and standards of literacy which we apply on an either-this-or-nothing basis? That is, do we believe that some literacy is better than none? Who is to make the decision as to curricular needs, and upon what principle? How much school attendance constitutes literacy? Who is included? children? adults? men? women? What body of literature do we use for people whose tradition has been entirely oral? Do we introduce our own classics, as a mission school did on the African Gold Coast, which proudly announced that every year its students performed a Greek play with all the odes in the original?[4]

In French Africa the policy at first was one of assimilation, based on ideas of equality of all men "before the law and before the future." At this time the school was transplanted from France, with all its syllabuses and legislation; the native languages were discarded and forbidden.[5] More recently, the policy has been to educate an *élite* group inspired with French ideals of civilization, who can then occupy administrative posi-

[1] Ibid. pp. 347-49.
[2] Ibid. p. 349.
[3] Ibid. p. 350.
[4] William Malcolm Hailey, 1938, p. 1245.
[5] *Fundamental Education*, op. cit. pp. 48-49; Hailey, op. cit. p. 1219.

tions; and, in separate schools, to educate the masses, mainly in areas of living. French is the medium of instruction in both types of school.[1]

In the Union of South Africa the colour bar, whether legislatively operative or not, means that there is no correspondence between attainment and reward.[2] It has been suggested, therefore, that because the great bulk of Africans are to be unskilled labourers, they should be educated realistically.[3] But this is not acceptable to the non-Europeans who want book-learning and want to be taught in English. The non-Europeans are not compelled to go to school, but they want to. Education represents to them the open sesame of progress. Their hunger for education is not met, however, as poor provision is made for their schooling.[4]

In many areas the introduction of a school system interferes with the established pattern of life. The Ngone of Nyasaland complain that their herds are in poor condition, since the boys who were the traditional herders now go to school.[5] In Basutoland and Bechuanaland there are twice as many girls as boys in school, as boys stay with the herds.[6] In some areas the level of health is too low to make school attendance easy; where there is little energy, as in many villages in India, the children are needed to do their share of the work.[7] In rural Mexico the children are said to have little energy because of inadequate diet; and they have to do hard work at home. Yet school often includes exhausting competitive games and gymnastics.[8] Turkey, faced with the necessity of establishing schools in its 40,-000 villages, adapted school work to the seasonal occupation of its villagers, "and class work, apart from the time devoted to practical training, has been reduced to 18 hours weekly."[9] Under the rural reconstruction scheme for the Menouf District of Egypt it was agreed to introduce schools working on a "full day system by which the pupils spend the first half of the day learning theoretical studies and the second half in practical training." [10]

To make schools a successful medium for literacy, the people have to be educated in the meaning of literacy; their co-operation must be enlisted, and incentives must be found or created. In many cultures there is no understanding of the need for continued attendance. Children will stay home for the

[1] Hailey, op. cit. p. 1282.
[2] *Fundamental Education*, op. cit. p. 73.
[3] Ibid. pp. 78-79.
[4] Ibid. pp. 70-71, 76; Hailey, op. cit. p. 1223.
[5] Margaret Read, 1938, p. 35.
[6] Hailey, op. cit. p. 1255.
[7] *Fundamental Education*, op. cit. p. 102.
[8] Alfredo Ramos Espinosa, 1942, p. 9.
[9] "Education in the New Turkey," 1950, p. 4; *Facts on Turkey*, 1950, pp. 14-15.
[10] Rural Reconstruction Scheme at Menouf District, Egypt.

slightest indisposition, or to keep a sick brother company, or because of a visitor or some family undertaking.[1] In Guatemala the one-crop economy does not require literacy, neither does the Church emphasize the need to read the Bible; the people do not see why they should become literate.[2] In the villages of India the co-operation of the older women—the mother-in-law and the grandmother—must be enlisted before the girls can attend school. And incentives must be created, strong enough to counteract the loss of a son who cannot now help in the fields, and will later feel above such work and will probably take a job in an urban centre. If the school can promise enough literacy to enable the son to read needed literature aloud to his illiterate father, and keep accounts, continuing his share in the familial system of interrelationships, a father might find enough incentive to encourage his son's attendance, because in this way the education would be for the family's welfare; it would not lead to separation, individual ends, atomization.[3] In Lebanon a visiting emigrant endowed his village with a school without first educating the villagers in the value of literacy; in three years, the school was in disuse.[4]

School attendance is not enough for literacy; and literacy itself is a means to education. It is also necessary, therefore, to introduce high-speed printing-presses for inexpensive reading matter, and to see to it that it reaches the people. It is reported from a number of areas that illiteracy increases with increasing age, because of forgetting.[5]

In some cultures, literacy seems to be an end in itself, because of past tradition, when it was the prerogative of an *élite* group. Higher education in areas involving manual labour is rendered useless by such attitudes. Agricultural schools in Burma and Latin America have not yet had sufficient effect in the agrarian picture because the graduates will not live with the peasants, will not soil their hands. After they study veterinary science or agronomy, they are ready to teach these subjects or work in laboratories, but not to set up demonstrations in rural areas or cultivate a demonstration plot.[6] In Panama teachers refused to help with sanitation problems; in the Netherlands Indies and Burma nurses refused to do rural work, since it involved manual work which in the urban hospitals was performed by menials.[7] In China higher education tended to create a group of unemployed, since it was beneath these people to

---

[1] Thurnwald, op. cit. p. 239.
[2] *Fundamental Education*, op. cit. p. 32.
[3] Ibid. pp. 99-101.
[4] Brunner, op. cit. p. 97.
[5] Frank Smothers and W. H. McNeill and E. D. McNeill, 1948, p. 117; Emilio Vásquez, 1943, p. 177.
[6] Charles P. Loomis, 1950, p. 125.
[7] Hooper, op. cit. p. 251; John Lee Hydrick, 1937, p. 49; Gordon S. Seagrave, 1943, pp. 44-45.

accept any non-academic position.[1] Specific cultural attitudes may make for difficulties in the specific area of instruction. In Afghanistan anatomy Las to be taught from charts and prepared specimens, as the religion does not permit human dissection or autopsy studies.[2] Where the native population had been assigned inferior status, higher education could not afterward be applied.

Fundamental education in living deals with a number of issues common to all areas. For example, co-operation in terms of new groupings and new ends is necessary to the introduction of new measures in land conservation and improvement, in agricultural mechanization, in production and marketing. For hygienic measures, co-operative participation is necessary before latrines will be built and used, since these are for the protection of others; it is needed for the application of general immunization, for quarantine measures on the local, national, and international levels, and for general hygienic precautions, as in food-preparation or garbage-disposal. The absence of such co-operative concepts is mentioned as an obstacle to industrialization.[3]

Experience has taught us that change can best be introduced not through centralized planning, but after a study of local needs. In China the mass-education programme was carried out by intellectuals who lived in the villages and learned the needs of the people.[4] When this principle is not followed, the education programme fails, or even works harm. In many Latin American demonstration farms, for example, ways of keeping records on the basis of tractors and combines are shown to farmers who use only a foot-plough,[5] and agronomists trained according to principles developed on the national level present to the cultivator material which is inapplicable on the local level.[6] In Indo-China, efforts at practical education in agriculture failed because they taught the value of fertilizer to people for whom it was too expensive to buy, at a time when they had to pay interest at the rate of about 80 per cent for three months if they were to finance the purchase of fertilizer by borrowing.[7] Actual harm was done when cultivators in Burma were persuaded to weed their rubber plantations, and found that this reduced the sap; and when they were persuaded to do deep ploughing in the rice-fields and thus broke the pan that held the water.[8] Again harm was done when young Turkish farmers were persuaded, also according to generalized princi-

[1] *Fundamental Education,* op. cit. pp. 85-86.
[2] J. C. Cutler, 1950, pp. 690-91.
[3] T. Bheemacharya, 1949, pp. 12-15.
[4] Buck, op. cit. pp. 3-7.
[5] Loomis, op. cit. p. 124.
[6] Ibid. p. 125.
[7] Erich H. Jacoby, 1949, pp. 152-53.
[8] J. S. Furnivall, 1948, p. 327.

ples, to remove from their wheat-fields the stones which had re-tained the moisture.[1] When Spanish Americans in New Mexico were requested by the health authorities to dig wells through 15 feet of solid rock so as to avoid the contaminated water of the ditches, without the accompanying education needed in this particular culture, the well-water was soon found to be con-taminated.[2]

Excellent results, on the other hand, are reported in cases where the programme of education was based on local needs. In the village of El-Manayel in Egypt the building of a school-house, carried out on the basis of discussions with the villagers, according to specific local needs, meant village co-operation in the filling in of an unhealthy pond for the school site, the level-ling of the village streets to get material for filling in the pond, and as an indirect result, better communication.[3]

When the specific needs of a locality or culture are dis-covered, it is often still necessary to teach the people to recog-nize them, and the desirability of improvement. Fellahin in a Middle East village had to be taught to see that trachoma was not part of the picture of health; their attitude was that tra-choma was part of a normal life, that it had always been with them; and even blindness was something to take for granted, since it was "from Allah."[4] In most areas people cannot be motivated to adopt new ways on the basis of logical evidence of better results or of charts or scientific arguments. Most people fear experimentation, or fear excursions into the unknown, since only the tried is known and safe; as when, for example, Chinese farmers refused to hatch the high-quality poultry eggs they had been given in exchange for their own inferior kind.[5] Everywhere, however, demonstration techniques carefully car-ried out have been found to be effective; in the Middle East they are indispensable, and have worked even when religious tenets threatened the effectiveness of the programme.[6] Demon-stration has been effective in India, Africa, Greece. Films of the entire process are sometimes effective, but only when they are taken against a local background.[7] Lambert showed New Guinea groups graphic representations of the progress of hook-worm through the intestinal tract, with good results. In the Middle East, however, where "slowly-slowly" is a maxim, movies are not entirely effective, as they move too fast for people who have to mull over things.[8]

[1] Nuri Eren, 1946, pp. 282-83.
[2] Loomis, op. cit. pp. 126-27.
[3] Mohamed M. Shalaby, personal communication, on introducing change into the rural Egyptian village of El-Manayel, 1939-44.
[4] Brunner, op. cit. pp. 94-95.
[5] Ibid. pp. 57-58.
[6] Shalaby, personal communication, op. cit. See also Marie Puhr, 1950.
[7] L. A. Notcutt and G. C. Latham, 1937, pp. 31-34, 52, 81; Loomis, op. cit. p. 124.
[8] Brunner, op. cit. p. 94; Shalaby, personal communication, op. cit.

Sometimes the traditional is so highly valued that no change is accepted as improvement. Workers find it difficult to motivate people in Latin America in terms of future benefits or an improved standard of living; and extra cash income through wages or cash crops is not used to raise the standard of living because this standard is not valued. In some regions of Africa, to ask the people to reduce their herds of cattle for the sake of their own better nutrition, or to exchange them for better breeds, or to sell some for cash to improve their own living-conditions, is like asking a mother to exchange her beloved child for a fairer or more robust one, or for two strange children.

Sometimes people resist new ways because the old have the sanction of the valued past or of religion. In such cases the worker often introduces change by using this sanction in support of it. When artificial insemination was introduced in Greece under the auspices of the Near East Foundation in 1945, the bulls were first blessed by high church dignitaries in the customary religious inaugurative ritual of "making sacred"; and women were persuaded to give their children the milk forbidden during Lent when Greek bishops themselves drank milk at this time. In Saudi Arabia the radio and telephone were made acceptable by first having verses of the Koran spoken over them.[1] In Lebanon the installation of a village pump which was needed to get uncontaminated water found sanction in quotations from the Koran to the effect that "cleanliness was required from every faithful Moslem";[2] and the Koran was likewise used to provide sanction for co-operation and land improvement.[3] When Kemal Ataturk made his sweeping changes in Turkey, he went about the villages talking with the people and showing them that he himself practised these things; for example, before he forbade the wearing of the fez, he visited the villages wearing a hat.[4] In the Middle East the glorious past is also used as a sanction, and conversely, an enemy's tradition is applied as an adverse sanction. Kemal, for example, told the Turks that the fez was the distinguishing head-gear of the Greeks. A Greek manual addressed to mothers urges that they suckle their own babies like the Homeric heroines, and that they stop swaddling them, as in doing so they are following the barbarous custom of the ancient Romans.

In many societies impersonality is abhorrent, or, at any rate, ineffective. Workers have found that programmes have a far greater chance of successful acceptance if they are personally introduced by people who show real concern. The expert may be held in high esteem; but the change will be accepted because of him, and not for its inherent merit; it will derive its validity

[1] Carl C. Taylor and others, 1949, p. 19; Richard S. Sanger, 1947, p. 181.
[2] Brunner, op. cit. p. 99.
[3] Afif I. Tannous, 1950, p. 269.
[4] Selma Ekrem, 1947, pp. 54-55.

through him, and the motivation for carrying it out will be rooted in loyalty to him: "I shall try it for your sake" is common phrasing in this situation. In the Netherlands Indies change was more readily accepted when the expert was physically and structurally on a level with the people, sitting as they did.[1] In Turkey and Lebanon, the expert comes in as a villager, cultivating his own land, building his own home, and teaching; his daily life affords a demonstration.[2] In China the forestry-planting expert who refused to go out to teach tree-planting in the rain lost out; and the professor who took his shoes off to work in the rice-seeding plot won.[3] The exact medium of communication may vary. There are groups where discussion has been the medium for reaching unanimous agreement.[4] In other cases, an oration may be more effective. Discussion may be merely a medium of entertainment and of the sharpening of wits. Questioning by the expert may be acceptable in some areas, and may be regarded with suspicion as prying in others. Or the questioning may itself be distrusted as a sign of ignorance by people who believe that the expert acts through divine revelation.[5] The words used by the expert have an emotional effect apart from their other content. An agricultural expert writing for specialists can speak without harm of the Scandinavian variety of cultured milk as "a thick, slimy product," and the Greek variety—that of his own culture—as "a custard-like curd of fine smooth, firm texture."[6] But in an educational situation, such linguistic discrimination may defeat one's ends.

The channel of communication also varies with the culture. In the United States the housewife has been the channel for nutritional education. In Latin American countries the co-operation of the community priest helps to accomplish a project of education in only a fraction of the time otherwise needed, and with more effectiveness.[7] Experience in fundamental education in a number of countries points to the importance of working through local leadership,[8] both for the acceptance of the project and for ensuring its continuing success. In Costa Rica the peasants look to both lay and church dignitaries for direction; but these must be their own dignitaries, with whom they are in an established *patrón* relationship.[9]

These are factors common to the introduction of change in most areas. There are specific factors to be considered in particular areas. Land reform, for example, has not always had

[1] Hydrick, op. cit. pp. 18-19.
[2] Eren, op. cit. pp. 284-85; Kitchen, op. cit. p. 34.
[3] Brunner, op. cit. pp. 54-55.
[4] Ruth Benedict, 1943, pp. 103-5; Redfield, op. cit. pp. 642-45.
[5] Alexander H. Leighton and Dorothea C. Leighton, 1944, p. 58.
[6] D. A. Soulides, 1949, pp. 10-11.
[7] Brunner, op. cit. pp. 123-24.
[8] Taylor, op. cit. pp. 15-19.
[9] Loomis, op. cit. p. 91.

the anticipated results because the people, as in Turkey in the nineteenth century, and in Mexico, had not been educated to proprietorship.[1] The attempt to teach isolation of the sick fails because it cannot be presented in the name of either the individual or the family. Where the family is not a collection of individuals but a unit in its own right, what is good for one is automatically good for the family; and since it is good for the sick to have loving companionship, this cannot be bad for the family.

Finally, it has been proved by experience that the vernacular is the most effective and the most emotionally satisfying medium of instruction. In this way literacy is not merely associated with the foreign, but becomes an instrument in familiar life. Learning to read and write can be experienced within the security of the known, and the hurdle of a new medium need not be surmounted. And in educating in areas of living, the use of the vernacular provides the greatest facilitation, as it can express immediately the meanings and specific concepts of the culture. What is true of the vernacular is true of all aspects of living. Working through the known patterns and the existing social groupings has proved to be the most effective procedure in fundamental education.

ADDITIONAL REFERENCES

Max A. Bairon, 1942; Hugh Hammond Bennett, 1945a; 1945b; "Case Studies in Applied Anthropology," n.d.; "Egypt Fights Illiteracy," 1947; "Egypt Menaced from Within," 1948; Erdman Harris, 1932; Victor George Heiser, 1936; Melville J. Herskovits, 1943; Charles S. Johnson, 1943; Apostolos Koskinides, 1948; S. M. Lambert, 1941; Charles P. Loomis, 1944; John F. Melby, 1942; *Near East Relief Consummated; Near East Foundation Carries On,* 1944; Elsie Clews Parsons, 1945; Donald Pierson, 1943; Ömer Celâl Sâre, 1948; Irwin T. Saunders, 1942; Mohamed M. Shalaby, 1950; Sol Tax, 1942; "The Road Comes to the Village," n.d.; E. W. F. Tomlin, 1946; A. Vandenbosch, 1943.

[1] Omer C. Stewart, 1950, p. 27; Nathan L. Whetten, 1948, p. 566.

IV. SPECIFIC MENTAL-HEALTH IMPLICATIONS OF TECHNICAL CHANGE

There are two aspects of the problem of technical change seen from the point of view of mental health: mental-health services themselves as one type of technical change, and a condition of mental health as the generalized goal of technical change. Technical change in its narrow sense includes not only technical advice on agriculture or animal-breeding, but also improved medical and public-health services, and these in turn are specifically and technically concerned with problems of the cure and prevention of mental illness and the cultivation of mental health. On a wider front, it may be said that the goal of technical change is to give to people of each country a way of life within which greater mental health may be achieved for all the members of that society.

Superficially, these two approaches may appear as separate. Under the heading of mental-health services fall such matters as the location of the mentally ill, the establishment of basic statistical data on the incidence of different types of mental illness, the exploration of the best methods by which those who are seriously ill can be treated, the way in which cultural factors must be taken into account in determining which forms of treatment are practical and likely to give results. These are the problems which face those world-wide governmental and voluntary agencies attempting to get a picture of the conditions of mental health in the world and to develop standards for the guidance of new international and local agencies. Under this heading comes the question of diagnosis: how to distinguish between some unfamiliar but culturally conventional forms of behaviour—such as seeing visions, hearing voices, believing that other people are killing one by magic—and symptoms of genuine mental illness. Even in Western countries where psychiatry is highly developed, the criteria are inadequate for distinguishing between mental illness and behaviour which is bizarre because the cultural context is not known—as when a former member of a secret society which operates by periodic assassination of members of a rival society informs the police in an American city that people are trying to kill him, and, until his nationality and society membership are known, is diagnosed as dangerously paranoid. Periods of customary religious fasting and withdrawal from all social intercourse may be very difficult to distinguish from attacks of catatonic schizophrenia. It may even be found that members of a society customarily fall into a benign deep stupor when they meet with frustrating or frightening situations—as is the case for the Balinese. Where psychiatry has existed side by side with religion for a long period, as in the West, a mutual accommodation takes place and it is possible for the religious leadership to develop criteria which will distinguish between individuals who may be regarded as supernaturally blessed, but not mentally unbalanced, and individuals whose mental illness has a high religious content. In introducing psychiatric practices into countries in which no such *modus vivendi* between religion and psychiatry has been worked out, a great deal of preliminary work needs to be done to establish criteria for diagnosis. This will be found to be true not only for such complex matters as trance and vision experience, but also for such simple matters as the accurate reporting on and localization of pain, or the evaluation of the psychogenic component in the healing of a wound. Among some peoples wound-healing is regularly delayed and a failure to heal will be significant only if it occurs beyond these delayed limits; among others, the rate of healing of a particular wound may have to be evaluated against a very high customary healing rate. So the whole range of somatic symptoms which modern psychiatry assumes to have, at least in some cases, a strong psychogenic component, have to be explored within the cultural setting before they can be evaluated diagnostically.

When there is any attempt to go beyond the diagnosis of psychotic states or of specific somatic symptoms to the diagnosis and treatment of neurosis, even greater caution is needed. Behaviour which would be regarded in the Western world as a sign of a highly developed obsessional neurosis, may be quite conventional in another culture—as, for example, ritual cleanliness or periods of extreme sexual licence. When it is also necessary to take inter-personal patterns of relationship into account, such as the degree of dependency or hostility which the child feels for the parent, even greater knowledge of the culture is needed. There are societies, for example, in which the only way in which the son can leave home is by having a terrific quarrel with his father; what would appear to be highly unbalanced and dangerously hostile behaviour if seen only once in a single individual will be found—when the whole cultural situation is known—to be a customary, dramatic way of breaking ties of dependency between one generation and another. Societies differ very much as to how and when the younger generation is weaned from the parent generation. Mothers may be permissive and permit a high degree of physical dependency, which is then followed by a harsh and sudden separation and an initiatory ceremony of some sort: being sent to boarding-school, being put on a régime of strict frugality and abstention from all gentleness, etc. The clinging affectionate behaviour of a boy of 12 to his mother cannot be evaluated as unusual and a sign of neurotic needs—on his or her part or both their parts—until the rest of the social maturation pattern is known.

So even for the very first step—a preliminary survey or collection of statistics on the incidence of different types of mental ill health—team work is needed between psychiatrists, clinical psychologists, sociologists and anthropologists, so that the whole cultural context can be taken into account, and tests and diagnostic criteria may be reformulated for the particular culture in such a way that the reports of incidence of mental illness may have some degree of comparability. At present, in spite of attempts to use existing sources, there is no valid information on the incidence of mental ill health outside the Westernized portions of the world.

When treatment of the mentally ill is the next step in procedures to be set up in a society, as part of a technical-assistance programme, there is even more acute need for inter-disciplinary team-work. In discussions in recent years, emphasis has been placed upon the virtual impossibility of treating the mentally ill by individual hospitalization in countries with huge populations such as India and China. Emphasized instead is concentration upon a general mental-health approach infused in the public-health practices and the educational systems of a country rather than upon clinics and hospitals for the mentally ill.[1] This emphasis has been combined with an attempt to skip some of the developmental stages through which the treatment of the mentally ill has gone in Western countries, and to avoid some of the less desirable features— such as separation of institutional care and community services—which have grown up historically. However, it is important to point out that the development of a genuine concern for mental health is dependent upon the development—among the people of a country, or at least those who make decisions— of the kind of sensitivity which can be aroused to the human suffering which the mentally ill inflict upon themselves and upon others. Unless some effort is made to provide for those acute cases of mental disturbance in which such suffering is conspicuous and unmistakable, it is difficult to develop within the general population the kind of concern for less conspicuous forms of mental suffering and malfunctioning.

If treatment programmes for the mentally diseased are to be developed in step with programmes of prevention, it is of course possible to combine them so that the serious cases, for which provision is being made, may be presented to an awak-

[1] United Nations, WHO, *Technical Report Series*, No. 9.
United Nations, WHO, *Technical Report Series*, No. 31.

ened public opinion as, in part at least, the consequences of the lack of preventive services. Then each mad beggar who disappears from the streets—as treatment services develop—will, by his absence, help to point up the possibility of a world in which not only are the streets empty of mad beggars and vagrants, but also in which such waste of human beings can be at least in part prevented. If the development of treatment centres is seen as a device for the cultivation of an enlightened and humane public opinion, then the apparent contradiction of spending time and effort on the care of a few—many of whom are hopelessly mentally diseased—instead of devoting all available skills and energies to preventive services, can be resolved.

Behind the movement for better mental health for all of mankind stands the finding of the psychiatrist, who has worked for a lifetime with individuals, through hundreds of hours of patient unravelling of lives which have been distorted and broken beyond any necessary expectation from heredity and constitutional weakness, the psychiatrist who says, *This need not happen.*

For each society and for each segment of society within which the psychiatrist finds his patients, he is able to provide new insights which, when translated with the help of educators and social scientists, become preventive measures to provide for the better mental health of future generations, suggestions for new social practices within which each growing child may be assured a better start. But the psychiatrist's practice must be local; it is not possible to go directly from the psychiatrist's insights in a large Paris hospital to the Burmese village or the Latin American plantation. The psychiatrists working in the industrialized West may come to emphasize the hazards of the weakened family structure and the broken home. But the psychiatrists working in unindustrialized sections of southern Europe or the Near East may simultaneously be emphasizing the hazards of a too closely knit family for the mental health of individuals who, later in life, must adapt to the impersonal system of human relations which will come with the introduction of modern industry.

We do not yet have a fully developed social psychiatry in which it is possible to say: Given such a type of family structure, such a sized population, with such a system of nutrition and succour, such a state of industrialization and type of agriculture, with such a degree of expected change in educational practice and ways of earning a living, *then,* in order to provide against the forms of mental illness now known and to prevent the development of new forms of mental illness, *do this.* Human culture is so complex that it seems unlikely that it will ever be possible to write prescriptions in such a form. Rather it is necessary to suggest—in the light of our present knowledge—practices which will set up processes within which the necessary psychiatric insights will develop for each situation, and will be made available.

The most practical step which can be recommended—on the basis of our present knowledge—is ensuring that, as psychiatric practice grows in a country in which there is as yet very slight psychiatric development, the psychiatrists have every opportunity to work closely with social scientists, both from outside and, wherever possible, inside the society, and also to work closely with those concerned with public health, educational and industrial and agricultural planning. In this way, the particular insights of the consulting-room, and the implications of such insights for the design of a school system, a maternity centre, or a factory may be high-lighted. For, while it may well be true that there are certain basic psychic nutrients which each human individual needs for his fullest and most harmonious development, these nutrients—of human love, care, stimulation, reassurance—are mediated so differently in each society that the most profound and detailed attention—on the spot—is needed to be sure that, instead of blanket prescriptions, which may involve serious errors, detailed adjustments to real situations are made.[1] Otherwise a great number of contradictions will develop, just as they have in the field of nutrition, where, in an attempt to prevent the danger of infection from the practice of pre-chewing the infant's supplementary food, mothers—themselves undernourished—have been told to stop supplementary feeding and rely only on breast milk; or where scheduled feeding has been introduced into a system of child-rearing where immediate food-giving was relied upon to balance expressions of temporary anger.

There are other aspects of the treatment situation, besides their great significance for the development of public awareness and receptivity, in which team-work with anthropologists and sociologists is essential. It is necessary to study carefully the patterns of human relationship before choices are made as to: whether out-patient or in-patient patterns of treatment will be most feasible; which types of patients may, with safety and promise, be hospitalized together; whether hospitalization of the mentally ill will, in fact, seem to the population kind and protective or, on the contrary, cruel and unnecessary and so defeat that development of popular sensitivity which it is believed to promote. When patterns of clinical practice are developed, *which* relative of a child under treatment is to be the one to receive guidance and help, or at least is to be scrutinized in order to understand the case better, will again be a matter which has to be worked out on the spot. The Western assumption that the mother is the crucial person for such consultation may have to be modified to include father, grand-

[1] J. Bowlby, 1951.

parents, etc., according to the age and sex of a child patient.

The role of the psychiatrist himself will have to be varied. Experience has shown that the European pattern of psychiatrist-patient relationship has to be modified in the United States to a more *fraternal* relationship; as experience accumulates of psychiatric practices in which the clergy and the psychiatrist work together, different divisions of role between the clerical and psychiatric professions develop. It is only necessary to raise the question of what model a psychiatrist would use in a country in which the gods are treated as children of the worshipping congregation, or in one in which a grandfather is to be treated as a joking relative, to demonstrate how patient-therapist relationships will have to be varied and modified as psychiatric practice develops in different parts of the world. But again, this can only be done on the spot, by foreign practitioners responding sensitively to experience with patients, and by physicians from the countries themselves, modifying the practices which they have learned in Western medical schools or from the imported medical practices of the urban West.

Throughout this discussion, it is important to realize that much of what has been said about the introduction of psychiatric practice into countries which have not previously had psychiatric services applies also to the rural and under-developed regions of countries where psychiatry has been highly developed but principally in urban areas. In such countries, only by working on the spot with the local inhabitants can practices be designed which are genuinely congruent with the habits and needs of the people—and such practices may differ sharply from those appropriate to urban populations even of the same nationality.

In summary, it is recognized that clinical practice by psychiatrists and care for the mentally ill are essential first steps in the development of a mental-health service in a new area or country, but that where these do not now exist, or exist in a very rudimentary form, they can best be developed parallel to the infusion of a mental-health approach in other health and educational services. However, in order to have this mental-health approach—in public health or education—accurately related to the particular habits and beliefs of a particular population, it is important to have psychiatrists—whether local or foreign—in local clinical practice, translating their clinical insights—on that exact population—into wider areas of prevention of mental illness and positive promotion of mental health.

TECHNICAL CHANGE AND MENTAL ILLNESS

Just as a first step in establishing any mental-health programme in a new area is the incorporation of clinical insights, so a first consideration—from the standpoint of mental health—in the introduction of any technical change should be the safe-guarding of the population against further mental ill health, against the expression in individual lives of the disorganization and disruption accompanying the introduction of new techniques and ways of living. The earlier chapters in this manual have been devoted to a consideration of methods and consequences of change seen on the social level: *which* cultural attitudes must be taken into account, *how* the cultural practices of a people may be used to facilitate change, how a people who resist hospitalization may come to use it, how a people whose food-habits prevent them from obtaining adequate nourishment may be persuaded to alter those habits. Throughout the discussion, we have made the major assumption that it is necessary to take into account the whole culture when a particular change is made and that unless this is done, various types of destructive changes may be set in motion in the society, in addition to the programme of change itself being resisted and sabotaged. The focus has been on changes in living-habits of large groups, rather than upon the implications for the mental health of particular individuals. The disciplines drawn upon have been cultural anthropology on the one hand, and on the other, the experience of a great variety of practitioners in the field of technical change.

But changes in living-habits are important because of what they mean in health and strength for individual human beings, not for the human race in the abstract. And it is to the disciplines of psychiatry and clinical psychology that it is necessary to turn for the frame of reference within which we can discuss the specific mental-health implications of technical change. Technical change disrupts old habits. What has the psychiatrist to say about the effects within the individual personality of such a disruption? Technical change makes it difficult for individuals to pattern their lives as adults on the lives which, as children, they watched their parents live. What can psychiatry say about the loss of parental models, or the conflicts involved in trying both to keep and to break away from parental models of behaviour? Technical change involves new learning, after adulthood, and changing types of behaviour which have been heavily reinforced by childhood experiences of reward and punishment. What can psychiatry say of the type of anxiety, conflict, and healthy stimulus which a challenge to new learning provides?

Here we do not have the detailed case histories of conflict and difficulty to parallel the accounts that we have of attempts to change food-habits or introduce new agricultural practices. We can assume that various types of psychological disturbances will occur, but the detailed clinical work is still to be done and recorded.

PSYCHOLOGICAL PRINCIPLES WHICH MAY BE UTILIZED DURING THE PROCESS OF TECHNICAL CHANGE

In this section we deal specifically with those findings of psychiatrists and psychologists concerning the behaviour of individuals which are relevant to the functioning of individuals within a situation of change. All those who are consciously concerned with technical change—whether the results are expressed in increase of yield per acre, or increases in total national export, or reduction in the infant death-rate—are of course concerned, in the final analysis, with individuals. But there is a definite difference in the level of this concern, and it is to the worker within the village or the school, the agricultural demonstration station and the local public-health clinic, who works day after day with a small number of identified human beings, that this discussion is specially directed.

1. The agents of change—the teacher, the agricultural extension worker, the nurse—must realize that their own behaviour, beliefs and attitudes are not universal and axiomatic. They must realize that their ways of counting, reckoning time, judging conduct, expressing enthusiasm or disgust, are—like the behaviour, beliefs and attitudes of those whom they are helping to change—learned and traditional.

2. The beliefs and attitudes of the people among whom they are working must be seen as having functional utility. For each individual, they give continuity to his personality, permit him to feel that he is a named, identified person, the same person—only older, or more important, although fatter, or just elected to office—that he was yesterday. They permit him to perceive his experiences as of the same order, to recognize a series of different activities as "gifts," as "changes," as "insults" to be resented, or as "expressions of deference." So he will hold on to his beliefs and practices because they help him to direct his daily behaviour and solve his daily problems of relating himself to other people. If the teacher or extension agent recognizes such clinging to old beliefs and practices as having real usefulness for an individual, rather than interpreting it as evidence of stubbornness, unco-operativeness, ignorance, inability to learn, etc., he will be better able to introduce changes.

3. Any change must be examined from the point of view of the individuals who are exposed to the change. Where a change may seem to the expert to be merely a better way of feeding cattle, or of disposing of waste, to the people it may seem to be a rejection of the commands of the gods,

or a way of giving their welfare and safety into the hands of sorcerers. An "improved" form of house may also be a house without the proper magical screens to baffle the demons who may enter and make one ill. Substitution of a more or less destructible cooking-pot may be seen as lowering the value of a bride because of a change in the cost of her dowry. It is, therefore, useful always to ask: How does this change look to those whom it will directly and indirectly affect?

If this question is asked, it will assist the experts in forecasting some of the difficulties which may occur, and in devising ways of compensating for them.

4. The experts must be on their guard against the apparently logical solution that because all the aspects of the life of a people are interrelated, the way to deal with a change in any one aspect of living is to make a complete blue-print for changes in the whole—a new educational system, new health and sanitation practices, a new form of transportation, new factories, etc. There is no available body of knowledge which makes it possible to predict in advance the way in which individuals will respond even to one far-reaching change, so that it is necessary to avoid master plans, while taking precautions against any one change's becoming so entrenched that it will actually block others. This is simply another way of stating that the sciences of human behaviour must take into account the complexity which results from historical accident, and recognize that while they can predict the range within which human beings will respond, they cannot predict the particular responses.

5. Any significant change in the life of an individual tends to introduce some degree of instability or disharmony in the way his life-activities, his beliefs and attitudes, are organized. Such instability can be described psychologically, as emotional tension.

A significant change results in tension either because old behaviour is found to be inadequate or by creating new situations for which new behaviour must be acquired. The old responses—the way a man handled a tool, or led a work party, or called in a shaman to cure a sick child— have usually been an essential part of the individual's sense of his "self"; now their inadequacy or uselessness may be felt as a threat to the whole hitherto prized way of life. Even if the individual is willing to give up his old responses for new ones, he will be in a state of tension while he unlearns the old responses. Here he will benefit from support given him, which can take a variety of forms: accounts of the difficulties which other people in similiar situations have encountered; group work in which individuals learning new habits can encourage each other by sharing accounts of difficulties and making suggestions for new habits; interpretations from experienced workers that the tensions experienced are to be expected.

Although we may expect that the existence of such tensions will be accompanied by changes in the individual's behaviour which tend to reduce the original tension, the dissipation of such tensions may take a considerable time, or may not be successful. If the dissipation of the tension is not successful, the individual remains in a state of maladjustment or frustration. A common consequence of such a state of frustration is that the individual returns to the old responses that he had begun to abandon. But these old responses are likely to seem less satisfactory than they once were, and so he may remain maladjusted. The illiterate who attempts to learn to read and fails is a very much less satisfied person than the peasant by whom learning to read was never considered a possible or even a suitable activity.

It is the general experience of psychiatrists that even when changes in an individual's life are very painful for him to achieve, if he has a strong wish to change, then the successful resolution of his tensions is quicker and more likely, and there are fewest returns to old and undesired responses. Also there may be less tension and reluctance to change if the new procedures deal with the recognized difficulties and sufferings of the people and will directly help to resolve those difficulties and reduce those sufferings which have long been endured as inevitable.

It follows that there is less reason to fear mental-health disturbances among those populations in which the individuals affected by the change have themselves desired the change. Hence the provision by the Specialized Agencies of the United Nations that requests for technical assistance be initiated in the countries involved is supported by psychiatric experience with the responses of individuals observed clinically.

6. Frustration may be discussed under four main headings: (a) physical environment; (b) biological limitations; (c) psychological make-up; and (d) social environment. After technical devices are available to relieve frustration of the first two types—to dam the rivers, or irrigate the land, to improve nutrition, or to eliminate yaws or tuberculosis— the frustration induced in individuals by conflicts within the social environment, the incompatibility between old beliefs and new practices, between old concepts of individual human worth and new medical practices, may remain as persistent sources of frustration.

The possible consequences of frustration are very numerous and they are not by any means all bad. The nature of the consequences depends partly upon the severity of frustration. If frustration has an intense consequence of one kind, other consequences are less likely to appear. Thus if a man customarily shows direct aggressive behaviour when he is frustrated, he is not as likely to withdraw from society, or to smile when he is angry, or to become bedridden, as a consequence of frustration. Also, workers who bend all their efforts to destroy new tools of production have little energy left to learn to use the new tools; oppressed and enslaved peoples who drown their sorrows in singing about a heaven in which all loads will be lightened are not as likely to welcome agitation for improved conditions on this earth. However, while a man who is mildly thwarted may show negligible changes in his behaviour, summation of many minor frustrations whose effects are cumulative can result in severe changes in behaviour. This should be remembered when a series of plans is made each one of which appears to involve only a slight change—getting to work a little earlier, being paid a little differently, obtaining supplies from a different spot, etc.

Many or most of the frustrations experienced in daily life are not harmful, and for this reason the term "blockade," which is neutral, has been proposed. The tensions set up by the new learning required, the old habit relinquished, the longer series of acts necessary to reach the goal, are resolved without disrupting the successful adjustment of the total person. Such frustrations or blockages may be regarded as beneficial. They alter the way in which the individual's energy is distributed among his daily tasks, help him reorient himself, learn and grow, by (a) leading to intensification of his efforts; (b) forcing him to re-examine the situation in which he is blocked; (c) leading to his finding some way around the difficulty, often a new way.

It is conceivable, then, that it is not harmful, from a mental-health point of view, to stimulate needs, desires, demands among peoples who now feel no such needs or desires, or who at least are not conscious of them or articulate about them. Such stimulation does, of course, create instability, disharmony and tension. If means are available for dissipating the tensions successfully, persistent frustration is to be expected. But if means are made available, then the created frustrations can become the basis for new, desired, and self-perpetuating behaviour, as in the case of increased use of cow's milk in Thailand or increased use of milk for babies in Greece. But if the desire to have new kinds of machinery, or new food, or new free education, is stimulated and then, because of poverty or lack of personnel, the desire cannot be realized, persistent frustration is to be expected, with possible return to old behaviours, which will then be less satisfactory than in the past. There are, then, clearly dangers here. In the advanced industrial nations the desire for longevity has been carried to the point where millions of people have the medical care to keep them alive, but no way of making these later years of life meaningful. Thus, mass frustration exists among the aged. The danger of cultivating "felt needs" which are unrealized under existing conditions can be diminished by keeping close to local conditions, to that which is immediately feasible, so that training teachers precedes building local schools, importing a minimum supply of a new seed precedes the demonstration of its superiority.[1]

Needs can be felt too intensely; people can be so highly motivated that it may be dangerous to assume they will achieve an adequate assimilation of a significant change with non-disruptive reorganization of their beliefs and attitudes. The man roused to anger is not the best social planner. People on a starvation diet are not likely to produce new and workable patterns of economic activity. So share-croppers, who have only fat meat to give their children, may force their children to like fat, because it is absolutely necessary that they learn to eat it; or parents in a country with meat rationing may forget all they have learned about not forcing their children to eat because that particular bit of meat cooked for the Sunday meal is all the meat the child will get. Immigrants from country to city may try to embrace every detail of the new way of life, losing all sense of continuity.

7. When frustration persists and is intensified, consequences not at all beneficial tend to occur. These consequences generally reduce the individual's tension, but while so doing, impair the healthy functioning of the whole personality and disrupt his successful adjustment to the society within which he lives. Of the many such consequences, the following are important in understanding social behaviour:

    (a) Return to old forms of behaviour, which, as has been discussed above, are now less satisfactory. Thus vil-

[1] Hugh H. Bennett, founder of the Soil Conservation Service of the United States Department of Agriculture, waited many years until he could interest American farmers in soil conservation, and was only really successful after the great floods and droughts of the 1930's swept the United States. He believed that he could not force men to become good stewards of their land, any more than he could prevent them from becoming good stewards once they realized its importance—"felt the need." (Wellington Brink, 1951.)

lage people who ignored the changes which took place in the larger towns may actively combat them when they have failed to incorporate them into village life. Young men who are given no chance to use a new form of education which they saw as designed to fit them for a higher form of work may return to unskilled work, but with new resentment.

(b) The individual's behaviour may become less mature, more childish; his feelings and emotions may be more poorly controlled, or new forms of dependency may develop.

(c) The accumulated tensions may find expression in aggressive acts, such as feelings and actions of anger and rage, actual physical violence against objects and people, verbal attacks, slander and denunciation, or preoccupations with thoughts of violence. The objects of such aggressive acts are often not at all connected with the frustrating situation or agent; so a man frustrated by a superior may spank his child, or denounce the tax-collector.

(d) The individual may withdraw psychologically or physically from the frustrating situation, as did some of the Indians of the North American Plains, who became apathetic after the disappearance of the buffalo. Withdrawal may be into apathy, into substitute activities such as alcoholism, drug addiction, or gambling, or into nativistic cults in which the former state, now seen as a golden age, is acted out symbolically. Adolescents who in the former way of life would have remained energetic and highly motivated suddenly cease to be able to learn, and so give rise to myths about the inability of peoples newly exposed to modern technology to acquire the necessary new knowledge.

(e) The individual may reduce his tensions by preventing the occurrence of a tension-provoking reaction. Partial prevention is even more common. It then happens that the unresolved tensions find expression in diverse and often unrelated ways, such as chronic fatigue, preoccupation with one's state of health, compulsive ritual, new activities which are socially approved, redefinition of the situation in a way that is more acceptable to oneself, assigning blame for the situation to others, retreat into endless thinking about the situation without any attempt to check the thinking with reality.

Little systematic information exists concerning the percentages of individuals who, under sustained tension, have developed this or that consequence of frustration, or one or another medically defined mental disorder. Even more inadequate than the scattered and contradictory studies which have been conducted in the West of the relationship between urban crowding, war, immigration, etc. and types of mental disorder, are the existing published materials on the rest of the world.[1]

MAKING TECHNICAL CHANGES ACCEPTABLE

In earlier sections of this survey, illustrations have been given of a variety of successful ways in which change has been introduced. In these illustrations dependence has been placed upon the actual experience with changes introduced into social groups. It is also possible to examine our present knowledge of psychological processes in the individual, which comes from clinical and experimental psychology, for principles which may be drawn upon in real-life situations.

It seems painfully evident that the most miserable living-conditions (from the viewpoint of industrial nations) do not of themselves make technical improvements acceptable, nor make disruption and maladjustment less likely once change is introduced. Over and over again, we see that attempts to remedy such conditions chiefly by knowledge and logic (as seen by the agents of change) fail. Those failures can be better understood if it is recognized that explanation and logical interpretation *alone* are often ineffective in changing behaviour because their application is blocked by the emotional satisfaction which the individual achieves through his present mode of life. The new knowledge can be put to use only as the old behaviours, beliefs and attitudes are unlearned and the appropriate new behaviours, beliefs and attitudes are learned.

An effective way to encourage the learning of new behaviours and attitudes is by consistent prompt attachment of some form of satisfaction to them. This may take the form of consistent praise, approval, privilege, improved social status, strengthened integration with one's group, or material reward. It is particularly important when the desired change is such that the advantages are slow to materialize—for example, it takes months or even years to appreciate a change in nutrition, or to register the effect of a new way of planting seedlings in the increased yield of an orchard. Here the gap between the new behaviour and results, which will not reinforce the behaviour until they are fully appreciated, has to be filled in other ways. The pleasure of belonging to a particular social group, or the delight in mastering a new skill which others can admire, can provide immediate rewards. Under conditions of satisfac-

[1] A recent investigation which centred on the mental effects of Trypanosomiasis in the Gold Coast, is an excellent illustration of the complexity of factors—social, cultural, and medical—which have to be taken into account in evaluating cases of even frank mental disorder. (Geoffrey Tooth, 1950.)

tion, the new behaviours become more deeply rooted, the new interests strengthened, the new purposes reinforced, the new attitudes more alive.

As such changes occur, there is more readiness to accept new facts, which are now identified with a situation in which satisfaction has been experienced; beliefs (knowledge, faith and opinion) then change as the people involved become freer to examine the new facts. The use of consistent approval or reward underlies the successful introduction of technical change in many parts of the world, as it has in the work of the Near East Foundation.[1]

The process of acceptance of change is more rapid if simultaneously the old behaviours and attitudes provide less satisfaction, or no satisfaction, or meet with disapproval or other punishment. (It must be understood that both reward and punishment are used in a technical, psychological sense; that is, a behaviour is punished if the individual who practises it is for any reason dissatisfied, or unhappy, rejected by a group whose aproval he seeks, or plunged into doubt and self-reproach, etc. It is not suggested that actual punishment, in the sense that an individual in authority metes out punishment to other individuals, is an effective way of introducing change, although as new behaviours become well established—such as new sanitary practices, for example—the group itself may pass new regulations which carry fines for infraction.) The punishment the individual derives from the situation need not be severe and may well be absent; if too severe, its only effect tends to be intense emotional disturbance, with blockage of the desired new behaviour. For example, a public-health nurse had been attempting to persuade a group of Mexican immigrant mothers in the United States to abandon their customary diet, and to feed their babies milk. She had been violently condemning their traditional diet, but finally, when she discovered that she was making no progress, she suggested that they feed their babies the water in which their beans were cooked. The babies began to thrive, and when the nurse later pointed out to the mothers the supposed effects of the bean-water, they replied: "Oh, but we are feeding them milk now too. We have followed your advice about the milk ever since you stopped calling all of our own food bad." When the effect of a punishing situation is only intense emotional disturbance, punishment may actually tend to stamp in deeper the undesired behaviour.

Satisfactions which are attached to a new behaviour may be intentional or unintentional; the learner may be aware of their relation to the new behaviour (or attitude) or unaware of such a relation; the form or degree of the satisfaction may vary. Such satisfactions, directly experienced, in themselves

[1] Cf. references to Near East Foundation in Section III on "Agriculture," *passim.*

strengthen new behaviour, and need not involve an individual's conscious memory of past rewards for similar behaviour. The learning that accompanies satisfaction goes on unconsciously; the learner does not know that a change is going on, nor that in the future he will tend to repeat the rewarded act.

It is important to remember that this way of encouraging new learning can be abused. It can be used to attach fear to all sorts of symptoms or behaviour, while promising relief of the aroused fear by the purchase of an advertiser's worthless or dangerous medicine. It can be used to stimulate purchases beyond a person's means by consistent verbal and non-verbal attachment of the purchases to the satisfactions of superior status, real or imagined. It can be used to cultivate hate as well as co-operation. It can be used to indoctrinate people so strongly with beliefs that the intellectual processes involved in knowledge and judgment are paralysed. It has been so used deliberately in many countries in which some interested group—private or public—has sought to manipulate people to a desired end. The strongest safe-guard against an undesirable use of these psychological principles will be in leaving new learning in the hands of the group involved and helping them to develop means of making the new learning rewarding, and the old learning, unrewarding. Where people do things themselves, for themselves, but with expert help in the psychological principles which they invoke, the dangers of exploitation and manipulation, although never absent, are minimized.

To summarize: The learning of desired new behaviours and attitudes can be achieved by the learner's living through a long series of situations in which the new behaviour is made highly satisfying—without exception if possible—and the old not satisfying.

In considering ways of advancing learning of new technologies, some reliance can be placed on the actual pleasure which flows from exercising a new skill. As Hegel says: "Man, in so far as he acts on nature to change it, changes his own nature." As the use of more complex devices intervenes between a felt need and its satisfaction, some satisfaction is experienced with the use of the complex devices themselves, with discovering their nature and their possibilities. Members of advanced industrial societies are likely to sentimentalize simple craft processes and forget the delight of first cutting with steel instead of stone, or of substituting machine reaping for hand reaping, or a power-driven flour-mill for the mortar and pestle. The new devices begin to play a part in the individual's experience; the idea of power which is not dependent on human sweat and effort, the possibility of repeating the same operation with absolute accuracy, the compensation for lack of individual skill or experience by the use of a machine, the sudden equalization of the gap between the mature man and the callow apprentice—all of these are exciting and thought-provoking. New ways of thinking appear. A willingness to regard the environment and man's relations to it in new ways develops. The American Indian with a modern mowing-machine, who formerly regarded cutting hay as a ruthless shearing of the tresses of his mother, comes to understand the new mysteries of the engine which drives a modern combine.

It is a matter of historical record that empirical use of the fundamental principles of mechanics long preceded the development of theoretical explanations.[1] As we now seek to introduce people who have had no experience either with tools, or with the scientific rationale which produced them, to the whole paraphernalia of modern industrialized living, we can place explicit reliance on the understanding which will develop from the use of the new techniques and tools. Hence an immediate complete intellectual reorientation is obviously not a necessary requirement for successful technical change.

We may also take into account psychological findings about resistance to new learning.

New information psychologically available to an individual, but contradictory to his customary behaviour, beliefs and attitudes, may not even be perceived. Even if he is actually forced to recognize its existence, it may be rationalized away, or almost immediately forgotten. Thus a people who insist that magic is necessary to grow yams may have it pointed out to them that the foreign missionaries are growing larger yams by using improved agricultural techniques instead of magic. They will counter the evidence of their senses about the size of the mission yams by insisting that the yams are a different kind, or that the missionaries used their own magic, not an improved technology.

So new information will tend to be assimilated in such a way as to produce the smallest effect in the whole meaningful interrelated structure of an individual's organized experience. This tendency to maintain order is of vital importance in giving constancy to perceptual life (otherwise human beings would be unable to recognize people, trees, dogs, etc., seen from different angles, in different illumination, etc., as the same objects). But it also makes possible the assimilation of new facts in such a way as to obscure their newness, break their impact, so that there is no noticeable resulting reorganization of the system. New Guinea peoples who have had an opportunity to work on machine-driven craft may then slowly relate airplanes and trains to these experiences, but those who have never seen any machine-driven contrivance, but who have heard Biblical stories, may instead perceive an airplane that is seen overhead as the chariot of God.

[1] Ernst Mach, 1893.

Individuals exposed to facts or experience contradicting a strong system of behaviours, beliefs and attitudes can withdraw themselves from them, sometimes even physically. Such withdrawal permits the system to remain unchanged. It is, as we have noted above, one of the less beneficial consequences of sustained tension or frustration. The dismissal of any political information which is uncongenial as the propaganda of an enemy country, which should not be attended to, is a common contemporary example of this mechanism.

Finally, as an individual's behaviour, belief and attitudes are shared with members of his cultural group, it may be necessary to effect a change in the goals or systems of behaviour of the whole group before any given individual's behaviour will change in some particular respect. This is particularly likely to be so if the need of the individual for group acceptance is very great—either because of his own psychological make-up or because of his position in society. Thus it may be the chief or prince who can most easily adopt a new practice, or on the other hand, a group may force such a leader to maintain the *status quo* after all the rest of the group have changed, providing a sort of anchorage for the rest of the group. No knowledge of the way an individual of a given constitution and capacity may be able to accept or reject change can ever be used alone without giving due weight to the nature of the culture of which he is a part, and his position in the particular social group within which he lives.

WAYS OF STUDYING THE HABITS OF INDIVIDUALS AMONG WHOM A CHANGE IS TO BE INTRODUCED

One of the necessary tools of the expert who is seeking to introduce technical change, or to protect and promote the mental health of those involved in technical change, is some way of analysing the traditional behaviour, so as to be able to estimate just where the changes are going to fall, which habits are going to change, which beliefs are going to be threatened, which attitudes will have to be altered. In earlier chapters the importance of taking the whole culture into account has been emphasized; it is also desirable to have a way of following a series of identified individuals which can be used as a basis for planning.

One very good method is to record very carefully the behaviour which individuals manifest over specified periods of time (14 days is a useful unit in modern society, where weekends are important). It will be found that each individual exhibits during his waking days a customary pattern of observable behaviours, together with the beliefs and attitudes which serve to explain these behaviours and are reinforced by them. One can observe the time spent in doing things by oneself (solitary activities) and the time spent in responsive contact (social activities with other people) during a waking day.

In any society, we may assume that for each individual there are limitations, during his waking day, upon the amount of responsive participation with others of which he is capable while experiencing sufficient over-all emotional satisfaction. There limitations will probably involve: (a) the total amount of interaction with other people; (b) the frequency of such interactions with other people; (c) their nature—that is, whether they are subordinate-superordinate relationships, affectional, hostility-provoking, etc. Thus, an individual's mental health at a given period in his life may depend upon a type of relationship with his peers which compensates or balances periods when he is under the orders of a superior, or is himself responsible for the activity of others. He may be depending upon a certain ratio of planned activity to unplanned, or of gregariousness to solitariness, or of using his hands to using words or symbols. Severe disturbances in such a customary pattern of distribution of time result in tension, which the individual seeks to relieve. Furthermore, while each individual has his own unique pattern, the patterns of interaction in a given culture will be found to show definite regularities, so that by sampling the lives of a given group of individuals, it will be possible to see what changes are likely to occur through new habits of work, different agricultural equipment, factory labour, etc.

Each technical change being considered can then be examined against this customary pattern, even when the change is the substitution of a single tool, or the simple introduction of a new method of transportation between home and work. The change may reduce the need to do a job, and so free more time for more jobs, or for other social or solitary activities. It may require that new relationships to people be developed, either to replace those disrupted by giving up the old working process or to carry out the new process. Associated with the old tool, or the old method of transport, will be old beliefs and attitudes. The agent of change can then ask whether the new change will alter the observable pattern of social interaction and associated beliefs and attitudes to such a degree as to strain the individual's capacity for readjustment. Workers on plantations who are well paid, but for whom no social activities are provided, may become involved in vice and alcoholism simply in an attempt to establish an expected ratio between work and relaxation.[1] Decreases in the length of the working-day may lead to maladjustment unless new ways of using time are available. Closer contact with other workers, when it replaces former solitariness of the

[1] Elizabeth Hoyt, 1951.

individual peasant working alone in a garden, may prove unbearable unless other changes are introduced. It may be possible for an individual to tolerate almost continuous inter-action with people whom he knows and can take for granted, while a much less prolonged contact with strangers may be taxing and may lead to strain and maladjustment. But in other cultures, it may be too close contact with relatives or neigh-bours, introduced by some change in working-habits, which proves hard to bear.

Since any one of these types of change may occur separately or in various combinations, it is necessary to find out by careful observation which changes have occurred or are likely to occur, and to appraise their possible effects on mental health. If in the recent past there have been any significant changes in the way people live, a knowledge of how these changes have occurred and how people felt about them may give some promising clues to the form their present readiness or re-luctance to change may take. Changes due to the use of new tools or materials, or to new power sources, are more obvious than changes which occur in individual work-habits or in patterns of social interactions. But the mental health of the individual tends to be more affected by the last two.

New methods of exchange of goods and payment for work, associated with an economy based on money and credit, may profoundly affect work patterns. If marked changes occur in the length of time between the completion of a particular task and the payment for that task, the individual worker's social relationships may be profoundly disturbed. He can no longer plan for his own or his sister's marriage, for illness or for funerals; debts mount up. He is no longer able to preserve a stable and habitual set of routines with people outside his work organization; he has lost a predictable pattern of life.

Careful observations of the customary pattern of life—how work is planned and paid for, what are the social relationships involved in doing it, what are the rules which govern it, etc.— made before changes are introduced, should make possible a better appraisal of the expected changes during work, or in other parts of the total system of human relationships, the degree of such changes, their impact upon the individuals concerned, thus laying the basis for helpful preventive or compensating measures.

Changes in work may be reflected in changes of the inter-actional pattern within the family. The worker may be away longer, he may not be able to provide in the same way for his children, new and irksome forms of supervision or speed-up may disturb him emotionally, and this may be reflected in his family life. The small farmer who now works in a factory may have fewer contacts each day with his wife, his children and other relatives with whom he used to do his farm-work.

New sources of emotional satisfaction must be developed during his working-day, if emotional stability is to be maintained.

In addition, technical changes not directly affecting individual workers' patterns of work relationships may produce serious alteration in work relationships. New types of housing may make it necessary to reduce the size of the family who live together; new types of water-supply may transform what was once a pleasant communal method of laundering into a solitary and hated domestic chore; factory-made instead of home-woven cloth may transform the wife's role; food which is bought ready-prepared may prevent the wife from demonstrating her wifely devotion by long hours over pot or kettle. With such changes in patterns of domestic work, of distribution of time, of distribution of interaction within the family, strain is experienced.

In medicine it has been discovered repeatedly that a specific remedy for a disease may have serious side-effects, creating organic disturbance or other ill effects not intended or expected. In the same way, a very useful new tool, practice, or technique may be highly effective for the specific purpose intended, but have disturbing side-effects upon the individual and the whole social organization. Further, the total system of an individual's relationships may be disturbed by technological changes which initially affect neither himself as a worker nor anyone in his immediate family. The public-health clinic may sever old relationships to midwife and medicine man and priest. The ratio of old men to young is upset by conscription of labour for distant mines or plantations. The introduction of a trading-post or store may cause a demand for cash where cash was not needed before. Wide-spread disturbances in an individual's habitual relationships within his community may occur as consequences of initially localized technical changes, wherever these may be—whether in the local economy, in the system of government, in the administration of public health, in the educational system, or elsewhere.

An attempt is made, therefore, to evaluate such proposed changes by gathering initial information about the total existing pattern of relationships of the individuals involved, and by asking whether a significant change in part or all of this pattern is a likely result of any specific technical change. Associated changes in beliefs and attitudes, as well as in habits, should be carefully considered. The observations can be obtained from detailed records of several consecutive days' waking activities. It is necessary to know the total amount of interaction an individual has with each other person (total number of minutes or hours per day per week), the number of contacts per day or per week with a particular person (coworker, supervisor, wife, priest, etc.), the quality or type of the contacts in a particular situation (for example, there may be a change from supervision by a local boss to hard-driving impersonal supervision by an outside boss).

Considerable changes in any of these three aspects of the pattern are easily noted; the associated changes in emotional states, beliefs and attitudes can then be inquired into, and some estimate can be formed of the expected strain upon the individuals concerned. Whether the most practicable form of compensation will be to build up new satisfaction within the disturbed area of relationship (as by substituting long annual vacations with one's family for previous longer daily periods with one's family) or to develop other relationships (new clubs or associations, labour-unions which compensate for the impersonality of the modern factory) or to provide new recreational forms for leisure time, it is impossible to predict in advance. But some estimate can be formed and promising procedures can be tried out.

These same methods can be used when much more fundamental changes occur—when whole families leave their villages to work, when fathers are away from their families for years, or when young boys go away for several years' work in mines or plantations. In such cases, careful records can chart the traditional pattern which preceded such a move, the pattern which operates after the move is made, and the habits and expectations which will be carried over first in the new environment and later if the migrants return to their original environment. These procedures can also be used at intervals during a period of change as a means of detecting unsuspected disturbances before they become too deep-seated and dangerous.

SUMMARY

1. As a rule, an individual's behaviour, beliefs and attitudes grow and change only to the minimal extent that is called for by the demands of his immediate situation in life. All that is required is that his daily behaviours and his daily perceptions have meaning and integration. So when a boy marries he must alter his behaviour to that of a married man; a married man must learn to be a father; a newly elected official must alter his behaviour to suit his new role. But when an individual is confronted not by an expected change in role, but by a chaotic external environment to which he cannot adjust with emotional satisfaction, and which he cannot explain to himself, he is impelled to seek a new adjustment—which relieves his tension. He tends also to seek a new explanation of his changed environmental situation, and this new explanation

also relieves his tension. A man thrown out of a job in an industrial society tries to adjust himself to living unemployed, and he may also for the first time feel a need to understand how the economic system works. Thus at times of individual or group crisis, the situation is more favourable for adaptive changes in habitual behaviours, beliefs and attitudes. Groups which have themselves felt and expressed a need for technical change are more likely to be aware of the crisis which develops in their lives as a result of the desired change, and so be able to make an effort to adapt to it constructively.

2. A technical change will be perceived by the affected individuals as a smaller change if the change can be incorporated into an unchanged larger pattern of relationships, thus taking advantage of the way in which human perception organizes objects or events together on the basis of proximity in time or space, or culturally determined similarity. Thus families may migrate a great distance but preserve their usual habits of family life. Or upon entering a new country an individual may begin to do new work, but of a type which has been defined   appropriate for anyone from his country, so that his sense of his national identity is strengthened even while the work itself is new and strange.

Even in very complicated situations, in which technical changes cannot be fitted into an existing community or family framework, it may be quite possible to find in operation institutions or existing patterns of interaction which have sufficient similarity to the new desired behaviours to make the introduction of change easier.

In any attempt to use old ways of behaviour to facilitate change, it is, however, important to keep in mind that sometimes a change will be accepted more easily if it is new in a new context. So a new kind of organization may be perceived as more appropriate for a new kind of activity—so that people will accept a factory and a union together where either one alone might be rejected. Paper cups may be accepted more readily if an unfamiliar beverage is served in them. New foods may be accepted if they are introduced together with a new kind of stove or fuel. Thus, the tendency of the human mind to organize and simplify may be invoked by grafting new forms of behaviour onto old forms so that the new seems old and familiar, or by letting one break in traditional behaviour carry a number of other breaks.

3. An individual's ability to learn is a function of the way in which he perceives a situation. Failure to understand this leads to unwarranted discouragement about the learning capacities of other peoples. "They can't learn from

experience," we say. This often simply means that what the expert or the innovator saw in a sequence of events differed sharply from what the people saw. Each person learns from the sequence as he perceives it.

A famous example of the operation of this principle was the unforeseen effect upon the American public of Upton Sinclair's novel *The Jungle*. Mr. Sinclair was a crusading friend of the overworked and underpaid; he hated cruelty, exploitation, and the cheating of the innocent. He observed how people lived in the Chicago stockyards and put his burning indignation down in vivid words. The facts which he was relating demonstrated to him the need for a co-operative commonwealth. The vast majority of his American readers, however, were not socialists, but they were meat-eaters. They perceived Mr. Sinclair's facts in their own way. They read about the human beings and the rats who had fallen into the lard vats and were then sold as food. They concluded that a new pure-food law was required, and Upton Sinclair's novel led to a reform in the handling of meat rather than men.

As memory is selective, just as perception is, great attention must be given, in all educational efforts, to allowing for sufficient time and enough repetition so that facts which are less easy to assimilate are not lightly forgotten.

Sometimes a perception will be so dependent upon an underlying set of fundamental beliefs that it will not be possible to change a practice without altering the whole structure of belief. Thus a desire to lower the infant death-rate may not develop until there is a new conception of the importance of each human individual, or a desire to compete with other nations in the field of vital statistics.

4. The agents of change have a wide choice of methods: they can attempt to influence the perceiving individual directly; they can alter the environment so that it will in turn alter his perception; they can create situations within which he will continue to remain in contact with the new situations; they can attempt to satisfy the needs and emotions which lie at the root of the existing behaviours in a way which will include the proposed change; they may create social support for the individual who adopts the new behaviours. Taken together, these methods involve working through many or all of the personality-forming agencies in a society —institutions, individual people, objects. Any programme aimed at successful change needs to be multidimensional.

Any programme of change whic⸛ has been shown to work on a small scale or in a given type of community or culture must be very carefully evaluated before any of the principles found can be applied in a different setting. It is particularly important to allow for the extensive qualitative

differences which quantitative changes in scale may introduce. A village is not a model for a province or a nation.

5. In this section we have dealt with the mental health of the
individuals actually involved in technical change at a given
moment—the man who must learn a new technique of agriculture, the woman who has her domestic routine disrupted, the worker who must learn to keep pace with a
machine or to accept some new form of association or
supervision.

But from the standpoint of mental health, the hazards
of change are actually not as great for those who are involved thus immediately as they are for their children. The
peasant who comes to the city brings with him all the
stability derived from a childhood spent within a traditional and coherent social order. His personality reflects that
experience and he often withstands enormous pressures,
and meets crisis after crisis with courage and imagination.
It is not among the first-generation immigrants from country to city, from agricultural country to industrial country,
from simple levels of life to complex levels, that we find the
principal disturbances which accompany technical change.
Rather, it is in the lives of their children, reared in conditions within which no stable patterns have been developed,
by parents who, while they may be able to weather the
storm themselves by drawing on a different childhood
experience, have no charts to give their children. Juvenile
delinquency, alcoholism, drug addiction, empty, defeated,
meaningless lives, lives which are a series of drifting rud-
derless activities, commitment to oversimplified political
programmes which promise relief from their feelings of inadequacy and lack of direction—these are the prices which
are paid not so much by the first as by the disturbed members of the second generation. Here there is urgent need for
agencies which will help parents develop new ways of being
parents, and children develop new ways of growing up.
Assuring mental health to the second generation, the children of the uprooted who have not yet themselves taken
root, requires more than the observation of sound psychological principles such as those outlined in the chapter for adjusting adults to change; it requires new social
inventions, most of which have not even been glimpsed
in outline.

Among such inventions are new methods of child care,
which substitute new flexibility for the rigid patterns appropriate to a stable, relatively unchanging society, so that
the child learns to fit together his internal rhythms and the
demands of his environment flexibly, safely—going to sleep
not only at a fixed time in a familiar bed, but also able to
sleep trustingly in new places, because he has learned to

trust even in a world that is not fixed and predictable. We need new methods of education which will leave the child's mind open longer, leave his muscular adjustments freer, less stylized, methods which teach him that safety lies not in knowledge but in knowing what could be but is not known.

In all technical change, even when it seems to be concerned with tools, machines and other impersonal objects, the individual person is both the recipient of change and the mediator or agent of change. His integrity as a person, his stability as a personality, must be kept ever in focus as the living concern of all purposive change.

V. PRINCIPLES INVOLVED IN DEVELOPING MENTAL HEALTH DURING TECHNICAL CHANGE

It is recognized that during technical change, difficulties and conflicts are inevitable. This survey does not offer "solutions" to these problems, but rather indicates how these problems can be approached so as to minimize the difficulties or conflicts creating problems of adjustment, preserve, and where possible promote, mental health.

We may now summarize the general principles which can be derived from the type of materials which have been examined for this survey:

1. The culture of each people is a living unity in the sense that a change in any one aspect will have repercussions in other aspects. This is true even in those cultures which, while in the process of very rapid change, are torn by conflicts and contradictions.

2. As each human individual embodies the culture through which he lives, discrepancies, inconsistencies, different rates of change of parts of culture, will have their expression in the personality organization of the individuals who live within changing cultures.

3. An active concern for the mental health of the peoples of the world includes an active concern for the ways in which technical change is taking place. When the introduction of technical change is purposively initiated, or promoted by individuals or responsible bodies, such purposiveness involves responsibility for the effects not only in improved living-conditions, but also upon the total way of life of the

people, for reintegration as well as a defence against dis-integration.

4. As each culture is unique, and as each particular situation within which a change is occurring or is to be made is unique, it is not possible to lay down prescriptions for what is to be done in any particular case. It is only possible so to identify and describe the process which occurs that each particular individual or team charged with responsibility for planning, or executing, or adjusting to some type of change, may be able to act in terms of this process. For example, it is possible to point out that in any programme involving popular education in public health, the problem of language is a serious one—exact meanings must be ex-plored, questions of adapting old words to new ideas, as opposed to coining new words, must be weighed, choice must be made among rival dialects, issues such as the use of a world-language or the elevation of a local language to a level at which the literature of the world may be expected to be translated into it—all must be taken into considera-tion. But after such details have been pointed out, whether all the public-health teaching in Sumatra is to be couched in the new national language of Indonesia (Bahasa Indo-nesia, an adaptation of Malay) would have to be worked out in active co-operation with members of the Indonesian health and education services who have an immediate knowledge of the local conditions in Sumatra. There is no possible prescription except this insistence upon taking into account the culture and the situation and the individual in-volved.

5. All changes should be introduced with the fullest possible consent and participation of those whose daily lives will be affected by the changes.

6. Every change, even such apparently conspicuous modifi-cations of the external environment as building a dam or a railroad, occurs through the mediation and for the benefit of living individuals, and it is with these living human beings, their aspirations and hopes, their historically given and environmentally limited capabilities, that this survey is concerned.

7. In the light of these general principles, we may consider in somewhat more detail a set of recommendations which should make it possible to observe these principles in any given case.

RECOMMENDATIONS

First

It is important to take into account the degree of congruence between different levels of planning, from the international or national level to the final expression of any change in the daily lives of some identified group of people in some part of the world. If there are serious discrepancies in the practices involved or in the goals sought at higher levels, these will be reflected in the way the changes are made which affect the lives of the people whose farming practices, methods of earning a living, or health attitudes are to be changed. For example, if a government is promoting a given change for purposes of prestige, as a way of establishing itself in the minds of the people as progressive, modern, with an active concern for the welfare of the population, while the technical experts who are involved in the next step of the planning are themselves out of sympathy with these governmental aspirations, and are only concerned with better nutrition, or more education for the people—so that what is a sub-goal for one group is a major goal for the second group—a type of internal sabotage and friction may be set up which will be reflected in discordant practices at a more local level, in literature produced, or plans which are drawn up. If, however, the several groups involved can agree on a particular sub-goal, such as increasing the agricultural production or the proportion of a marketable crop, or the lowering of the infant death-rate, so that each interest group is able to focus on a common problem, many of these discrepancies and disharmonies can be avoided. (This is, of course, only a sub-head of the general principle of the interrelatedness of culture: all those who become involved in purposive change share together a sort of temporary sub-culture within which inconsistencies become a hazard.)

As there are bound to be great differences between main goals at different levels and in different sorts of planning—international, national, scientific, humanitarian, educational, engineering, etc.—the identification of a common sub-goal—such as universal vaccination—may prove impracticable. Those concerned with population growth may well point out that reduction in the infant death-rate before adequate changes have been made in agricultural and industrial practice to support the increased population, or before educational practices have been introduced to raise the standard of living and reduce the desire for large families, may only bring more misery. At the same time, those concerned with the immediate welfare of each child born today may feel that to withhold or to fail to promote measures now available for saving human lives would violate those very principles of concern for human welfare on which the whole programme of purposive change is based. Such a conflict, serious though it seems, may be minor compared with the conflict between modern Western values—in which each individual is seen as unique and with but one life to live, so that every effort must be made to promote the survival and health of each individual born—and the values of religious systems which, while affirming the value of individual human souls, disallow this tremendous emphasis upon the human life-span of each individual. Issues such as these lie back of discussions about industrialization, immigration, immunization, etc.—often inexplicit and inarticulate—troubling to the exponents of each point of view just to the degree that they are unrecognized and unadmitted. Attempts to resolve such issues, in which the leading political and religious ideologies of the world of the twentieth century are involved, will inevitably colour decisions which are made to build a giant irrigation project in one country, to build factories in some agricultural area, to start the modernization programme with schools or with public-health clinics.

In this manual we are considering not the resolving of such issues as they relate to the most fundamental concerns of human beings in the world today, but with making recommendations which will protect and preserve individual men, women and children whose whole way of life is being affected and altered, from the ill effects of such conflicts. The only way we now know of in which planning on high levels—involving conflicts of the most fundamental sort—can be handled so as to protect the individual lives affected is to be sure that as much of the implementing action as possible is put into effect by members of the same culture and of the same locality.

For example, in the 1940s there was a series of discussions, in which members of different nationalities participated, on child welfare and nutrition in China. Working from Western assumptions about the need to preserve each individual Chinese infant, the conference emphasized the need in China for cow's milk, canned if necessary. Chinese participants were able to oppose these demands from two points of view, whether the economic or the nutritional emphasis was given. Chinese nutritionists—unencumbered by the Western insistence that if infants are not fed human milk, they must be fed animal milk —had experimented successfully with diets based on vegetables and eggs; Chinese economists were wary of a plan which, while nominally promoting nutritional goals, was economically unrealistic. Those who are themselves members of a culture within which a change is being introduced will be able, often unwittingly, to block suggestions which proceed from quite different value systems than their own, and which would eventuate in destructive changes.

It may be asked how such blockings by the members of a culture, or by the members of a local community or of a particular professional group, are to be distinguished from the type of resistance to change which is offered by those groups who have a vested interest—economic or psychological—in the preservation of the *status quo,* or in the promotion of conditions which are antithetical to the best mental health of the members of the society. Here again the question of sub-goals comes in. If the entire group involved in making a plan is committed to the particular sub-goal, the alteration of the plans in the direction of genuine cultural considerations may more safely be relied upon. Thus in a conference on nutrition, while one cannot with safety rely upon a representative of a manufacturer of synthetic baby foods, or the advocate of a change in the agricultural production pattern of a country to a crop of which he is the principal exporter, or the representative of a group whose particular services will disappear if any action is taken, one can rely upon *nutritionists* of different cultural backgrounds to introduce the necessary precautions into any nutritional plan made.

As a general recommendation, then, it is possible to say that it is dangerous ever to make any plan, or to try to execute any plan, without the active participation of members of the culture, of the particular professions, and of the administrative apparatus concerned; as soon as any planned change has a specific population group as its object, members of that group —through demonstration villages, pilot projects, etc.—must be brought into the planning.

Whether we focus on the need for homogeneity in type of practice or on the need for reconciling widely different basic ideologies and values, this procedure is necessary. The arrogant self-assurance which makes more industrialized countries force their methods on the less industrialized, the touchy eagerness to prove themselves that characterizes young nations, the missionary zeal of the apostles of the scientific point of view, and the defensive measures of the religiously orthodox, may all be welded into a working whole if exponents of each position plan together.

Certain other recommendations follow. It is desirable that all groups involved with planning the introduction of technical change—either in its technological aspects or in making those necessary changes in education, social organization, and family life which will protect and promote the mental health of those among whom the change is being introduced—should consist of members of more than two cultures. Such a group would include, of course, the members of the culture in which the change is being made, members of the culture whose developed professional skills or economic know-how and resources are being drawn upon, and members of a third culture, who can maintain a certain objectivity and prevent the consuming group and the resource group from becoming dead-locked or developing an isolated bit of behaviour in which the conflicts— between, for example, Indonesian and American, or Burmese and Dutch, value systems—may become frozen. This same recommendation applies to the composition of every type of team within a country; if the national level and rural communities are the focus of the planning, the inclusion as a third participant of someone who has worked in cities will similarly help maintain a certain measure of objectivity.

What applies to the involvement of members of different cultures and different levels of organization applies equally to the inclusion of different professions; having more than two professions and including one with less involvement again will provide steadiness of team-work.

Such measures are a protection against the organization of bias, and a certain guarantee that the programmes developed and the steps taken can both embody and be to a degree unhampered by the vested interests and old and new, conscious and unconscious, prejudices of all those concerned.

It will be recognized that this recommendation is again based on the principle that culture is mediated through persons, and that a culture, or a profession, or a level of administration, or a point of view, cannot be represented by a charter, a diagram, or a printed description, but only by living human beings who themselves embody the position which is to be taken into account.

Second

Where specific technical practices are to be introduced into a culture or a part of a society which has not hitherto used them, it is desirable to strip these technical practices of as many extraneous cultural accretions (from the lands of origin) as possible. This recommendation applies to such varied matters as mass production, methods of immunization, development of alphabets for unwritten languages, methods of antisepsis or of sanitation, etc. It is realized that the technologies and inventions of modern science are themselves the outgrowth of a very particular historically limited type of culture—a culture in which the focus of interest has been upon the observable, the repeatable, the measurable, upon using the external world as a model even when processes within the body were concerned. Without this focus of modern science—this discontent with any except the "scientific" explanation, this attempt to investigate all types of phenomena so that lawfulness in nature could be identified—the particular benefits of modern medicine and of modern industrial processes, which are coveted by and for all the peoples of the world, could not have developed in the way they have. However, once invented, a particular device may be used effectively by peoples within whose culture that particular invention might never have been made. It is also probable that too much emphasis upon the whole complex of cultural attitudes surrounding such inventions as clocks, thermometers, shock therapy, printing, caloric food-counts, assembly-line production, Diesel engines, or electronic self-corrective devices, may slow down the possibility of invention in the world, because the members of the new cultures who import and adopt the invention are prevented from making a contribution to its further development. If in order to use a certain type of machine it is necessary to adopt all the attitudes towards punctuality of Western factories and school systems, absorbing this alien type of education may act selectively within the new culture, so that only the deviant or only the obedient and frightened learn, and the gifted and creative may turn away. An alien technology, supported by forms of education and inter-personal relations which are also alien, is likely to separate the practitioner of the new skill from his cultural roots, prevent the new practice from becoming integrated in the living-habits of the mass of the people, and produce populations who are confused and disoriented because they do not participate meaningfully in the new forms of their society. We see this happening every day in workers who emigrate from country to city, from a peasant to an industrial country, who learn to comply with the alien ritual of factory or clinic, but who are themselves lost and disoriented.

Western-trained professionals carry about with them an enormous amount of cultural baggage which could very well be discarded. We may illustrate this again from the field of nutrition, where, instead of taking the basic principles of nutrition and examining a given local dietary pattern for the actual nutrients, the caloric content, in relation to the growth and work patterns of the population, there is instead an insistence upon ideas like three meals a day, balance of the diet within 24 hours, the importance of animal milk for infants, and so the use of the findings of nutritional science is compromised and confused in other parts of the world. Sanitarians may impose the ideas of their own culture on the proprieties of age and sex standards of privacy, or even introduce systems of behaviour which involve culturally special ideas about the whole process of digestion, or which violate the trust of a particular culture in the goodness of human nature. Extraneous and culturally destructive effects can be avoided by stripping each scientific technique to the bone, to the absolute essentials which will make it possible for other people to learn to use it, and to handle it in a living, participating, creative way.

This recommendation applies not only to stripping scientific practices bare of the particular habits of the members of the Western society within which a practice was developed, but also to the advisability of leaving behind the particular rationalizations and sanctions, both religious and scientific, with which a specific practice may have been associated in a given Western country. For example, the insistence that individual will-power should be invoked in teaching good nutritional usage is the result of a blend of Protestant Christian conceptions of the human will and scientific findings as to the best way to utilize a given set of food resources. In another culture, pleasure in eating, or customary compliance with ritual arrangements of food, may be invoked instead.

To carry out this recommendation, reliance must again be placed on mature human beings. Instead of saying that in order to train a public-health nurse we must first have an elementary-school system patterned on the school system of the West—in which children will be rebuked and rewarded for the same sort of mistakes, learn to read the same kinds of directions, learn to fear the same kinds of errors in arithmetic and to hate the same kinds of tasks—we may experiment with how to teach particular practices to the most educated young adults we can find.

Instead of bringing beginners from the countries wishing to introduce new public-health practices, to learn a pattern in a country with more developed practice, we can bring more mature students who will participate—sometimes with the help of seniors who have worked as foreigners in their country and with representatives from other countries with different types of practice—in making a new pattern which is congenial and meaningful to them, as representatives of their own culture.

The model for such a procedure, by which the end product of modern technology is reinterpreted in terms of particular cultures, was established in the United States during World War II, when the question was raised how recipes were to be developed for using new dried-food products which resembled no known kind of food. As long as recognized food staples were distributed by the nationals of a country carrying out a food-relief programme, a question like this was seldom raised, and the result was the kind of misery and ill feeling which came from assuming that European populations would eat maize. But these new synthetic foods were as strange to Americans as they would be to Greeks or Japanese. Because they were relatively unencumbered with traditional sentiments, were in fact stripped down to the barest essentials, the question of what to do with them could be asked. Experimental groups were set up among women from different countries for whom these were designed as relief foods, to explore the range of different ways in which the same synthetic food might be used as hot soup or cold dessert, or simply as an ingredient in a made dish. Once this exploration was completed, although it did yield suggestive recipes and insights about differences in cultural practice, it seemed clear that the best advice was: (a) Do not set up any fixed way of using the new foods which will inevitably be special to American food-habits and; (b) in each country get local cooks, who may be trusted, if given support and latitude, to work out ways of adopting the new strange materials, of turning what was food only in the scientific sense—in that it had been demonstrated to contain the necessary nutrients for human beings—into food in the cultural sense, something that people would eat and be nourished by.

In this instance, the synthetic food, because it was new, had as yet little weight of cultural meaning, except in matters like colour. But for most of the technological change which is introduced from one part of the world to another, the burden of the habits and beliefs of the people who developed a particular technique is heavy. It will be necessary to set about stripping each practice down, as well as building up training and development methods which permit each new culture which takes over a particular technique to contribute new patterns of use. This means a style of analysis which asks of each procedure: What is the scientifically essential, the minimum core, of this operation? In regard to a thermometer questions would be asked about size, shape, colour, the use of the particular system of measurement, the way "normal" was marked; the preference for a mouth or a rectal thermometer; the phrasing of high and low temperatures; the phrasing of the meaning of temperature deviations as showing that an individual was sick, or that an individual was putting up a fight against disease, etc.

In building a factory questions would be asked about such matters as size and shape—Does a factory have to have walls? Should the assembly line move the object or should a moving platform move the men along with the objects? How long is a shift? What should control the tempo of the operation?—as well as the more obvious question of how an operation of a factory type should be set up in a society with entirely different patterns of human relations.

But one of the great advantages of first stripping each technological change to the core, of querying the most time-honoured accretions and practices, is that the experts then genuinely need constructive thinking by members of the culture where they are going to work. Because the situation is new, no one can give them a recipe, and usually the culturally workable answer can only be arrived at by experiment—with living human beings from the culture in question. If a thermometer is not even to *look* like our thermometer, then what is it to look like? If a factory is not a building with walls, what is it? If dried beans are not bean-soup, what are they? The scene is then set for the participation of the members of the other culture, in which the experts with experience—knowing their helplessness in this area of re-design—will welcome help, and the gifted members of the culture in which the device or process has never been used will be able to contribute imaginatively. By this very contribution they will lay the groundwork for the mental health of all the members of their society who must learn to take temperatures or work in factories.

Obversely, a sensitive attention to the way in which the existing techniques of the country to which change is being brought are interwoven with the local value system is also important. So it may be found that agricultural practices are tied up with an image of the earth as a mother who gives food and is fed, and an image of mutual giving—by man, care and fertilizer; by the earth, food for man—may be used for the new agricutural techniques.

Third

When the particular values of a given culture are to be used as vehicles for change, such a use should be planned and applied by those members of the culture who share the belief or the aspiration which is to be used. Those who are engaged either in introducing technological change or in providing for a cushioning or muting of the effects of technological change, have become increasingly aware, during the last few years, of the advantages of couching a change in terms which are familiar to a given society, in supporting a new practice by quoting an old sacred text. At the same time, many discussions among experts reveal a deep disquiet about such a procedure, a disquiet which manifests itself in questions, such as whether it is possible to imbed modern scientific practices in age-old systems of religious values. Or is it not necessary, many specialists ask, to plan to introduce a secular, scientific point of view right through a society, if men are to use the inventions and machines of the Western world, with their superior capacity to provide food and shelter, education, and medical care for the masses of the people? These questions reveal a dilemma, in which the secularized expert asks how in fact he—who does not believe in a particular system of values, and shows, by his every act, his adherence to a secularized scientific system of values—can with any integrity use these values, which he believes to be outmoded and wrong, to accomplish such ends as the introduction of literacy and public health.

This problem, however, is also soluble if it is referred to the general principles of cultural integrity. If members of the group of people who are to use the new technology themselves do the planning, then they will be adapting their own beliefs, and quoting their own sacred texts, restructuring their own lives, in accordance with the common sub-goal of infant welfare or universal literacy, which they share with the technical experts from the city, from the modernizing sector of the population, from another country, or from an international agency. For a man who himself believes in no God to search the Koran for an appropriate text to support methods of preventing well-pollution will, at best, limit his efficiency and make his commitment to the effort of guaranteeing a population pure water less whole-hearted. At worst, it introduces an element of manipulation into the operation which reduces the dignity of those whose holy texts are quoted to the level of puppets whose strings are pulled by an arrogant and alien hand. But if the people themselves, steeped in the traditional wisdom of their scriptures, transform the new knowledge into a new expression of an ancient and beloved revelation, then the dangers of lack of spontaneity, falseness, manipulation and degradation are avoided.

Careful attention to this principle of participation will also help to deal with one of the most serious dangers in the purposive introduction of new technologies among peoples who have newly come to trust in and desire the scientifically based achievements and values of the West. Among such peoples a great many of those who acquire an education in medicine, or engineering, or agriculture, will have had to make a considerable break with their own traditions, and will have compensated for this by embracing—with the self-protective zeal and blindness of the convert—the beliefs and practices which they associate with the new knowledge. Their willingness to assume a whole series of symbols—from fountain-pens, rain-coats and brief-cases to an insistence upon marriage for love, and the disregard of traditional patterns of inter-personal relations—is often an essential step in the particular path of modernization or Westernization on which they have determined, or for which their own society has selected them. But they are, for this very reason, seldom the appropriate persons to adapt the new practices to the traditions which are still shared by the masses of the people. To the extent that they are committed to the new form of their society, they will wish to bring their fellow-nationals with them, to use some new public-health practice or method of transportation as a device to wean them from all their old beliefs.

For example, a critical observer, watching from a distance, may be impressed with the way in which local officials in the Indonesian Republic have adapted the traditional shadow-play to their programmes of keeping the people of the villages informed about the changes which are being vigorously pursued throughout Indonesia. This new shadow-play has ordinary human characters and has been stripped of supernatural elements. But this use of the shadow-play is viewed with deep and genuine scepticism by young political leaders, who feel that the shadow-play itself should be eradicated as lending inevitably an inappropriate aura of religious awe to the modern national leadership. For an educator who felt this way to plan to use the shadow-play would mean either a compromise with his principles or an expression of pessimism and contempt for the villagers who, from his point of view, are steeped in age-old mysticism. If, however, some programme of information is entrusted to village leaders, who entertain no such scepticism and who themselves feel the shadow-play to be a most appropriate way of educating the people to take part in the work of developing their country, then there is no such question as compromise or insincerity. The play will be furnished with new lines, and, in time, as the characters explain to the people the advantages of new agricultural practices and new health measures, in the mind of the script-writer and in the minds of his audiences, a new synthesis will take place, which is organic because it has occurred within the same human organisms, which is harmonious because it is an expression of individual human beings' efforts to make sense of their own lives.

Fourth

As each culture is a whole, however sorely torn at the moment—whole in the sense that it is the system by which and through which its members live—in all relationships between cultures, each must be accorded dignity and value. Much of the present phrasing of technical-assistance planning, and much of the present evaluation of change within a country, is conducted with explicit or implicit denial of the dignity of members of those countries which, while often the inheritors of much older traditions, have not been in the vanguard of those aspects of culture which stem from modern science. This is self-defeating, in that it arouses violent resistances and attempts at compensation and retaliation from those whose feelings of self-esteem have been violated; it is also contrary to the findings of modern psychiatric practice, which insist on the recognition of the patient's validity as a human being. Phrases which divide the world into the "haves" and the "have-nots" overvalue bread and plumbing and devalue music and architecture. Those whose status is defined as a "have-not" may come to repudiate the possibility of learning anything at all, or of sharing anything at all except "bread" with those who have so denigrated their cherished ways of life. Phrases like "under-developed," "backward," "simple"—to the extent that they cover a whole culture—are equally defeating. If, instead, we draw on an image in which two adults—one experienced in one skill, another in a different skill—pool their knowledge so that each can use the skill of the other for a particular task, as when foreign explorer and local guide venture together into a forest, much more viable relationships can be set up. Leaders of the newest countries, only recently established by revolution or mandate or negotiation, are young adults, not children— less experienced but not less adult than those upon whose skills and resources they need to draw. Indeed, it is possible to contrast the often childlike dependence of members of old societies towards their governments, which they feel ought to look after them, protect them and provide for them, and the responsible adulthood of the members of some new nations who regard their young governments as institutions which must be protected and cherished by the citizenry. A very little scrutiny, if the whole culture is taken into account, is enough to do away with assumptions of superiority, and to permit the establishment of working partnerships in which engineer and architect, scientist and sage, pool their different but not incompatible wisdoms. The most complex invention of the Western world—radar or psychoanalytic therapy—is still only part of a way of life, to which others who are skilled in ways of life which have developed differently may be expected to contribute new insights. The sensitive application of a gadget, or the rejection of some use to which it has callously been put, may be as great or even greater a contribution than the invention of the gadget itself.

Fifth

Every effort should be made to design the introduction of measures to facilitate or compensate for or provide for benefits from technical change in such a way that the process is circular, and all those involved at every level are able to participate and experience the changes as they occur.

One of the serious difficulties experienced by human beings who attempt to change the culture within which they live is that the very fact of planning itself makes it possible to force through a single-line change in disregard of the hundreds of side-effects which are taken care of in unplanned change which occurs within a society unsupported by disproportionate governmental or industrial pressure. Where a system of piped-on water is gradually spread through a country, with each village taking responsibility for its own water-supply, the changes may be very slow, but problems of landownership, of where the clothes are to be washed, of combining watering cattle and arranging business transactions, etc., will be thrashed out slowly, and the disruption of old ways of life will be less serious. When a new impulse towards better water, or better roads, or better land-use sweeps the country, implemented by funds and personnel from outside the community, its effective progress is rapid, but fewer such adjustments can take place.

This was vividly illustrated by an episode in which housing was planned at the national level, and the architects, anxious to conserve labour and materials (which meant massive savings when thousands of dwelling units were concerned in the plans), reduced the traditional space allotted to stairways only to find that they had built houses in which a coffin could not be carried down the stairs. Harassed housing-managers had to send mildly sick people off to already over-crowded hospitals, afraid of the effects of a death in which traditional burial ritual would be violated. When houses are built within a community on a normal scale, the architects do not take coffins into account, but long experience in human living has brought about an accommodation between the dimensions of the houses and the traditional ceremonials which take place within them. The porte-cochère disappears with the open carriage and the closed motor car stands, itself roofed, before an unroofed doorway.

It is possible to say that in all old and habitual enterprises, with slow and traditional introduction of small changes, the side-effects of a change can be felt and responded to by the members of that society. When change is introduced by external forces, however beneficent in intent, these protective behaviours cannot operate, and changes may go much too far in some given direction before compensatory measures can be taken.

Two inventions which have been made in the last century attempt to deal with these problems: the model or the pilot project, and provision for "feed-back" from an area where any new activity is introduced. In the model, or pilot, or demonstration project, a desired change is introduced on a small scale and meticulous observations are made of the process. These observations can be used as the basis for modifications of the original plan, new provisions for flexibility, and compensatory measures which are necessary. This method is now becoming a commonplace over much of the world, part of the equipment of administrators, educators and planners; but one element is still neglected—the recognition that the experts who inaugurate a given change are so much a part of the project, that they themselves should be observed, and their behaviour should be recorded and analysed. A next step in the use of demonstration, model and pilot projects is the introduction of recorders, and the use of the records of the roles of experts, or representatives of higher administrative levels on the local scene. Thus those who are charged with making innovations—in addition to the observations which they themselves make—can learn what they themselves are doing. Their own behaviour is "fed back" to them and becomes part of the planning process.

There are a variety of other ways in which the "feed-back" process can be elaborated, so that, for example, no planning conference is held without provision for the planners later being fully informed of the outcome of their plans. Modern methods of sound-recording and moving pictures can be tried to increase the insight of practitioners, and function in lieu of the older, slower methods by which the practitioner—educator or physician or engineer—who failed to respond to the needs of a local situation was disciplined and educated by "experience."

In brief, if there is to be purposive change, directed by those with power and resources, to introduce programmes of vast scope with unprecedented speed, so as to add 20 years to the expectation of life within a single generation, or alter the level of literacy from 10 per cent to 90 per cent within a decade, it is necessary to develop substitutes for "experience," so that people may learn in a few weeks what they once learned in a lifetime, and yet learn it with all of the complexity of genuine human experience. Failure to provide such corrections carries automatic penalties, for either the desired changes cannot be carried out at all, or methods of force and manipulation have to be used which, while introducing a particular technology, decrease the well-being of the people as a whole.

Sixth

In the choice of methods to be used for introducing change, whether technical or compensatory, the criteria of involvement of the whole personality should be used. A great deal of discussion is wasted over the relative desirability of using print or radio, films or discussion groups, cartoons or dramas, practice or demonstration or illustration, as ways of teaching new procedures and attitudes. These discussions tend to ignore the fact that all media for dissemination of new knowledge are to be judged in terms of effectiveness, and effectiveness in turn is a function of the extent to which the new practice becomes part of the way of life of the people among whom the change is to be introduced. Any reliance on a method which is purely intellectual or purely aesthetic, purely emotion, or purely moralistic, purely social or purely individual, will necessarily restrict the area of involvement. Whether, in a given culture, films or group discussions will evoke a more whole participation in adults or children, in the educated or the uneducated, on weekdays or on a holy day, are matters which have to be decided by experiment, with the full participation of the particular population on the spot. If this is recognized, preparation of teaching and demonstration materials will take the form of suggestions of ways of developing materials rather than the provision of ready-made, rigid, untranslatable devices. In the preparation precautions may be undertaken which make local adaptation inescapable—as in a film which has a sound-track which must be translated into a local idiom, or an exhibit with gaps in it which must be filled in with local materials.

Seventh

In order to preserve the process of change in each culture as a living one through which each generation of human beings increasingly is able to use the knowledge of every part of the human race to solve their emerging problems and advance towards a realization of their highest aspirations, efforts should be directed towards the establishment within each country— and often within each locality—of institutions which will make it possible to assay this ongoing process. Instead of working out blue prints for health and welfare, nutrition and longevity, towards the fulfillment of which populations are relentlessly propelled, it is possible to establish patterns of social evaluation, so that communities and countries may take stock of themselves, assess the present state of nutrition against the present state of agricultural resources and present state of community facilities, match the projected population curve against the present rate of building elementary schools or homes for the aged, project needs for new kinds of personnel and begin to train them 10 years before the need develops.

To preserve and promote mental health in the midst of technical change then emerges as a way of stating a goal of cultural renewal as each group of people undertakes to utilize technical advances for the purpose of creating and maintaining institutions which will cherish and protect the lives of men in world-wide community.

APPENDIX A

THE INTERNATIONAL SETTING OF TECHNICAL CHANGE

GENERAL OBJECTIVES OF THE UNITED NATIONS

With the establishment of the United Nations on 24 October 1945, the idea that the well-being of mankind is an international responsibility was laid down in the Charter. Peace based on fundamental and equal human rights, freedom, justice and welfare, with full recognition of the dignity and worth of the human person, is the basic aim of the world organization as expressed in the preamble to the United Nations Charter in the name of the peoples of the Member Nations. "To promote social progress and better standards of living in larger freedom" to which end "to employ international machinery for the promotion of the economic and social advancement of all peoples" is among the stated objectives of the world organization.[1]

[1] The full text of the preamble reads:
We the peoples of the United Nations determined
to save succeeding generations from the scourge of war, which twice in our lifetime has brought untold sorrow to mankind, and
to reaffirm faith in fundamental human rights, in the dignity and worth of the human person, in the equal rights of men and women and of nations large and small, and
to establish conditions under which justice and respect for the obligations arising from treaties and other sources of international law can be maintained, and
to promote social progress and better standards of life in larger freedom, and for these ends

The Economic and Social Council, under the authority of the General Assembly and supported by the Specialized Agencies of the United Nations, became the arm of the world organization to promote "higher standards of living, full employment, and conditions of economic and social progress and development." [1] All Member Nations pledged themselves to take joint and separate action in co-operation with the United Nations to achieve these purposes. [2]

Greater development of all resources, human and material, was recognized as a prerequisite to the attainment of better standards of living in different parts of the world. Accordingly, among the functions of the Economic and Employment Commission of the Economic and Social Council is the promotion of full employment and advice to the Council on "problems of economic development in less developed areas and of economic expansion in general."

"The less developed areas," which are now generally referred to as "economically under-developed areas," comprise the larger portion of the world. North America and Western Europe, whose peoples have mastered scientific techniques to control their environment, improve their health, and develop their production of material goods, stand out in strong contrast to vast areas of South America, Africa, the Middle East, and Asia, where malnutrition and disease undermine the strength and shorten the life-span of the predominantly agrarian and illiterate masses who, for a number of geographic, cultural and historical political reasons, do not benefit much or at all from the inventions of modern science and technology. It has become increasingly clear that the wide gap between wealth and relative welfare ascribed to economic development in a few countries, and grinding poverty in most of the others, constitutes a basic source of economic and social

---

to practice tolerance and live together in peace with one another as good neighbors, and

to unite our strength to maintain international peace and security, and

to ensure, by the acceptance of principles and the institution of methods, that armed force shall not be used, save in the common interest, and

to employ international machinery for the promotion of the economic and social advancement of all peoples,

have resolved to combine our efforts to accomplish these aims.

[1] From Article 55 of the United Nations Charter. The whole article reads:
With a view to the creation of conditions of stability and well being which are necessary for peaceful and friendly relations among nations based on respect for the principal of equal rights and self-determination of peoples, the United Nations shall promote:

(a) higher standards of living, full employment, and conditions of economic and social progress and development;

(b) solutions of international economic, social, health and related problems; and international cultural and educational cooperation; and

(c) universal respect for, and observance of, human rights and fundamental freedoms for all without distinction as to race, sex, language, or religion.

[2] United Nations Charter, Art. 56.

instability in the world and is, in fact, a threat to peace. It has been recognized that accelerating the economic development in the less advanced areas is imperative from the standpoint of all countries alike and that increase in productivity in the under-developed areas is a prerequisite to raising the living-standards of their peoples.[1]

This idea was strongly expressed by the President of the United States in his inaugural address of 20 January 1949, which launched the "Point Four" programme. President Truman stated that "greater production is the key to prosperity and peace. And the key to greater production is a wider and more vigorous application of modern scientific and technical knowledge." The United States invited other countries "to pool their technological resources" to "help the free peoples of the world, through their own efforts, to produce food, more clothing, more materials for housing, and more mechanical power to lighten their burdens." [2]

Prior to this statement the subject of technical assistance in general, and with special reference to under-developed countries in particular, had been receiving increasing attention in the United Nations.

In December 1946, the General Assembly, considering that "the Members of the United Nations are not yet all equally developed" and may need expert advice, instructed the Economic and Social Council to "study the question of providing effective ways and means for furnishing, in co-operation with the Specialized Agencies, expert advice in the economic, social, and cultural fields to Member Nations who desire this assistance." [3] At the same session the Assembly empowered the Secretary-General to assist and advise governments requesting such help on "new technical methods in any branch of social welfare," including the training of local welfare officials outside their own countries.[4]

The Economic and Social Council took a number of steps to stimulate in the United Nations the development of facilities for technical assistance such as may be necessary—as, for instance, in the fields of public finance, statistics, public administration, and cartography.

In December 1948, the Assembly, noting that the lack of expert personnel and the lack of technical organization are among the factors that impede the economic development of under-developed areas, appropriated funds to enable the Secretary-General, in co-operation with the Specialized Agencies:

(a) to arrange for international teams of experts to advise Governments in connexion with their economic development programmes,

[1] United Nations, Economic and Social Council, E/1327/Add. 1.
[2] United States Department of State Publ. 3719, "Point Four . . ."
[3] United Nations, General Assembly, A/64/Add. 1, Resolution 51 (I).
[4] Ibid., Resolution 58 (I).

(b) to arrange for facilities for the training abroad of experts of under-developed countries,

(c) to arrange for the training of local technicians within the under-developed countries, and

(d) to "provide facilities designed to assist governments to obtain technical personnel, equipment and supplies, and to arrange for the organization of such services as may be appropriate in the promotion of economic development."

Among the instructions to the Secretary-General, it was stipulated that the technical assistance furnished shall "(1) not be a means of foreign economic and political interference in the internal affairs of the country concerned and shall not be accompanied by any considerations of a political nature; (2) be given only to or through governments; (3) be designed to meet the needs of the country concerned; (4) be provided, as far as possible, in the form which that country desires; and (5) be of high quality and technical competence." [1]

The Assembly simultaneously (a) requested the International Labour Organisation to examine, in consultation with the United Nations, "the most appropriate arrangements for facilitating the admission to the world's centres of training for apprentices and technical workers of qualified persons from countries which suffer from a lack of technicians and specialists necessary to the development of their national economy." [2] and (b) resolved to establish an International Centre for Training in Public Administration mainly for candidates from countries "in greatest need of access to principles, procedures and methods of modern administration." [3]

The announcement of the "Point Four" programme by the United States gave a strong impetus to further international action. In March 1949, the Economic and Social Council requested the Secretary-General, in consultation with the Specialized Agencies and with due consideration to suggestions by Member Governments, to prepare a report setting forth a comprehensive plan for "an expanded programme of technical assistance for economic development of under-developed countries." The Council recommended that this be done "paying due attention to questions of a social nature which directly condition economic development." [4] The report [5] was considered by the Council in August 1949, whereupon the Council adopted a resolution with recommendations to the General Assembly including a set of observations and guiding principles which remain basic in the approach to the implementation of technical assistance by any United Nations body within the

[1] United Nations, General Assembly, A/810, Resolution 200 (III).

[2] Ibid., Resolution 201 (III).

[3] Ibid., Resolution 246 (III).

[4] United Nations, Economic and Social Council, /E/1310, Resolution 180 (VIII).

[5] United Nations, Economic and Social Council, E/1327/Add. 1 and Add. 2.

framework of the Expanded Programme.[1] The Assembly adopted these recommendations in November 1949,[2] including the suggestion to convoke a conference on technical assistance. Such a conference was held in June 1950, where funds equivalent to about 20,000,000 United States dollars were pledged by 50 nations for the operation of the Expanded Programme until the end of 1951. These funds were allocated in varying proportions to the United Nations and to five Specialized Agencies:

United Nations	23 per cent
Food and Agriculture Organization	29 per cent
International Civil Aviation Organization	1 per cent
International Labour Organisation	11 per cent
United Nations Educational, Scientific and Cultural Organization	14 per cent
World Health Organization	22 per cent

The close interrelationship between economic and social development is heavily stressed in the report prepared by the Secretary-General, mentioned earlier.[3] It is stated therein that "it is impossible to define economic development precisely or in absolute terms." As a process, which is nowhere complete and nowhere absent, "it is the product of simultaneous developments in many fields." It is stated that it involves in particular "an increase in productivity—a more efficient use of resources to produce more and better food, clothing, shelter and the other necessaries and amenities of life, at a less heavy cost in human toil and hardship." It is further stated:

Economic development has far-reaching implications for all aspects of life. It makes possible higher standards of nutrition, health, and education. It permits an increase of leisure and opens up new intellectual frontiers. Given a wide and equitable distribution of its benefits, it is likely to result in a substantial increase in the security of the individual and in social stability.

In the discussion devoted to the objectives and nature of the Expanded Programme, the passages below are noteworthy in reference to the social aspects.[4]

Preceding a statement that too great and too long, continued dependence on foreign capital and technicians may impede rather than accelerate development along sound lines, is the following:

The effective organisation of more rapid economic development

[1] United Nations, Economic and Social Council, E/1553, Resolution 222A (IX), Annex I.

[2] United Nations, General Assembly, A/1251, Resolution 304 (IV). Related to above are also ibid., Resolution 305 (IV), Resolution 306 (IV), Resolution 307 (IV), and Resolution 308 (IV), par. 4 and 10.

[3] United Nations, Economic and Social Council, E/1327/Add. 1 and Add. 2.

[4] United Nations, Economic and Social Council, E/1327/Add. 1, pp. 52 and 53.

will require broad vision and sustained effort on the part of both the under-developed and the developed countries and on the part of the United Nations and the Specialized Agencies. Patterns of economic development which fit the economic and social structure of the technically more advanced countries cannot be applied without modification to those which have remained under-developed. In every country development must be brought about mainly through the efforts of the local population, with the help of domestic resources, and by means of appropriate changes in economic and social structure.

Noting that the accumulation of capital and the organization of technical skills on the scale necessary for effective economic development are often possible, especially in under-developed countries, only through governmental action, the report states:

These facts impose a heavy responsibility on the governments of countries seeking rapid development. Inevitably the process involves serious social and economic stresses, which reach into every aspect of the nation's life. An unusual measure of social vision, political courage and administrative competence will be needed to keep these stresses within manageable limits, and to make necessary adaptations in the social institutions and practices of the developing countries.

Among the prerequisites for the effectiveness of a technical-assistance programme in stimulating and accelerating sound economic development are mentioned (a) practical approach; (b) favourable environment; (c) personnel; (d) supplies and equipment; and (e) continuity. With reference to (b), favourable environment, it is stated in part:

Any comprehensive programme of economic development will involve far-reaching changes in the social and economic structure of an under-developed country . . .

In some countries existing social institutions may hamper economic modernization. Obsolete and oppressive systems of land tenure, and inadequate credit and marketing facilities may retard agricultural development . . .

Far-reaching changes may also be necessary in the attitudes and habits of the people. Workers for newly developed industries must be drawn largely from the farm population, whose families may have lived on the land for centuries; they must adjust themselves to new surroundings and learn new work habits and disciplines. Individuals possessed of financial resources must be prepared to invest in new productive enterprises, and not merely to hold their wealth in land, precious metals or commodity stocks. Merchants must learn to think in terms of wider markets and narrow profit margins instead of maximum profits on a small volume of sales. Traditional methods of soil cultivation and handicraft must often be modernized. New crops and new breeds of livestock may be introduced. These changes will often impose considerable psychological and social strains but those strains may be greatly eased and their duration shortened if an effort is made to make the economic development programme itself and the changes which are necessary for its success as widely understood as possible among those whose interests are affected.

And, finally, among the points that establish the premises for the proposals by the United States, there is a point clarifying the reference to "questions of a social nature" to which the Economic and Social Council wished due attention to be given:

The reference to "questions of a social nature" in the Economic and Social Council resolution of 4 March 1949 is understood to mean that the programme must take account of: (a) the probable consequences of proposed economic developments in terms of the welfare of the population at large; (b) the social conditions, customs and values in a given area that will directly influence the kinds of economic development that may be feasible and desirable; (c) the specific social improvements that may be necessary in order to permit effective economic developments; (d) the social problems, particularly problems of dislocation of family and community life, that may arise as a concomitant of economic change. It is not understood that existing social programmes of the United Nations shall become part of the technical assistance programme for economic development, but rather that through it there shall be such specific additional activities in the social field as are directly required for the economic development programme, to be carried out in close co-ordination with activities in the economic field.

The United Nations, therefore, definitely envisaged that:

. . . Under-developed countries may need assistance in analysing their population problems and in dealing with population movements; in devising appropriate means for introducing changes that are necessary to improve standards of living and enjoyment of basic human rights; and in strengthening their social welfare services to meet new demands arising from economic development. It is essential that proper measures be taken to ensure that economic changes do not in fact create social distress; that families in areas undergoing industrialization are properly housed and settled and that slums are avoided; that socially pathological conditions, such as delinquency and narcotic addiction, do not undermine the efficiency of the population. International organizations, able to draw upon the experience and cultural backgrounds of all their members, are perhaps especially qualified to supply outside technical assistance in these social fields.[1]

OBJECTIVES OF THE SPECIALIZED AGENCIES

Each of the Specialized Agencies (see Chart, p. 315) in its charter has made a separate declaration of its philosophy, aims, and functions. Their work in the fields of technical assistance is in consonance with their individual basic objectives. They all aim at welfare in the broadest sense, but each agency approaches it from its own specialized angle and narrows down its functions to some important aspect of welfare.

The principles and objectives of each Specialized Agency can be summarized as follows:

ILO (INTERNATIONAL LABOUR ORGANISATION)

Social justice is a prerequisite for peace. The ILO will promote
[1] Ibid., p. 56.

improvement of labour conditions, especially where injustice, hardship and privation to large numbers of people exist, by furthering:

regulation of hours of work, including the establishment of a maximum working day and week;

the regulation of the labour supply;

the prevention of unemployment;

the provision of an adequate living wage;

the protection of the worker against sickness, disease, and injury arising out of employment;

provision for old age and injury;

the protection of children, young persons, and women;

protection of the interests of workers when employed in countries other than their own;

recognition of the principle of freedom of association;

the organization of vocational and technical education and other measures.[1]

FAO (FOOD AND AGRICULTURE ORGANIZATION)

Common welfare will be promoted by the FAO by means of action

toward raising levels of nutrition and standards of living of the peoples . . .

securing improvements in the efficiency of the production and distribution of all food and agricultural products;

bettering the condition of rural populations and thus contributing toward an expanding world economy.[2]

UNESCO (UNITED NATIONS EDUCATIONAL, SCIENTIFIC AND CULTURAL ORGANIZATION)

The nations who established Unesco believe in "full and equal opportunities for education for all," "unrestricted pursuit of objective truth," and "free exchange of ideas and knowledge." Unesco believes that the intellectual and moral solidarity of mankind is essential for lasting peace and that the "education of humanity for justice, liberty, and peace" is the sacred duty which all nations must fulfill. Unesco will further:

mutual knowledge and understanding of peoples;

popular education and the spread of culture;

maintenance, increase and diffusion of knowledge.

(A special clause in Article I, on Purposes and Functions of Unesco, states:

With a view to preserving the independence, integrity and fruitful diversity of the cultures and educational systems of the States Members of this Organization, the Organization is prohibited from intervening in matters which are essentially within their domestic jurisdiction.)[3]

WHO (WORLD HEALTH ORGANIZATION)

"Attainment by all peoples of the highest possible level of health" is the principal objective of WHO, and health is defined as a state

[1] United Nations, ILO, *Constitution* . . .
[2] United Nations, FAO, *Constitution* . . .
[3] United Nations, Unesco, "*Constitution* . . .*"

of "complete physical, mental, and social well-being and not merely the absence of disease or infirmity."

The aims of WHO are not only to further protective measures, such as the elimination of reservoirs of communicable diseases, but also to promote measures toward positive health by means of public-health education in the widest sense.

Among the principles enunciated by Member States of WHO in its charter, the following are directly relevant to the social aspects:

Healthy development of the child is of basic importance; the ability to live harmoniously in a changing total environment is essential to such development.

Governments have a responsibility for the health of their peoples which can be fulfilled only by the provision of adequate health and social measures.[1]

UNICEF (UNITED NATIONS INTERNATIONAL CHILDREN'S EMERGENCY FUND)

By its own definition, Unicef is "an international co-operative on behalf of children" and is designed to make a permanent contribution to child welfare. From concentration on child feeding to meet post-war emergency needs following cessation of Unrra activities in 1946, when Unicef came into being, the organization is increasingly turning toward long-standing problems of maternal and child welfare and works closely with WHO in this field.[2]

ICAO (INTERNATIONAL CIVIL AVIATION ORGANIZATION)

This organization is responsible for drawing up and maintaining the basic code of international practice in all matters pertaining to civil aviation, and among its objectives is to ensure the safe and orderly growth of international civil aviation throughout the world, as another important facet of international co-operation conducive to peace.[3]

BANK (INTERNATIONAL BANK FOR RECONSTRUCTION AND DEVELOPMENT)

The International Bank was established "to assist in the reconstruction and development of territories of Members by facilitating the investment of capital for productive purposes, including the restoration of economies destroyed or disrupted by war, the reconversion of productive facilities to peace-time needs, and the encouragement of the development of productive facilities and resources in less developed countries." The promotion of long-range balanced growth of international trade and the maintenance of financial equilibrium in Member countries "thereby assisting in raising productivity, the standards of living and conditions of labour in their territories" are among the principal purposes of the BANK.[4]

FUND (INTERNATIONAL MONETARY FUND)

Established for the purpose of consultation and co-operation on international monetary problems, FUND, like BANK, hopes to

[1] United Nations, WHO, *"Constitution . . ."*, pp. 29-43.
[2] United Nations, UNICEF, *UNICEF.*
[3] United Nations, ICAO, "International Civil Aviation Conference, Final Act and Related Documents . . ."
[4] United Nations, FUND and BANK, *Articles of Agreement . . .*

facilitate the "expansion and balanced growth of international trade" which, in turn, would contribute to the "maintenance of high levels of employment and real income and to the development of the productive resources" of Member countries.[1]

In addition to the above-listed Specialized Agencies the International Telecommunications Union (ITU) and the Universal Postal Union (UPU) can be invited to advise and co-operate in such phases of technical assistance as call for expert experience in their particular fields. Potentially, such organizations as the International Trade Organization (ITO) and the proposed Inter-governmental Maritime Consultative Organization (IMCO) may also have a role in technical-assistance programmes.

GUIDING PRINCIPLES

The principles to guide the United Nations and the Specialized Agencies in extending technical assistance under the Expanded Programme have been formulated by the Economic and Social Council as follows:[2]

OBSERVATIONS ON AND GUIDING PRINCIPLES OF AN EXPANDED PROGRAMME OF TECHNICAL ASSISTANCE FOR ECONOMIC DEVELOPMENT

The Council recommends the following principles to serve as guides to the United Nations and Specialized Agencies participating in the expanded programme[3] of technical assistance, hereinafter called the "participating organizations":

GENERAL PRINCIPLES

The participating organizations should, in extending technical assistance for economic development of under-developed countries:

1. Regard it as a primary objective to help those countries to strengthen their national economies through the development of their industries and agriculture, with a view to promoting their economic and political independence in the spirit of the Charter of the United Nations, and to ensure the attainment of higher levels of economic and social welfare for their entire populations;

2. Observe the following general principles laid down in General Assembly Resolution 200 (III):

    (a) Technical assistance for economic development of under-

[1] Ibid.

[2] United Nations, Economic and Social Council, E/1553, Resolution 222 A (IX), Annex I.

[3] Although the word "programme" is employed in this connexion, it is not contemplated that all projects described in the "programme" would or should be executed; rather what is contemplated is that the United Nations and the Specialized Agencies should hold themselves ready to render to the under-developed countries, at their request, the types of technical services which are described in the "programme" and which are designed to assist them in their economic development.

developed countries shall be rendered by the participating organizations only in agreement with the governments concerned and on the basis of requests received from them;

(b) The kinds of services to be rendered to each country shall be decided by the government concerned;

(c) The countries desiring assistance should perform, in advance, as much of the work as possible in order to define the nature and scope of the problem involved;

(d) The technical assistance furnished shall:

  (i) Not be a means of foreign economic and political interference in the internal affairs of the country concerned and not be accompanied by any considerations of a political nature;

  (ii) Be given only to or through governments;

  (iii) Be designed to meet the needs of the country concerned; and

  (iv) Be provided as far as possible in the form which that country desires;

3. Avoid distinctions arising from the political structure of the country requesting assistance, or from the race or religion of its population.

STANDARDS OF WORK AND PERSONNEL

1. The highest professional competence should be maintained in all services undertaken by the participating organizations in rendering technical assistance to requesting countries.

2. Experts should be chosen not only for their technical competence, but also for their sympathetic understanding of the cultural backgrounds and specific needs of the countries to be assisted and for their capacity to adapt methods of work to local conditions, social and material.

3. Adequate preparation of experts should be provided before assignments are undertaken; such preparations should be designed to give understanding of the broad objectives of the common effort and to encourage open-mindedness and adaptability.

4. Experts and groups of experts visiting a country should not engage in political, commercial, or any activities other than those for which they are sent. The scope of their duties should be strictly defined in each case by agreement between the country requesting assistance and the organizations providing assistance.

5. Even when allocations are committed, projects should not be commenced unless properly qualified experts and assistants have been secured and trained.

6. All governments should be invited to co-operate in the securing and selecting of qualified staff and to facilitate, when necessary, arrangements for their temporary release and for their continued employment on return.

7. Universities, technical schools, foundations, research institutions and other non-governmental sources from which experts may be drawn should be encouraged to release experts for field assignments under the programme, to arrange for their continued employment on return and to undertake special research projects on problems related to economic development.

PARTICIPATION OF REQUESTING GOVERNMENTS

The requesting governments should be expected to agree:
1. To facilitate the activities requested from the participating organizations by assisting them to obtain the necessary information about the problems on which they have been asked to help, such information to be limited strictly to questions directly related to the concrete requests for technical assistance; and, whenever appropriate, to facilitate their contacts with individuals and groups, in addition to government agencies, concerned with the same or related problems;
2. To give full and prompt consideration to the technical advice they receive as a result of their co-operation with the participating organizations in response to the requests they have initiated;
3. To undertake to maintain or set up as soon as practicable such governmental co-ordination machinery as may be needed to ensure that their own technical, natural and financial resources are mobilized, canalized in the interest of economic development designed to improve the standard of living of their peoples and through which the effective use of major international technical assistance resources could be assured;
4. Normally to assume responsibility for a substantial part of the costs of technical services with which they are provided, at least that part which can be paid in their own currencies;
5. To undertake the sustained efforts for economic development, including continuing support and progressive assumption of financial responsibility for the administration of projects initiated at their request under international auspices;
6. To publish information or provide for study and analysis material suitable for publication regarding the results of the technical assistance rendered and the experience derived therefrom, so that it may be of value to other countries and to the international organizations rendering technical assistance;
7. To inform the participating organizations, whenever technical assistance is requested, of all assistance which they are already receiving or requesting from other sources in the same field of development;
8. To give publicity to the programme within their countries.

CO-ORDINATION OF EFFORT

1. The projects falling within the competence of participating organizations should be carried out by them, and the co-ordination of their work should be effected, with due regard to their constitutions and the relations established between them.
2. The work undertaken by the participating organizations under the expanded technical assistance programme should be such as to be suitable for integration with their normal work.
3. Arrangements should be made for requests for assistance within the sphere of two or more organizations to be handled jointly by the organizations concerned, and there should be co-ordination among the participating organizations at the planning level before commitments by them are entered into with governments.

4. Technical assistance activities which are not at the present time the special responsibility of any Specialized Agency, such as certain aspects of industrial development, manufacturing, mining, power, and land and water transport, should be undertaken by the Secretary-General of the United Nations.

5. All requests for technical assistance which involve comprehensive or regional development projects falling within the purview of more than one organization should first be submitted to joint examination by the organizations concerned; such requests should be directed to the Secretary-General of the United Nations.

6. Programmes of training should be the subject of co-operative action among participating organizations.

CONCENTRATION AND ECONOMY

Within the wide range of activities envisaged, the participating organizations should practise, especially in the initial stages of their programmes, concentration of effort and economy. The participating organizations should also ensure the fullest use of any existing facilities.

SELECTION OF PROJECTS

1. The participating organizations, in deciding on a request for assistance, should be guided solely by the Charter of the United Nations, by the principles of the United Nations programme for technical assistance and by appropriate resolutions of the General Assembly and of the Economic and Social Council. The services envisaged should aim at increased productivity of material and human resources and a wide and equitable distribution of the benefits of such increased productivity, so as to contribute to the realization of higher standards of living for the entire populations. Due attention and respect should be paid to the national sovereignty and national legislation of the under-developed countries and to the social conditions which directly affect their economic development. Requests for technical assistance may therefore be approved which will help governments to take account of the probable consequences of proposed projects for economic development in terms of the welfare of the population as a whole, including the promotion of full employment, and also to take account of those social conditions, customs and values in a given area which would directly influence the kinds of economic development that may be feasible and desirable. Similarly, requests may also be approved for technical assistance to governments desiring to undertake the specific social improvements that are necessary to permit economic development and to mitigate the social problems—particularly problems of dislocation of family and community life—that may arise as a concomitant of economic change. As in any national programme for economic development any increased services undertaken by the government can be maintained, in the long run, only out of national production, special attention should be given in timing and emphasis to activities tending to bring an early increase in national productivity of material and human resources.

2. The participating organizations, when reviewing and placing in order of priority the requests which they receive, should, so far as possible, ensure that due regard is paid to the urgency of the needs of the various applicants and to their geographical distribution.

3. In response to requests from governments, especially in connexion with plans for economic development, special consideration should be given to resources and methods of financing the development. It is recommended therefore that participating organizations, before undertaking work of an extensive character involving substantial cost, should assure themselves that governments requesting such assistance are giving full consideration to major capital investment or large continued governmental expenditure which may be needed as a result of this technical assistance. Governments may also require advice concerning conditions and methods of financing appropriate to such projects. Close co-operation among the participating organizations in responding to requests for technical assistance can facilitate the attainment of this objective.

4. Requests for the furnishing of equipment and supplies may be considered in so far as they form an integral part of a project of technical assistance.

CHART
International Bodies concerned with Technical Assistance

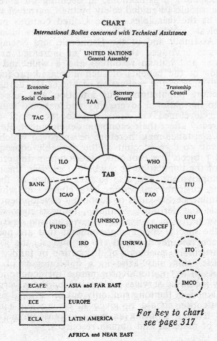

For key to chart see page 317

KEY TO CHART

On this chart the *circled units* are those actually or potentially concerned with the implementation of technical assistance. Basic units are linked by *solid lines*. *Closed-line circles* indicate functioning units; *open-line circles* are potentialities.

ABBREVIATIONS

United Nations Specialized Agencies and International Organizations

BANK: International Bank for Reconstruction and Development
FAO: Food and Agriculture Organization
FUND: International Monetary Fund
ICAO: International Civil Aviation Organization
ILO: International Labour Organisation
IMCO: Intergovernmental Maritime Consultative Organization
IRO: International Refugee Organization
ITO: International Trade Organization
ITU: International Telecommunication Union
UNESCO: United Nations Educational, Scientific and Cultural Organization
UNICEF: United Nations International Children's Emergency Fund
UNRWA: United Nations Relief and Works Agency for Palestine Refugees in the Near East
UPH: Universal Postal Union
WHO: World Health Organization

United Nations Bodies created for the Expanded Programme of Technical Assistance

TAA: Technical Assistance Administration (UN)
TAB: Technical Assistance Board
TAC: Technical Assistance Committee of the Economic and Social Council

Regional Commissions of the Economic and Social Council

ECAFE: Economic Commission for Asia and the Far East
ECE: Economic Commission for Europe
ECLA: Economic Commission for Latin America

EXPLANATORY REMARKS

TAB is the central co-ordinating body for technical assistance to under-developed countries. Its chairman is the Secretary-General or his representative; its permanent members are the UN, (TAA), FAO, ICAO, ILO, UNESCO, and WHO—the six organizations among which UN funds for the expanded programme of technical assistance have been allocated. While ILO, ICAO, FAO, UNESCO, and WHO are bodies responsible to their own conferences, TAA is an integral part of the UN, virtually one of its departments. On the other hand, through TAA the UN in a sense functions like a Specialized Agency, but renders assistance of a type that is outside the competence of any other single Specialized Agency. The BANK and FUND, which have budgets of their own, are participating members of TAB. UNICEF, an independent organization, works closely with WHO in many technical-assistance projects. IRO and UNRWA, both temporary agencies concerned with refugees, are called upon to render services in connexion with some projects. ITU has an observer in the TAB and could be called upon for specialized advice, as could such an old international organization as UPU and incipient ITO and IMCO. The TAB is responsible to TAC, which reviews TAB's regularly reported programme and plans. Neither the Trusteeship Council nor the Regional Commissions of the Economic and Social Council—ECAFE, ECE, and ECLA—are directly concerned with the planning and implementation of technical assistance under the expanded programme, though liaison is maintained with the Regional Commissions.

ORGANIZATION AND DIVISION OF FUNCTIONS

The preceding chart and accompanying notes show the various United Nations bodies concerned with technical assistance, and their interrelationships. The division of functions among them is reflected in the following list of subjects in which technical assistance is or may be rendered. The fields of assistance are divided as follows:[1]

UNITED NATIONS[2]

General Economic Development

Comprehensive development surveys
Combined resource development of an area or region, including the economic and technical as well as the organizational and administrative aspects
Community organization for economic development

Industrial Development

Appraisal of opportunities for the establishment of new industries
Power development:
   Hydraulic and thermal resource appraisal
   Control of water resources in relation to power development and flood-control; planning, construction and operation of installations
   Power-plant construction and operation; transmission and distribution; industrial, urban, and rural
Appraisal of mineral resources, including geological, geophysical and other techniques of location
Extractive industries: mining and milling
Metallurgical techniques and processes
Manufacturing industries: processing and fabricating, efficiency of production and distribution of output
Industrial organization and management

[1] United Nations, Technical Assistance Board, 1951, pp. 7-10.
[2] The Technical Assistance Administration of the United Nations.

Transport

Appraisal of the potentialities of various means of transport in relation to needs and possibilities
Road transport
Railroad transport
Inland water transport
Shipping

Public Finance and Fiscal policies

Fiscal administration and management
Budgeting and financial reporting
Revenue administration and policy
Public-debt management
Fiscal machinery for development projects

Statistics

Statistical operations (collection, compilation and presentation) in relation to economic development, in such fields as census work and trade, production, national income, transport and price statistics

Public administration

Organization and co-ordination of central and local administrative services
Standardization of administrative procedures
Personnel selection and training

Social Welfare and Development

Social-development policies
Research in social fields as an aid in policy formulation (surveys of standards of living, social structure, popular attitudes affecting development, etc.)
Social-welfare services—organization, administration, operation of services, training of staff
Population and migration questions in relation to economic and social development
Housing, community development, town and country planning
Measures for dealing with social problems such as delinquency, drug addiction, status of minorities and aboriginal populations, and the physically handicapped
Community, family and child welfare

INTERNATIONAL LABOUR ORGANISATION

The relation of economic development policies to labour income and employment
Employment, training and migration
Industrial relations, including machinery for the settlement of industrial disputes
Industrial safety
Occupational health
Enforcement of labour legislation including labour inspection
Employment problems of women and young workers

Development of labour statistics
Social security
Wages policy; systems of wages payment; machinery for the
   determination of minimum rates
Co-operation and handicrafts
Employment, wages and conditions of work in agriculture
Maritime labour problems
Labour problems in specific industries
Labour and social problems of indigenous populations

FOOD AND AGRICULTURE ORGANIZATION OF THE UNITED NATIONS

Agriculture (including irrigation, soil management, farm machinery, crop production, insect-control, animal breeding and
   diseases, agricultural-research institutes)
Forestry and forest products (including conservation, marketing
   and industrial utilization of timber)
Fisheries
Nutrition (in collaboration with World Health Organization)
Rural institutions and services (including extension services, rural
   industries and amenities, co-operatives)
Economic and statistical services (including credit, insurance and
   marketing in agriculture, forestry and fisheries)

UNITED NATIONS EDUCATIONAL, SCIENTIFIC AND CULTURAL ORGANIZATION

Technical education
Elementary education
Fundamental and adult education
Materials for education and mass communications
Technical needs for press, film and radio
Training of teachers
Scientific research and training
Survey of natural resources (in collaboration with United Nations
   and Specialized Agencies concerned)
Protection of local cultures

INTERNATIONAL CIVIL AVIATION ORGANIZATION

Organization of national civil-aviation departments
Economic and technical surveys to ascertain civil-aviation requirements
Design, construction and installations of air-navigation facilities
   and airports
Organization of air-traffic control, aeronautical communications
   and radio aids to navigation, flight operations, aeronautical
   meteorology and other ancillary services required by civil aviation
Air-transport organization and administration
Training in all branches of civil aviation

WORLD HEALTH ORGANIZATION

Malaria
Venereal diseases
Tuberculosis
Other communicable diseases (plague, cholera, typhus, schisto-
  somiasis, yellow fever, trachoma, leprosy, etc.)
Professional and technical training and education
Assistance to educational institutions
Fellowships and exchange of scientific information
Public-health administration
Environmental sanitation
Nursing
Maternal and child health
Social and occupational health
Health education of the public
Nutrition
Mental health
Health statistics
Antibiotic and insecticide production

INTERNATIONAL BANK FOR RECONSTRUCTION AND DEVELOPMENT

Preparation of long-term development programmes, including investment priorities and economic, fiscal and administrative
  measures necessary for achievement of programme goals
Financial and economic policies related to development
Means for mobilizing local capital and channelling it into productive investment
Advice on other important development problems

INTERNATIONAL MONETARY FUND

Monetary and banking problems
Balance-of-payments problems
Exchange policies and practices, including exchange rates, re-
  strictions, special arrangements, etc.
Fiscal and public finance matters related to the above
Financial and monetary statistics
Legislative, administrative and economic aspects of the foregoing

In certain fields, work is undertaken co-operatively by more
than one organization. So, for instance, assistance toward raising the levels of food production in malarial areas simultaneously involves the raising of health standards and is undertaken jointly by FAO and WHO. Similarly, FAO and WHO
co-operate in certain projects involving nutrition, a field in
which Unicef is concerned especially with reference to child
health. An advisory mission requested by a national government to survey needs and assist in the formation of an
economic development programme may be composed of representatives of the United Nations and of one or more of the

Specialized Agencies. Expert advice by FAO in the field of agriculture may involve agricultural-labour problems falling within the competence of ILO , while the latter's recommendations in the field of technical training might be supported by the work of Unesco. The United Nations and the Specialized Agencies also consult with a number of non-governmental international and national organizations,[1] and co-operate with such regional organizations as, for instance, the Institute of Inter-American Affairs.

With special reference to the social aspects of economic development, the list above shows that assistance in the social fields falls most directly within the competence of the United Nations. However, such subjects as "labour and social problems of indigenous populations" (ILO), "rural institutions and services" (FAO), "protection of local cultures" (Unesco), and "mental health" (WHO), all indicate that the Specialized Agencies also have each developed an approach of their own to social and cultural questions.

FORMS OF TECHNICAL ASSISTANCE

Technical assistance can take several different forms. Individual "experts" or a group of experts, joint "missions" and expert "teams" provide advice and practical assistance. An individual expert may be called upon to survey conditions in a special field such as irrigation and to assist the requesting government in assessing the needs, to plan measures toward their alleviation, and the best possible methods for realizing the necessary steps. A group of experts may be concerned with one wider aspect of a country's economy, such as the whole field of agriculture or fundamental education or finance; while a joint mission composed of different experts, after a comprehensive survey, may assist in formulating a long-range economic-development plan and make recommendations for its phases of implementation. The actual performance of technical services, apart from advice and planning, can be executed by individuals as well as teams. An individual expert may have to help organize a central statistical service or establish a laboratory or give a training course for social workers or for nurses. An expert team, often incorporating local personnel, may engage in field demonstration work, as in maternal and child health, or malaria-control, or control of animal diseases. In many of these activities the experts must co-operate not only with officials of the national government or of local administrations, but also with local professional organizations and individuals and, when operating in the field, must secure the co-operation of the local people.

[1] United Nations, Economic and Social Council, E/C. 2/INF/1.

Assistance in training, to help under-developed countries in building up a domestic corps of technical and specialized personnel, takes the form of fellowships and scholarships made available by the United Nations and the Specialized Agencies to government-approved candidates from these countries, as well as local seminars and training courses given within a country. Training institutes and seminars are also being established on a regional basis, such as, for example, the Latin American Training Center for Agricultural Statistics in Costa Rica, or the Training Institute on Economic Appraisal for Development Projects at Lahore, Pakistan, which was attended by members from various countries of South Asia.

Demonstration projects, intended to serve as models to show how advanced techniques can be beneficially adapted and applied to the special needs and circumstances of under-developed countries, simultaneously serve as aids in technical training and offer local personnel opportunities for practical experience. These demonstration projects are also vehicles for spreading knowledge among the population about the nature and application of new technological methods.

Development and dissemination of technical information is furthered by practically all United Nations organizations concerned with technical assistance by means of publication and sometimes by reference services. They also further scientific research in their special fields and in the organization of conferences on technical subjects.

Experimental "pilot plants" to ascertain the type of equipment and processes most suitable for local needs and conditions, available raw materials and other resources, have been envisaged as one of the means of furthering industrial development in under-developed countries.

Technical equipment and supplies needed for carrying out technical-assistance projects are furnished by the organizations rendering technical assistance at their expense but only as an integral part of the project.[1] In problems of major capital investments, or large continuing governmental expenditures which may be needed for the continuance and further development of projects that could be initiated by technical-assistance experts, advice concerning methods and conditions of financing such projects can be obtained from organizations like BANK and FUND.

PLANNING AND CO-ORDINATION

The co-ordination of technical assistance for any one country requires at least three planning centres; each of these, condi-

---

[1] Such equipment remains the property of the organization that renders technical assistance unless or until it is handed to the government on the completion of the project.

tioned by its own resources and outlook, must interact harmoniously with the others in evolving a project whose nature, scope and timing can ensure maximum effectiveness and permanence of benefit to a country's economy. In the previously cited report of the Secretary-General, it is stated:[1]

The general objective of co-ordination would be to ensure that the programmes of the several international organizations will effectively reinforce and supplement the economic development activities of the government concerned, that overlapping is avoided, that gaps are filled and that co-operative action is taken when needed. Effective co-ordination in carrying out expanded programmes of technical assistance will require the establishment and strengthening of working relationships between (i) recipient government and the international organizations, (ii) between these organizations themselves, and (iii) between the "multilateral" programmes of these organizations and the "bilateral" technical assistance activities of individual governments.

The first planning centre is at the source of the request for assistance—the national government. There the effectiveness in planning the measures to raise the people's standard of living through economic development depends on the general internal policies, on the degree of competence in and co-operation among its various departments or ministries, and the government's resources. In some countries, special bodies have been set up to deal with all aspects of technical assistance. In certain countries, advice on the formulation of plans for comprehensive development is the first subject of requests for technical assistance. In such a case, a mission composed of different experts makes an exploratory survey and, in consultation with the government, works out recommendations. If, however, the government has already developed effective planning mechanisms through which it has gained thorough insight into the developmental problems of its country, the task of a survey mission is to review, in consultation with local authorities, the specific fields in which the immediate assistance of experts may be desired. In some cases, the national government welcomes the appointment of a "resident representative" to represent several Specialized Agencies jointly. It is among the duties of such a representative to "advise and assist governments in formulating requests to the organizations, in light of the latter's resources, and, on the other hand, to assist experts sent in by the organizations to work effectively and in a co-ordinated manner."[2]

When a government has requested and is receiving technical assistance not only from the United Nations and its Specialized Agencies, but from other sources also—such as under

[1] United Nations, Economic and Social Council, E/1327/Add. 1 and Add. 2.
[2] United Nations, Technical Assistance Board, op. cit. p. 12.

the United States technical co-operation programme, from a regional organization, or a programme furthered by a private foundation—the problems of correlation become more complex. Much depends on the degree of liaison and agreement between the organizations involved, the degree of co-operation which develops between the representatives of the respective organizations in the field, and the role which the national government can play in stressing its own integrated approach. The impact and effectiveness of any one operational technical-assistance project in local communities, where pressure for action or stimulation toward new attitudes may be coming from different sources without a unifying focus, depends heavily upon the co-ordination facilities of the national government. The responsibility of the national government with regard to national planning is also heavy; if it cannot ensure the continuation of services or the practice of new methods initially introduced by the technical experts or teams of experts, and if certain innovations, once satisfactorily demonstrated, remain unfeasible or inaccessible thereafter because of lack of funds, services, or official channelling of materials, tools and other equipment, the "felt needs" have been intensified, and so has frustration.

Each Specialized Agency has its own programme-planning procedures (which is some cases are under constant revision) within the limitations of its budget, and must consider each request for technical assistance in relation to other requests, availability of resources and personnel, and a variety of other factors. In considering a project for a given country, the agency is concerned with the relation of that project to the wider field of its specialization as developed in that country. For example, the entire field of public health and the manner of the administration of a programme must be considered by WHO when a specific project, such as one concerned with maternal and child health, or one for the prevention of venereal diseases, is involved. Likewise, any FAO project aimed at the intensification or diversification of crops may immediately pose questions about the adequacy of storage and marketing facilities, of farm credits, or developing resettlement schemes, etc. The interdependence of these and similar elements, and the fact that many of them directly or indirectly may require extensive financing—which may not be immediately feasible— renders the problems of co-ordination, integration, and articulation very complex.

Finally, the central international technical-assistance unit, TAB, where programmes are reviewed and major projects are approved, stresses co-ordination between the different Specialized Agencies and liaison with other organizations, whether regional or governmental, that are concerned with technical assistance.[1]

To conclude, each technical-assistance project that comes to fruition will have been considered in at least three centres by various criteria, all of which will have been evolved in the light of the total needs and resources as these are viewed from within each of the centres. The combined application of these criteria must yield proper selection, timing, and effective interaction of projects for any one given country.

Most of the programmes are still relatively new. Many of the organizations, much of their personnel, and some of the governments involved are just beginning to acquire experience in this co-operative venture. As the programmes develop further, methods and approaches may be modified, procedures refined, criteria sharpened, and some of the very difficult problems may gradually approach solution.

APPENDIX B

ORIGINAL PLAN PRESENTED TO UNESCO BY THE WORLD FEDERATION FOR MENTAL HEALTH

MEMORANDUM

To: Social Sciences Department, Unesco.
From: World Federation for Mental Health.
Subject: Technological Change and Mental Health.
Problem: To explore the mental-health implications of the changes in living-habits resulting from technological development.

Background of Problem. In the past the introduction of new techniques and practices into the life of so-called under-developed peoples has usually been undertaken without adequate consideration of the effects of such changes on mental health and social adjustment. The changes planned will undoubtedly affect many areas of activity—sanitation, nutrition, wages and conditions of labour, agricultural techniques, pediatrics, ob-

[1] Among such regional and governmental organizations are: the Organization of American States (Co-ordinating Committee on Technical Assistance); the Council for Technical Co-operation in South and South-East Asia; the Commission for Technical Assistance South of the Sahara; the South Pacific Commission; the Caribbean Commission. (Ibid., p. 17.)

The Board also receives information on bi-lateral technical assistance projects.

stetrics, preventive medicine, etc. Such changes are bound to alter the "way of life" of the group, the relations between parents and children, the hierarchy of authority, the acquisition of status and prestige, etc. These are precisely aspects of existence which are important for personality development and which give to individuals their feelings of happiness or unhappiness, security or insecurity, respectively. No programme of technological development can hope to succeed in the long run if it leaves people unhappy and maladjusted. In the long run also, such unhappy and maladjusted people are the ones who are more likely to turn to violence and even war, because of their dissatisfaction with the conditions under which they live. This is not a necessary consequence of technological development, but it is a possible one. It can be rendered much less probable if adequate attention is paid to the effect of technological development on people. The most important single fact to be kept in mind is that new techniques must be introduced with proper regard for the existing culture and with as little violence as possible to the folkways of the groups concerned.

For example, if a people have been accustomed to pre-chew food and feed it as supplementary during breast feeding, two quite different courses are open in public-health education. The public-health innovator who has neither interest nor respect for native custom may insist that the "disgraceful and dangerous" habit be given up and the infants fed only from the breast, without recognizing that the maternal nutritional status may be inadequate, and severe infant malnutrition may result. Alternatively, after an investigation of the whole pattern of infant feeding, the innovator may recommend mashing up food and continued supplementary feeding, in which a minimum of change is introduced into the maternal habits.

A society may depend upon a new mother being trained by her mother, after a child is born, in the care of the child; hospitalization for deliveries may separate the new mother and the grandmother, and while increasing the chances of survival of the infant at birth, so impair the mother's care of her child, as to decrease or compromise its survival chances. It should be possible to introduce hospitalization while continuing to utilize at least some of the techniques upon which the society has depended in the past.

There are many examples of both successful and unsuccessful introductions of changes in these and other respects. A collection of such examples should serve a useful purpose as a guide to those who will be responsible for future innovations in the life of so-called under-developed peoples.

The Project. It is proposed, therefore, to prepare a manual or guide, utilizing existing source material which is at present scattered and relatively inaccessible, in order to aid those who will introduce and carry out the processes of technological change. This manual would contain sample techniques to be followed, as well as indications of methods which could be used in different countries to obtain the necessary information about food-habits, hygiene, agriculture, family organization, methods of sharing of household expenses, which would be needed in order to facilitate and expedite the process of change, while at the same time protecting and advancing mental health.

Technique. The World Federation for Mental Health will undertake to place this problem in the hands of a committee of experts, representing not only the field of psychiatry but related disciplines as well, who would supervise the preparation of such a manual. The actual work of writing the manual would be done by an expert who combines a knowledge of anthropology with familiarity with the principles and problems of psychiatry and mental hygiene. The manual will give special attention to the mental-health aspects of technological change, especially as these affect attitudes in the field of international relations. Care will be taken to co-ordinate this activity with similar activities on the part of the United Nations and the Specialized Agencies.

APPENDIX C

SELECTED BIBLIOGRAPHY ON CULTURE CHANGE

ALLAN, William. 1949. *Studies in African Land Usage in Northern Rhodesia.* Published for the Rhodes-Livingstone Institute. Capetown, New York, Oxford University Press.

ALLAN, William and others. 1948. *Land Holding and Land Usage among the Plateau Tonga of Mazabuka District: A Reconnaissance Survey, 1945.* The Rhodes-Livingstone Papers, No. 14. Capetown, London, New York, Oxford University Press.

ALLEN, Harold B. 1943. *Come Over into Macedonia.* New Brunswick, Rutgers University Press.

BECKETT, W. H. 1944. *Akokoaso.* Monographs on Social Anthropology, No. 10. Published for the London School of Economics and Political Science. London, Percy Lund, Humphries.

BRUNNER, Edmund de S. and others, editors. 1945. *Farmers of the World.* New York, Columbia University Press.

BUSIA, K. A. 1950. *Sociology: Report on a Social Survey of Secondi-Takoradi* (Gold Coast). Published by Colonial Office, Great Britain, Crown Printing.

COLSON, Elizabeth and GLUCKMAN, Max, editors. Forthcoming. *Seven Tribes of British Central Africa.* Published for the Rhodes-Livingstone Institute. London, Oxford University Press.

DAI, Bingham. 1944. "Divided Loyalty in War." *Psychiatry,* vol. 7, no. 4, pp. 327-40.

ELKIN, A. P. 1951. "Reaction and Interaction: A Food Gathering People and European Settlement in Australia." *American Anthropologist,* vol. 53, no. 2, pp. 164-86.

EMBREE, John F. 1946. "Military Government in Saipan and Tinian. A Report on the organization of Susupe and Churo, together with notes on the attitudes of the people involved." *Applied Anthropology,* vol. 5, no. 1, pp. 1-39.

FORDE, C. Daryll and SCOTT, Richenda. 1946. *The Native Economies of Nigeria.* London, Faber.

FORTES, Meyer. 1936. "Culture Contact as a Dynamic Process." *Africa,* vol. 9, no. 1, pp. 24-55.

———. 1948. "The Ashanti Social Survey: A Preliminary Report." *Rhodes-Livingstone Journal,* no. 6, pp. 1-36.

FORTES, Meyer. 1949. "Time and Social Structure." *Social Structure.* Studies presented to A. R. Radcliffe-Brown, edited by Meyer Fortes. Oxford, Clarendon Press, pp. 54-84.

FORTES, Meyer, STEEL, R. W. and ADY, P. 1947. "Ashanti Survey, 1945-46: An Experiment in Social Research." *Geographical Journal,* vol. 110, nos. 4-6, pp. 149-79.

FRANKEL, Sally Herbert. 1938. *Capital Investment in Africa.* London, New York, Oxford University Press.

Fundamental Education. Report of a Special Committee to the Preparatory Commission of Unesco, 1947. New York, MacMillan.

GEDDES, W. R. 1945. "Acceleration of Social Change in a Fijian Community." *Oceania,* vol. 16, no. 1, pp. 1-14.

GLUCKMAN, Max. 1943. *Essays on Lozi Land and Royal Property.* Livingstone, Rhodes-Livingstone Institute.

HANCOCK, William Keith. 1942. *Survey of British Commonwealth Affairs,* vol. 2: Problems of Economic Policy 1918-1939, Part 2. London, Oxford University Press. (See Chapter II: "Evolution of the Traders' Frontier, West Africa.")

HATCH, Spencer. 1950. *Toward Freedom from Want.* London, Oxford University Press.

HAYDEN, Lyle J. 1949. "Living Standards in Rural Iran." *Middle East Journal,* vol. 3, no. 2, pp. 140-50.

HELLMANN, Ellen. 1948. *Rooiyard.* The Rhodes-Livingstone Papers, No. 13. Cape Town, Oxford University Press.

———, editor. 1949. *Handbook on Race Relations in South Africa.* Published for South African Institute of Race Relations. Cape Town, Oxford University Press.

HOGBIN, Herbert Ian. 1939. *Experiments in Civilization: The effects of European culture on a native community of the Solomon Islands.* London, G. Routledge.

HYDRICK, John Lee. 1937. *Intensive Rural Hygiene Work and Public Health Education of the Public Service of the Netherlands, India.* Java, Netherlands India, Batavia-Centrum.

INSTITUTE OF PACIFIC RELATIONS. 1938. *Agrarian China: Selected Source Materials from Chinese Authors.* Chicago, University of Chicago Press.

INTERNATIONAL INSTITUTE OF AFRICAN LANGUAGES AND CULTURES. 1938. "Methods of Study of Culture Contact in Africa." *International Institute of African Languages and Cultures Memorandum 15.* London, Oxford University Press. Reprinted from *Africa,* vol. 7 (1934), vol. 8 (1935), and vol. 9 (1936).

JOSEPH, Alice. 1942. "Physician and Patient." *Applied Anthropology,* vol. 1, no. 4, pp. 1-6.

KEESING, Felix M. 1939. *The Menomini Indians of Wisconsin: A Study of*

Three Centuries of Cultural Contact and Change. Philadelphia, The American Philosophical Association.

KEESING, Felix M. 1941. *The South Seas in the Modern World*. Institute of Pacific Relations. New York, John Day.

KUPER, Hilda. 1947a. *An African Aristocracy*. Published for International African Institute. London, Oxford University Press.

——. 1947b. *The Uniform of Colour*. Johannesburg, Witwatersrand University Press.

LAMBERT, S. M. 1941. *A Yankee Doctor in Paradise*. Boston, Little, Brown.

LEIGHTON, Alexander H. and LEIGHTON, Dorothea C. 1944. *The Navaho Door*. Cambridge, Harvard University Press.

LEWIS, Oscar. 1951. *Life in a Mexican Village: Tepoztlán Restudied*. Urbana, Illinois, University of Illinois Press.

LINTON, Ralph, editor. 1940. *Acculturation in Seven American Indian Tribes*. New York, D. Appleton-Century.

LITTLE, K. L. 1947. "Mende Political Institutions in Transition." *Africa*, vol. 17, no. 1, pp. 8-23.

——. 1948. "Social Change and Social Class in the Sierra Leone Protectorate." *American Journal of Sociology*, vol. 54, no. 1, pp. 10-21.

LOMMEL, Andreas. 1950. "Modern Culture Influences on the Aborigines." *Oceania*, vol. 21, no. 1, pp. 14-24.

LOOMIS, Charles P. 1950. *Studies in Applied and Theoretical Social Science*. East Lansing, Michigan State College Press.

MACMILLAN, William Miller. 1929. *Bantu, Boer, and Briton*. London, Faber & Gwyer.

——. 1930. *Complex South Africa*. London, Faber & Faber.

MEAD, Margaret. 1932. *The Changing Culture of an Indian Tribe*. New York, Columbia University Press.

OLIVER, Douglas L. 1951. *The Pacific Islands*. Cambridge, Harvard University Press.

PEDLER, F. 1948. "A Study of Income and Expenditure in Northern Zaria." *Africa*, vol. 18, no. 4, pp. 259-71.

READ, Margaret. 1938. "Native Standards of Living and African Culture Change." *International Institute of African Languages and Cultures Memorandum*, no. 16. London, Oxford University Press. Supplement to *Africa*, vol. 11, no. 3.

REDFIELD, Robert. 1950. *A Village That Chose Progress*. Chicago, University of Chicago Press.

REED, Stephen W. 1943. *The Making of Modern New Guinea*. Memoirs of the American Philosophical Society, vol. 18. Philadelphia.

Report of the Committee on Food Habits, 1941-1943. 1943. "The Problem of Changing Food Habits." *Bulletin of the National Research Council*, no. 108. Washington, D. C.

Report of the Committee on Food Habits. 1945. "Manual for the Study of Food Habits." *Bulletin of the National Research Council*, no. 111. Washington, D. C.

RICHARDS, Audrey Isabel. 1939. *Land, Labour and Diet in Northern Rhodesia*. International Institute of African Languages and Cultures. London, Oxford University Press.

——. 1940. *Bemba Marriage and Present Economic Conditions*. The Rhodes-Livingstone Papers, no. 4. Livingstone, Rhodes-Livingstone Institute.

RICHARDSON JR., F. L. W. Special Issue editor. 1943. "Five Case Studies of Successful Experiments in Increasing Food Production." *Applied Anthropology*, vol. 2, no. 3, entire number.

RUESCH, Jurgen and BATESON, Gregory. 1951. *Communication, the Social Matrix of Psychiatry*. New York, Norton.

SCHAPERA, Isaac. 1943. *Native Land Tenure in the Bechuanaland Protectorate*. Lovedale (S. Africa), Lovedale Press.

SCHWEITZER, Albert. 1931. *The Forest Hospital at Lambaréné*. Translated by C. T. Campion. New York, Henry Holt.

SIMEY, Thomas Spensley. 1946. *Welfare and Planning in the British West Indies.* Oxford, The Clarendon Press.

TANNOUS, Afif I. 1944. "Extension Work among the Arab Fellahin." *Applied Anthropology,* vol. 3, no. 3, pp. 1-12.

THOMPSON, Laura. 1950 a. *Culture in Crisis.* New York, Harper.

——. 1950 b and 1951. "Personality and Government." *America Indígena,* vol. 10, no. 1, pp. 7-45, no. 2, pp. 135-79, no. 3, pp. 233-63, no. 4, pp. 335-63; vol. 11, no. 1, pp. 69-82, no. 2, pp. 147-81.

THURNWALD, Richard C. 1935. *Black and White in East Africa.* London, Routledge.

USEEM, John. 1945. "Governing the Occupied Areas of the South Pacific: Wartime Lessons and Peacetime Proposals." *Applied Anthropology,* vol. 4, no. 3, pp. 1-10.

HORST VAN DER, Sheila T. 1942. *Native Labour in South Africa.* London, Oxford University Press.

WILSON, Godfrey and WILSON, Monica Hunter. 1945. *The Analysis of Social Changes.* Cambridge, Cambridge University Press.

WILSON, Monica Hunter. 1936. *Reaction to Conquest.* Published for International Institute of African Languages and Cultures. London, Oxford University Press.

YANG, Hsin-Pao. 1949. "Planning and Implementing Rural Welfare Programs." *Human Organization,* vol. 8, no. 3, pp. 17-21.

YANG, Martin. 1945. *Chinese Village.* New York, Columbia University Press.

EDITORIAL STAFF

Lawrence K. Frank
Eliot D. Chapple
Claire Holt
Dorothy Demetracopoulou Lee
Margaret Mead
George Saslow
John Useem

ADVISORY COMMITTEE

Chairman:
Lawrence K. Frank (IPAC)[1]
Former Director, Caroline Zachry
Institute for Human Development

John Adair, Ph.D.	Assistant Professor of Anthropology Department of Sociology and Anthropology Cornell University Ithaca, New York
Leona Baumgartner, M.D.	Assistant Commissioner in charge of Maternal and Child Welfare New York City Department of Health 125 Worth Street New York, New York
Carl Binger, M.D.	Director, Mary Conover Mellon Foundation for the Advancement of Education Vassar College Poughkeepsie, New York 125 East 73rd Street New York, New York

[1] IPAC: American Regional Interprofessional Advisory Committee, World Federation for Mental Health.

Eliot Chapple, Ph.D.   President, the E. D. Chapple Company
                              61 West 55th Street
                              New York 19, New York

Bingham Dai, Ph.D.   Professor of Mental Hygiene and
(IPAC)   Psychotherapy
                              Medical School, Duke University
                              Durham, North Carolina

Frank Fremont-Smith,   Medical Director, Josiah Macy Jr.
M.D. (IPAC)   Foundation
                              565 Park Avenue
                              New York, New York

Elizabeth Hoyt, Ph.D.   Professor of Economics
                              Iowa State College
                              Ames, Iowa (on leave of absence at
                                  present at the Institute of Social
                                  Research, Makerere College, Kam-
                                  pala, Uganda)

Otto Klineberg, M.D.,   Professor of Psychology
Ph.D. (IPAC)   Columbia University
                              New York 27, New York

Mary Fisher Langmuir,   Professor of Child Study
Ph.D.   Vassar College
                              Poughkeepsie, New York
                              also Director of Vassar Summer
                                  Institute
                              also President, Child Study Associa-
                                  tion of America

Margaret Mead, Ph.D.   Associate Curator of Ethnology
(IPAC)   American Museum of Natural History
                              New York 24, New York

William Menninger, M.D.   General Secretary, Menninger
                                  Foundation
                              Topeka, Kansas

Michel Pijoan, M.D.   Chief of Medical Service
                              Navaho Medical Center
                              Fort Defiance, Arizona

Nina Ridenour, Ph.D.   Director, Division of Education
(IPAC)   National Association of Mental Health
                              1790 Broadway
                              New York, New York

Nathan Sinai, M.D.   Professor of Public Health
                              University of Michigan
                              Ann Arbor, Michigan

Edward Spicer, Ph.D.   Professor of Anthropology and
                                Sociology
                            University of Arizona
                            Tucson, Arizona

George S. Stevenson, M.D.   Medical Director
(IPAC)   National Association for Mental
                            Health
                            1790 Broadway
                            New York, New York

John Useem, Ph.D.   Associate Professor
                            Department of Sociology and
                            Anthropology
                            Michigan State College
                            East Lansing, Michigan

Note. Biographical and bibliographical details are as of June, 1951.

BIBLIOGRAPHY[1]

AARONOVITCH, S. and K. 1947. *Crisis in Kenya.* London, Lawrence and Wishart.

ABBOTT, G. F. 1903. *Macedonian Folklore.* Cambridge, Cambridge University Press.

ABRAHAM, Roy Clive. 1940. *The Tiv People.* Second edition, London, published on behalf of the Government of Nigeria by the Crown Agents for the Colonies.

AGARWAL, Shriman Narayan. 1949. "Ghandian Economics." *Indian Review,* vol. 50, no. 4, pp. 182-86.

ALLEN, Harold B. 1943. *Come Over into Macedonia.* New Brunswick, Rutgers University Press.

ANDRUS, J. R. 1947. *Burmese Economic Life.* Stanford, Stanford University Press.

ARENSBERG, Conrad. In preparation. Intercultural Transfer of Techniques, Manual of Applied Social Science for Point IV Technicians Overseas. Prepared by the American Anthropological Association for the Foreign Service Institute and the Technical Co-operation Administration of the United States Department of State.

AZIZ, M. 1947. "A Brief Account of the Anopheles (Malaria) Eradication in Karpas . . . Cyprus, 1946." *Journal of the Royal Sanitary Institute,* vol. 67, no. 5, pp. 498-509.

BAEHR, H. A. 1950. "Wheat Processing and Uses in the Far East." *Foreign Agriculture,* vol. 14, no. 9, pp. 204-8.

BAIRON, Max A. 1942. "La Educación del Indio en Bolivia." *America Indígena,* vol. 2, no. 3, pp. 7-10.

BARNETT, S. A. 1948. "Principles of Rodent Control." In *Preservation of Grains in Storage,* edited by Stephen S. Easter. "*FAO Agricultural Studies,*" no. 2. Washington, D. C., Food and Agriculture Organization of the United Nations, pp. 129-48.

BARTON, R. F. 1922. "Ifugao Economics." *University of California Publications in American Archaeology and Ethnology,* vol. 15, no. 5, pp. 385-446.
————. 1946. "The Religion of the Ifugaos." *American Anthropological Association Memoirs,* no. 65.

BEALE, Wilbert. 1935. "Turkey's Ten-Year Health Plan." *Asiatic Review,* vol. 44, no. 157, pp. 88-90.

BELL, E. J. 1950. "Far Eastern Food Preferences." *Foreign Agriculture,* vol. 14, no. 7, pp. 161-63.

BELSHAW, Horace. 1950. "Industry and Agrarian Reform." Reprinted in

[1] This master bibliography contains full references to all works cited in the footnotes throughout the volume.

New Forces in Asia, edited by Bruno Lasker. New York, Wilson, pp. 45-52.

BENEDICT, Ruth. 1943. "Recognition of Cultural Diversities in the Postwar World." *The Annals of the American Academy of Political and Social Science,* vol. 228, pp. 101-7.

———. 1949. "Child Rearing in Certain European Countries." *American Journal of Orthopsychiatry,* vol. 19, no. 2, pp. 342-50.

BENNETT, Hugh Hammond. 1939. *Soil Conservation.* New York, McGraw-Hill.

———. 1945 a. "Answering an SOS from South Africa." *Land Policy Review,* vol. 8, no. 2, pp. 27-30.

———. 1945 b. *Soil Erosion and Land Use in South Africa.* Pretoria, Department of Agriculture and Forestry.

BHEEMACHARYA, T. 1949. "Cottage Industries in India." *Indian Review,* vol. 50, no. 1, pp. 12-15.

BOWLBY, J. 1951. "Maternal Care and Mental Health." *"World Health Organization Monograph Series,"* no. 2. Geneva.

BRANT, Charles. Memorandum on Burma. (MS.)

BRINK, Wellington. 1951. *Big Hugh, Father of Conservation.* New York, Macmillan.

BRUNNER, Edmund de S. and others, editors. 1945. *Farmers of the World.* New York, Columbia University Press.

BUCK, Pearl S. 1945. "Mass Education in China." *American Council, Institute of Pacific Relations Pamphlets,* no. 16. New York.

"Burma Facts and Figures." 1946. *Burma Pamphlets,* no. 9. Calcutta, Orient-Longmans.

Burma Handbook. 1943. Simla, Government of Burma.

Burma Handbook. 1944. Simla, Government of Burma.

Burma Village Manual. n.d. Revised edition. Government of Burma.

BURTON, Margaret E. 1918. *Women Workers of the Orient.* West Medford, Mass., The Central Committee on the United Study of Foreign Missions.

BUXTON, P. A. 1949. "Presidential Address on Control of Tsetse Flies by Human Settlement." *Journal of the Royal Sanitary Institute,* vol. 69, no. 5, pp. 615-16.

CARMEN, John S. 1936. *Rats, Plague and Religion.* Philadelphia, Judson Press.

"Case Studies in Applied Anthropology." n.d. Comments by Herrell de Graff. Cornell University. (Mimeographed report, SA 690, Ah 50:30).

CASTRO POZO, Hildebrando. 1942. "El 'Ayllo' peruano debe transformarse en cooperativa agropecuaria." *America Indígena,* vol. 2, no. 12, pp. 11-16.

CHANG YU-SUI. 1938. "The General Economic Decline in Fuan in Northern Fukien." Reprinted in *Agrarian China,* edited by Institute of Pacific Relations. Chicago, University of Chicago Press, pp. 251-55.

CHATTERJEE, Anathanath and DAS, Tarakchandra. 1927. *The Hos of Seraikella,* Part I. Calcutta, University of Calcutta.

CHARITAKI, Koste. 1948. *To Vivlio tes Meteras (The Book of the Mother).* Athens, Petrou Demetracou.

CHEN HAN-SENG. 1947. "Gung Ho: The Story of the Chinese Co-operatives." *American Institute of Pacific Relations Pamphlets,* no. 24. New York, Institute of Pacific Relations.

CHI PING. 1938. "The Effects of Commercialization of Agriculture in Southern Hopei." Reprinted in *Agrarian China,* edited by Institute of Pacific Relations. Chicago, University of Chicago Press, pp. 160-67.

CHRISTIAN, John Leroy. 1942. *Modern Burma.* Berkeley, University of California Press.

COLLIER, Jr., John and BUÍTRON, Aníbal. 1949. *The Awakening Valley.* Chicago, University of Chicago Press.

COMAS, Juan. 1942. "El Regimen alimenticio y el mejoramiento Indígena." *America Indígena,* vol. 2, no. 2, pp. 51-56.

"Contrast in Method." 1950 (Summer). Report of the American Farm School. Thessalonica, Greece. (MS.)

Coon, Carleton S., editor. 1948. *A Reader in General Anthropology.* New York, Henry Holt.

"Co-operative Stores in Ceylon." 1944. Article by a "Ceylonese." *Indian Review,* vol. 45, no. 10, p. 493.

Corbyn, E. N. 1945. "Soil Conservation in the Anglo-Egyptian Sudan." *Foreign Agriculture,* vol. 9, no. 12, pp. 188-89.

Cutler, J. C. 1950. "Venereal Diseases in Afghanistan." *Bulletin of the World Health Organization,* vol. 2, no. 4, pp. 687-703.

Das, Moses. 1947. "Rural Uplift through Industrialization." *Indian Review,* vol. 48, no. 6, pp. 298-300.

Dennis, Wayne. 1940 a. "Does Culture Appreciably Affect Patterns of Infant Behavior?" *Journal of Social Psychology,* vol. 12, 2nd half, pp. 305-17.

——. 1940 b. *The Hopi Child.* New York, Appleton-Century.

Dolivet, Louis. 1946. *The United Nations.* New York, Farrar Straus.

Downes, Roger Meaden. 1933. *The Tiv Tribe.* Kaduna, printed by the Government Printer.

East, Rupert, translator and annotator. 1939. *Akiga's Story, the Tiv Tribe as seen by one of its Members.* London, Oxford University Press.

Edmonson, Munro. 1950. Field Notes. (MS.)

"Education in the New Turkey." 1950. *Turkey Today,* no. 5. New York, Turkish Information Office.

"Egypt Fights Illiteracy." 1947. *Middle East Opinion,* vol. 1, no. 33, pp. 20-21.

"Egypt Menaced from Within." 1948. *Middle East Bulletin,* vol. 1, no. 2, pp. 1-3.

Ekrem, Selma. 1947. *Turkey, Old and New.* New York, Scribner's.

Elwin, Verrier. 1939. *The Baiga.* London, J. Murray.

Embree, John F. 1950. Cultural Cautions on Liberia. (MS.)

Enlow, Charles R. 1948. "Malye Desert—A Turkish 'Combine' Farm." *Foreign Agriculture,* vol. 12, no. 12, pp. 268-71.

Enochs, Elisabeth S. 1943. "Transformations in Remote Places." *Land Policy Review,* vol. 6, no. 2, pp. 20-24.

Eren, Nuri. 1946. "The Village Institutes of Turkey." *Journal of the Royal Central Asian Society,* vol. 33, Parts 3 and 4, pp. 281-88.

Espinosa, Alfredo Ramos. 1942. "La alimentación en el campo y los niños." *America Indigena,* vol. 2, no. 4, pp. 7-10.

Ethridge, Willie Snow. 1947. *It's Greek to Me.* New York, Vanguard Press.

"European Programs for Expanding Farm Production—Turkey." 1949. *Foreign Agriculture,* vol. 12, no. 2, pp. 34-37.

Evans-Pritchard, E. E. 1940. *The Nuer.* Oxford, Clarendon Press.

Facts on Turkey. 1950. New York, Turkish Information Office.

Fong, H. D. 1937. "Industrial Organization in China." *Industry Series,* Bulletin No. 10. Nankai Institute of Economics, Tientsin. Tientsin, Chihli Press.

Fosdick, Raymond B. 1947. *The Rockefeller Foundation, A Review for 1947.* New York.

Francis, René. 1948. *Social Welfare in Egypt.* Cairo, Imp. MISR, S.A.E.

Fundamental Education. Report of a Special Committee to the Preparatory Commission of Unesco. 1947. New York, Macmillan.

Furnivall, J. S. 1943. *Educational Progress in Southeast Asia.* New York, Institute of Pacific Relations.

——. 1948. *Colonial Policy and Practice.* Cambridge, Cambridge University Press.

Gamio, Manuel. 1942. "Consideraciones sobre la problema indígena en America." *America Indigena,* vol. 2, no. 2, pp. 17-23.

Garnett, Lucy M. J. 1896. *Greek Folk Poesy.* London, David Nutt.

Garnham, P. C. C. 1949. "Modern Concepts in Malaria Control," *Journal of the Royal Sanitary Institute,* vol. 69, no. 5, pp. 617-22.

Gear, James H. S. 1949. "The Virus of Poliomyelitis, Its Distribution and Methods of Spread." *Journal of the Royal Sanitary Institute,* vol. 69, no. 3, pp. 149-53.

GIBBERD, Kathleen, compiler. 1944. *British Survey Handbooks: Greece.* Cambridge, Cambridge University Press.

GILLANDERS, George. 1940. "Rural Housing." *Journal of the Royal Sanitary Institute,* vol. 60, no. 6, pp. 230-40.

GOMME, A. W. 1945. *Greece.* New York, Oxford University Press.

GORER, Geoffrey. 1943. Burmese Personality. New York, Institute for Intercultural Studies (mimeographed).

GRANQUIST, Hilma. 1947. *Birth and Childhood among the Arabs.* Helsingfors, Söderström.

GRAY, Peter. 1942. *People of Poros.* New York, Whittlesey House, McGraw Hill.

GREEN, O. M. 1950. "Japan, 1945-1949." Reprinted in *New Forces in Asia,* edited by Bruno Lasker, New York, Wilson, pp. 74-79.

GUNN, G. H. 1947. "The Mobile Loud-Speaker Unit in Health Education for the Bantu." *Journal of the Royal Sanitary Institute,* vol. 67, no. 5, pp. 513-14.

HADARY, Gideon. 1949. "Iran—A Survey of Agriculture." *Foreign Agriculture,* vol. 13, no. 9, pp. 210-15.

HAILEY, William Malcolm. 1938. *An African Survey.* London, Oxford University Press.

HALL, H. Fielding. 1906. *The Soul of a People.* London, Macmillan.

——. 1908. *The Inward Light.* New York, Macmillan.

HALLOWELL, A. Irving. 1937. "Temporal Orientation in Western Civilization and in a Preliterate Society." *American Anthropologist,* vol. 39, no. 4, pp. 647-60.

——. 1948. "The Social Function of Anxiety in Primitive Society." Reprinted in *Personal Character and Cultural Milieu,* compiled by Douglas G. Haring. Syracuse, pp. 331-43.

HANKS, L. M. 1949. "The Quest for Individual Autonomy in the Burmese Personality." *Psychiatry,* vol. 12, no. 3, pp. 285-300.

HARING, Douglas G., compiler. 1948. *Personal Character and Cultural Milieu.* Syracuse.

HARRIS, Erdman. 1932. *New Learning in Old Egypt.* New York, Association Press.

HASKINGS, F. 1944. *Burma, Yesterday and Tomorrow.* Bombay, Thacker.

HATCH, D. Spencer. 1944. "Rural Reconstruction in Mexico." *Agriculture in the Americas,* vol. 4, no. 3, pp. 51-53, 57.

HAYDEN, Lyle J. 1949. "Living Standards in Rural Iran." *Middle East Journal,* vol. 3, no. 2, pp. 140-50.

HEISER, Victor George. 1936. *An American Doctor's Odyssey.* New York, Norton.

HERSKOVITS, Melville J. 1943. "Education and Cultural Dynamics." *American Journal of Sociology,* vol. 48, no. 6, pp. 737-49.

HERTIG, Marshall. 1950. "Observations on the Density of Phlebotomus Populations Following DDT Campaigns." *World Health Organization Bulletin,* vol. 2, no. 4, pp. 629-36.

HO, F. L. 1931. "Population Movement to the Northeastern Provinces in China." *Chinese Social and Political Review,* vol. 15, no. 3, pp. 346-401.

HOOPER, Ofelia. 1943. "Rural Panama, Its Needs and Prospects." *Rural Sociology,* vol. 8, no. 3, pp. 247-53.

HOYT, Elizabeth. 1951. "Tiquisate: a Call for a Science of Human Affairs." *Scientific Monthly,* vol. 72, no. 2, pp. 114-19.

HU NAI-TSIU. 1938. "Internal Chinese Migration." Reprinted in *Agrarian China,* edited by Institute of Pacific Relations. Chicago, University of Chicago Press, pp. 255-58.

HUNTER, Monica. 1936. *Reaction to Conquest.* London, Oxford University Press.

HYDRICK, John Lee. 1937. *Intensive Rural Hygiene Work and Public Health Education of the Public Health Service of the Netherlands, India.* Java, Netherlands India, Batavia-Centrum.

INSTITUTE OF PACIFIC RELATIONS. 1938. *Agrarian China: Selected Source Materials from Chinese Authors.* Chicago, University of Chicago Press.

ISSAWI, Charles. 1947. *Egypt: an Economic and Social Analysis.* London, Oxford University Press.

JACOBY, Erich H. 1949. *Agrarian Unrest in Southeast Asia.* New York, Columbia University Press.

JAREMILLO, Gabriel Giraldo. 1942. "Aspectos históricos de la alimentación indígena." *America Indígena,* vol. 2, no. 3, pp. 49-55.

JOHNSON, Charles S., editor. 1943. "Education and the Cultural Process." *American Journal of Sociology,* vol. 48, no. 6, pp. 629-32.

JOSEPH, Alice. 1942. "Physician and Patient." *Applied Anthropology,* vol. 1, no. 4, pp. 1-6.

KALOYEREAS, Socrates A. 1948. "The Milk Industry in Greece." *The Milk Dealer,* October.

KARMOULE, Georgion I. 1926. "Tragoudia Kretika." *Laographia,* vol. 9, no. 1-2, Athens.

KATSIGRA, Anna. n.d. *Trophe Kai Zoe (Food and Life).* Athens.

KAZAVE, Georgion N. 1940. *Nisyrou Laographica.* New York, Diury.

KELMAN, Janet Harvey. 1923. *Labour in India.* London, Allen and Unwin.

KENYA COLONY AND PROTECTORATE. 1932. *Crime Committee Report.* Nairobi, Government Printer.

————. 1939. *Report of the Commission of Inquiry appointed to Examine the Labour Conditions in Mombasa,* Nairobi, Government Printer.

KITCHEN, Helen A. editor. 1950. *Americans and the Middle East: Partners in the Next Decade.* Washington, D. C., Middle East Institute.

KLUCKHOHN, Clyde. 1947. "Some Aspects of Navaho Infancy and Early Childhood." *Psychoanalysis and the Social Sciences,* vol. I. New York, International Universities Press, pp. 37-86.

KLUCKHOHN, Florence. c. 1941. Los Atarquenos. Dissertation, Radcliffe College. (MS.)

————. 1949. "Dominant and Substitute Profiles of Cultural Orientations: Their Significance for the Study of Social Stratification." Harvard University. (Mimeographed).

KOENIG, Nathan. 1949. "World-Wide Gap between Science and Practice." *Foreign Agriculture,* vol. 13, no. 8, pp. 171-76.

KOKKOLATOS, N. C. and KOKKOLATOS, C. N. 1947. *Dia tas Nearas Meteras* (For the Young Mothers), sixth edition. Athens, A. A. Papaspyrou.

KOSKINIDES, Apostolos. 1948. "How the Greeks are Saving Greece." *Reader's Digest,* vol. 53, no. 318, pp. 112-15.

KUMARAPPA, J. C. 1949. "Mechanisation in Our Country." *Indian Review,* vol. 50, no. 9, pp. 449-50.

LADEJINSKY, W. I. 1942. "Thailand's Agricultural Economy." *Foreign Agriculture,* vol. 6, no. 5, pp. 165-84.

————. 1950. "Land Reform in Japan." Reprinted in *New Forces in Asia,* edited by Bruno Lasker. New York, Wilson, pp. 83-88.

LAMBERT, S. M. 1941. *A Yankee Doctor in Paradise.* Boston, Little, Brown.

LAMPRELL, B. A. and RAMSAY, G. C. 1939. *Conservance for Tea Estate Labourers in India.* London, Ross Institute of Tropical Hygiene, London School of Hygiene and Tropical Medicine.

LASKER, Bruno, compiler. 1950. *New Forces in Asia.* New York, Wilson.

LAW YONE, Edward M. and MANDELBAUM, David G. 1950 a. "Pacification in Burma." *Far Eastern Survey,* vol. 19, no. 17, pp. 182-87.

————. 1950 b. "The New Nation of Burma." *Far Eastern Survey,* vol. 19, no. 18, pp. 189-94.

LEAKEY, L. S. B. 1936. *Kenya Contrasts and Problems.* London, Methuen.

LEE TSE-TSIAN. 1938. "The Decline of Chinese Handicrafts." Reprinted in *Agrarian China,* edited by Institute of Pacific Relations. Chicago, University of Chicago Press, pp. 224-29.

LEIGHTON, Alexander H. and LEIGHTON, Dorothea C. 1944. *The Navaho Door.* Cambridge, Harvard University Press.

LEIGHTON, Dorothea C. and KLUCKHOHN, Clyde. 1947. *Children of the*

People, The Navaho Individual and His Development. Cambridge, Harvard University Press.

LEONARD, Olen and LOOMIS, Charles P. 1941. "Culture of a Contemporary Rural Community: El Cerrito, New Mexico." *Rural Life Studies*, no. 1. Washington, D. C. United States Department of Agriculture, Bureau of Agricultural Economics.

LINTON, Ralph. 1936. *The Study of Man*. New York, D. Appleton-Century.

LO-CHUN. 1938. "Peasant Women and Hand Weaving in Kiangyin." Reprinted in *Agrarian China*, edited by Institute of Pacific Relations. Chicago, University of Chicago Press, pp. 239-42.

LOOMIS, Charles P. 1944. "Extension Work at Tingo María." *Agriculture in the Americas*, vol. 4, no. 2, pp. 23-26, 36.

——. 1950. *Studies in Applied and Theoretical Social Science*. East Lansing, Michigan State College Press.

LOOPER, Don. 1950. "Liberian Agricultural Progress." *Foreign Agriculture*, vol. 14, no. 5, pp. 110-13.

MACH, Ernst. 1893. *The Science of Mechanics: a Critical and Historical Exposition of Its Principles*. Translated from the second German edition by T. J. McCormick. Chicago, Open Court.

MAES, Ernest E. 1942. "Indian Farming in South America." *Agriculture in the Americas*, vol. 2, no. 12, pp. 233-36.

MALINOWSKI, Bronislaw. 1926. *Myth in Primitive Psychology*. New York, Norton.

——. 1935. *Coral Gardens and Their Magic*. Two vols. New York, American Book.

MARKETOS, B. J., compiler and editor. *A Proverb for It: 1510 Greek Sayings*. Translated by Ann Arpajoglou. New York, New World Publishers.

MARRIOTT, Alice. 1949. *The Valley Below*. Norman, University of Oklahoma Press.

MATTHEWS, Roseric and AKRAWI, Matta. 1949. *Education in Arab Countries of the Near East*. Washington, D. C., American Council on Education.

MAUROGORDATO, John. 1931. *Modern Greece, Chronicle and Survey*. London, Macmillan.

McDOUGALL, J. B. 1947-1948. "Tuberculosis in Greece." *Bulletin of the World Health Organization*, vol. 1, no. 1, pp. 103-96.

McWILLIAMS, Carey. 1949. *North from Mexico*. Philadelphia, Lippincott.

MEAD, Margaret. 1946. "Professional Problems of Education in Dependent Countries." *Journal of Negro Education*, vol. 40, no. 3, pp. 346-57.

——. 1950 a. "Cultural Contexts of Nutritional Patterns." In *Centennial*. Washington, D. C., American Association for the Advancement of Science.

——. 1950 b. "Food and the Family." *"Unesco Food and People Series,"* no. 1, New York, Manhattan Publishing.

MELBY, John F. 1942. "Rubber River, An Account of the Rise and Collapse of the Amazon Boom." *Hispanic American Historical Review*, vol. 22, no. 3, pp. 452-69.

Memorandum on Land Nationalization Act, 1949. Washington, D. C., Embassy of Burma.

MENON, K. G. 1949. "Our Plans for Industrialization." *Indian Review*, vol. 50, no. 6, pp. 298-300.

MINTZ, Sidney W. 1951. "Cañamelar: The Contemporary Culture of a Rural Puerto Rican Proletariat." Dissertation, Columbia University. (MS.)

MORGENTHAU, Henry. 1929. *I was sent to Athens*. Garden City, Doubleday Doran.

MORRIS, K. R. S. 1950. *Fighting a Fly*. Publications of the Public Relations Department, Acora, Gold Coast Colony.

NEAR EAST FOUNDATION. 1949 a. "Annual Report on Livestock Improvement Program," by John Halpin. New York, Near East Foundation. (Mimeographed.)

——. 1949 b. "Annual Report of the Educational Director," by Harold B. Allen. New York, Near East Foundation. (Mimeographed.)

————. 1950 a. "Annual Report of the Educational Director," by Harold B. Allen. New York, Near East Foundation. (Mimeographed.)

————. 1950 b. "Final Report on Livestock Improvement Program in Greece," by John Halpin. New York, Near East Foundation. (Mimeographed.)

Near East Relief Consummated; Near East Foundation Carries On. 1944. A Committee of Trustees of Near East Relief.

NELSON, H. 1949. "Poliomyelitis—Epidemiology and Preventive Measures." *Journal of the Royal Sanitary Institute*, vol. 69, no. 3, pp. 160-70.

NIEH, C. L. 1933. *China's Industrial Development, Its Problems and Prospect.* Shanghai, China Institute of Pacific Relations.

NORTHROP, F. S. C. 1949. *Ideological Differences and World Order.* New Haven, Yale University Press.

NOTCUTT, L. A. and LATHAM, G. C. 1937. *The African and the Cinema.* London, published for the International Missionary Council by the Edinburgh House Press.

ONABANIRIO, S. D. 1949. *Why Our Children Die, the Causes, and Suggestions for Prevention of Infant Mortality in West Africa.* London, Methuen.

OPLER, Morris and SINGH, Rudra Datt. 1948. "The Division of Labor in an Indian Village." In *A Reader in General Anthropology*, edited by Carleton S. Coon. New York, Henry Holt, pp. 464-96.

PARSONS, Elsie Clews. 1936. *Mitla, Town of the Souls,* Chicago, University of Chicago Press.

————. 1945. *Peguche.* Chicago, University of Chicago Press.

PERHAM, Margery. 1937. *Native Administration in Nigeria.* London, Oxford University Press.

PHIPSON, E. S. 1939. *Tribal Beliefs concerning Tuberculosis in the Hills and Frontier Tracts of Assam.* Assam Government Press.

PIERSON, Donald. 1943. "The Educational Process and the Brazilian Negro." *American Journal of Sociology*, vol. 48, no. 6, pp. 692-700.

PIJOAN, Michel and GOUBAUD, Antonio. 1942. Food and Culture: A Nutritional Study of Cañon de Taos. (MS.)

PILLAY, A. I. 1931. *Welfare Problems in Rural India.* Bombay, D. B. Tataporevala.

POLITES, N. P. 1914. *Eclogae apo ta Tragoudia tou Ellenicou Laou* (Selections from the Songs of the Greek People). Athens, Estia.

PSATHA, D. 1937. *E Themis Echei Kephia* (Themis Enjoys Herself). Athens, Demetracou.

PUHR, Marie. 1950. "Co-op Idea takes Root in Near East." *News for Farmer Co-operatives.* Washington, D. C., United States Department of Agriculture, Farm Credit Administration.

PURVES, C. M. and HOBBES, John C. 1951. "Philippine Agriculture and Its Position and Problems." *Foreign Agriculture*, vol. 15, no. 1, pp. 3-10.

QUATE, Graham S. 1950. "Petch Barrage." *Foreign Agriculture*, vol. 14, no. 9, pp. 199-204.

QUINTANA, Epaminondas. 1942. "El problema dietético del Caribe." *America Indígena*, vol. 2, no. 2, pp. 25-29.

RAMAH PROJECT. n.d. Comparative Study of Five Cultures: Files and Field Notes. Harvard University, Peabody Museum. (MS.)

RAYMOND, E. R. 1949. "An Egyptian Modernizes a Roman Irrigation System." *Foreign Agriculture*, vol. 13, no. 7, p. 152.

READ, Margaret. 1938. "Native Standards of Living and African Culture Change." *International Institute of African Languages and Cultures Memorandum*, no. 16. London, Oxford University Press. Supplement to "*Africa*," vol. 11, no. 3.

REDFIELD, Robert. 1943. "Culture and Education in the Midwestern Highlands of Guatemala." *American Journal of Sociology*, vol. 48, no. 6, pp. 640-48.

REDFIELD, Robert and WARNER, W. Lloyd. 1940. "Cultural Anthropology and Modern Agriculture." In *Farmers in a Changing World*, 1940 *Year-*

book of Agriculture. United States Department of Agriculture. Washington, D. C., Government Printing Office, pp. 983-93.

"Report of a Trip to Langada, Sohos, Sckepasto, Mavrouda and Pente-Vrysses." 1950. Made in July 1950, by one of the teachers at the American Farm School, accompanied by Mr. Constantinides. (MS.)

Report of the Committee on Food Habits, 1941-1943. "The problem of Changing Food Habits." *Bulletin of the National Research Council,* no. 108. Washington, D. C.

Report of the Committee on Food Habits. 1945. "Manual for the Study of Food Habits." *Bulletin of the National Research Council,* no. 111. Washington, D. C.

Report of the First National Sanitation Clinic, July 1948. 1948. Ann Arbor, Michigan. National Sanitation Foundation.

ROBERTS, Lydia J. and STEPHANI, Rosa Luisa. 1949. *Patterns of Living in Puerto Rican Families.* Rio Piedras, University of Puerto Rico.

ROEST, Peter K. 1942. "A Review of Farm Policy, Production and Trade." *Foreign Agriculture,* vol. 6, no. 3, pp. 83-108.

RONDON, Candido M. da Silva. 1943. "Problema Indígena." *America Indígena,* vol. 3, no. 1, pp. 23-37.

"Rural Reconstruction Scheme at Menouf District, Egypt." n.d. Fellah Department Research Section. (Memorandum, MS.)

SALVANOU, Malvina I. 1926. "Tragoudia, Moirologia Kai Lazarika." *Laographia,* vol. 9, no. 1-2. Athens.

SAMPATH, P. N. 1939. "Our Agriculture." *Indian Review,* vol. 50, no. 9, pp. 467-69.

SANGER, Richard S. 1947. "Ibn Saud's Program for Arabia." *Middle East Journal,* vol. 1, no. 2, pp. 180-90.

SARE, Ömer Celâl. 1948. "Economic Policy of the New Turkey." *Middle East Journal,* vol. 2, no. 4, pp. 430-46.

SAUNDERS, Irwin T. 1942. "The Folk Approach in Extension Work." *Applied Anthropology,* vol. 2, no. 4, pp. 1-4.

SCHAPERA, Isaac. 1941. *Married Life in an African Tribe.* New York, Sheridan House.

SCHRIVER, Joanne Lee. 1947. Notes on the Culture of the Greeks of Nisyros. (MS.)

SCHMIDT, Carlos B. 1943. "Systems of Land Tenure in São Paulo." *Rural Sociology,* vol. 8, no. 3, pp. 242-47.

SCHWEITZER, Albert. 1931. *The Forest Hospital at Lambaréné.* Translated by C. T. Campion. New York, Henry Holt.

⸻. 1933. *Out of My Life and Thought.* Translated by C. T. Campion. New York, Henry Holt.

SCOTT, Sir George (Shway Yoe). 1910. *The Burman, His Life and Notions,* third revised edition. London, Macmillan.

SEAGRAVE, Gordon S. 1943. *Burma Surgeon.* New York, Norton.

"Self-Government in Turkey." n.d. *Turkey Today,* no. 6. New York, Turkish Information Office.

SHALABY, Mohamed M. 1950. *Rural Reconstruction in Egypt.* Cairo, Egyptian Association for Social Studies.

SHARP, Lauriston. 1950. "Peasants and Politics in Thailand." *Far Eastern Survey,* vol. 19, no. 15, pp. 157-61.

SHIH KUO-HENG. 1944. *China Enters the Machine Age, A Study of Labor in Chinese War Industry.* Edited and translated by Hsiao-tung Fei and Francis L. K. Hsu. Cambridge, Harvard University Press.

SILVA, José. 1943. "Economic Policy in Agriculture." *Rural Sociology,* vol. 8, no. 2, pp. 180-87.

SMITH, Edwin H. 1943. "Indigenous Education in Africa." In *Essays Presented to C. G. Seligman,* edited by E. E. Evans-Prichard and others. London, Kegan Paul, Trench Trubner, pp. 319-34.

SMITH, Marian W. 1946. "Village Notes from Bengal." *American Anthropologist,* vol. 48, no. 4, part 1, pp. 574-92.

SMITH, Thomas Lynn. 1946. *Brazil, People and Institutions*, Baton Rouge, Louisiana State University Press.

SMOTHERS, Frank, MCNEILL, William Hardy and MCNEILL, Elizabeth Derbishere. 1948. *Report on the Greeks*. New York, Twentieth Century Fund.

SOULIDES, D. A. 1949. "Better Utilization of Milk." *FAO Agricultural Studies*, no. 7. Washington, D. C., Food and Agricultural Organization of the United Nations.

SPATE, O. H. 1941. "Beginnings of Industrialization in Burma." *Economic Review*, vol. 17, no. 1, pp. 75-92.

SPICER, Edward H., editor. 1952. *Human Problems in Technological Change*. New York, Russell Sage Foundation.

SPIELMAN, Henry W. 1950. "India Can Feed Itself." *Foreign Agriculture*, vol. 14, no. 5, pp. 95-98.

STEPHANIDES, C. S. 1948 a. "Where Lack of Fuel Means Food Shortage." *Foreign Agriculture*, vol. 12, no. 3, pp. 60-62.

————. 1948 b. "Sheep—Man's Best Friend in Greece." *Foreign Agriculture*, vol. 12, no. 7, pp. 153-55.

————. 1948 c. "Agricultural Machinery in Greece." *Foreign Agriculture*, vol. 12, no. 11, pp. 250-53.

————. 1949. "Turkey—An Expanding Agricultural Economy." *Foreign Agriculture*, vol. 13, no. 9, pp. 196-201.

STEVENSON, H. N. C. 1944. "The Hill People of Burma." *Burma Pamphlets*, no. 6. Calcutta, Longmans, Green.

STEWART, Omer C. 1950. "Social Scientists and the Point Four Program." *Human Organization*, vol. 9, no. 3, pp. 26-27.

TAEUBER, Irene B. 1950. "Population Increase and Manpower Utilization in Imperial Japan." *Milbank Memorial Fund Quarterly*, vol. 28, no. 2, pp. 273-93.

TANNOUS, Afif I. 1943. "Food Production and Consumption in the Middle East." *Foreign Agriculture*, vol. 7, no. 11, pp. 243-55.

————. 1944 a. "Agricultural Production and Food Consumption in Iran." *Foreign Agriculture*, vol. 8, no. 2, pp. 27-42.

————. 1944 b. "Agricultural Co-operation in the Middle East." *Foreign Agriculture*, vol. 8, no. 6, pp. 131-44.

————. 1945. "Wartime Food Situation in the Middle East." *Foreign Agriculture*, vol. 9, no. 3, pp. 34-45.

————. 1947. "Agricultural Collaboration in the Middle East." *Foreign Agriculture*, vol. 11, no. 4-5, pp. 69-72.

————. 1948. "The Middle East Challenges Modern Agricultural Technology." *Foreign Agriculture*, vol. 12, no. 5, pp. 101-5.

————. 1949 a. "Egypt, Ancient and Agrarian." *Foreign Agriculture*, vol. 13, no. 9, pp. 202-7.

————. 1949 b. "The Village in the National Life of Lebanon." *Middle East Journal*, vol. 3, no. 2, pp. 151-63.

————. 1950. "Land Ownership in the Middle East." *Foreign Agriculture*, vol. 14, no. 12, pp. 263-69.

TARSOULE, Athena. 1947, 1948, 1950. *Dodecanesa*, 3 vols. Athens, I. M. Skazike.

TAX, Sol. 1942. "Ethnic Relations in Guatemala." *America Indígena*, vol. 2, no. 4, pp. 43-48.

TAYLOR, Carl C. and others. 1949. (November). *Experience with Human Factors in Agricultural Areas of the World*. United States Department of Agriculture, Extension Service, no. 1018. (Multilithed.)

The Industrialization of the African. 1937. London, The Anti-Slavery and Aborigines Protection Society.

"The Road Comes to the Village." n.d. *Sketches from Turkish Life*, no. 1. New York, Turkish Information Office.

THOMPSON, Laura. 1949. "Relations of Men, Animals and Plants in an Island Community (Fiji)." *American Anthropologist*, vol. 51, no. 2, pp. 253-67.

————. 1950. *Culture in Crisis.* New York, Harper.

THOMPSON, Laura and JOSEPH, Alice. 1945. *The Hopi Way.* Chicago, University of Chicago Press.

THOMPSON. Virginia. 1937. *French Indo-China.* New York, Macmillan.

————. 1943. Memorandum on Burma's Politics, Minorities, and Labor Problems. New York, Institute of Pacific Relations. (Mimeographed.)

THORP, Willard L. 1950. "New International Programs in Public Health." *American Journal of Public Health and the Nation's Health,* vol. 40, no. 12, pp. 1479-85.

THURNWALD, Richard C. 1935. *Black and White in East Africa.* London, Routledge.

Time. 1951. Vol. 57, no. 4, p. 74.

Time. 1951. Vol. 57, no. 8, p. 39.

TOMLIN, E. W. F. 1940. "Turkey: The Modern Miracle." *The Thinker's Forum,* no. 3. London, Watts.

————. 1946. *Life in Modern Turkey.* London, Thomas Nelson.

TOOTH, Geoffrey. 1950. "Studies in Mental Illness in the Gold Coast." *Colonial Research Publications,* no. 6. London, His Majesty's Stationery Office.

TRONCOSO, Moises Poblete. 1940. "Socio-Agricultural Legislation in the Latin-American Countries." *Rural Sociology,* vol. 5, no. 1, pp. 15-16.

TROWELL, H. C. 1950. "Problems Raised by Kwashiorkor." Condensed in *Nutrition Reviews,* vol. 8, no. 6, pp. 161-63.

"Turkey's Agricultural Land." 1945. *Foreign Agriculture,* vol. 9, no. 9, pp. 142-44.

UNITED NATIONS. 1946. *Charter of the United Nations and the Statute of the International Court of Justice.* New York.

————. General Assembly. 1947. *Official Records, 1st Session, Resolutions* A/64/Add. 1, 31 January 1947).

————. General Assembly. 1948. *Official Records, 3rd Session, Resolutions* (A/810, December 1948).

————. General Assembly. 1949. *Official Records, 4th Session, Resolutions* (A/1251, 28 December 1949).

————. Economic and Social Council. 1949. *Technical Assistance for Economic Development: Plan for an expanded co-operative programme through the United Nations and the Specialized Agencies* (E/1327/Add. 1, May 1949; United Nations Publications Sales No.: 1949. II. B. 1).

————.Economic and Social Council. 1949. *Economic Development of Under-developed Countries: Plan for an expanded co-operative programme through the United Nations and the Specialized Agencies,* (E/1327/Add. 2).

————. Economic and Social Council. 1949. *Official Records. 8th Session, Supplement No. 1* (E/1310, 15 March 1949).

————. Economic and Social Council. 1949. *Official Records, 9th Session, Supplement No. 1* (E/1553, 15 August 1949).

————. Economic and Social Council. 1950. "List of Non-Governmental Organizations in Consultative Relationship with the Economic and Social Council" (E/C.2/INF/1, 9 November 1950).

————. Secretariat, Department of Social Affairs. 1948. *Child and Youth Welfare, Annual Report.*

————. Secretariat, Department of Social Affairs. 1949. *Child and Youth Welfare, Annual Report.*

————. Statistical Office in collaboration with the Department of Social Affairs. 1949. *Demographic Yearbook,* 1948. Lake Success, New York.

————. Technical Assistance Board. 1951. *The Expanded Programme of Technical Assistance for Economic Development of Under-developed Countries.* New York.

————. FAO. 1951 (February). *Constitution, Rules and Regulations.* Washington, D. C.

————. FAO. 1947. *Report of the FAO Mission for Greece.* Washington, D.C.

————. FAO. 1949. *The State of World Food and Agriculture*. Washington, D. C.

————. FAO. 1949. *Training Rural Leaders*. Shantan Bailie School, Kansu Province, China. Washington, D. C.

————. FAO. 1949. *Yearbook of Food and Agricultural Statistics*, Part I. Washington, D. C.

————. ICAO. 1945. "International Civil Aviation Conference. Final Act and Related Documents, Chicago, November 1 to December 7, 1944." Department of State Publication 2282, Conference Series 64. Washington, D. C., U. S. Government Printing Office.

U. N. Bank and Fund. 1944. *Articles of Agreement, International Monetary Fund and International Bank for Reconstruction and Development*. United Nations Monetary and Financial Conference, Bretton Woods, N. H., July 1-22, 1944. Washington, D. C. U. S. Treasury.

————. ILO. 1949. *Constitution and Rules of the International Labour Organisation*. Conference edition. Geneva.

————. ILO. 1950 (November). "Information on the Development of the Expanded Programme of Technical Assistance." (G.B.113/T.A.C./D.1). Brussels.

————. ILO. 1938. "Labour Conditions in Indo-China." *International Labour Office-Studies and Reports Series B* (Economic Conditions), No. 26. Geneva.

————. UNESCO. 1945. *Constitution of the United Nations Educational, Scientific and Cultural Organization* (Unesco publication 367). Paris, 16 November 1945. (Available through Columbia University Press.)

————. UNESCO. 1951. 25 EX/19, Paris, 8 January 1951.

————. UNICEF. 1950 (June). *UNICEF*, A compendium of information about the United Nations International Children's Emergency Fund: its origin and development; policies; and operations in Asia, Europe, Latin-America, the Middle East and North Africa. New York.

————. WHO. 1947. "Constitution of the World Health Organization." *Chronicle of the World Health Organization*, vol. 1, no. 1-2. Geneva. (United Nations Document E/155, October 1946.)

————. WHO. 1950 (October). *World Health Organization Newsletter*, no. 10.

————. WHO. 1950. "Report of the First Session." *Technical Report Series*, no. 9. Expert Committee on Mental Health, Geneva.

————. WHO. 1951. "Report of the Second Session." *Technical Report Series*, no. 31. Expert Committee on Mental Health, Geneva.

UNITED STATES. Department of Agriculture. 1940. *Farmers in a Changing World, 1940 Yearbook of Agriculture*. Washington, D. C., U. S. Government Printing Office.

————. Department of Agriculture. Soil Conservation Service. 1935. *"Conservation Economic Series,"* no. 2. (Processed.)

————. Department of Agriculture. Soil Conservation Service. 1937 (May). "Destruction of Villages at San Marcial." *Soil Conservation Service Regional Bulletin* no. 38, *"Conservation Economic Series,"* no. 11. (Processed.)

————. Department of Agriculture. Soil Conservation Service. 1937 (July). "Handling of a Cash Crop (Chili)." *Soil Conservation Service Regional Bulletin*, no. 46, *"Conservation Economic Series,"* no. 19. (Processed.)

————. Department of Agriculture. Soil Conservation Service. 1937 (July). "Village Dependence upon Migratory Labor in the Upper Rio Grande Area." *Soil Conservation Service Regional Bulletin*, no. 47, *"Conservation Economic Series,"* no. 20. (Processed.)

————. Department of State. 1950. "Point Four . . ." *"Economic Cooperation Series,"* no. 24 (U. S. State Department of Publication 3719). Washington, D. C., U. S. Government Printing Office.

————. Navy Department, Office of the Chief of Naval Operations. 1948. *Handbook on the Trust Territory of the Pacific Islands*. Washington, D. C.

————. Office of Indian Affairs, Indian Land Research Unit. 1939. *Tewa*

Basin Study, 1935. 3 vols. Albuquerque, N. M., released by Soil Conservation Service, Region 8, Division of Economic Survey.

USEEM, John. 1945 a. "Governing the Occupied Areas of the South Pacific: Wartime Lessons and Peacetime Proposals." *Applied Anthropology,* vol. 4, no. 3, pp. 1-10.

————. 1945 b. "The American Pattern of Military Government in Micronesia." *American Journal of Sociology,* vol. 51, no. 2, pp. 93-102.

————. 1945 c. "The Changing Structure of a Micronesian Society." *American Anthropologist,* vol. 47, no. 4, pp. 567-88.

————. 1946. "Social Reconstruction in Micronesia." *Far Eastern Survey,* vol. 15, no. 2, pp. 21-24.

————. 1947. "Applied Anthropology in Micronesia." *Applied Anthropology,* vol. 6, no. 4, pp. 1-14.

————. 1948 a. "Human Resources of Micronesia." *Far Eastern Survey,* vol. 17, no. 1, pp. 1-4.

————. 1948 b. "Institutions of Micronesia." *Far Eastern Survey,* vol. 17, no. 2, pp. 22-25.

————. 1950. "Structure of Power in Palau." *Social Forces,* vol. 29, no. 2, pp. 141-48.

VANDENBOSCH, A. 1943. "The Effect of Dutch Rule on the Civilization of the East Indies." *American Journal of Sociology,* vol. 48, no. 4, pp. 498-502.

VAN DER EERDEN, Sister M. Lucia. 1948. "Maternity Care in a Spanish-American Community of New Mexico." *"Catholic University of America Anthropological Series,"* no. 13. Washington, D. C.

VÁSQUEZ, Emilio. 1943. "Preparación del Magisterio Rural en el Peru." *America Indígena,* vol. 3, no. 2, pp. 173-79.

WAGLEY, Charles and GALVÁO, Eduardo. 1949. *The Tenetehara Indians of Brazil.* New York, Columbia University Press.

WALTER, Jr., Paul Alfred Francis. 1938. A Study of Isolation and Social Change in Three Spanish Speaking Villages of New Mexico. Dissertation, Stanford University. (MS.)

WHETTEN, Nathan L. 1948. *Rural Mexico.* Foreword by Manuel Gamio. Chicago, University of Chicago Press.

WHIPPLE, Clayton E. 1944. "The Agriculture of Greece." *Foreign Agriculture,* vol. 8, no. 4, pp. 75-96.

WHITING, John W. M. 1938. *Becoming a Kwoma: Teaching and Learning in a New Guinea Tribe.* New Haven, Yale University Press.

WILSON, Charles Morrow. 1949. *One Half the People.* New York, William Sloan Associates.

WISDOM, Charles. 1940. *The Chorti Indians of Guatemala.* Chicago, University of Chicago Press.

WONG YIN-SENG, CHANG HSI-CHANG, and others. 1938. "Change in Land Ownership and the Fate of Permanent Tenancy." Reprinted in *Agrarian China,* edited by Institute of Pacific Relations. Chicago, University of Chicago Press, pp. 21-25.

WORLD FEDERATION FOR MENTAL HEALTH. 1948. *Mental Health and World Citizenship: A statement prepared for the International Congress on Mental Health, London, 1948.* London, distributed by H. K. Lewis.

YANG HSIN-PAO. 1949. "Planning and Implementing Rural Welfare Programs." *Human Organization,* vol. 8, no. 3, pp. 17-21.

YANG, Martin. 1945. *Chinese Village.* New York, Columbia University Press.

YU, James Y. T. 1948. "Chinese Agriculture and Its Mechanization." *Agricultural Engineering,* vol. 29, no. 7, pp. 297-98, 300.

INDEX

346

348